PRAGMATISM, PRINCIPLE, AND POWER IN COMMON LAW CONSTITUTIONAL SYSTEMS

Professor Bruce Harris

This book has been made possible with the support
of the New Zealand Law Foundation

PRAGMATISM, PRINCIPLE, AND POWER IN COMMON LAW CONSTITUTIONAL SYSTEMS

Essays in Honour of Bruce Harris

Edited by

Sam Bookman
Edward Willis
Hanna Wilberg
Max Harris

INTERSENTIA

Cambridge – Antwerp – Chicago

Intersentia Ltd
8 Wellington Mews
Wellington Street | Cambridge
CB1 1HW | United Kingdom
Tel: +44 1223 736 170
Email: mail@intersentia.co.uk
www.intersentia.com | www.intersentia.co.uk

Distribution for the UK and
Rest of the World (incl. Eastern Europe)
NBN International
1 Deltic Avenue, Rooksley
Milton Keynes MK13 8LD
United Kingdom
Tel: +44 1752 202 301 | Fax: +44 1752 202 331
Email: orders@nbninternational.com

Distribution for Europe
Lefebvre Sarrut Belgium NV
Hoogstraat 139/6
1000 Brussels
Belgium
Tel: +32 (0)800 39 067
Email: mail@intersentia.be

Distribution for the USA and Canada
Independent Publishers Group
Order Department
814 North Franklin Street
Chicago, IL 60610
USA
Tel: +1 800 888 4741 (toll free) | Fax: +1 312 337 5985
Email: orders@ipgbook.com

Pragmatism, Principle, and Power in Common Law Constitutional Systems.
Essays in Honour of Bruce Harris

Artwork on cover: Greg Balfour Evans - World History Archive - Ian Hogg / Alamy Stock Photo

ISBN 978-1-83970-198-6
D/2022/7849/1
NUR 823

British Library Cataloguing in Publication Data. A catalogue record for this book is available from the British Library.

FOREWORD

The year was 1977. I was studying contract at Otago and the lecturer for the whole course was one Bruce Harris. He was just beginning his academic career and it was, as we discovered later, his very first year teaching contract. But you would never have guessed it. He demonstrated a mastery of the subject and best of all, as far as the class was concerned, he was able to impart that knowledge clearly and in an interesting, thought-provoking and at times amusing way. He was also extremely approachable and supportive. He cared about the class and that was very evident. Different viewpoints were encouraged. No question was ever too silly. In short, it was the best possible learning environment. And gave us the best possible grounding.

By the end of that year, Bruce was firmly established as one of the most popular and respected teachers in the law school. It was no coincidence that the following year the numbers in our advanced contract course were much bigger than usual. Bruce was, as John Ip so aptly describes it,[1] the 'fount of avuncular assurance'.

Fast forward to 2015 when I took part in a seminar for one of Bruce's honours classes at Auckland, having almost forgiven him for leaving Otago. The same qualities and easy teaching style which had earned him so much respect and affection at Otago were very apparent. The vibe in the room was enthusiastic, the students were engaged, and they impressed with the depth of their knowledge and their critical thinking.

Not that I was surprised. For not only was their professor a superb teacher but since those fledgling days at Otago he had become a top constitutional and public law scholar with both a national and international reputation.

Festchriften are reserved for pre-eminent scholars. Bruce is unquestionably in that category. His work has attracted high praise as well as a great deal of attention. It is erudite and insightful but, importantly, also accessible. It is of huge importance to our country and never more so. And

1 See John Ip's contribution to this volume.

how fitting it is that the contributions in this collection to honour him not only reflect the breadth of his work but are themselves of a high calibre.

We do right to honour Bruce. His has been a truly outstanding career. He has established himself as a leading academic and has made a very significant contribution to legal education, the development of the law and public discourse on the future of the New Zealand constitution. I am both proud and grateful to have been taught by him and very proud to be asked to contribute this foreword.

Christine French
Judge of the New Zealand Court of Appeal

PREFACE

Bruce Harris is a stalwart of the New Zealand legal community and epitomises the very best of legal academia. His dedication to teaching in his 23 years at the University of Auckland, in addition to his previous tenure at the University of Otago, has inspired hundreds of lawyers, especially those who have completed his legendary public law honours seminar. His research has sparked new fields of scholarly inquiry from republicanism to judicial conduct, and his suggestion of the 'third source of executive power' has been cited and developed in judicial decisions across the Commonwealth. His administrative service – as dean, university councillor and work with the New Zealand Vice Chancellors' Committee – has been influential and prolific.

But more than a list of achievements, Bruce's career has been marked by remarkable kindness and dedication to his students and colleagues. Anyone who has met Bruce will know of his extraordinarily calm, patient and inclusive approach. Colleagues at both Auckland and Otago universities credit him with making the faculty lounge a warmer place to be. In emails and in person, he insisted on referring to his undergraduate honours students as his 'colleagues'. But his calm and cordial manner has never been a barrier to passion when necessary. Bruce was known as a champion of student and staff welfare in both the law school and the university at large and was never afraid to speak out against corporatising governance reforms. In class there were certain topics – the Kerr/Whitlam saga, the *Saxmere* cases, and Henry VIII clauses – which sparked his righteous indignation. And Bruce's career has also been marked by a quiet but mischievous humour. His public law honours seminars were full of quips and witty critiques, and he encouraged a spirit of jovial camaraderie. With a glint in his eye and deadpan demeanour, he was known for bringing a box of fried chicken to class to illustrate aspects of contract law, or an antique model of the Queen to explain his theory of the third source. He seems to take joy in eliciting surprised reactions to the unexpected.

Bruce's academic work is impressive in both substance and depth. But the breadth and method of his scholarship is equally impressive. Bruce sees public law as a system and avoids the tendency to think too narrowly in terms of administrative law, human rights, or Te Tiriti o Waitangi: for Bruce, no subfield can make sense detached from another. As a senior academic with significant control over his teaching load, Bruce nevertheless insisted on teaching the entire public law syllabus himself. His most recent monograph – *New Zealand Constitution: An Analysis in Terms of Principles* – demonstrates the value and surprising simplicity that can be drawn from this approach.

As several contributions in this volume attest, Bruce's thinking is distinctively pragmatic. He has no pretensions to a grand theory of what public law should be: instead, he expertly unpicks the ways in which it is shaped incrementally by different actors. But this should not be confused with a lack of innovation or progressive spirit. Bruce has always been forward-thinking and farsighted. In his scholarship, he has long championed a greater role for Te Tiriti o Waitangi in New Zealand's constitutional arrangements and has adopted an unabashedly normative tone in advocating for more republican, accountable and representative forms of government. This progressive spirit has carried over from his scholarship to his teaching and administration. Bruce has been a champion of junior scholars trying to balance the demands of academia and raising young children, and together with Nin Tomas, introduced Te Reo Māori classes for faculty long before this was common in public life. As a teacher, he was never afraid to challenge students on normative positions that lacked rigour or justification.

In different ways, all four of us have had our professional and intellectual outlooks shaped by Bruce's patient, understated and longstanding support. Bruce has a way of soaking up the ideas and anxieties of students and junior academics, carefully chewing them over, and responding with the calm, generous and assured advice that can change the course of a paper or career. A simple question from Bruce in the margins of an honours thesis draft – 'but where is the law in this argument?' – continues to be a mantra for one of us ten years after it was scribbled down. For at least two of us, his advice that we complement our interest in public law with a solid grounding in at least one field of private law, has been career-defining. We hope that the breadth and quality of contributions to this volume can do justice to the immense debt of gratitude that we each owe to Bruce.

There are several people without whose help the publication of this volume would not have been possible. First, we would like to thank the authors for their thoughtful contributions and responsiveness to feedback. We also wish to thank Anna Crowe, who provided assistance in the early stages of this book project. Lauren Millington provided extremely helpful editorial assistance, and we are grateful to the New Zealand Law Foundation for financial support. Ann-Christin Maak, Ella Brice-Jeffreys and their team at Intersentia enthusiastically accepted this book proposal and have helped shepherd it to completion. Finally, we thank Bruce Harris for providing the intellectual and personal inspiration for this volume.

Sam Bookman, Edward Willis,
Hanna Wilberg and Max Harris
November 2021

CONTENTS

PART II. ISSUES CONCERNING THE JUDICIARY

The Nature of Judicial (and Executive) Power

Creativity and Pragmatism in Judicial Method

THE WRITINGS OF PROFESSOR BRUCE HARRIS

1. BOOKS

New Zealand Constitution: An Analysis in Terms of Principles (Thomson Reuters, Wellington, 2018).

Executive Law-Making Under the Economic Stabilisation Act 1948 (Legal Research Foundation Inc, Auckland, 1984).

2. CHAPTERS IN BOOKS

"Remedies and Accountability for Unlawful Judicial Action in New Zealand: Could the Law Be Tidier?" in J Berryman and R Bigwood (eds) *The Law of Remedies* (Irwin Law, Toronto, 2010) 493–532.

"Towards a Written Constitution" in Raymond Miller (ed) *New Zealand Government and Politics*, (5th ed, Oxford University Press, Melbourne, 2010) 91–104.

"Judicial Activism and New Zealand's Appellate Courts" in Brice Dickson (ed) *Judicial Activism in Common Law Supreme Courts* (Oxford University Press, Oxford, 2007) 273–322.

"Constitutional Change" in Raymond Miller (ed) *New Zealand Government and Politics* (4th ed, Oxford University Press, Melbourne, 2006) 115–129.

"The Law-making Power of the Judiciary" in Philip A Joseph (ed) *Essays on the Constitution* (Brookers, Wellington, 1995) 265–285.

"The Constitutional Base" in Hyam Gold (ed) *New Zealand Politics in Perspective* (3rd ed, Longman Paul, Auckland, 1992) 56–76.

"The Constitutional Base" in Hyam Gold (ed) *New Zealand Politics in Perspective* (2nd ed, Longman Paul, Auckland, 1989) 34–53.

"The Constitutional Base" in Hyam Gold (ed) *New Zealand Politics in Perspective* (Longman Paul, Auckland, 1985) 28–42.

3. JOURNAL ARTICLES

"A Call to Maintain and Evolve the Third Source of Authority for Government Action" (2017) 27 New Zealand Universities Law Review 853–871.

"The Coherent Zeal that Nin Tomas Brought to her Responsibilities as a Law Teacher and Researcher" (2017) 5 Te Tai Haruru – Journal of Māori and Indigenous Issues 15–22.

"The Continuing Struggle with the Nuanced Obligation on Judges to Provide Reasons for Their Decisions" (2016) 132 Law Quarterly Review 216–235.

"A Judicial Commission for New Zealand: A Good Idea that Must Not Be allowed to Go Away" [2014] New Zealand Law Review 383–422.

"Recent Judicial Recognition of the Third Source of Authority for Government Action" (2014) 26 New Zealand Universities Law Review 60–81.

"The Resignation of Wilson J: A Consequent Critique of the Operation of the Judicial Conduct Commissioner and Judicial Conduct Panel Act 2004" [2011] New Zealand Law Review 625–662.

"New Zealand: Supreme Court judge resigns. Saga raise questions about recently enacted judicial complaints legislation" [2011] Public Law 436–439.

"Government 'Third Source' Action and Common Law Constitutionalism" (2010) 126 Law Quarterly Review 373–402.

"The Irish President, the New Zealand Governor-General and the Head of State in a Future New Zealand Republic" [2009] New Zealand Law Review 605–657.

"Replacement of the Royal Prerogative in New Zealand" (2009) 23 New Zealand Universities Law Review 285–314.

"Remedies and Accountability for Unlawful Judicial Action in New Zealand: Could the Law Be Tidier?" [2008] New Zealand Law Review 483–521.

"The 'Third Source' of Authority for Government Action Revisited" (2007) 123 Law Quarterly Review 225–250 (awarded the Sir Ian Barker Prize for best published contribution to New Zealand law in 2007).

"The Treaty of Waitangi and the Constitutional Future of New Zealand" [2005] New Zealand Law Review 189–216.

"The Constitutional Future of New Zealand" [2004] New Zealand Law Review 269–312.

"Judicial Review, Justiciability and the Prerogative of Mercy" (2003) 62 Cambridge Law Journal 631–660.

"The New Supreme Court" [2003] New Zealand Law Journal 15–17.

"Employment Changes for Judges" (2003) 83 Employment Today 44–45.

"Final Appellate Courts Overruling their Own 'Wrong' Precedents: the Ongoing Search for Principle" (2002) 118 Law Quarterly Review 408–427.

"Equal Access to Justice: A Constitutional Principle in Need of a Higher Profile" [1995] New Zealand Law Review 282–309.

"Sustainable Management as an Express Purpose of Environmental Legislation" (1993) 8 Otago Law Review 51–76.

"Parliamentary Sovereignty and Interim Injunctions: *Factortame* and New Zealand" (1992) 15 New Zealand Universities Law Review 55–79.

"The 'Third Source' of Authority for Government Action" (1992) 108 Law Quarterly Review 626–651.

"Judicial Review of the Prerogative of Mercy?" [1991] Public Law 386–407.

"A Changing Perception of the Law-making Powers of Parliament?" [1988] New Zealand Law Journal 394–398.

"Bill of Rights: Redistribution of Power" [1985] New Zealand Law Journal 49–53.

"The Law-making Powers of the New Zealand General Assembly; Time to Think About Change" (1984) 5 Otago Law Review 565–602.

"The Temporary Constitutional Crisis" [1984] New Zealand Law Journal 302–306.

"Interim Relief Against the Crown" (1981) 5 Otago Law Review 92–113.

"Interim and Interlocutory Injunctions: Assessment of Probability of Success" [1979] New Zealand Law Journal 525–536.

"*Australian National Airways Commission v Commonwealth of Australia and Canadian Pacific Airlines Ltd*: Crown Privilege – a Widening Immunity?" (1976) 3 Otago Law Review 619–625.

"*Lower Hutt City Council v Bank*: The Principles of Fairness" (1975) 3 Otago Law Review 405–410.

"Administrative Law" (1974) 3 Otago Law Review 245–247.

"Constitutional Law" (1973) 3 Otago Law Review 107–110.

"Land Law" (1972) 2 Otago Law Review 497–499.

LIST OF CASES

NEW ZEALAND

UNITED KINGDOM

CANADA

UNITED STATES

INTERNATIONAL LAW

LIST OF CONTRIBUTORS

Sam Bookman, SJD Candidate, Harvard Law School and Staff Attorney, Cyrus R. Vance Center for International Justice. Sam graduated BA/LLB (Hons) from the University of Auckland in 2015, where Bruce Harris supervised his honours research. He worked as a Judge's Clerk for the Chief District Court Judge of New Zealand before completing LLM studies at Harvard Law School. His research focuses on constitutional responses to environmental challenges.

Taylor Burgess practises group litigation with London-based firm PGMBM. Before joining PGMBM in 2020, Taylor was a Yale University Bernstein Human Rights Fellow and an Assistant Crown Counsel in NZ's Crown Law Office.

Claire Charters, University of Auckland. Ngāti Whakaue, Ngā Puhi, Tūwharetoa, Tainui. Claire is an Associate Professor at Auckland Law, teaching and researching mainly Indigenous peoples' and comparative constitutional law and international law. Claire has taught around the world including at Columbia University and the University of Copenhagen. She combines her research with advocacy and appointments to the United Nations, including as advisor to the President of the General Assembly.

Paul Craig, Emeritus Professor of English Law, St John's College, Oxford. His principal areas of research and teaching have been administrative law, constitutional law, EU law and comparative administrative law. He was the UK Alternative Member on the Venice Commission from 2010–2018.

John Dawson is a Professor of Law at the University of Otago. His specialisation, since the 1980s, is mental health law, especially the law and practice of compulsory community care. He also teaches jurisprudence and public law, including courses on Treaty of Waitangi settlements and comparative federalism. He was a student of Bruce Harris at Otago in the 1970s.

Caroline E Foster, Faculty of Law, University of Auckland. Dr. Caroline Foster is a Professor at the University of Auckland Law Faculty. She recently completed a new monograph *Global Regulatory Standards in*

Environmental and Health Disputes: Regulatory Coherence, Due Regard and Due Diligence (Oxford University Press, 2021) complementing her previous book *Science, Proof and Precaution in International Courts and Tribunals: Expert Evidence, Burden of Proof and Finality* (Cambridge University Press, 2011). Caroline was formerly with the New Zealand Ministry of Foreign Affairs and Trade, and holds a graduate diploma from the Academia Diplomática de Chile as well as an LLM and a PhD from the University of Cambridge.

Max Harris's DPhil (PhD), completed at the University of Oxford as an Examination Fellow, was on the prerogative and third source, including the work of Bruce Harris. He holds a BA/LLB(Hons.) from the University of Auckland, and BCL and MPP degrees from the University of Oxford, where he was a Rhodes Scholar.

John Ip, Faculty of Law, University of Auckland. John Ip is an Associate Professor at the University of Auckland Faculty of Law, which he joined in 2005. John graduated with BA and LLB(Hons) degrees from the University of Auckland, and obtained his LLM degree from Columbia University where he was a James Kent Scholar. Previously, John worked on Guantánamo Bay and death penalty litigation at an NGO in the United States, and as a Judge's Clerk at the Auckland High Court. His research interests are in public and constitutional law, with a particular focus on legal issues arising out of post-9/11 counterterrorism measures, and in law and popular culture. He has published extensively on these subjects in the United States, the United Kingdom, and New Zealand.

Paul Rishworth is a Professor at the Faculty of Law, University of Auckland and practises as a barrister from Britomart Chambers in Auckland. His research interests and legal practice are in the field of constitutional and human rights law. He serves as a member of the Legislation Design and Advisory Committee.

ATH Smith, LLD; Professor, Victoria University of Wellington; Fellow, Gonville and Caius College, Cambridge.

He became a Fellow of Gonville and Caius College, Cambridge in 1973, and am a Life Fellow of that College. His final position in the UK (after holding posts at Durham and Reading) was "Professor of Criminal and Public Laws" at Cambridge, which he left to return to New Zealand in 2007 after a long absence, to become the Pro Vice Chancellor and Dean of the Law Faculty at Victoria. He was the Arthur Goodhart Distinguished Visiting Professor at Cambridge for 2015–2016, and has held Visiting

Professorships at Otago and Auckland, at Iowa USA, Northwestern (Chicago), City University (London) and Paris 2 (Pantheon Assas).

EW Thomas, LLB(NZ) LLD(VUW) KNZM QC. The Rt Hon. Sir Ted Thomas KNZM QC is a retired judge of the Court of Appeal of New Zealand and a former acting judge of the Supreme Court of New Zealand. He was appointed Queen's Counsel in 1981 and was appointed to the High Court of New Zealand in 1990 where he served for five years before being elevated to the Court of Appeal. He retired in 2001 but was appointed as an acting Judge of the Supreme Court in 2005. Sir Ted was made a member of the Privy Council in 1996. In 2002 he was appointed a Knight Companion of the New Zealand Order of Merit. Following his retirement Sir Ted was Distinguished Fellow at the Law School at the University of Auckland. He retired from that position in February of 2018.

Nicola R Wheen is a Professor in the Faculty of Law / Te Kaupeka Tātai Ture, University of Otago / Te Whare Wānanga o Otāgo, where she teaches public law, environmental law and international environmental law. She was a student of Bruce Harris in the late 1980s, and took over his newly-developed environmental law paper when he moved to Auckland in the early 1990s. She is interested in the law about nature conservation, environmental law and the Treaty of Waitangi / Te Tiriti o Waitangi, and law in New Zealand's environmental history. Her recent research focuses on legal issues in wildlife protection, the regulation of genetically-modified organisms, and contemporary environmental institutions in New Zealand. She has an on-going research focus on law and the conservation of New Zealand dolphins and sea lions.

Hanna Wilberg is an Associate Professor at the University of Auckland. Her main research areas are administrative law and the tort liability of public authorities.

Edward Willis, Faculty of Law, University of Auckland. Edward Willis is a Senior Lecturer in Public Law at the University of Auckland Faculty of Law. Before joining the Auckland Law Faculty he spent over a decade as a solicitor in private practice. He has broad interests in administrative law, constitutional theory, Indigenous rights, competition law and regulation. His recent research focuses on the nature of unwritten constitutions and the public law dimension in economic regulation.

INTRODUCTION

Edward Willis and Hanna Wilberg

No doubt there are many different markers of success for an academic career. If pressed to articulate some of them, many of us might point to one or more of these common standards for intellectual achievement: breadth and depth of scholarship, engagement from critics and interlocutors, development of novel ideas and avenues for research, and perhaps the everyday usefulness to society of one's intellectual contribution.

Bruce Harris's academic career has more than seen these standards met. He is expert in New Zealand public law, having taught and published in the field for more than 40 years. Harris graduated with a Bachelor of Laws degree (with Honours) from the University of Otago in 1974 and a Master of Laws degree from Harvard University in 1975. He was admitted as a barrister and solicitor the following year, and spent two years in practice with a focus on resource management law (a focus reflected in his early academic work).[1] Harris then returned to the University of Otago Faculty of Law where he would teach and research for the next 17 years, before moving to join the Faculty of Law at the University of Auckland in 1994. His commitment to faculty life saw him appointed Dean of Law at each of those two proud universities during his tenure. And, of course, a number of academic accolades have followed, including the Sir Ian Barker Prize for Best Published Article in 2007, and the conferral of a Doctor of Laws degree from the University of Otago in 2012.

In terms of scholastic output, the culmination of Harris's expertise and experience was the publication of *New Zealand Constitution: An Analysis in Terms of Principles*,[2] which provides a comprehensive yet highly accessible account of how New Zealand's constitution operates. It also

---

1 Bruce Harris "Sustainable Management as an Express Purpose of Environmental Legislation" (1993) 8 Otago L Rev 51; "Land Law" (1972) 2 Otago L Rev 497.

2 Bruce Harris *New Zealand Constitution: An Analysis in Terms of Principles* (Thomson Reuters, Wellington, 2018).

reflects Harris's highly pragmatic style of public law scholarship, which strips the law of pretence while somehow losing very little of its nuance. One colleague noted not long after its publication that it deserved to sit alongside the *Cabinet Manual* as an essential resource for all new Members of Parliament. Experience already tells us that a number of law students also now rely on it as a first port of call when examining constitutional issues for the first time.

Such a remarkable book rests on many years of top-class scholarship and publications. Major themes in Harris's work include the nature of executive and judicial power within the constitution, judicial accountability, and constitutional reform. There has also been a willingness to wrestle with the Māori rights aspects of New Zealand public law. Each of these topics merit at least a brief comment.

One of Harris's main areas of expertise is executive power that is not authorised by statute or sourced in the prerogative. Indeed, Harris coined the label 'third source' of authority for government action, and any scholar seriously engaging with that fraught topic, which goes to the heart of the nature of executive government, is required to engage with his treatment of the matter in UK and New Zealand publications.[3] While it seems that Harris's primary motivation for addressing this topic is simply to describe and acknowledge an under-studied area of public law practice, he has notably maintained a stance as a strong advocate of third source doctrine, even in the face of significant normative controversy surrounding its acceptability.

While the third source is perhaps what he is best known for, Harris's intellectual contribution is much wider than this single issue. Continuing with the theme of executive power, Harris has written about the royal prerogative,[4] particularly in the context of the reviewability of the prerogative of mercy,[5] and reform of New Zealand's Head of State arrangements.[6]

3 Bruce Harris "A Call to Maintain and Evolve the Third Source of Authority for Government Action" (2017) 27 NZULR 853; "Recent Judicial Recognition of the Third Source of Authority for Government Action" (2014) 26 NZULR 60; "Government 'Third Source' Action and Common Law Constitutionalism" (2010) 126 LQR 373; "The 'Third Source' of Authority for Government Action Revisited" (2007) 123 LQR 225; "The 'Third Source' of Authority for Government Action" (1992) 108 LQR 626.

4 Bruce Harris "Replacement of the Royal Prerogative in New Zealand" (2009) 23 NZULR 285.

5 "Judicial Review, Justiciability and the Prerogative of Mercy" (2003) 62 Cambridge LJ 631–660; "Judicial Review of the Prerogative of Mercy?" [1991] PL 386–407.

6 "The Irish President, the New Zealand Governor-General and the Head of State in a Future New Zealand Republic" [2009] NZ Law Rev 605–657.

Some early work examined the infamous Economic Stabilisation Act 1948,[7] which was responsible for much executive domination of the New Zealand constitutional system.

While aspects of Parliamentary government have also caught Harris's attention,[8] it is the nature of judicial power that has become another dominant theme in Harris's work. Judicial accountability is an especially under-explored topic in New Zealand where Harris has become a leading and welcome commentator,[9] but his work also addresses judicial law-making and the ever-present spectre that accompanies such law-making – judicial activism.[10] These are difficult areas of the law to address both in terms of bringing coherence to any substantive analysis and being sensitive to the sometimes delicate nature of the subject matter. Harris's pragmatic style of writing and analysis seems especially well suited to this task.

The public law scholar is always interested in the question of reform. Imagining the constitutional future of a nation is perhaps an act of courage – the imaginer is almost certainly going to find that they are wrong to a material extent as events unfold – but in many ways it is also a vital act of optimism. Knowing that we can make things better for ourselves encourages us to take action. Harris's two articles on New Zealand's constitutional future, the first addressing general issues and the second focused on the Treaty of Waitangi,[11] have become the

7 *Executive Law-Making Under the Economic Stabilisation Act 1948* (Legal Research Foundation Inc, Auckland, 1984).

8 "Parliamentary Sovereignty and Interim Injunctions: Factortame and New Zealand" (1992) 15 NZULR 55–79; "A Changing Perception of the Law-making Powers of Parliament?" [1988] NZLJ 394–398; "The Law-making Powers of the New Zealand General Assembly; Time to Think About Change" (1984) 5 Otago L Rev 565–602.

9 Bruce Harris "The Continuing Struggle with the Nuanced Obligation on Judges to Provide Reasons for Their Decisions" (2016) 132 LQR 216; "A Judicial Commission for New Zealand: A Good Idea that Must Not Be allowed to Go Away" (2014) 26 NZ L Rev 383; "The Resignation of Wilson J: A Consequent Critique of the Operation of the Judicial Conduct Commissioner and Judicial Conduct Panel Act 2004" [2011] NZ L Rev 625; "Remedies and Accountability for Unlawful Judicial Action in New Zealand: Could the Law Be Tidier?" [2008] NZ L Rev 483.

10 "Judicial Activism and New Zealand's Appellate Courts" in Brice Dickson (ed) *Judicial Activism in Common Law Supreme Courts* (Oxford University Press, Oxford, 2007) 273; "The Law-making Power of the Judiciary" in Philip A Joseph (ed) *Essays on the Constitution* (Brookers, Wellington, 1995) 265.

11 "The Treaty of Waitangi and the Constitutional Future of New Zealand" [2005] NZ L Rev 189; "The Constitutional Future of New Zealand" [2004] NZ L Rev 269.

starting point for thinking about responsible and effective constitutional change. Maybe part of the reason for this is that, consistent with Harris's academic style more generally, these works are not overly normative in a morally laden sense. Instead, they deliberately centre the needs and desires of the people whom the constitution is intended to serve.

Harris has also reviewed major works in the field of New Zealand public law including the first two editions of Philip Joseph's seminal text on constitutional and administrative law,[12] and the recent contribution by Alison Quentin-Baxter and Janet McLean on the nature of the Crown.[13] And it is certainly worth mentioning the willingness Harris has always had to learn from his colleagues and even his students, who often bring very different perspectives to issues of public law than his own. His honouring of Nin Tomas is a high-profile example,[14] but there are many others.

This *Festschrift* celebrates all of these remarkable achievements, and the contributions to this collection pick up three of the core themes emerging from Harris's body of scholarship: sources of executive power, a range of issues concerning the judiciary, and the nature of unwritten constitutions and their future.

As already noted, among Bruce Harris's most high-profile contributions is his work on the 'third source' of authority for government action – the power to do what is not prohibited, in addition to statutory and common law powers. In this volume, Claire Charters and Edward Willis take another look at this topic, each in the context of a contribution that also tackles broader constitutional issues.

Charters queries whether the source of executive power is an appropriate focus, suggesting that the more pressing concern is holding the executive to account and restraining its power, particularly vis-à-vis Māori. The broader constitutional question she is concerned with is the illegitimacy of Aotearoa's present constitution, unauthorised as it is by Te Tiriti o Waitangi, and the best route towards remedying this. She notes that Bruce Harris on the one hand has given greater recognition to these issues than most other New Zealand constitutional scholars, especially of his generation, but on the other hand has tended to favour a conservative incrementalist approach to change. Among Māori constitutional scholars

12 Published at [1993] PL 551 and (2003) 20 NZULR 533 respectively.

13 Published at [2018] PL 560.

14 Bruce Harris "The Coherent Zeal that Nin Tomas Brought to her Responsibilities as a Law Teacher and Researcher" (2017) 5 Te Tai Haruru – Journal of Māori and Indigenous Issues 15.

such as herself, Charters notes a common ambivalence between working within the colonial legal framework to achieve as much change as is possible, and rejecting such work as ultimately merely serving to legitimate the present illegal New Zealand state.

Approaching the topic of executive power from that perspective, Charters queries the significance of the distinction between statutory and non-statutory powers on the basis that the former are legitimated by a democratic mandate. In relation to Māori as the indigenous minority in a system without any constitutional guarantees of minority rights, majority authorisation represents a weak justification for power. On the other hand, anything that enlarges rather than restrains executive power is of concern, hence third source power with its lack of a requirement of prior authorisation is problematic. The central issue, however, is that while rights from various sources constrain executive power (whether statutory or not), Māori rights are generally insufficiently 'legal' to be enforceable. As a final thought, Charters raises the question as to possible non-judicial methods for holding the executive to account with respect to Māori claims and rights.

Edward Willis takes another look at the legitimate extent of third source power. He does so in the context of a contribution evaluating constitutional pragmatism, widely considered the dominant approach in New Zealand. The potential concern that such an approach entails simply a lack of a coherent theory and of meaningful normative commitments may be addressed, he argues, by a functionalist version of constitutional pragmatism exemplified by Bruce Harris's work, which includes space for normative and theoretical considerations. On this approach, the law is understood as a social institution serving the social purpose of serving society and its interests and goals. Constitutional practices are evaluated in light of the norms that govern them, and conversely the norms are evaluated in light of the practices they generate. The value of this approach, Willis argues, is that it avoids the 'unreal and contestable abstraction' of pure normativism, but equally avoids the 'bare descriptivism of constitutional realism'. Its strength lies in 'its ability to reconcile actual constitutional practice with theoretical perspectives that legitimise that practice'.

Willis then takes the debate about 'third source' power as his case study to demonstrate what a normative version of constitutional pragmatism can accomplish; applying it as the basis for a conceptually sound and constitutionally defensible account of 'third source' authority. He argues that the availability of this power should be conditioned by five considerations that he adapts from Harris's approach to determining justiciability: whether there is a public purpose; whether a statutory power is available to use instead; the constitutional appropriateness of the action (does it risk upsetting the prevailing constitutional balance, does it impinge on any extra-legal constitutional restrictions such as Treaty of Waitangi guarantees?); the agency's institutional capacity for the particular action; and the range and effectiveness of alternative accountability mechanisms. This framework, he argues, serves to reconcile the pragmatic desire to facilitate effective government with normative concerns about the constitutional appropriateness of executive power that has not been positively authorised by law.

Turning to the next of our three themes from Bruce Harris's work – issues concerning the judiciary – Harris's early work on the Resource Management Act 1991 (RMA) was an instance of his concern with the nature of both executive and judicial power.

This work is the starting point for Nicola Wheen's contribution to this volume. The RMA enshrined a purpose of sustainable management. However, soon after it was enacted, critics including Harris predicted that the vague and indeterminate wording of the relevant provision would result in that purpose being balanced against competing economic and social objectives in an exercise of broad discretionary judgment. Harris worried this would render controversial the Environment Court's merits review jurisdiction, and would cause problems with insufficiently impartial local-level decision-making authorities.

Wheen outlines experience with the RMA since then, demonstrating that these concerns have been borne out. Although the more recent Supreme Court decision in *King Salmon* established that high-level plans and policy statements set bottom lines that confine discretion in lower-level plans and decisions,[15] that 'bottom lines' approach has not been extended to apply to the sustainability purpose of the Act itself. Given the failure of successive governments to exercise their powers to lay down prescriptive standards in national policy statements, the discretionary balancing approach continues to apply to most decision-making. Beyond the institutional concerns expressed by Harris, the substantive effect has been to facilitate significant environmental deterioration during the life of the RMA. Wheen calls for Parliament to take responsibility for laying down more prescriptive standards of environmental protection.

---

15 *Environmental Defence Society Incorporated v The New Zealand King Salmon Co Ltd* [2014] NZSC 38, [2014] 1 NZLR 593.

Next under the heading of the judiciary, there are four contributions to this volume exploring aspects of creativity and pragmatism in judicial method – a strong theme in Harris's work. The first contribution concerns the newly recognised remedy of declarations of inconsistency with the New Zealand Bill of Rights Act 1990. Unsurprisingly this receives attention in several contributions to this volume (those of Smith, Rishworth and Bookman). Readers looking for detailed discussion of this development, however, should turn to John Ip's chapter.

Employing the framework set out in Bruce Harris's piece on judicial creativity or activism, Ip's main argument is that the recognition of the new remedy amounts to judicial creativity, but that it is justified and hence avoids the charge of illegitimate judicial activism. Beyond that, Ip contrasts the reasoning of the Court of Appeal and Supreme Court for the new remedy, with the former emphasising inherent judicial powers and institutional dialogue, while the latter focused on implication from the text and structure of the Bill of Rights, and on vindication of rights. On the one hand, the Supreme Court's approach is less vulnerable to accusations of judicial activism and could thus plausibly be seen as designed to ensure the new remedy's acceptance and legitimacy. On the other hand, the Supreme Court's assertion that a declaration of inconsistency is a declaration of law and of rights is a significant assertion of the Bill of Rights' status and of the judicial role in relation to it.

Taylor Burgess calls for greater judicial engagement with questions about creativity, and for greater willingness to engage in creativity, in cases involving social policy questions. Her case study concerns family forms – access to marriage and adoption – but her discussion of creativity is of more general relevance. She notes that courts have been comfortable innovating in contexts where social change has already occurred and the law merely needs to catch up, and in such cases they have tended not to acknowledge their social policy creativity. On the other hand, they have tended to decline innovation, and to simply treat 'social policy' as a no-go area, in contexts where they were asked to spear-head change.

Adopting Harris's analysis, Burgess accepts that there are limits to the appropriate level of judicial creativity, and that deference to Parliament on matters of social policy is a good starting point. However, there are always competing factors to weigh up. Where vulnerable minorities claim protection against discrimination, a lack of social acceptance should not be a reason for non-intervention, provided the relevant Bill of Rights tests are met: that is, provided there is no competing public interest that on balance justifies the disadvantage (s 5), and provided Parliament has not spoken clearly against the innovation (s 6). Furthermore, Burgess argues that regardless of whether creativity is determined to be appropriate in the particular context or not, judicial accountability requires clear articulation of the issue and the reasons for the determination one way or the other.

Paul Rishworth draws attention to the less-noted phenomenon of judicial creativity in the service of judicial restraint, which has featured in New Zealand in cases engaging significant moral controversies such as about abortion, assisted suicide and same-sex marriage. By way of comparison, he surveys the varying approaches of US, Canadian and UK courts to these matters. Appropriately, in Rishworth's view, New Zealand courts have found creative ways to reserve such moral controversies to Parliamentary resolution. This approach, he argues, is also consistent with the principle underlying the New Zealand Bill of Rights model – that on social policy decisions the last word should be left to Parliament. While a declaration of inconsistency with the Bill of Rights, which has recently been confirmed as being available, would not be dispositive of the matter, it would nonetheless represent a formal statement of law, and as such would have a distorting effect on such moral controversies.

Caroline Foster examines judicial creativity in the context of international courts and tribunals. The powers of such bodies are limited to interpreting and applying provisions agreed by States parties. However, in contexts where international law constrains States' domestic regulatory activities, for instance where environmental protection or public health are at issue, such bodies have found it necessary to flesh out the bare terms of the relevant provisions. They have done so by developing standards and tests such as a requirement of a reasonable relationship of a challenged measure to its stated objective – a standard which notably has not so far been extended to a full proportionality test. The relevant contexts include certain parts of the International Court of Justice's jurisdiction; the work of the World Trade Organisation's Appellate Body; and Investment Treaty arbitration. Foster presents specific case studies on these three, involving whaling, plain packaging of tobacco and contracts for the supply of renewable energy. As illustrated by these case studies, she suggests there is a sufficient convergence of various tribunals' jurisprudence to talk of emerging global regulatory standards. She concludes by raising a question as to the legitimacy of such a development in the absence of opportunities for public engagement.

Staying with the judiciary, the final topic is judicial appointment and accountability, addressed by two contributions to this volume. Sir Edmund Thomas outlines, examines and endorses Harris's proposal to introduce an independent judicial appointments commission. He is persuaded by the argument that judicial power is so immense that appointment to judicial office requires a more formal process, and one that is much more independent of the executive.

Tony Smith is concerned that the judiciary's constitutional status – its independence as part of the separation of powers – is not well understood, nor entirely adequately protected, in New Zealand. He explores possible reasons for the lack of understanding, and then surveys issues concerning our appointment system, security of tenure along with complaints and removal procedures, the role of judges in the protection of rights, and the extent to which the law of contempt of court protects judges from harmful attacks. Particular concerns about compromising the constitutional status of judges arise from the potential lack of confidentiality in the complaints process and from the failure to enforce available laws against false and harmful public attacks on judges.

The final one of the three broad themes addressed in this volume is the nature of unwritten constitutions and their future. Three contributions address aspects of this.

A fundamental part of Aotearoa New Zealand's unwritten constitution is Te Tiriti o (the Treaty of) Waitangi. The issues around its status and effect exemplify the issues arising from unwritten constitutions. In this volume, John Dawson casts these issues in terms of jurisprudential debates on the concept of law. The usual account of the legal status and effect of the Treaty presents it as lacking direct legal effect, but requiring statutes to be interpreted consistently where possible and public powers to be exercised only after taking it into account. Dawson proposes a better conceptualisation of this legal status, drawing on Ronald Dworkin and Mayo Moran's work. Law according to Dworkin includes not only rules with determinative effect, but also principles that exert their force on legal reasoning. Similarly, Moran has observed that the law includes aspects that have influential authority – an intermediate category between binding authority and mere persuasive authority. Instead of the usual insistence that the Treaty is not part of New Zealand law, Dawson argues, the legal effect of the Treaty can be conceived in terms of either Dworkinian principles or Moran's influential authority.

Paul Craig explores how the modalities of constitutional change differ between superior law constitutions and constitutions recognising Parliamentary sovereignty. Before turning to the question of change, Craig contrasts the content of such constitutions. Both types have horizontal, vertical and structural dimensions, but in a constitution recognising

Parliamentary sovereignty, that doctrine is central. In the context of a superior law constitution, over-constitutionalisation can be a concern; Parliamentary sovereignty by contrast is more likely to entail a danger of under-constitutionalisation.

Craig notes that Parliamentary sovereignty has not always been part of the UK constitution, and traces the different normative justifications that have been given for it in different centuries since it became part of the constitution. Turning finally to the modalities of change, a superior law constitution can change through constitutional amendment, judicial interpretation, changes to constitutional legislation and also through constitutional practice. In contrast, Parliamentary sovereignty constitutes the core of a constitutional system's rule of recognition. This can change, but such change requires acceptance by all key players within the polity.

It is appropriate to conclude a tribute to one of our leading constitutional scholars with a reflection on the role of constitutional scholars. Sam Bookman argues that constitutional scholars are themselves constitutional actors, especially so in an unwritten constitution. He situates this point as part of a wider literature recognising the constitutional roles of public officials, integrity agencies and knowledge institutions. He identifies three distinct but related and overlapping functions of constitutional scholarship, and gives New Zealand examples of each. The first is interpretive/descriptive – analysing existing sources and practices to help define what the constitution is. The role of the scholar in this regard is especially central in an unwritten constitution. The second role is evaluative/normative – this may involve critique and reform proposals, or in some cases outright rejection of the status quo as incoherent or illegitimate. The final role is educative, not only vis-à-vis students but also vis-à-vis other constitutional actors and the public. Bookman calls for constitutional scholars to candidly acknowledge these roles and to be conscious of the power inherent in their exercise; for other actors to support and resource them; and for scholars to discharge these functions in a collaborative and inclusive fashion.

Bruce Harris has made a leading contribution in all three roles. His work has helped to shape public law in New Zealand and beyond, and he has exercised that power with a clear sense of responsibility as well as his characteristic integrity and humility. The contributions to this *Festschrift* help carry forward the continuing exploration of some of the central themes in Harris' scholarship.

PART I

THE NATURE OF EXECUTIVE POWER

A MĀORI PERSPECTIVE ON CONSTITUTIONAL ISSUES, ESPECIALLY EXECUTIVE POWER

Claire CHARTERS

1. INTRODUCTION

In his book *New Zealand Constitution: An Analysis in Terms of Principles*, in the chapter on te Tiriti o Waitangi, Harris concludes that 'the perspective of each of the three branches of government in determining what is law and what is not does, however, remain that of the Anglo-New Zealand lawyer rather than that of the Māori-New Zealand lawyer'.[1] Here, I attempt to bring a Māori perspective to New Zealand constitutional law and Harris's specific contribution to scholarship on constitutional legal issues here and elsewhere.

Harris's recognition of, and explicit drawing attention to, Māori lawyer perspectives on New Zealand law is remarkable.[2] It epitomises Harris's support for the long-time claim by Māori that orthodox accounts of law ignore Māori views on New Zealand's constitution and the ways in which it – illegitimately – continues to subject us to law that is not our own. He clearly sees the structural racism. It also reflects that Harris, and arguably mainstream scholarship more widely, now sees and encourages spaces for Māori perspectives to contribute to orthodox understandings of New Zealand public law. This is significant. Shifting of orthodox constitutional law contributes to positive incremental change of New Zealand's constitution to better realise Māori legitimate claims and rights. This is particularly important in a context where incrementalism is the primary modus operandi for changing New Zealand's constitution.

However, as I will reflect on later in this contribution, Harris remains somewhat conservative in his assessment of Māori claims for constitutional transformation. He appears to be sitting inside the Western-constitutional box presenting only options from the Anglo-constitutional tradition as credible and/or realistic. Here, I hope, Harris is out of step with developing political and social context and law, and there is more scope for creativity, and justice, than he might suggest.

Harris is a pre-eminent public law scholar here and internationally. This is especially evident in his work on what he terms the third source of executive power. Bringing my Māori lawyer's lens to this issue, I wonder whether the more pressing question for New Zealand constitutional lawyers in this space might be a different one, namely how to ensure the executive is held to account to the honour of the Crown with respect to Māori. Nonetheless, I also delve a little deeper into the nuances of this work to provide some specific comments from my Māori lawyer perspective.

---

1 Bruce Harris *New Zealand Constitution: An Analysis in Terms of Principles* (Thomson Reuters, Wellington, 2018) at 50.

2 I oftentimes hear Nin Tomas's voice here, too, about whom Harris wrote, 'Nin taught me a lot about how Māori really feel and think about things. She helped me to better appreciate how Māori see New Zealand's colonial history, the Treaty of Waitangi and the development and organisation of New Zealand society since 1840': BV Harris "The Coherent Zeal that Nin Tomas Brought to her Responsibilities as a Law Teacher and Researcher" (2017) 5 Te Tai Haruru – Journal of Maori and Indigenous Issues 15 at 15.

2. WHAT IS A MĀORI PERSPECTIVE?

There is no singular Māori-New Zealand lawyer perspective on New Zealand's constitution. I stress, emphatically, that mine is only one. Māori views on New Zealand's constitution, authority and power today and over centuries span a spectrum from an exclusively tikanga perspective and rejection of state claims to authority in New Zealand to relatively orthodox, Anglo accounts of New Zealand law as it emanates from Westminster Parliament and the common law. Some Māori-New Zealand lawyers engage critically with mainstream accounts and with specific public law issues while others argue that New Zealand's constitution is structurally, at heart, racist and incapable of realising Māori aspirations. Today, although it took some time coming, many Māori lawyers have undertaken years of study of New Zealand's constitution in New Zealand, and legal systems in North American and European law schools and beyond, which have historically taught almost exclusively and always predominantly very un-Indigenous understandings of law. Some Māori lawyers, like me, have only a superficial understanding of our own Māori legal systems and belatedly devote time now to learning more about them.

Nonetheless, at a more general level, Māori often ask similar questions of constitutional law and scholarship. For example, where is Māori sovereignty and authority? Why isn't the main and most pressing issue in New Zealand constitutional law that Māori just claims, including to authority, do not have legal force in state law nor over these territories and the peoples residing on them? Does attention to other constitutional issues, either within state or Māori law, detract our attention from the ongoing injustice of colonisation and a colonial legal system in New Zealand? The more we gloss over the question of the basic illegality of the state, the more we support the assumption that the Anglo state is legitimate, and the result is that the executive (and Parliament) remain ultimately and effectively all powerful over Māori.[3] And, the more we adopt a realist, pragmatic and/or practical approach to the constitution, the more we avoid the normatively challenging question of the state's claim to authority.[4]

A response to this is, of course, that despite the questions about the basic legality of the state, historically and today, it is authoritative in fact in New Zealand: that is the reality. However, specific legal issues about the

---

3 Indeed, even those who do not gloss over the question of legality might also assume the legitimacy of the state, for example, Brookfield.

4 See Edward Willis's contribution to this volume.

source of executive power, and restraint on power, matter very much to individual and collective freedom and deserve attention from a Māori perspective: because the exercise of that power impacts on Māori. Avoid it at your peril! Turning to Harris's work on the source of executive power specifically, Māori-New Zealand lawyers interested and/or operating in New Zealand state law have good reason to be interested in executive power, albeit often for the wrong reasons. Executive power, and judicial deference to it, are at the heart of the Crown's claim, illegitimate but unpoliced, to sovereignty over Māori and much taking of Māori land contrary to aboriginal title doctrine. Even here we see from a Māori perspective, working inside the state system, that the wrong questions are being asked: why is the focus not more on restraints on power, and Crown obligations, rather than the source of power?

In sum, there is a messiness in Māori thinking about New Zealand's constitution and scholarship because, below the fundamental question of the legitimacy of the New Zealand state, it *is* messy. I share the dual perspective of many Māori constitutional scholars, simultaneously questioning the system at its core, from outside, while also seeking to critique the operation of the system, from the inside – legitimising it in so doing – but in an attempt to illuminate and eliminate it of its structural inequity, if that is possible. This dual perspective colours my specific comments on Harris's scholarship here, and the constitution generally.

3. MĀORI PERSPECTIVES INSIDE ORTHODOX ACCOUNTS, NOT TRANSFORMATIVE CONSTITUTIONAL CHANGE

Harris's support for Māori claims, be they based on the te Tiriti, tikanga Māori, international norms and/or wider understandings of justice, is evident throughout his career but particularly in his book on New Zealand's constitution, published in late 2018.[5] In his understanding of state law, and the ways in which it might develop to better respect Māori claims, Harris is progressive. Profoundly, unlike many other constitutional scholars and actors, Harris makes it clear that there is uncertainty 'as to the legal underpinning of the claimed United Kingdom sovereignty'.[6]

5 See Harris, above n 1; BV Harris "The Treaty of Waitangi and the Constitutional Future of New Zealand" [2005] NZ L Rev 189.

6 Harris, above n 1 at 10.

In explaining New Zealand's constitution in terms of 15 principles, the second principle, after the rule of law, is 'the principle of legislative, executive and judicial respect for the Treaty of Waitangi'.[7] Indeed, it is the approach to the constitution based on principles that illuminates the many non-legal rules in play, comparatively emphasising the moral and political obligations.[8] By focusing on principles, Māori rights are visible within the constitution even though they are rarely enforceable as a matter of hard law. Harris includes discussion of the Declaration on the Rights of Indigenous Peoples, a formally non-binding but legally influential international instrument setting out Indigenous peoples' rights, including to self-determination.[9] Harris also carefully avoids portraying the Treaty as Māori consent to British sovereignty – related to the above point about the uncertainty underlying New Zealand's constitution. He sees the Treaty in judicial review under a number of existing grounds for review and concludes '[i]t may be that the Supreme Court at some time will be called upon to review the legal status of the Treaty of Waitangi, independent of its selective recognition in statute, with a view to possibly holding that it has status on its own as justiciable positive law'.[10]

Harris puts the question of the Treaty in the centre of his discussion of the future of New Zealand's constitution, arguing it should be the 'first step' in any constitutional development.[11] More recently, he adds that public acceptance of reform in relation to the Treaty is a prerequisite to 'successful development of other aspects of the constitution' such as adoption of a written constitution.[12]

Nonetheless, Harris might be classified as more of an incrementalist – in favour of step-by-step change that does not challenge the basic structure of the constitution. While Harris is more receptive and open than many of his contemporaries to Māori perspectives on state constitutional law, he still works within the confines of Western constitutional design. To Harris, the key questions remain, first, entrenchment of a written constitution with strong-form review and, secondly, the temperament of the non-Māori

7 At ch 3.

8 At 41.

9 For discussion see Claire Charters "The Declaration on the Rights of Indigenous Peoples in New Zealand Courts: A Case of Cautious Optimism" in Centre for International Governance Innovation *UNDRIP Implementation: Comparative Approaches, Indigenous Voices from CANZUS* (Ottawa, 2019) 43.

10 Harris, above n 1, at 42.

11 Harris, above n 6, at 190.

12 Harris, above n 1, at 314.

majority that might view Māori rights, including in the Treaty of Waitangi, as a source of inequality. He comments that:[13]

> The analyses will expose the essential choice that the New Zealand community must make between: giving the Treaty of Waitangi a justiciable status in a written constitution that may allow it to constrain legally the legislature, the executive, and the judiciary; not providing such higher law constitutional status in the interests of leaving protection of Treaty and other Maori interests to regular statute and common law; or, as a third option, furthering the ideal of equality in society by removing from the law all differential protection for Maori interests.

Positively, Harris considers, in more depth than many mainstream texts, the *Report of Matike Mai Aotearoa – the Independent Working Group on Constitutional Transformation* (the Matike Mai report),[14] devoting over two pages to it in his book. The Matike Mai report was commissioned by the iwi chairs and is the result of 252 consultation hui held with Māori on constitutional change. It outlines a structure for constitutional transformation, and realisation of Māori tino rangatiratanga. Harris concludes, 'The major policy issue as to whether aspects of the law should provide differently for Māori, or there should be no special provision for Māori, appears increasingly to be resolved in favour of a degree of pluralism being accepted in justified circumstances'.[15]

Yet, the future constitutional change options outlined in Harris's book are notably devoid of serious consideration of how the Matike Mai report, or other Māori ideas to realise te Tiriti, including Māori governance, might be realised, even via the possibility of incremental steps. For example, there is no discussion of how Māori rights might be related to greater provision for human rights in the future or realised in a bicameral legislature or efforts to move to a republic. In confining his consideration of Māori rights to a single question of entrenchment, or not, some opportunities for important change within the system are missed.

Moreover, Harris might be thinking about some of the questions that preoccupy Anglo-constitutional lawyers in an Anglo way. There are other

---

13 Harris, above n 6, at 190.

14 See Matike Mai Aotearoa – The Independent Working Group on Constitutional Transformation *He Whakaaro Here Whakaumu mō Aotearoa: The Report of Matike Mai Aotearoa – The Independent Working Group on Constitutional Transformation* (2016).

15 Harris, above n 1, at 314.

ways to think about them. For example, Harris wrote in relation to the judicial creativity needed to make sense of the Treaty:[16]

> In a system of government founded on the rule of law, and where the doctrine of the separation of powers is regarded as relevant, creativity by the courts is quickly recognised as law-making and open to criticism as inappropriate for a non-elected, and therefore democratically unaccountable, body. Accusations of judicial activism are easily made in New Zealand.

He is suggesting that such creativity may be contrary to the rule of law. From where I sit, judges are not required to be creative to interpret the Treaty.[17] Adopting the international legal rule of contra proferentem when interpreting treaties, the te reo Māori text takes precedence, and it is clear: the Crown acquired some authority over its citizens, Māori retain authority over Māori, and the Crown agrees to respect all Māori rights in relation to our taonga. The focus in more recent times on the principles of the Treaty and the perceived 'confusion' around the Treaty comes, in my view, from the uncomfortable conflict between te Tiriti (not to forget international obligations to recognise Māori self-determination) on the one hand and New Zealand's constitution and the political sovereignty exercised by the Crown.[18]

The clearest indication that Harris provides as to *why* he dismisses grander constitutional transformation recommended in the Matike Mai

---

16 Harris, above n 6, at 201.

17 For example, I disagree with the following passage: 'If the Treaty in its original versions, or its principles, were included in a written constitution that was intended to constrain the law-making of Parliament, the nature of the content of the Treaty is such that the courts would have a stark choice between either being creative or giving little effect to the Treaty. The general principles in written constitutions, especially the guarantees of entrenched bills of rights, inevitably compel courts to give practical content in particular contexts to generic aspirations. With so little assistance from the texts of the Treaty, and with little available precedent from New Zealand and overseas jurisdictions, the courts' task would be difficult. The 30 years of jurisprudence in reports of the Waitangi Tribunal would be of some assistance. The courts would face a dilemma between failing to fulfil their responsibility to give effect to the constitution and being perceived as so creative as to undermine the confidence the community must have in them if they are to retain their perceived legitimacy. It is necessary to question whether an impossible or inappropriate task would be asked of the courts': Harris, above n 6, at 201–202.

18 See Claire Charters "The Elephant in the Court-room: An Essay on the Judiciary's Silence on the Legitimacy of the New Zealand State" in Simon Mount and Max Harris (eds) *The Promise of Law: Essays Marking the Retirement of Dame Sian Elias as Chief Justice of New Zealand* (LexisNexis NZ, Wellington, 2019) 91.

report is in his discussion of majority intolerance and equality. On the first point, he argues, '[c]onsistent as the models suggested in the report may be with the Māori ethos surrounding the original signing of the Treaty, they are unlikely to be acceptable to a majority of the contemporary New Zealand community'.[19] On the equality point, he states:[20]

> The availability of the Treaty, or its principles, to constrain the law-making of Parliament could be argued to be giving one racial group in New Zealand a constitutionally privileged position that would deny fundamental ideals of equality and the arguably simplistic principle of 'one law for all'. The tension is between the justifications for the recognition in an overriding constitution of a different position for Maori in New Zealand law, and the principle that all races, all individuals, in a multi-racial and increasingly pluralistic community should be treated equally. The tension would be heightened by the specific protection of Maori interests being provided in an overriding constitution, and not just ordinary enactments of Parliament.

And:[21]

> The potential justifications for the different position in the law of Maori are: the obligations undertaken and expectations created by the United Kingdom Crown and the representatives of Maori when in 1840 they entered into the Treaty of Waitangi; the indigenous status of the Maori people; and the fact that Maori continue to fail to achieve social and economic parity with the non-Maori New Zealand community. The policy question is whether these justifications should outweigh the principle that the law-making process and the law should treat all of New Zealand's peoples equally. Some may argue that, without special constitutional protection, Maori cannot be treated equally because of their current inherently disadvantaged position. Positive discrimination is needed to facilitate equality.

He concludes that, given the respective normative positions, 'the current approach, involving multifarious provisions in law for justified Māori interests in relevant contexts is likely to continue to evolve in an incremental way ...'.[22]

Harris's focus on equality became particularly apparent in his work post the government's decision to extinguish potential Māori title in

---

19 Harris, above n 1, at 316.
20 Harris, above n 6, at 207.
21 Harris, above n 6, at 207.
22 Harris, above n 1, at 316.

the foreshore and seabed, then enacted in legislation. Māori argued that it was discriminatory to extinguish only (potential) Māori title to the foreshore and seabed yet retain freehold titles. On the other hand, many – arguably the majority – opposed to Māori title argued that Māori title was discriminatory. Citing the work of some of those most opposed to Māori title,[23] Harris wrote, 'compliance with unqualified equality principles would require the formal legal and informal protection of Maori interests to be deliberately dismantled'.[24]

While there is, arguably, almost universal commitment to equality in principle, the meaning of equality is notoriously difficult to pin down, and there are very different views on how it might be achieved in theory and in practice. Typically, there are distinctions between formal and substantive equality, with the former more favoured by liberal-leaning scholars and the latter by critical scholars of colour. What is true, whatever one's assessment of the merits of different approaches to equality, is that equality is not a simple and easy-to-achieve objective.

A point that is rarely appreciated in orthodox understandings of equality in Aotearoa New Zealand is that Māori continue to be regulated by an imposed system that is non-Māori, belonging to the ancestors and heritage of the dominant, most powerful and colonising group in New Zealand society, Pākehā. Moreover, equality is not a neutral concept, and it is important to recognise that the prevailing ideal of equality in the law of Aotearoa New Zealand is a liberal, 'pākehā' one. The idea of equality that Harris, and many others, is concerned about, at least on the basis of their writing, is ensuring individuals – individual Māori (the colonised) and individual non-Māori – are treated identically, *under the law of the coloniser*. When we start our analysis of equality from an appreciation that Māori continue to live under a foreign legal system and imagine the reaction to the converse – Pākehā being regulated under tikanga Māori – the assessment of the equality of Māori 'rights' under New Zealand's constitution, and how to achieve it becomes more complex. To Harris's points above, cited as supportive of legal protections of Māori rights, I would add that it is important to understand New Zealand's outlier position in not providing for legally enforceable (by the judiciary against the legislature), constitutional rights designed to protect minorities against the 'tyranny of the majority'.

---

23 Harris, above n 1, at 314, citing Don Brash *Incredible Luck* (Troika Books, Auckland, 2014).

24 Harris, above n 6, at 193.

Moreover, many of our liberal democratic settler state friends include much stronger – legal – protections of Indigenous peoples' rights in their constitutional and legal systems.[25]

4. EXECUTIVE POWER

Harris is well known for his work on executive power, its source and constraints. His arguments related to the 'third source' of executive power, additional yet independent from statutory and prerogative power, were published no less than three times in the Law Quarterly Review with a related argument on the prerogative published in the Cambridge Law Review.[26]

It is a pertinent time to consider executive power with respect to Māori rights: as I write, the High Court is considering substantive arguments in the dispute over Crown decisions determining mana whenua in specific areas in Tāmaki Makaurau. The majority of the Supreme Court stated at the outset of the earlier – unsuccessful – strike out proceedings that, '[t]he principal issue for determination on the appeal is whether the claim should be permitted to proceed on the basis that it is properly characterised as a claim for the recognition of various rights rather than as a challenge to the decision to legislate'.[27] The case follows a recent line of cases where the courts have reviewed Crown action in Treaty settlements, and other areas, narrowing the circumstances where courts show deference to the executive.

4.1. THE CLAIM TO CROWN SOVEREIGNTY IS AN EXPRESSION OF EXECUTIVE POWER, RATHER THAN LAW

The key point about Crown executive power is the illegality of the assertion of sovereignty over Aotearoa. While Harris does not perhaps dwell on this point in any scholarly way, he is open and transparent about it:[28]

---

25 The Constitution of Canada 1982, especially s 35.

26 BV Harris "Government 'Third Source' Action and Common Law Constitutionalism" (2010) 126 LQR 373; "The 'Third Source' of Authority for Government Action Revisited" (2007) 123 LQR 225; "The 'Third Source' of Authority for Government Action" (1992) 108 LQR 626; "Judicial Review, Justiciability and the Prerogative of Mercy" (2003) 62 Cambridge LJ 631.

27 *Ngāti Whātua Ōrākei Trust v Attorney-General* [2018] NZSC 84, [2019] 1 NZLR 116 at [2].

28 Harris, above n 1, at 10.

> Notwithstanding the entering into the Treaty, there is uncertainty as to the legal underpinning of the claimed United Kingdom sovereignty. The question is whether it followed from cession through the Treaty, occupation by the United Kingdom settlers, discovery by James Cook, or a combination of these events. Irrespective of whatever outcome may result from formal legal analysis, there is no doubt that United Kingdom sovereignty was effectively asserted over New Zealand as a political fact.

Harris is right, and right to point out that there is no satisfactory legal explanation of the transfer of sovereignty from Māori to the Crown under relevant British or international law applicable at the time (and certainly not under tikanga Māori). The reasons for the uncertainty around the Treaty as a source of cession of sovereignty is that it did not amount to consent to the transfer of Māori authority anywhere close to the level understood by British lawyers by the word 'sovereignty'. At best, it amounted to a cession of some power to the Crown to regulate its own people.[29] Occupation is a poor legal explanation of transfer, at least at the time when sovereignty was proclaimed, because there was little settlement in 1840, with estimates of around 2000 non-Maori residents. Discovery would assume Aotearoa to have been terra nullius, which is implausible factually but also legally given the long-time official recognition of Māori by the Crown, not least in *He Whakaputanga*. Conquest is also a legal justification for a transfer of sovereignty under British law, in 1840 at least, but there was no evidence of that. This means that the Crown's 1840 proclamations of sovereignty, under prerogative, is the only plausible official explanation of transfer of sovereignty from Māori to the Crown.[30] However, proclamation around acquisition of territory does not amount to a legal source of transfer and is not lawful. It is simply a political claim that the courts will not legally review.[31] It is a quintessential example of unchecked executive power. Concern about executive power, therefore, colours my perspective as a Māori lawyer on all issues involving the executive.

---

29 Ned Fletcher "A Praiseworthy Device for Amusing and Pacifying Savages?: What the Framers Meant by the English Text of the Treaty of Waitangi" (PhD Thesis, University of Auckland, 2014); "Foundation" in Simon Mount and Max Harris (eds) *The Promise of Law: Essays Marking the Retirement of Dame Sian Elias as Chief Justice of New Zealand* (LexisNexis NZ, Wellington, 2019) 67.

30 Paul McHugh in *The Māori Magna Carta: New Zealand Law and the Treaty of Waitangi* (Oxford University Press, Auckland, 1991) at 32.

31 Harris "The 'Third Source' of Authority for Government Action Revisited", above n 25.

4.2. IS A DEMOCRATIC MANDATE FOR EXECUTIVE ACTION RELEVANT?

Moving forward, a key question in executive decision-making, very relevant to the contemporary courts' approach to review, is the democratic source of the executive's authority to act. Clearly there is democratic direction in statutory authorisations, which is missing, at least explicitly,[32] in exercises of prerogative power and use of the third source. Harris, other scholars and the judiciary consider the normative arguments for review in cases where the legislature has directed or authorised the executive to act in the way being challenged, compared to when it has not. Democratic authorisation is used to justify executive incursions on individuals' rights. Putting Māori to the fore, democratic authorisation is a weak justification. In New Zealand's constitutional structure, there is no formal legal restriction on the majority's will to protect Indigenous peoples, or other minorities' rights. In such a system the courts should be considerably more careful and proactive to hold the executive to rights standards irrespective of legislative authorisation for the executive's action. While New Zealand courts are also, at heart, a state construct in a colonial system, and hence imperfect, structurally they are better placed to protect rights than a majoritarian-driven legislature or executive.

4.3. THE THIRD SOURCE IS BASICALLY PROBLEMATIC AS IT PROVIDES THE EXECUTIVE WITH MORE POWER RATHER THAN LESS

Like others, I share the concern that the third source effectively authorises the executive's freedom to act unless restrained, broadening the executive's power. The converse – the need for authorisation before action is permitted – is at least basically more restrictive. Limiting the power of state institutions with the power to encroach on Māori rights is positive, at least from my perspective, for the reasons I have canvassed. Harris's arguments for recognition of the third source include that pragmatic requirements of the modern state to enter into contracts, for example. Pragmatic arguments

[32] There is some debate about whether the use of prerogative power is implicitly authorised by Parliment where Parliament has not legislated over prerogative power: see BV Harris "Replacement of the Royal Prerogative in New Zealand" (2009) 23 NZULR 285 at 303.

do not, in my view, outweigh the more substantive and normative point about the need to restrain power, even noting Willis's comments about the normativity of pragmatism in this volume.[33]

4.4. THE SOURCE OF EXECUTIVE POWER IS THE LESS PRESSING QUESTION

I am not convinced that the source of executive power is the central question from a Māori perspective. Whether statutory, prerogative or third source, the more interesting questions in terms of outcomes are (1) whether there is a clear, straightforward and strong judicial review ground on which Māori claimants might peg review when our rights are compromised by executive action; and (2) how much deference the courts show to executive decision-making and/or when proximate to legislative action.

On the first point, source matters less now than it did previously in influencing a court's decision to review, or not,[34] and courts are increasingly reviewing exercises of power in areas formerly considered out of bounds.[35] Further, as I have argued elsewhere,[36] there is increasing momentum towards review of executive action against the Treaty, tikanga Māori and Māori just claims, and the ongoing *Ngāti Whātua ki Ōrākei* case will bear on this point too.

On the second point, that of deference, Harris has this to say:[37]

> Deference is controversial. First, because, if the discretion to defer is exercised, the courts are choosing, as with all findings of non-justiciability, not to fulfil their important role of upholding the rule of law against the public decision-maker. ... Deference is controversial, second, because there will inevitably be differing opinions as to where the line should be drawn in each circumstance between exercise of deference to the government decision-maker and a court assuming responsibility for supervising the executive

---

33 See Edward Willis's contribution to this volume.

34 Harris "The 'Third Source' of Authority for Government Action Revisited", above n 25.

35 *R (Miller) v The Prime Minister* and *Cherry v Advocate General for Scotland* [2019] UKSC 41. An example from New Zealand involving Treaty settlements is *Ririnui v Landcorp Farming Ltd* [2016] NZSC 62, [2016] 1 NZLR 1056.

36 Claire Charters "*Wakatū* in Peripheral Vision: Māori-Rights Based Judicial Review of the Executive and the Courts' Approach to the United Nations Declaration on the Rights of Indigenous Peoples" [2019] NZ L Rev 85.

37 Harris, above n 1, at 210.

> decision-making. The line between what the court may appropriately supervise and what should be left to the discretion of the public authority decision maker and their non-judicial accountability paths will not always be bright.

The glaring issue in relation to both questions – related to judicial review grounds and deference – is, in my view, the same: that Māori collective and individuals' rights are potentially at stake, and the need for courts to have the legal tools available to enforce them.[38] A review of scholarship on executive action in New Zealand law quickly reveals that all executive action must be subject to rights, including statutory rights, such as in the New Zealand Bill of Rights Act 1990,[39] and common law rights, unless rights-abridging action is authorised by legislation.[40] Why, then, are Māori rights – in te Tiriti, under tikanga Māori, under international law and in common law (including aboriginal title) – for the most part insufficiently 'legal' to be enforceable? It means that the executive remains relatively free to act inconsistently with te Tiriti, the Indigenous Declaration and so on, just as it did when claiming sovereignty over New Zealand in 1840. Why does this remain the constitutional reality today, in 2021? For this contribution, my question is more directed: why is this ongoing injustice not the central focus of New Zealand's public lawyers examining the executive (or constitutional law more generally) today?

4.5. THE SOURCE OF EXECUTIVE POWER MAY CONTINUE TO MATTER SYMBOLICALLY

Equally, if the source of executive power is important, maybe it is for a different reason. The source of executive authority might matter more

---

38 I also outline normative reasons for court intervention in Charters, above n 36. I also note that this raises, of course, the normative question of whether courts, and law rather than political negotiation, are 'better' at realising Māori rights and claims than political arms of government, an interest also of Harris: see "Government 'Third Source' Action and Common Law Constitutionalism", above n 25. These are long-standing issues debated regularly for over many centuries, and issues in which I have an intense interest. However, I just remind us of Justice Joseph Williams' recent caution against the executive being the arbiter of its own justice: *Port Nicholson Block Settlement Trust v Attorney-General* [2012] NZHC 3181 at [63].

39 I note, here, as many others also have, the under-utilisation by Māori of the BORA, and especially the s 20 right to culture. Claire Charters "Finding the Rights Balance: A Methodology to Balance Indigenous Peoples' Rights and Human Rights in Decision-making" [2017] NZ L Rev 553.

40 Harris "Government 'Third Source' Action and Common Law Constitutionalism", above n 25.

symbolically than practically, at least from a Māori perspective. If the source of executive authority to act in its dealings with Māori, iwi, hapū and whānau, including in Treaty settlements, is the prerogative act of state power, then the logical legal consequence must be that Māori retain their state-like qualities, consistently with Māori claims to rangatiratanga.[41] Māori remain a foreign state as a matter of state domestic law, or at the least an entity with separate and independent authority from the state. While it may be irrelevant, from a tikanga perspective, whether or not the state recognises iwi, hapū or whānau tino rangatiratanga – explicitly, implicitly, or any other way – it supports Māori claims to self-determination and authority under state law.[42]

4.6. OPTIONS FOR FUTURE: NON-JUDICIAL OVERSIGHT OF THE EXECUTIVE?

Harris highlights in his work non-judicial methods of holding the executive to account.[43] Here, in this penultimate paragraph, I simply note that there might be appropriate non-judicial ways to hold the executive, and Parliament, to account with respect to Māori claims and rights based on te Tiriti, the UN Indigenous Declaration, under tikanga Māori and so on. One is a kind of pre-review of executive decision-making by an entity expert in such matters, such as the Waitangi Tribunal or Māori senate, or similar entity, providing their recommendations are binding.[44]

5. CONCLUSION

In this contribution, drawing on Harris's scholarship and responding to his implicit invitation in his most recent major piece of work, I have

---

41 See Claire Charters "Recognition of Tikanga Māori and the Constitutional Myth of Monolegalism: Reinterpreting Case Law" in Richard Benton and Robert Joseph (eds) *Waking the Taniwha: Māori Governance in the 21st Century* (Thomson Reuters, Wellington, 2021) (forthcoming).

42 See John Dawson and Abby Suszko "Courts and Representation Disputes in the Treaty Settlement Process" [2012] NZ L Rev 35.

43 See, for example, BV Harris "The 'Third Source' of Authority for Government Action Revisited" (2007) 123 LQR 225 at 237–238.

44 I note here, too, the potential of Matthew Palmer's ideas around a Treaty court or similar as suggested in Matthew SR Palmer *The Treaty of Waitangi in New Zealand's Law and Constitution* (Victoria University Press, Wellington, 2008).

attempted to illustrate how we might examine constitutional issues from a Māori legal perspective. While I find the direction of orthodox constitutional legal development pleasing, as it incrementally shifts to better accommodate Māori concerns, claims and rights, it remains largely preoccupied with legal questions that are less relevant to, and thus effectively side-line, Māori concerns, claims and rights. It is for this reason that I agree with Moana Jackson, Margaret Mutu and other leading Māori constitutional scholars that, for real justice in New Zealand's constitution, nothing short of normatively driven constitutional transformation is essential.

CONSTITUTIONAL PRAGMATISM AND 'THIRD SOURCE' EXECUTIVE AUTHORITY

Edward WILLIS*

1. INTRODUCTION

For at least 20 years the language of pragmatism has been used to describe New Zealand's constitution. Charlotte Macdonald argued in 2000 that our constitutional arrangements 'have tended to favour the simple, accessible

* Thanks to Nicole Roughan, Sam Bookman, Max Harris and Hanna Wilberg for commenting on an early draft, although all errors and omissions are my own.

and pragmatic'.[1] Dame Silvia Cartwright noted in her inaugural year as Governor-General that 'constitutional change in New Zealand is often the result of a pragmatic and practical response to events'.[2] The description of New Zealand's approach to constitutional development as one of 'pragmatic evolution' by the Constitutional Arrangements Committee of the House of Representatives appeared especially apt at the time – a convenient shorthand for both the lack of the kind of organising framework provided by a written constitution and a propensity to address constitutional matters on an as-needed basis.[3] In hindsight, this official endorsement of the description marked a tipping point in our constitutional discourse. It is now almost second nature to invoke some concept of pragmatism when attempting to describe New Zealand's constitutional arrangements.

Nonetheless, I detect some dissatisfaction with the prominence pragmatism occupies in our constitutional thinking. Part of this dissatisfaction seems to stem from an understanding of pragmatism as a way of understanding our constitution independently of inquiries into its normative (and in particular, its moral) content. Rather than serve as a theory of constitutional practice, pragmatism stands as an empty justification – or perhaps an apology – for a lack of coherent constitutional theory.[4] And our comfort with relying on such empty vessels has been seriously shaken. We must acknowledge a comparative context where naked populism and ad hoc political manoeuvring has struck at the foundations of democratic constitutionalism.[5] The institutions of constitutional government can fail where underlying normative considerations are ignored, challenged or perceived as inadequate. One of the lessons of this international experience may be that coherent constitutional theory buttresses wide acceptance for the moral norms that support institutional resilience and strength. Over-reliance on pragmatism at the expense of this type of normative

1 Charlotte Macdonald "What Constitutes Our Nation? How Do We Express Ourselves?" in Colin James (ed) *Building the Constitution* (Victoria University of Wellington Institute of Policy Studies, Wellington, 2000) 81 at 87.

2 Dame Silvia Cartwright "The Role of the Governor-General" (New Zealand Centre for Public Law Occasional Paper, Wellington, 2001) at 15.

3 Constitutional Arrangements Committee *Inquiry into New Zealand's Existing Constitutional Arrangements: Report of the Constitutional Arrangements Committee 1.24A* (House of Representatives, 10 August 2005) at 12.

4 See Christopher Pouwels "Does New Zealand Have a 'Pragmatic' Constitution?" (2015) 21 AULR 41.

5 See generally Tarunabh Khaitan "Executive Aggrandizement in Established Democracies: A Crisis of Liberal Democratic Constitutionalism" (2019) 17 Int'l J Con L 342.

grounding can appear quaint given the state of the world, and perhaps even increasingly naïve.

However, I would argue that anti-normativism is not the only frame of reference for understanding pragmatic accounts of our constitution. It is also possible to place our constitutional practice within a rich philosophical tradition that understands pragmatism as a particular branch of knowledge, with its own intellectual goals and methods.[6] This approach retains a strong focus on instrumental efficacy, but it does not imply a rejection of constitutional theory. Instead, theory itself is treated as a means for ensuring that actual constitutional outcomes best serve the needs and interests of society. In this contribution I suggest that this strand of pragmatism may well provide useful insights into our constitutional practice and the norms that guide it. Perhaps it can even reconcile the instinct to describe the constitution in pragmatic terms with our apparent unease regarding the consequences of that particular choice of language.

This contribution takes the work of Professor Bruce Harris as exemplary of this richer, more credible account of constitutional pragmatism in a New Zealand context. Adherents to constitutional pragmatism, as with legal pragmatism more generally, form a broad church. One feature that pragmatists share is a scepticism that legal and constitutional matters can be understood or determined primarily on the basis of a priori reasoning. Instead, constitutional law is best understood as a problem-solving exercise where the law is deployed to achieve social goals.[7] Systemic considerations of the kind with which normative theory is concerned still play a role, but they must be balanced against the need to do justice in the particular circumstances of the individual case. Harris's work comes within this definition because he views the constitution as a system with the aim of contributing towards and maintaining an ordered and stable society, and it is informed by political reality and moral theory as much as by positive legal rules.[8] This outlook is also what distinguishes

---

6 Compare Richard A Posner *Law, Pragmatism and Democracy* (Harvard University Press, Cambridge, 2003) at 49–56, who distinguishes between philosophical and 'everyday' pragmatism for the purposes of legal theory.

7 For an account of legal pragmatism along these lines see David Landau "Legal Pragmatism and Comparative Constitutional Law" in Gary Jacobsohn and Miguel Schor (eds) *Comparative Constitutional Theory* (Edward Elgar Publishing, Northampton, 2018) 208.

8 Bruce Harris *New Zealand Constitution: An Analysis in Terms of Principles* (Thomson Reuters, Wellington, 2018) at 1.

Professor Harris's approach from other similar perspectives, such as constitutional realism,[9] that do not really engage with normative constitutional theory.

This contribution seeks to demonstrate the utility of this richer, more normative account of pragmatism with particular reference to 'third source' authority for executive government action. Third source authority has been a persistent motif in Harris's scholarly work.[10] It is also controversial. If a constitution's normativity emphasises the authority of positive law, then the residual nature of third source authority can appear anomalous or even dangerous.[11] The traditional response from proponents of third source authority is to claim that the practical value of an empowered, responsive government outweighs any rule of law concerns.[12] This response leans on normatively thin pragmatic justifications for the ad hoc administration of government, but I believe that pragmatism has more to offer in this debate. It can engage with the rule of law and other normative critiques more directly, and so offer a conceptually sound account of third source authority that can be better reconciled with rule of law values.

Or at least, that will be my argument in the sections that follow. That argument is broadly divided into two parts. The first part sets constitutional pragmatism in its theoretical context. The discussion frames pragmatism as a response to the difficulty of coherently engaging with the normative dimension of an unwritten constitution, but also distinguishes pragmatism from primarily descriptive or 'realist' approaches to constitutional analysis. This shows constitutional pragmatism as sensitive to normative considerations even though such considerations are not afforded paramount importance. The second part then uses constitutional pragmatism to

---

9 See Matthew SR Palmer "New Zealand Constitutional Culture" (2007) 22 NZULR 565; "Using Constitutional Realism to Identify the *Complete* Constitution: Lessons from an Unwritten Constitution" (2006) 54 Am J Comp L 587; "What is New Zealand's Constitution and Who Interprets it? Constitutional Realism and the Importance of Public Office-holders" (2006) 17 PLR 133.

10 Harris, above n 8, at 154–161; "A Call to Maintain and Evolve the Third Source of Authority for Government Action" (2017) 27 NZULR 853; "Recent Judicial Recognition of the Third Source of Authority for Government Action" (2014) 26 NZULR 60 ("Recent Judicial Recognition"); "Government 'Third Source' Action and Common Law Constitutionalism" (2010) 126 LQR 373; "The 'Third Source' of Authority for Government Action Revisited" (2007) 123 LQR 225 ("The 'Third Source' Revisited"); "The 'Third Source' of Authority for Government Action" (1992) 108 LQR 626.

11 See especially Philip A Joseph *Constitutional and Administrative Law in New Zealand* (4th ed, Thomson Reuters, Wellington, 2014) at 652–658.

12 See Harris "Recent Judicial Recognition", above n 10, at 80.

explain the legitimate use of third source executive authority. This includes tangible guidance for the courts to consider when assessing the lawfulness of government action based on the third source.

2. THREE PERSPECTIVES

In the American legal tradition, legal pragmatism is often understood in terms of its opposition to legal formalism.[13] In this section I seek to understand constitutional pragmatism by contrasting it with two other jurisprudential viewpoints more familiar to New Zealand legal scholarship: constitutional normativism and constitutional realism. My purpose here is elucidation rather than definition. All three viewpoints sit on a spectrum and are not separated by neat conceptual boundaries, but we can generally say that constitutional pragmatism occupies the space between normativism's idealised commitment to substantive values and realism's anti-theoretical descriptivism. Pragmatism is distinctive because it is instrumental in its orientation, but it can and does acknowledge the influence of moral and political theory on the constitution's efficacy. In other words, constitutional principle matters to the pragmatist, as long as it supports the standards of social practicality and functionality that pragmatism holds dear.

2.1. NORMATIVISM

I have always been of the view that there is something quintessentially normative about the concept of a constitution. What I mean by this is that, while part of the function of any constitution is to describe the nature and allocation of public power within the state, genuine constitutions also tend to have something to say about the relationship between public power and certain underlying substantive principles or values that the state recognises as fundamental.[14] In this sense a constitution sets out an abstract framework of political and moral values for the conduct of legitimate government. A credible account of constitutional government, I would argue, will make this substantively normative dimension more or less explicit.

13 Landau, above n 7, at 209.

14 Charles Howard McIlwain *Constitutionalism: Ancient and Modern* (Cornell University Press, Ithaca, 1940) at 5.

We might label this constitutional perspective 'normativism', following in part Loughlin's terminology associated with the ideal of constitutional legality.[15] On this view, constitutional law is necessarily motivated by a kind of 'institutional morality' – that is, an institutional commitment to the realisation of principles and values that justify or legitimate government.[16] These principles and values form the starting point for deductive reasoning to resolve constitutional disputes and inform ongoing constitutional practice. When I speak of a normative approach to constitutional law in this contribution, it is this thick, morally laden normativism that I have in mind.

Written constitutions,[17] particularly those that have inspired or been inspired by a tradition of liberal constitutionalism, do a very good job of making at least some important principles and values explicit.[18] In contrast, the Westminster tradition, with its unwritten form, and its Diceyan emphasis on Parliamentary sovereignty, often seems to struggle to integrate this implicitly normative dimension. John Griffith controversially argued that the UK constitution is 'no more and no less than what happens'.[19] This statement has been understood as a denial of the existence of any moral content to the constitution,[20] but more pertinently it reveals an uncomfortable truth about the nature of normative constitutional analysis in the Westminster tradition. Unlike written constitutions premised on consistency with a higher-order law (however conceived), the normative principles informing constitutional practice in an unwritten constitution are themselves inherently contestable, as well as being difficult to access and only vaguely articulated. Vernon Bogdanor essentially reiterated Griffith's core point in much less ambiguous terms by contrasting Westminster constitutional analysis that usually proceeds 'only in descriptive terms, as a summation of past experience' with analysis engaging in 'genuinely

---

15 Martin Loughlin *Public Law and Political Theory* (Clarendon Press, Oxford, 1992) at 60.

16 Joseph, above n 11, at 2.

17 I prefer the terms 'written constitution' and 'unwritten constitution' as terms of art to the modern tendency to refer to 'codified' and 'uncodified' constitutions. A full justification for my insistence on using these terms will need to wait for another occasion.

18 See generally Beau Breslin *From Words to Worlds: Exploring Constitutional Functionality* (Johns Hopkins University Press, Baltimore, 2009).

19 JAG Griffith "The Political Constitution" (1979) 42 MLR 1 at 19.

20 See, for example, JWF Allison *The English Historical Constitution: Continuity, Change and European Effects* (Cambridge University Press, Cambridge, 2007) at 34; Adam Tomkins *Our Republican Constitution* (Hart Publishing, Oxford, 2005) at 52.

constitutional terms as representing the recognition of certain normative principles'.[21]

This apparent difficulty with analysing Westminster-type constitutions in terms of their substantive normative content has not prevented theorists from engaging in debate as to the most morally appealing version of our constitutional practice. Trevor Allan, for instance, influenced by the interpretivist approach of Ronald Dworkin,[22] has forcefully advocated that formal sources of law such as Parliamentary legislation take their authority through a process of application that brings those sources into line with fundamental constitutional values.[23] John Laws has presented an explicitly Kantian account of an implied fundamental common law based on human dignity and individual autonomy.[24] In New Zealand, Philip Joseph has developed a 'thick' account of the rule of law that overtly conditions the exercise of state authority in order to give effect to fundamental values.[25] Such richly normative accounts can appear compelling in the abstract, but moral desirability is not sufficient for a viable theory of constitutional government. The realities of Westminster government – Parliamentary sovereignty, political determination of rights issues, an absence of constitutional review – set themselves in direct opposition to these theoretical normative accounts. Further, the basis in the constitution for these moral prescriptions is often less than clear. Advocates for a normative account of constitutional government therefore risk substituting their own views in place of those of the wider community the constitution is intended to serve.[26] This apparent gap between the ideal and the actual poses a genuine challenge to the coherence of normativism in a Westminster constitutional context.

I think that this challenge of meaningful engagement at the level of normative principle goes some way towards explaining the predilection for pragmatism as a characterisation of New Zealand's constitutional arrangements. Pragmatism is often defined in opposition to 'formalism'

---

21 Vernon Bogdanor *The New British Constitution* (Hart Publishing, Oxford, 2009) at 19.

22 See, for example, Ronald Dworkin *Law's Empire* (Harvard University Press, Cambridge, 1986).

23 TRS Allan *Constitutional Justice: A Liberal Theory of the Rule of Law* (Oxford University Press, Oxford, 2001); *The Sovereignty of Law: Freedom, Constitution, and Common Law* (Oxford University Press, Oxford, 2013).

24 John Laws "Constitution: Morals and Rights" [1996] PL 622.

25 See especially Philip A Joseph "The Rule of Law: Foundational Norm" in Richard Ekins (ed) *Modern Challenges to the Rule of Law* (LexisNexis NZ, Wellington, 2011) 47.

26 Harris, above n 8, at 21.

in the sense of reasoning from ex ante, normative principles,[27] and so provides an organising framework for constitutional practice that is not necessarily tethered to a particular set of external norms, values or principles.[28] This reflects pragmatism's origins as a philosophical discipline, which is motivated by suspicion of the idealist tendency towards abstraction that in turn gives rise to normative phenomena.[29] Instead, the clear emphasis is on developing a practical and empirical approach.[30] Pragmatism counsels that the constitution should be approached as it is, not as we would like it to be. Further, the pragmatist perspective argues that this practical and empirical framework for analysis is completely appropriate. Constitutional pragmatism tends to the view that constitutional analysis ought to be instrumental in the sense that '[r]eflective, deliberative, even contemplative thinking originates in the practical need to solve real problems'.[31] There is, in contrast, little value in relying on the abstract rationalisations we have created to seek to justify that practice after the fact.[32]

The difference between pragmatism and normativism in New Zealand constitutional practice is not always stark. The adoption of a Parliamentary bill of rights or the judicial creation of a remedial jurisdiction for breaches of the New Zealand Bill of Rights Act 1990 each tap into a rich vein of normative ideals while proving to be pragmatic approaches to difficult constitutional issues. Nonetheless there is a clear pragmatic bent to much New Zealand constitutional analysis. For example, Keith Jackson's analysis of the New Zealand Parliament takes on a distinctively pragmatist hue when he states that '[t]here is no neat theory of Parliament. Parliaments were not based on theory, certainly not democratic theory: they evolved and continue to evolve'.[33] Dean Knight's proposals for republican constitutional reform are deliberately framed in incremental terms rather than engaging

27 See, for example, Posner, above n 6, at 19; Gary Jacobsohn *Pragmatism, Statesmanship, and the Supreme Court* (Cornell University Press, Ithaca, 1977) at 56–57.

28 Richard Warner "Why Pragmatism? The Puzzling Place of Pragmatism in Critical Theory" [1993] U Ill L Rev 535 at 542.

29 Thomas F Cotter "Legal Pragmatism and the Law and Economics Movement" (1996) 84 Georgetown LJ 2071 at 2074.

30 Rachael Gray *The Constitutional Jurisprudence and Judicial Method of the High Court of Australia* (Presidian Legal Publications, Adelaide, 2008) at 99.

31 Thomas C Grey "Holmes and Legal Pragmatism" (1989) 41 Stan L Rev 787 at 802.

32 Contrast AW Burks (ed) *Collected Papers of Charles Sanders Pierce* (Vol. 8, Harvard University Press, Cambridge, MA, 1958) at 16–17.

33 Keith Jackson "Parliament" in Raymond Miller (ed) *New Zealand Government and Politics* (3rd ed, Oxford University Press, Auckland, 2003) 77 at 79.

more broadly with the moral framework of the constitutional order.[34] This is despite the fundamental nature of the proposed reform. Cleaving the republican movement from any association with broader constitutional and civic questions is very much in line with New Zealand's pragmatic approach to constitutional development. Mai Chen offers a proposal for greater use of manner and form entrenchment of legislative provisions as an alternative to more fundamental reform that would involve the adoption of a written constitution, which is seen as both unwanted and undesirable.[35] These are pragmatic responses to current and emerging constitutional challenges and demonstrate the depth and breadth of pragmatism as a constitutional perspective in New Zealand. In many respects, they can be seen as a natural response to the distinctive nature of our unwritten constitutional arrangements. I would even go as far as to argue that these responses align neatly with the way we imagine ourselves as a nation and how we see our constitutional analysis best unfolding.

2.2. REALISM

So far, I have argued that normativism is an important perspective within public law that approaches constitutional analysis with reference to substantive underlying principles and values, and that one way of understanding constitutional pragmatism is as a response to the difficulty of approaching an unwritten constitution in primarily normative or theoretical terms. What then of the relationship between pragmatism as a school of thought and the ideals that inform constitutionalism more generally? One answer to this question is to claim that pragmatism and constitutionalism are completely at odds, so that one must be embraced at the expense of the other. On this understanding, pragmatism is a strict alternative to normativism.

The work of Matthew Palmer is a prominent New Zealand example of pragmatism exhibiting this non-normative tendency. Palmer's intellectual

34 Dean Knight "Patriating our Head of State: A Simpler Path?" in Caroline Morris, Jonathon Boston and Petra Butler (eds) *Reconstituting the Constitution* (Springer, Heidelberg, 2011) 107.

35 Mai Chen "The Advantages and Disadvantages of a Supreme Constitution for New Zealand: The Problem with Pragmatic Constitutional Evolution" in Caroline Morris, Jonathon Boston and Petra Butler (eds) *Reconstituting the Constitution* (Springer, Heidelberg, 2011) 123. Despite the title of Chen's chapter, the analysis she employs is distinctly pragmatic.

project aims to describe New Zealand's constitution in more or less comprehensive terms. Over the course of a number of works this has included both a granular catalogue of constitutional precepts,[36] as well as more fluid, contextual accounts of lived constitutional experience.[37] Palmer's approach has been an influential one in New Zealand scholarship,[38] and deserves its own specific treatment on another occasion. For the moment I wish to highlight only that this descriptive analysis is undertaken dispassionately, emphasising the practical operation of a constitution in a realistic context to the exclusion of abstract values or constitutional ideals. This purely descriptive analysis is worth highlighting because it is not necessarily obvious on an initial reading of Palmer's body of work.[39] There is an idiosyncratic reliance on constitutional 'norms' where one might expect to see normative critique or prescriptive analysis to guide constitutional development.[40] On a close reading, it becomes apparent that these norms refer to usual (that is, normal) constitutional practice rather than serving as a statement of fundamental principle. Such principles, while essential to a normativist reading of the constitution, presumably fall into the 'form and fiction of a law or constitution' that Palmer seeks to penetrate with his own analysis.[41]

Palmer self-describes his approach as 'constitutional realism', drawing inspiration from the American realist school of thought.[42] Elsewhere, Palmer has been characterised as an 'ad hoc pragmatist', a characterisation I consider apt.[43] It accurately reflects Palmer's disinterest with over-arching

36 Palmer "What is New Zealand's Constitution and Who Interprets It?", above n 9.

37 Palmer "Using Constitutional Realism to Identify the *Complete* Constitution", above n 9.

38 For example, see references in Janet McLean "The Unwritten Political Constitution and its Enemies" (2016) 14 Int'l J Const L 119 at 125; Paul Rishworth "Writing Things Unwritten: Common Law in New Zealand's Constitution" (2016) 14 Int'l J Const L 137 at 141; Oliver Hailes and Andrew Geddis "The Trans-Pacific Partnership in New Zealand's Constitution" (2016) 27 NZULR 226 at 239; MB Rodriguez Ferrere "Standing Orders in the New Zealand House of Representatives" (2014) 34 *Parliaments, Estates and Representation* 228 at 231; Claudia Geiringer "The Dead Hand of the Bill of Rights? Is the New Zealand Bill of Rights Act 1990 a Substantive Legal Constraint on Parliament's Power to Legislate?" (2007) 11 Otago L Rev 389 at 414.

39 Compare Jim Evans "Questioning the Dogmas of Realism" [2001] NZ L Rev 145 for a normatively richer account of realism.

40 See especially Palmer "New Zealand Constitutional Culture", above n 9.

41 Palmer "New Zealand Constitutional Culture", above n 9, at 566.

42 See especially KN Llewellyn "The Constitution as an Institution" (1934) 34 Colum L Rev 1. For a broad-brush account of American legal realism more generally, see Brian Leiter "American Legal Realism" in Dennis Patterson (ed) *A Companion to Philosophy of Law and Legal Theory* (2nd ed, Blackwell Publishing Ltd, Malden, 2010) 249.

43 Pouwels, above n 4, at 43–45.

theory and external standards for measuring constitution propriety. It also hints at Palmer's implicit dismissal of the instrumental goals we usually associate with pragmatism. For instance, take this passage where Palmer addresses the question of why it matters if something is considered to be constitutional:[44]

> [I]t matters because people think it matters. The symbolism of the term "constitutional" seems to matter to the New Zealand public and to constitutional decision-makers in New Zealand. Whether a matter is "constitutional" can affect the behaviour and decisions of those able to make decisions in relation to that matter – politicians, officials and judges.

A pragmatist would expect the constitution to be put to some instrumental work. Palmer prefers to leave constitutionalism untethered from instrumentalism so that it matters for its own sake. There is undoubtedly a Hartian, positivist quality to this passage.[45] If we were to emphasise that quality, we might take Palmer's point to be that those in authority share a conception of how public power should be organised, and that this shared conception in turn influences how it is organised in practice. But the passage also has other jurisprudential overtones. It offers little in the way of relevance for constitutional matter outside of their own status as being constitutional. An alternative reading might therefore emphasise a more Schmittian interpretation.[46] On this reading constitutional norms, such as they exist on Palmer's realist approach, are essentially determined by their acceptability to those in positions of authority. The constitution is, in turn, simply whatever practice prevails at the time. The normative ground here is very thin indeed, as reflected in the evident circularity Palmer relies on to describe his realist perspective. There is no appeal to particular substantive values or even instrumental outcomes that might break this circularity. We can therefore characterise Palmer's realism as a purely descriptive approach to constitutional analysis because there is no need to investigate further why conferral of 'constitutional' status might be appropriate or beneficial.

This account of constitutional realism as a kind of 'bare pragmatism' may come across as unduly critical, so let me clarify that Palmer's approach does have certain merits. It helps to identify constitutional changes and

---

44 Palmer "Constitutional Realism", above n 9, at 139.

45 See HLA Hart *The Concept of Law* (Oxford University Press, Oxford, 1961).

46 See Carl Schmitt *Constitutional Theory* (1928) (Jeffrey Seitzer (trans), Duke University Press, Durham, 2008).

the effects of those changes, for instance.[47] But Palmer's realism has fundamental weaknesses as a general constitutional theory that we might look to in order to gain wider insights (if indeed it is intended to be treated as a general theory in these terms). It overcompensates for the difficulty of approaching an unwritten constitution in normative terms by electing not to directly engage in normative analysis at all. This, I would argue, leaves out something essential about New Zealand's constitutional practice. If we wish to incorporate pragmatism into our constitutional reasoning then we need a normatively richer account of pragmatism, if one is available.

2.3. PRAGMATISM

It is a mistake to treat Palmer's descriptive, atomised realist perspective as the only contribution that pragmatism makes to New Zealand constitutional scholarship. Pragmatism need not be synonymous with either anti-intellectualism or anti-normativism.[48] Other strands of pragmatism can and do seek to place constitutional practice more fully in its normative context. A pragmatic philosophy of this kind still emphasises a practical and empirical approach to constitutional scholarship and decision-making,[49] and as such often advocates an instrumentalist approach to constitutional analysis. But in doing so it recognises that the need to solve real constitutional problems in a pragmatic way is necessarily linked to deep, reflective thinking about constitutions at the theoretical level. Something more than pragmatism understood as ad hoc realism is in play when this type of constitutional thinking is invoked.

The 'functionalist' account of pragmatism is one strand of this normatively richer account of our constitutional tradition.[50] As Ted Thomas puts the matter:[51]

> I regard pragmatism as being essentially functional. The law is viewed as a social institution in its social setting and vested with the social purpose of serving society and furthering the interests and goals of society.

---

47 Palmer "What is New Zealand's Constitution and Who Interprets It?", above n 9, at 141; Hailes and Geddis "The Trans-Pacific Partnership in New Zealand's Constitution", above n 38, at 239.

48 Compare Pouwles, above n 4.

49 Gray, above n 30, at 99.

50 On the functionalist style see generally Martin Loughlin "The Functionalist Style in Public Law" (2005) 55 U Toronto LJ 361.

51 EW Thomas *The Judicial Process: Realism, Pragmatism, Practical Reasoning and Principles* (Cambridge University Press, Cambridge, 2005) at 308.

There are two essential elements implicit in this definition. There is, of course, the instrumentalist, empirical commitment to working out tangible answers to social problems that we naturally associate with pragmatism. But it is coupled with a meaningful conception of the social good that imbues constitutional practice with important normative goals. On this conception, pragmatism views constitutional law as a valuable institution to the extent that as a whole it produces normatively valuable social effects. Pragmatism holds that '[t]he final cause of law is the welfare of society',[52] and constitutional law is crucial to achieving that goal.

Normative goals of this kind make constitutional theory relevant even as pragmatism rejects adherence to any single over-arching 'grand theory' of the kind implied by constitutional normativism.[53] There are no prior moral ideals that constitutional law ought to achieve for their own sake – indeed, pragmatists often adhere to the view that there is no single conception of the public good. This means that acceptance that the constitution serves social goals still leaves room for the influence of a variety of normative perspectives without compromising pragmatism's essential nature. At the thick end of the spectrum are accounts that 'recognize that normative presuppositions are inherent within any exercise of constitutional creation, reform, or practice'.[54] Stephen Tierney labels this brand of scholarship 'functional normativity', an approach which seems to imply that the functioning of the constitution cannot be cleanly separated from political theories about the proper functioning of the state.[55] Jules Coleman, a committed pragmatist although not a constitutional theorist, refers to the similar idea that legal norms are best understood 'not only in the abstract, but also in light of their concrete embodiment in practice'.[56] But for present purposes it is not necessary to unpack the pragmatic legal method into this level of detail. It is enough that, as Martin Loughlin has put it, 'theories become instruments'.[57] On this approach, the principles, values and other abstract concepts that inform normative constitutional analysis are incorporated into the

52 Benjamin N Cardozo *The Nature of the Judicial Process* (Yale University Press, New Haven, 1921) at 66.
53 Cotter, above n 29, at 2083.
54 Stephen Tierney *Constitutional Referendums: The Theory and Practice of Republican Deliberation* (Oxford University Press, Oxford, 2012) at 2.
55 At 2.
56 Jules Coleman *The Practice of Principle: In Defence of a Pragmatist Approach to Legal Theory* (Oxford University Press, Oxford, 2003) at 6.
57 Loughlin, above n 50, at 389.

evaluation and re-evaluation of pragmatic constitutional practice without subsuming it:[58]

> Theory and practice evolve together with a context of human purpose and activity; the practice informs the theory while the theory, in turn, informs the practice. Thus the hall-mark of a pragmatic method is its continual re-evaluation of practices in the light of norms that govern them and of the norms in light of the practices they generate.

Normative considerations are a valuable part of the toolkit for achieving the important social ends implied by the existence of any self-organised, political society. A functionalist rather than a realist understanding to constitutional pragmatism accepts this ongoing interaction between actual practice and the inherently normative theorising of that practice.

I take Harris's work to be an example of this functionalist style of pragmatic analysis in a New Zealand context. I offer two examples here – one specific and one more general – which serve to illustrate the point but are far from exhaustive. The specific example concerns Harris's defence of justiciability as an analytical tool in the context of judicial review of the prerogative of mercy.[59] Prerogative issues involve political imperatives that make it difficult to determine how deferential or robust the courts should be when exercising their review function. In this context, Harris suggests two complementary reasons for using justiciability as the appropriate lens through which to assess the merits of judicial intervention. The first is that for practical reasons there are issues on which the courts are not best placed to determine the issue. Justiciability as an analytical concept reflects the need for limitation on the availability of judicial review for instrumental reasons. This justification is baldly pragmatic, but the second reason for a focus on justiciability is that it places the issue of judicial decision-making in its appropriate constitutional context. It allows for 'big picture' consideration of the issues in a way that abstracts away from the specific issue under consideration, bringing constitutional theory squarely into play. What is the role of the courts in the constitution, and does it extend to intervention of the type the applicant seeks? This question is essential to judicial review of prerogative matters, and its answer can only

---

58 Catharine Pierce Wells "Improving One's Situation: Some Pragmatic Reflections on the Art of Judging" (1992) 49 Wash & Lee L Rev 323 at 331.

59 BV Harris "Judicial Review, Justiciability and the Prerogative of Mercy" (2003) 62 Cambridge LJ 631 at 633.

come from a theory of legitimate constitutional government. Harris then advances a particularly pragmatic model of justiciability that encompasses five core considerations governing a decision to intervene judicially: the subject matter of the decision under review, legislative restrictions on justiciability, constitutional appropriateness, institutional capability and objective criteria for measuring the decision-making.[60] It is through these five considerations, Harris argues, that the constitutional and instrumental aspects of judicial review can be appropriately determined. This neat reconciliation of instrumental and theoretical perspectives is the hallmark of pragmatic constitutionalism,[61] and Harris's analysis deftly sounds in both registers.

The general example comes from Harris's analytical approach in his recent textbook on the New Zealand constitution.[62] The analysis in this case is squarely structured around the notion of a set of organising principles that lend coherency and consistency to disparate and apparently unsystematised practice. For example, this approach allows Harris to deal with the inconvenient distinction between justiciable positive law and non-justiciable manifestations of constitutional propriety (conventions being the primary example). Both are able to be given appropriate emphasis as the underlying principle justifying the relevant constitutional rule is the same in each case. This approach links examples of constitutional practice into a coherent whole, again melding the theoretical and the pragmatic in constitutional terms.

We might still question, however, whether Harris struggles to integrate a thick normativity into his constitutional analysis. For example, the importance of the rule of law as a basic constitutional principle is supported by the matter of fact claim that if it were otherwise it is 'likely that there would be little order'.[63] The normative language of rights is notably absent, and the result is that Parliamentary consideration of rights issues is not presented in compelling or aspirational terms.[64] The question that remains for those (including myself) steeped in the normative tradition is whether constitutional pragmatism ultimately lacks the critical and normative resources to address the desirability of government action in even the most foundational terms. But perhaps this

60 At 634–643.
61 Posner, above n 6, at 60–64.
62 Harris, above n 8.
63 At 20.
64 At 286.

misses the point. For pragmatists like Harris, the constitution is a system, informed by political theory as much as positive legal rules, with the aim of contributing towards and maintaining an ordered and stable society.[65] Indeed, this emphasis on the constitution as an instrument to deliver on societal expectations is made plain right from the beginning:[66]

> The constitution is not an end in itself, but rather has instrumental value in allowing society to have the order that it wants. The rules and decisions made by the system ideally are all ultimately for the benefit of the electorate and all others living in New Zealand. Development of the system tends to be incremental in response to the ever-changing expectations of New Zealand society and the world community. Context plays a decisive role in what is accepted as currently provided by constitutional law, conventions and political theory.

This is the perspective that pragmatism contributes to our constitutional practice and scholarship. It has goals, and a broadly conceived normative orientation, but it remains grounded in reality. Theory and practice both serve the ends of the constitutional pragmatist, avoiding the unreal and contestable abstraction of normative analysis and the bare descriptivism of constitutional realism. The question that remains is whether this pragmatic perspective can be usefully deployed to address issues in contemporary constitutional practice. That question is examined in the following section.

3. 'THIRD SOURCE' AUTHORITY

The third source of authority for executive action is usually understood to be the residual freedom of the executive government to take action where it is not prevented from doing so by positive law.[67] It can be distinguished from positive authority to take action under statute or the prerogative, the first and second sources of authority respectively. Third source authority is a recognised part of the law in New Zealand and the UK,[68] although its existence is controversial. In this section I seek to describe third source authority and frame its controversial nature in terms of a clash

65 At 1.

66 At 3.

67 Harris "Recent Judicial Recognition", above n 10, at 60.

68 *Hamed v R* [2011] NZSC 101, [2012] 2 NZLR 305; *R (New London College Ltd) v Secretary of State for the Home Department* [2013] UKSC 51, [2013] 1 WLR 2358.

between normativist and pragmatic interpretations of our constitution. Notably, the pragmatic defence of third source authority is normatively thread-bare – it does not situate the third source in any extensively developed theory of constitutional government over and above the fact of executive convenience. I suggest that constitutional pragmatism can do more work here, broadening our understanding of when reliance on third source authority is constitutionally appropriate.

3.1. THIRD SOURCE AUTHORITY DESCRIBED

Under the common law, an individual may do anything that does not conflict with the established rights of others and that he or she is not prohibited from doing. This residual freedom is important to ensure individual liberty. The third source thesis suggests that this same residual freedom is also enjoyed by the executive branch of government. Government officials may do anything that does not conflict with the established rights of private individuals and which those officials are not prohibited from doing.

This third source 'residual freedom' in respect of government action has been something of a background rule in the UK since at least 1945, influencing the practice of government as well as framing the context in which positive law such as statute is required to operate.[69] Based on legal advice received at that time, the UK government's position is that positive authorisation in law is not needed for Ministerial action where equivalent powers are available to individuals at common law.[70] However, despite its war-time origins the doctrine only rose to prominence following the decision in *Malone v Metropolitan Police Commissioner*.[71] In that case, the Post Office acted on the instructions of the police to intercept private telephone communications. Although there was no positive source of authority permitting police interception in this manner, the Court held that the actions were lawful because no rights were violated and there was no specific legal prohibition preventing such action.

---

69 McLean, above n 38, at 132.

70 This interpretation is sometimes known as the 'Ram doctrine'. See Matthew Weait and Anthony Lester "The Use of Ministerial Powers Without Parliamentary Authority: The Ram Doctrine" [2003] PL 415.

71 *Malone v Metropolitan Police Commissioner* [1979] Ch 344.

Malone clearly creates a troubling precedent, but the existence of third source authority is of immense practical importance to the government. It supports the ability of the government to take such actions as appointing committees, organising departments, conducting inquiries, publishing information, entering into contracts and employing staff. In the absence of such authority the scope of government action could be severely limited, particularly in response to developments or problems that have not been anticipated and therefore not addressed in positive law. We can see a clear example of this in the case of government agencies that sit at arm's length from core Crown departments, who in New Zealand at least do not enjoy third source authority.[72] When the Commerce Commission, an independent Crown entity, undertook an inquiry into the state of competition in the telecommunications sector, the incumbent service provider challenged the lawfulness of the inquiry.[73] The Court of Appeal upheld the challenge on the basis that the inquiry could not be construed as incidental to the Commission's statutory functions.

That a broad-based inquiry power, not specifically tied to the exercise of other statutory functions, is beneficial to the Commission's work was subsequently recognised with the enactment of s 9A of the Telecommunications Act 2001. In this sense, although the oversight was eventually corrected, the inability to rely on third source authority impeded the development of the regulatory regime for telecommunications for a period of time. Avoiding this same type of impediment for core government departments is one of the key reasons that such reliance is placed on third source authority.

3.2. THE CONTROVERSIAL NATURE OF THIRD SOURCE AUTHORITY

Perhaps unsurprisingly, proponents of third source authority are quick to point out precisely these kinds of tangible benefits. Harris has put the matter in the following terms:[74]

> The main argument in favour of the government being free to do that which does not conflict with other legal rights, or is not prohibited by positive

72 This principle is implicitly recognised in Crown Entities Act 2004, s 17.

73 *Commerce Commission v Telecom Corporation of New Zealand Ltd* [1994] 2 NZLR 421 (CA).

74 Harris "The 'Third Source' Revisited", above n 10, at 237.

> law, is that this legal position meets the practical day-to-day needs of the government. The government is able to respond quickly, flexibly and relatively unhindered with the action it considers appropriate to meet, sometimes unexpected, social needs.

The pragmatic benefit of effective government therefore serves as the key justification for third source authority.

As already foreshadowed, however, judicial recognition of third source authority is controversial. The implicit normativity of most constitutional analysis readily conflates the rule of law with positive law empowerment of executive action. The lack of any positive source in law for third source executive authority is inherently concerning at the constitutional level.[75] Executive action that is not positively authorised risks abuse because it has not received the benefit of conscious scrutiny from responsible law-making authorities. As a result, a normativist conception would deem executive action not positively authorised in law, including third source authority, to be unconstitutional.

This is the essential approach taken by Joseph in his critique of third source authority. While individual citizens enjoy residual freedom to act, Joseph considers that government officials acting in an official capacity do not.[76] From here, Joseph develops an account of executive authority that he terms 'positive empowerment theory'.[77] He argues that it is 'inimical to the rule of law and constitutional government' for the executive to pursue purposes not expressly authorised in law.[78] The residual freedom doctrine allows for the 'malevolent exercise of public functions', provided that they are not positively prohibited or interfere with recognised interests.[79] The risk here is a result of the fundamental difference in nature between public authorities and private individuals. The power imbalance is such that a richly normative conception of constitutionality would act to restrain the public authority, thereby protecting individual liberty, in the absence of the endorsement of positive law.

The concern of abuse of third source authority is neatly demonstrated in *Malone v Metropolitan Police Commissioner*.[80] Joseph labels the police

---

75 See *R v Somerset County Council, ex parte Fewings* [1995] 1 All ER 513 (QB) at 524.
76 Joseph, above n 11, at 658.
77 At 652–658.
78 At 657.
79 At 654.
80 *Malone v Metropolitan Police Commissioner* [1999] Ch 344.

actions in that case 'distasteful'.[81] The clear effect of the decision was to reduce the scope of effective liberty enjoyed by private persons without clear positive authorisation. Justifying the actions on the basis of third source residual freedom to act ignores the significant power imbalance between the government and individual citizens who may be affected by the government's actions. The risk of coercive interference is manifestly greater in respect of government action, especially in respect of departments that exercise law-enforcement functions. This essential difference in the practical impact on individual citizens where the government enjoys the residual freedom of an ordinary person leaves the decision in *Malone* constitutionally questionable regardless of the precise legal position.

Indeed, the positive law has been updated since *Malone* to reflect the changing views and beliefs of the community. But the issue can still arise. In *Hamed*,[82] the police engaged in video surveillance by placing recording equipment on private land without consent. The primary issue in that case concerned the admissibility of the video surveillance evidence, but Chief Justice Elias took the opportunity to reject completely the third source theory of executive government authority.[83] This rejection engaged normativist analysis, with principles of the protection of individual liberty at the forefront. Her Honour's concern is that individual liberty of the kind prized in a free and democratic society would be unduly inhibited if public authorities had residual freedom to act where they were not prohibited from doing so. To protect the individual from arbitrary and unjustified state interference, third source authority must be rejected.

This is a powerful normative argument. With respect, the conventional response from third source proponents is less than convincing. The broad approach is to retrench the pragmatic necessity of third source authority. For example, Harris responds to the Chief Justice's critique specifically in the following terms:[84]

> In an ideal world the Chief Justice's point of view in expecting democratic pre-action approval for all executive action should prevail. However, in the real world there are good practical reasons for recognising that the government should be free to do that which is not prohibited by positive law. It is not possible for Parliament to anticipate all needed government authority, or for it to provide for all needed government authority with appropriate prescription.

---

81 Joseph, above n 11, at 653.

82 *Hamed v R* [2011] NZSC 101, [2012] 2 NZLR 305.

83 At [28].

84 Harris "Recent Judicial Recognition", above n 10, at 80.

We see here the characteristic rejection of idealism as a basis for legal decision that defines the pragmatic instinct. But in an important sense this rejection rings hollow. The modern-day risks associated with ignoring the normative dimension of constitutionalism in favour of ad hoc political power are all too apparent. Those risks are precisely the reason that there is such disquiet conceiving of our constitutional practice in thinly pragmatic (that is, realist) terms. Bare adhocracy does not promote either constitutional propriety or institutional resilience, and it offers the genuine potential for widespread abuse of public power. In that context, I would argue that it is not sufficient to lean on the pragmatic advantages to government officials of third source authority. A more fully articulated constitutional case for the existence of third source authority is needed.

It seems odd to me, at least, that a pragmatic case in favour of third source authority has not been put in a way that addresses the obvious constitutional concerns that arise when positive empowerment is absent. Instead, when pressed on the matter, the response seems to be to simply note that third source authority is 'not the result of deep constitutional theory'.[85] Even more unusually, there even seems to be a willingness to rely on a normatively thin conception of constitutional authority that largely ignores pragmatism's ability to engage in more extensive normative critique. Harris, for example, ultimately defends third source authority in a way that largely divorces it from normative considerations:[86]

> From a practical, or realist, point of view the prevailing understanding is that the government does have residual liberty, and this has not resulted in a groundswell of public opinion criticising any compromise of the negative liberties of the individual. Both the theoretical and practical reason for this is that in most circumstances the individual may legally ignore government action taken under the third source and continue to exercise his or her freedom.

This realist case for third source authority leaves the debate rather unresolved. I think pragmatism has more to offer here. Addressing the genuine normative concerns raised by Professor Joseph and Chief Justice Elias requires more direct engagement with constitutional theory. The pragmatic benefits of third source authority do not stand on their own merits. If such benefits are to be defended, they must be melded to a wider conception of constitutionally legitimate government action.

---

85 Harris, above n 8, at 156.

86 Harris "Recent Judicial Recognition", above n 10, at 67.

3.3. A PRAGMATIC ACCOUNT OF THIRD SOURCE AUTHORITY

Constitutional pragmatism of the normatively engaged kind I have advocated for in this contribution does not uncritically accept the practical value of relatively unconstrained executive authority. If such authority can be defended, an account of it ought to engage both instrumental and constitutional grounds. In this section I seek to offer a pragmatic account of third source authority that links instrumental and constitutional considerations in precisely this way.

Useful frameworks for this kind of account are in fact readily available from across the constitutional spectrum. If we conceive of third source authority as the executive branch determining its own purposes and limits, then a model could be drawn from other instances where a different branch of government is required to determine the nature and limits of its own intrinsic authority. For example, third source authority has an 'ephemeral quality' that could be seen as analogous with the principles that govern and limit the courts' inherent jurisdiction.[87] In keeping with the pragmatic impulse that motivated this contribution, I suggest that the nature and limits of third source authority can be seen as closely analogous to the concept of justiciability in judicial review. We have already seen when analysing examples of Harris's pragmatic analysis that justiciability usefully determines when it is instrumentally valuable and constitutionally sound for the courts to intervene in executive decision-making. Harris has suggested that consideration of the subject matter of the decision under review, any legislative restrictions on justiciability, the constitutional appropriateness of review, institutional capability of the courts to assess the decision and objective criteria for measuring the legality of decision-making.[88] I propose to recalibrate these five core considerations to sketch a pragmatic model to determine whether third source authority is legitimate. Where it is not, the courts on review ought to rule the reliance on third source authority unlawful.

The five core considerations I propose are: (1) the purpose of the government action; (2) legislative treatment of the subject matter; (3) the constitutional appropriateness of relying on the third source (particularly from a rule of law perspective); (4) the institutional capacity of the officials undertaking the action; and (5) the other accountability mechanisms in place. I address each of these considerations in turn.

87 See, for example, MB Rodriguez Ferrere "The Inherent Jurisdiction and Its Limits" (2013) 13 Otago L Rev 107 at 142.

88 Harris, above n 60, at 634–643.

3.3.1. Purpose

A key concern is that third source authority may be relied on to act for an arbitrary or cynical purpose. A pragmatic response would not be to ignore this risk, but to acknowledge that some actions taken under the third source are legitimate government purposes while others are disproportionate or arbitrary. It should be a requirement for officials relying on third source authority that they can demonstrate some public benefit in their actions.

This requirement is far from controversial. It accords closely with the constitutional pragmatist's instinct that constitutional power 'has instrumental value in allowing society to have the order that it wants'.[89] It is also an emerging feature of the case law on third source authority. In *Shrewsbury*,[90] Carnwath LJ argued in his Honour's dissenting judgment that third source authority should be limited to such actions that are 'for the public benefit, and for the identifiably "governmental" purposes within limits set by the law'.[91] This might be seen by some as limiting the practical utility of third source authority,[92] but it is difficult to see why any executive action should be allowed if it is not motivated by some public purpose. If there is no instrumental value in the action being taken, then it represents the kind of naked political power where the courts are required to intervene.

It is appropriate in any judicial assessment that a margin of appreciation is afforded to the executive decision-maker. This may raise concerns of the breadth of the residual power, but alternative approaches share the same issue. Joseph's positive empowerment thesis, for instance, is predicated on an exceptionally wide reading of incidental and implied powers.[93] This tracks the case law on improper purpose, where the underlying concept of statutory authorisation is stretched to say the least.[94] In that case, I would argue that it is better to engage with the issue of assessing the governmental

89 Harris, above n 8, at 3.

90 *R (Shrewsbury and Atcham Borough Council) v Secretary of State for Communities and Local Government* [2008] 3 All ER 548 (CA).

91 At [48].

92 At [74] per Richards LJ.

93 Joseph, above n 11, at 655–657.

94 See, for example, *Unison Networks Limited v Commerce Commission* [2007] NZSC 74, [2008] 1 NZLR 42; *Attorney-General v Ireland* [2002] 2 NZLR 220 (CA). The law on improper purpose is currently unclear and subject to debate. For example, in respect of the *Ireland* case see the criticisms advanced in Philip A Joseph "Constitutional Law" [2012] NZ L Rev 515 at 533–537 and the response to those criticisms in Hanna Wilberg "The *Ireland* Principle on Unauthorised but not Improper Purposes: An Exploration and Defence" [2016] NZ L Rev 95.

purpose of executive action directly.[95] That is what this first consideration seeks to achieve.

3.3.2. *Legislative Treatment*

Where legislation addresses the matter in question, government officials should not be able to avoid the strictures and procedural protections imposed by legislation by relying in the alternative on third source authority. This would be contrary to the rule of law as it would simply undermine legal protections that Parliament has deliberately made available.

This principle mirrors the common law's approach to prerogative powers. In *De Keyser's*, the House of Lords was unequivocal on this point:[96]

> It is quite obvious that it would be useless and meaningless for the Legislature to impose restrictions and limitations upon, and to attach conditions to, the exercise by the Crown of the powers conferred by a statute, if the Crown were free at its pleasure to disregard these provisions, and by virtue of its prerogative to do the very thing the statutes empowered it to do. One cannot in the constructions of a statute attribute to the Legislature (in the absence of compelling words) an intention so absurd.

The same reasoning applies in respect of third source authority.[97] Indeed, the New Zealand Supreme Court cited this passage with approval in respect of its application to third source authority in the *Quake Outcasts* case.[98] The extensive legislative checks enacted in respect of the Canterbury earthquake recovery effort could not be circumvented by relying on third source authority.[99] This close assessment of legislative purpose and effect was entirely appropriate in all the circumstances, and provides important guidance on future judicial consideration of third source authority.

---

95 This approach may, of course, simply mean that in practice that the law relating to the improper purpose doctrine is applied in the context of non-statutory decision-making power. I am grateful to Hanna Wilberg for this point.

96 *Attorney-General v De Keyser's Royal Hotel* [1920] AC 508 (HL) at 539.

97 Mark Elliott *The Constitutional Foundations of Judicial Review* (Hart, Oxford, 2001) at 172.

98 *Quake Outcasts v Minister for Canterbury Earthquake Recovery* [2015] NZSC 27, [2016] 1 NZLR 1 at [111].

99 At [112]–[121].

3.3.3. *Constitutional Appropriateness*

The third consideration is the constitutional appropriateness of the action taken in reliance on the third source of authority. One manifestation of this constitutional appropriateness is already evident in the literature on the third source: the residual freedom of government cannot be used to interfere with legally protected rights, including common law rights.[100] To fully ensure constitutional appropriateness, however, a broader inquiry is necessary. Any actions or decisions that risk upsetting the prevailing constitutional balance should require express authorisation in positive law before being taken. The third source cannot authorise such decisions or actions.

The breadth of the inquiry I am envisaging here requires some explanation. There may be important individual interests or constitutional imperatives that do not formally qualify as legal rights, but still warrant some degree of protection from government interference. The lack of a positive basis in law for executive action should not permit the government to abuse its residual authority to the prejudice of individual citizens.[101] New Zealand law does not recognise a general right to privacy, for example, but there is a clear and widespread expectation that activities on private property attract a high degree of privacy. This presumption is not lightly displaced, and in all the circumstances it may be that an interest in personal privacy is sufficiently strong that interference will not be tolerated under the third source. The plaintiffs in *Hamed* may have had just this type of expectation of privacy, for example.

Another possibility is that the constitutional context is such that only positive authorisation in law could ever be appropriate. While this example is more speculative, if action purported to be taken under the third source was especially prejudicial to recognised interests under the Treaty of Waitangi, where initial work was being undertaken in respect of dealing with disputed land or natural resources for instance, then it would be at least arguable that judicial invalidation of that action would be warranted. Some caution needs to be exercised here. As Claire Charters points out in her contribution to this collection,[102] third source authority has the potential to be used to entrench Western perceptions of constitutional propriety. This can frustrate the ability of Māori to legally challenge Crown

---

100 Harris "Common Law Constitutionalism", above n 10.

101 Elliott, above n 100, at 192.

102 See the contribution of Claire Charters to this volume.

action that is inconsistent with standards of legitimacy derived from broader constitutional thinking that incorporates te ao Māori. I cannot address the detail of this important line of argument here but note that in such circumstances a careful inquiry into constitutional substance will need to be undertaken. The essential point here is that third source authority is not only residual in the sense of there being an absence of legal restriction. Because every exercise of public power has the potential to touch on constitutional issues, any residual authority must equally rely on the absence of non-legal, constitutional restrictions on government action. This is the crucial difference in character between the residual freedom enjoyed by the government and residual freedom enjoyed by an individual.

3.3.4. *Institutional Capacity*

The fourth consideration can be briefly stated. The executive branch of government is organised broadly according to function. That scheme of organisation should be broadly adhered to when third source authority is relied upon. Accordingly, we would not expect the police to unilaterally distribute information on public health matters, or the education department to undertake inquiries into the matters of economic policy. The institutional expertise and knowledge of each relevant department must be respected, or the risk of arbitrary or abusive use of public power grows unacceptably large. The purpose of any action taken in reliance on third source authority should be logically connected with the office undertaking the relevant action. If no such connection is evident, then on review the courts should find that third source authority is not available in that instance.

3.3.5. *Accountability*

The final consideration is the range and effectiveness of alternative accountability mechanisms in place. Constitutional accountability is always broader than standards of legality,[103] and so the exercise of third source authority should be situated within its full institutional context. There are a range of accountability mechanisms within government that effectively condition and constrain officials' reliance on third source authority. These accountability mechanisms include ex post

[103] See Edward Willis "Political Constitutionalism: The 'Critical Morality' of Constitutional Politics" (2018) 28 NZULR 237 at 239–240.

Parliamentary scrutiny, assessment by the Ombudsman's office, civil proceedings and judicial review.[104] There may also be department-specific or issue-specific accountability mechanisms, such as the Health and Disability Commissioner and the Police Complaints Authority. These mechanisms may be sufficient to provide confidence that third source authority will not be exercised arbitrarily or systematically abused. Of course, it may equally be the case that none of these accountability mechanisms can effectively substitute for authorisation in positive law. In that case, the courts would be obliged to find that third source authority is not an available justification for government action. The answer in each case will depend on context.

3.4. TOWARDS A MODEL OF LEGITIMATE THIRD SOURCE AUTHORITY

The foregoing five considerations represent a tentative generic model for assessing the availability of third source authority for government actions. If accepted, the model is likely to bite hardest in respect of judicial scrutiny of executive action through judicial review. However, the model could also function as a useful ex ante assessment in the hands of the executive itself. Close assessment of the merits and implications of reliance on third source authority before the fact is likely to be a key component in the ongoing legitimacy of the government's residual freedom. The model is tentative and stands to be refined, but it has been carried so far as to provide an important proof of concept.

My proposed model is unlikely to be particularly controversial – at least, beyond the ongoing debate between normativists and pragmatists concerning the appropriateness of third source authority more generally – because it draws on existing case law and established institutional expectations. That said, the ultimate success or otherwise of this proposed model is not the primary concern of this section. All that is intended is to demonstrate that there are pragmatic ways of reconciling specific instances of the instrumentality of third source authority (represented by principles 1 and 4 in the scheme above) with broader normative concerns about the constitutional appropriateness of executive power that has not been positively authorised in law (principles 2, 3 and 5). My contention is that constitutional pragmatism, properly understood as an approach that is quite distinct from

104 Harris "The 'Third Source' Revisited", above n 10, at 229.

ad hoc realism, provides the ideal conceptual framework for this attempted reconciliation. Pragmatism recognises that no single perspective or consideration addresses all of the relevant issues in play in all circumstances. Contextual assessment is warranted, rather than the normativist tendency to assert categorical conclusions in the abstract. In that sense constitutional pragmatism has something valuable to offer our constitutional practice, and we should take its contribution seriously.

4. CONCLUSIONS

This contribution has argued for the value of constitutional pragmatism. The difficulty of engaging directly with normative constitutional standards in the absence of a written constitution means that constitutional pragmatism is particularly influential in New Zealand. It is a coherent and vibrant philosophy animated by constitutional theory as much as by the instrumental needs of the political community. In that sense it extends well beyond realist descriptivism.

One of constitutional pragmatism's particular strengths, I have argued, lies in its ability to reconcile actual constitutional practice with theoretical perspectives that legitimise that practice. I have used the example of the controversy over third source authority within New Zealand's constitutional arrangements to demonstrate that this is case. Realism tells us that third source authority exists. Normativism often argues that it ought not to exist, given its sometimes quite serious rule of law implications. Pragmatism straddles these two positions. It asks how the need for flexible and effective executive government can be aligned with expectations about the constitutional propriety and protection of liberty. In doing so it acknowledges the benefits of a firm normative grounding for constitutional doctrine, and so does not ignore the very difficult real modern challenges to democratic constitutionalism. We should not resile from descriptions of our constitution as pragmatic if we mean to use the term in this normatively engaged sense. If third source authority is to remain a feature of Westminster constitutional systems, then constitutional pragmatism represents our best attempt to explain that doctrine's ongoing development.

PART II

ISSUES CONCERNING THE JUDICIARY

The Nature of Judicial (and Executive) Power

SUSTAINABILITY, INDETERMINACY AND THE ABDICATION OF ENVIRONMENTAL RESPONSIBILITY

Nicola R Wheen

1. INTRODUCTION

The Resource Management Act 1991 (RMA) has been New Zealand's principal piece of environmental legislation for three decades. It was enacted following an extensive law reform process to 'restate and reform [New Zealand] law relating to the use of land, air, and water'.[1] The RMA promised to bring great change to resource management in New Zealand: among its novel elements were referring expressly to the principles of the Treaty of Waitangi,[2] providing a framework for integrated resource planning and decision-making to be implemented by local government with policy guidance from central government and adopting a purpose

1 Resource Management Act 1991, Long Title.
2 Of the numerous Acts the Resource Management Act repealed and replaced only one, the Town and Country Planning Act 1977, made any express reference to Māori values or the Treaty of Waitangi.

of 'promot[ing] the sustainable management of natural and physical resources'.[3]

The RMA's purpose was a response to the emergence of 'sustainable development' as a policy goal on the world stage in the 1987 World Commission on Environment and Development's report, *Our Common Future*. The report's release coincided with the re-election of the fourth Labour government (1984–1990) and the launch of its resource management law reform process. The report's 'main theme' was a call for states to integrate environment and economic factors in pursuit of sustainable development,[4] which it defined as development that meets present generations' needs, without compromising future generations' abilities to meet their needs.[5] Given that the fourth Labour government was 'one of New Zealand's great reforming governments',[6] it is no surprise that these international developments influenced its resource management law reforms. However, the government stopped short of integrating environmental sustainability goals into the economic and social sectors, as intended by the World Commission, but it did adopt 'sustainable management' as the purpose of its new natural and physical resource management bill. Because of this, when it was eventually enacted, the RMA became 'one of the most ambitious and comprehensive products' of the 'hopeful' 1990s, 'an era of wholesale environmental law and policy reform'.[7] The hope was simply that the RMA's purpose would herald a change of direction in resource management, resulting in improved environmental outcomes.[8] Everything would depend on how the new legislation was interpreted and applied by decision- and rule-makers, and analysis of its terms began immediately. Unsurprisingly, the focus was on the RMA's definition of 'sustainable management' and a debate about its meaning and how it would be applied began.

---

3 BV Harris "Sustainable Management as an Express Purpose of Environmental Legislation: The New Zealand Attempt" (1993) 8 Otago L Rev 51.

4 Ian G McChesney *The Brundtland Report and Sustainable Development in New Zealand* (Information Paper no 25, Centre for Resource Management, Lincoln University and University of Canterbury, 1991) at 8.

5 World Commission on Environment and Development *Our Common Future* (Oxford University Press, Oxford, 1987).

6 Jonathan Boston and Martin Holland *The Fourth Labour Government: Politics and Policy in New Zealand* (Oxford University Press, Melbourne, 1990) at back cover.

7 Elizabeth Fisher "Towards Environmental Constitutionalism: A Different View of the Resource Management Act?" [2015] Resource Management Theory and Practice 63 at 63–64.

8 John Milligan "The Resource Management Act – 9 Months on" [1992] NZLJ 351 at 351.

As an academic in the Faculty of Law at the University of Otago in Dunedin, New Zealand when the RMA was enacted, Bruce Harris played an active part in the early debate on the statutory meaning and implications of sustainable management. Harris's close and practical analysis of s 5 (in the context of the rest of Part 2 of the Act) contributed significantly to discussion at the time, and his insightful discussion of the likely effect and implications of section 5 (hereafter s 5) (which defines sustainable management for the purposes of the Act) has unfortunately proved to be right in many ways, as this contribution explains. Before beginning it is helpful to provide a little background about the RMA and, in particular, s 5.

2. THE RESOURCE MANAGEMENT ACT AND SECTION 5

The RMA replaced a raft of other legislation, including the Town and Country Planning Act 1977 (previously the main statute governing land use), the Water and Soil Conservation Act 1967 (previously provided for freshwater management and the allocation of rights to use water) and the Clean Air Act 1972 (previously provided mechanisms for controlling localised air pollution).[9]

The RMA establishes a framework for the integrated management of natural and physical resources throughout New Zealand. The framework provides for a four-tier hierarchical scheme of standards, policies and plans made by central government (the top tier, national policy statements and national standards), regional councils (the middle two tiers, regional policy statements and regional plans) and district or city councils (the bottom tier, district plans). These policies and plans set objectives, strategies and methods for resource management in their respective geographical locations. National standards prescribe technical standards or methods. New Zealand coastal policy statements, regional policy statements and district plans are mandatory. While the RMA focuses on the effects of activities on the environment, rules in plans can categorise identified activities as permitted, controlled, discretionary or prohibited. Discretionary activities require resource consent. As a matter of law or best practice, the process of making standards, policies and plans is a public process in which anyone can participate by making submissions.

9 This section relies and draws on Ceri Warnock and Maree Baker-Galloway *Focus on Resource Management Law* (LexisNexis NZ, Wellington, 2015).

Any person can apply for a change to a provision in a regional, or district or city, plan.

The RMA also sets the basic rules for resource use and provides exceptions for some existing uses. Land can be put to any use that does not contravene a regional or district plan or is allowed by resource consent. Water use, discharges of contaminants into the air and activities in the coastal marine area (such as reclamation or disturbing the foreshore or seabed) are prohibited unless allowed by a standard, plan or resource consent. Applicants for resource consent provide an assessment of the likely effects of the proposed activity on the environment, and applications may be publicly notified. Applications are determined in the first instance by consent authorities within regional and district or city councils.

The RMA provides wide rights of merits appeal against provisions in plans, or decisions to refuse applications for plan changes or resource consents made by local authorities. Appeals are heard de novo by the Environment Court, formerly the Planning Tribunal.

The RMA's purpose and principles guide and direct policy-, plan-, rule- and decision-making. These are set out in Part 2, ss 5–8. Section 5 sets out and defines the RMA's purpose:

> **5 Purpose**
>
> (1) The purpose of this Act is to promote the sustainable management of natural and physical resources.
>
> (2) In this Act, sustainable management means managing the use, development, and protection of natural and physical resources in a way, or at a rate, which enables people and communities to provide for their social, economic, and cultural well-being and for their health and safety while—
>
> (a) sustaining the potential of natural and physical resources (excluding minerals) to meet the reasonably foreseeable needs of future generations; and
>
> (b) safeguarding the life-supporting capacity of air, water, soil, and ecosystems; and
>
> (c) avoiding, remedying, or mitigating any adverse effects of activities on the environment.

'Environment' is defined very widely in s 2 as *including* 'ecosystems and their constituent parts, including people and communities', 'all natural and physical resources', 'amenity values' and 'the social, economic, aesthetic, and cultural conditions which affect [those] matters … or which are affected by those matters'.

Sections 6 and 7 list other matters that are relevant to achieving this purpose. The matters in s 6 are of 'national importance' and policy-, plan-, rule- and decision-makers must recognise and provide for them. They include 'the protection of outstanding natural features and landscapes from inappropriate subdivision, use, and development' and 'the protection of areas of significant indigenous vegetation and significant habitats of indigenous fauna'. Section 7 lists 'other matters' that must be given 'particular regard', including 'the efficient use and development of natural and physical resources' and 'intrinsic values of ecosystems'. Section 8 requires policy-, plan-, rule- and decision-makers to 'take into account the principles of the Treaty of Waitangi'.[10]

3. THE DEBATE ON SECTION 5 BEGINS

The early debate on s 5 and the purpose of the RMA began with a discussion between Douglas Fisher and John Milligan.[11] Fisher suggested there were two possible and 'importantly different' readings for s 5, depending on the meaning of 'while'.[12] A subordinating meaning for 'while' would generate

10 The Treaty of Waitangi is New Zealand's foundational document, in which Māori ceded powers of government to the Crown while the Crown promised to protect Māori chieftainship, lands, waters, forests and other 'taonga' (values and valued things). The principles are defined by context, but are generally accepted to include partnership (between the Crown and Māori), active protection of Māori rights and interests, consultation and Māori involvement in decision-making, the provision of reasonable redress for past breaches of the Treaty by the Crown, and the Crown's right to govern in the national interest.

11 D Fisher "The Resource Management Legislation of 1991: A Juridical Analysis of its Objective" [1991] Resource Management 13; "Clarity in a Little 'While'" (1991) 50 Terra Nova; J Milligan "Pondering the 'While'" [1992] Terra Nova 50. The debate on s 5 involved/is discussed by many others including Inga Carlman "The Resource Management Act 1991 Through External Eyes" (2007) 11 NZJEL 181; Peter Fuller "The Resource Management Act 1991: 'An Overall Broad Judgment'" (2003) 7 NZJEL 243; Peter Skelton and Ali Memon "Adopting Sustainability as an Overarching Environmental Policy: A Review of section 5 of the RMA" (2002) 10 Resource Management Journal 1; Nicola R Wheen "The Resource Management Act: A 'Greener' Law for Water?" (1997) 1 NZJEL 165; David P Grinlinton "Integrating Sustainability into Environmental Law and Policy in New Zealand" in Klaus Bosselmann, David P Grinlinton and Prue Taylor (eds) *Environmental Law for a Sustainable Society* (2nd ed, New Zealand Centre for Environmental Law, Auckland, 2013) 21; Martin Philipson "Judicial Decision Making under the Resource Management Act 1991: A Critical Assessment" (1994) 24 VUWLR 163; Kerry James Grundy "In Search of Logic: s 5 of the Resource Management Act" [1995] NZLJ 40.

12 Milligan, above n 8, at 352.

an environmental, or ecological, 'bottom lines' approach to sustainable management. It would also arguably fit better with the government's economic policy and had received apparent support from the Minister for the Environment on the Third Reading of the Resource Management Bill. He had said that the RMA was not 'intended to be a comprehensive social-planning statute' but would allow for development so long as s 5's 'biophysical bottom-lines' (the matters in paragraphs (a)–(c)) were maintained.[13] Alternatively, a coordinating meaning for 'while' would generate a 'balancing' approach similar to that applied under the previous legislation. A bottom lines approach would limit the role of decision-makers to 'narrow discretionary or even quasi factual determinations' about whether or not proposals met the standards in paragraphs (a)–(c).[14] Balancing would ask them to weigh up all the matters in s 5, 'balancing the interests in the first and second parts of s 5(2) .... This interpretation would mean that the development interests in the first part may in some circumstances override the sustainability interest in the second part'.[15] Fisher argued the subordinating meaning of 'while' was grammatically correct but less likely to be adopted, given the legislative history, where balancing was the norm.[16]

The discussion on s 5 was continued by others including Janet McLean and Bruce Harris. Broadening their focus from 'while' (the importance of which Harris thought had been overstated in the debate thus far[17]) but still operating in the absence of any meaningful judicial analysis of the legislation, both McLean and Harris relied on close textual analysis of s 5 as a whole and in context and tried to apply it to hypothetical fact situations. McLean's hypothetical was a factory emitting air pollution that it could not afford to control. Her conclusion was that s 5 is vague and provides little guidance on when the factory should be required to close down and how bad the pollution would have to get.[18] McLean suggested that by enacting ambiguous legislation that failed to clarify 'how much

13 Third Reading of the Resource Management Bill (4 July 1991) 516 NZPD 3018–3021, discussed in Milligan, above n 8, at 351.

14 Bret C Birdsong "Adjudicating Sustainability: New Zealand's Environment Court" (2002) 29 Ecology Law Quarterly 1 at 45.

15 Harris, above n 3, at 60.

16 IH Williams "The Resource Management Act 1991: Well Meant but Hardly Done" (2000) 9 Otago L Rev 673 at 678.

17 Harris, above n 3, at 61.

18 Janet McLean "New Zealand's Resource Management Act: Process with Purpose?" (1992) 7 Otago L Rev 538 at 547.

weight social and economic factors are to be given as against physical factors', central government had effectively delegated the hard decisions to local government and the Planning Tribunal.[19] While devolution of resource management decision-making was undoubtedly a core goal of the resource management reforms, the idea was that those exercising devolved powers would obtain guidance from the RMA's purpose and principles, and subsequently from national policies set by central government.[20]

4. HARRIS'S ANALYSIS

Harris's hypothetical was a proposal to construct a hydro-dam on a river to meet consumer demand for electricity, but with likely effects of the extinction of a rare native duck species and damage to the spiritual significance of the river to local Māori. Harris did not say why he chose these hypothetical facts, but they may have reminded him of the facts in *Royal Forest and Bird Protection Society of New Zealand Inc v Bay of Plenty Regional Water Board*.[21] In that case, the Town and Country Planning Appeal Board (predecessor of the Planning Tribunal) controversially dismissed an appeal against the grant of water rights enabling use of the waters of the Rangitaiki and Wheao rivers for hydro-electric generation, despite evidence that this would result in the loss of a 'superb' trout fishing river and the destruction of nationally 'unique' habitat of four endemic water bird species, two of which were endangered.[22] Critics including Tony Black saw this decision as a good illustration of the 'difficulties of those who would defend the environment' under the Water and Soil Conservation Act, where decisions on water right applications were made using a 'beneficial use' test, which involved balancing and not bottom lines.[23] Black's view was that this test gave land and water management in New Zealand 'a decided bias towards resource development as opposed to environmental conservation. … For in the process of balancing tangible economic benefits and tangible social benefits against intangible and

19 At 555.

20 Commensurate with its role as a goals-based statute: see McLean, above n 18, at 543–544.

21 *Forest and Bird Protection Society of New Zealand Inc v Bay of Plenty Regional Water Board* (1978) 6 NZTPA 361.

22 Tony Black "Defending the Environment" [1978] NZLJ 153 at 153.

23 At 153. The beneficial use test was established in *Keam v Minister of Works and Development* [1982] 1 NZLR 319 (CA).

generally misunderstood environmental benefits the tangible wins out every time'.[24] If the RMA, with its new purpose of sustainable management, had indeed brought change, it might yield different results in a similar case.

After applying s 5 to his hypothetical, however, Harris concluded that 'bottom lines are inappropriate, and will not work. Situations will inevitably arise where a rational assessment of competing interests will overwhelmingly support a compromise of the so-called environmental bottom lines'.[25] Harris agreed that s 5 is complex and vague and concluded that 'Parliament has deliberately left the wording indeterminate. The courts [are] being left to give a more definite content to the purpose of the Act'. Drawing on his constitutional background,[26] Harris argued:[27]

> Parliament should not have abdicated its law-making responsibility in this way. The principles determining the priorities between development and maintenance of the natural environment are based on matters of high policy for which the elected government and parliament should be politically accountable. These principles should not be settled by the executive appointed and considerably less accountable judiciary.

Finally, Harris argued that the complexity and vagueness of s 5 could affect the quality of resource management rule- and decision-making under the RMA.[28] Harris suggested that s 5 would be difficult for the elected lay councils required to implement the RMA to understand and apply, and that – because they are elected and conferred with a wide discretion given s 5's loose criteria – councils 'may not bring a sufficient impartiality to the decision-making'.[29] Harris also implicitly acknowledged the implications for the Planning Tribunal, which would be charged with exercising the wide discretion conferred by s 5 when hearing and deciding merits appeals de novo. Harris reflected on the Tribunal's role under the Town and Country Planning Act 1977, when it was also asked to make discretionary decisions by balancing competing interests. He recalled his former days as a practitioner, 'marvelling at the power of the unelected executive appointed

24 Black, above n 22, at 153.
25 Harris, above n 3, at 68.
26 BV Harris "Judicial Activism and New Zealand's Appellate Courts" in Brice Dickson (ed) *Judicial Activism in Common Law Supreme Courts* (Oxford University Press, Oxford, 2007) 273; "The Law-making Power of the Judiciary" in Philip A Joseph (ed) *Essays on the Constitution* (Brookers, Wellington, 1995) 265.
27 Harris, above n 3, at 68.
28 At 68–71.
29 At 69–70.

members of the Planning Tribunal. They could stop or allow, for example, the building of supermarkets, hydro-electric dams, skifields – all decisions which had huge social, economic and environmental consequences'.[30] On Harris's analysis, the Tribunal's task under the new Act would be just as discretionary, but bigger. Harris simply observed that the background of the Tribunal's judges and commissioners might make them 'some of the persons in society best equipped to perform this task'.[31]

5. THE DEBATE ON SECTION 5 CONTINUES

The debate on the meaning of s 5 continued as the two Ministers responsible for the RMA re-expressed their support for bottom lines. Simon Upton (the Minister in charge of the Resource Management Bill when it was enacted) referred back to his comments made on the Bill's Third Reading about s 5 having 'bottom lines'[32] in a 1993 article[33] and again in his keynote speech at the second annual Resource Management Law Association conference in 1994.[34] In 1995, Geoffrey Palmer (the Minister who devised and developed the Bill, and introduced it to Parliament) confirmed in his own book that 'the virtue of establishing bottom lines in respect to development ... was always the broad policy aim of the Act's framers'.[35] Palmer went on to express frustration that some four years following the RMA's enactment, it was still 'difficult to discern what difference the paradigm shift in policy will make'.[36] Responding directly to Harris's claims that Parliament had abdicated its law-making responsibility by failing to make clear its intentions in s 5, Palmer added: 'The time when Parliament can spell everything out in black-letter law in statutes has passed ... and I would argue that the intended policy is clear enough'.[37]

30 At 71.
31 At 71.
32 Third Reading of the Resource Management Bill (4 July 1991) 516 NZPD 3018–3021 where the Minister said it 'is not a question of trading off those responsibilities [the matters in s 5(2)(a)-(c)] against the pursuit of well-being'.
33 SD Upton "Purpose and Principle in the Resource Management Act" (1995) 3 Waikato L Rev 17.
34 SD Upton "The Resource Management Act, Section 5; Sustainable Management of Natural and Physical Resources" (paper presented to the Second Annual Conference of the Resource Management Law Association Inc, Practice Makes Perfect, 1994).
35 GWR Palmer *Environment – The International Challenge* (Victoria University Press, Wellington, 1995) at 173.
36 At 169.
37 At 172.

Palmer's view was that the Planning Tribunal was dragging its feet, its judges having shown 'hostility to the Act' in extra-judicial utterances.[38] He opined that 'There appears to be reluctance among some of the judges of the Tribunal to boldly follow the intent of the legislation and strike out on new and creative paths', adding, 'In hindsight I regret that Parliament did not abolish the Planning Tribunal when the new legislation was framed'.[39]

I remember discussing the meaning of s 5 with Harris as he supervised my Master of Laws research on the implications of the enactment of the RMA for freshwater in 1994. I was taken by bottom lines, but Harris was right. The Planning Tribunal (which was replaced by the Environment Court in 1996) ultimately did reject bottom lines, albeit after first testing them out, in favour of a more discretionary approach. Many of the issues that Harris – and McLean – predicted would arise from s 5's ambiguity did in fact eventuate. In particular, local government decision-making and the adjudicatory function of the Planning Tribunal/Environment Court have both been the subject of considerable challenge, with tensions arguably exacerbated by the failure of successive governments to provide adequate national-level policy guidance under the RMA for a good 20 years following its enactment.[40]

6. THE OVERALL BROAD JUDGMENT APPROACH

As Harris had anticipated, although the Tribunal tried out a bottom lines approach in some early cases,[41] it transitioned to what has come to be known as the 'overall broad judgment' approach to sustainable management in 1996. This transition occurred largely because the broad terms of s 5(2)(a)–(c) alone did not serve well as bottom lines and because 'many cases do not permit a clear determination of whether bottom lines are met'.[42]

The first step towards adopting the overall broad judgment approach came when the High Court interpreted s 5 and the rest of Part 2 of the

38 At 170.

39 At 170.

40 Simon Upton "RMA Reform: Coming Full Circle" (Resource Management Law Association Salmon Lecture 2020, Auckland, 12 October 2020).

41 Birdsong, above n 14, at 44, citing *Plastic and Leathergoods Company Ltd v Horowhenua District Council* PT Levin W26/94, 9 April 1994). See also *Foxley Engineering Ltd v Wellington City Council* PT Wellington W12/94, 16 March 1994; *Shell Oil New Zealand Ltd v Auckland City Council* PT Auckland W8/94, 2 February 1994; *Campbell v Southland District Council* PT Invercargill W 14/94, 14 December 1994.

42 At 45–46.

RMA for the first time in 1994. It noted the 'deliberate openness about the language, its meanings, and its connotations which ... is intended to allow the application of policy in a general and broad way'.[43] This judgment opened the way for *North Shore City Council v Auckland Regional Council*, where then Principal Environment Court Judge Sheppard held that all parts of s 5 must be considered, along with the rest of Part 2, and an 'overall broad judgment' made of whether a proposal would promote sustainable management.[44] This approach, said the Judge, 'allows for comparison of conflicting considerations and the scale or degree of them, and their relative significance or proportion on the final outcome'.[45] This is obviously very close to Harris's suggestion that the correct approach to sustainable management as expressed in s 5 was 'one of evaluating the specified considerations and weighing them against each other'.[46]

The significance of adopting the overall broad judgment approach is that it confers a wide discretion on decision-makers presented with competing values 'to choose which value to prefer on the facts'.[47] The implications for decision-makers if s 5 was interpreted in this way included – as Harris had pointed out back in 1993 – making it more difficult for local authorities to make sound and sufficiently impartial decisions, and having unelected judges making important, but essentially political, decisions. The next sections show how the implications Harris anticipated have eventuated and discuss what has become of them since.

7. IMPLICATIONS FOR THE ENVIRONMENT COURT

The Environment Court is the successor of the Planning Tribunal, which was itself the successor of the Town and Country Planning Appeal Board

43 *New Zealand Rail Ltd v Marlborough District Council* [1994] NZRMA 70.

44 *North Shore City Council v Auckland Regional Council* (1996) 2 ELRNZ 305, [1997] NZRMA 59. This was subsequently approved on appeal in the High Court, see Williams, above n 16, at 681, n 52, citing *Green and McCahill Properties Ltd v Auckland Regional Council* [1997] NZRMA 519 at 527.

45 At 94.

46 At 68.

47 Ceri Warnock "Reconceptualising the Role of the New Zealand Environment Court" (2014) 26 Journal of Environmental Law 507 at 511, citing John Fogarty "Giving Effect to Values used in Statutes" in Jeremy Finn and Stephen Todd (eds) *Law, Liberty and Legislation: Essays in Honour of John Burrows QC* (LexisNexis, Wellington, 2008) 1.

and the Town Planning Board. The original Town Planning Board was chaired by the Minister of Works and was clearly part of the executive arm of government.[48] In 1953, the Board took on new functions hearing appeals against regional planning schemes by affected district councils and appeals against district planning schemes by affected property owners, and became the Town and Country Planning Appeal Board. This Board was 'substantially an appellate body, with the primary decision-maker being the territorial authorities'.[49] The Appeal Board comprised a barrister or solicitor and two local government nominees appointed on the recommendation of the Minister, and was empowered to vary, cancel or confirm planning schemes made by elected authorities about the 'conservation and economic development' of regions and the development of districts for the 'economic and general welfare' of their inhabitants.[50] In 1977, the Planning Tribunal replaced the Board, assumed its appellate function and became the final decision-maker on the merits of whether proposed uses of water were beneficial, or whether or not an elected council's plan met the Act's purpose of the 'wise use and management' of resources. The Tribunal essentially made value-judgments on activities with significant social, economic and environmental repercussions.

When the RMA was enacted, the Planning Tribunal's powers were continued and expanded. Its judges and commissioners hear de novo merits appeals from planning and consent decisions, allowing it to replace provisions in plans and decisions made by elected councils that, in its overall broad judgment, do not promote sustainable management. Adopting the overall broad judgment approach confirmed that decision-makers – including the Tribunal – have a wide discretion in choosing which values in Part 2 of the Act to prefer in deciding whether or not sustainable management is promoted by a policy, plan or proposal.

The constitutional ramifications of the Tribunal's powers were highlighted when the Tribunal was re-named the Environment Court in 1996, overtly confirming its place in the judicial arm of government, albeit as a court with specialised jurisdiction. In 2002, Birdsong, a visiting academic from the US, was moved to comment:

> The issue of political decisionmaking by unelected judges with life tenure raises the question of the proper balance between expertise and accountability in a

48 Sian Elias "Righting Environmental Justice" [2014] Resource Management Theory and Practice 47 at 53 and 63.

49 At 53.

50 Town and Country Planning Act 1953, ss 3(1), 18, 39 and 42(3).

> system of environmental governance. New Zealand's approach to environmental adjudication shifts substantial power from politically accountable government entities to the judiciary. In the New Zealand eye, the perceived benefits of an Environment Court both technically expert and experienced in making decisions about sustainability subjectively outweigh any concerns about fundamentally political decisions being made by a court that is not politically accountable in any direct way. ... New Zealand's choice to vest broad powers of environmental policymaking in a court of law raises longstanding questions about whether unelected expert judges, rather than expert administrative agencies that are arguably more politically accountable, should bear ultimate responsibility for environmental decisions.[51]

Birdsong further opined that New Zealanders accepted this situation owing to 'a profound belief that environmental decision-making ... is essentially a technocratic exercise ... even though, in the context of sustainable management under the RMA, decisions encompass a range of social, economic, cultural and ecological factors whose balancing might well be described as the essence of political governance'.[52] In fact, the scope of the Environment Court's decision-making under the overall broad judgment approach was not quietly accepted, and did raise deep questions. By 2009, 'various commentators and policy advisors were specifically questioning the expansive role of the Environment Court. Critics argued that the scope of the decision-making by the Court blurred Montesquieu's separation of the executive and judicial powers'.[53]

However, rather than suggesting a change to the overall broad judgment approach to remedy this problem, a Technical Advisory Group to the Minister suggested abolishing some rights of appeal to the Environment Court. The Minister for the Environment herself then proposed 'wholesale reform' of the Court because '[t]he judiciary should not be placed in the position of having to determine values or policy – this role should be played by publicly-accountable, elected representatives'.[54] These suggestions moved Dame Sian Elias (then the Chief Justice of New Zealand but writing extra-judicially in this instance) to remind the Environment Court's

---

51 Birdsong, above n 14, at 64–65. Birdsong notes at 66 that 'the Environment Court is required to exercise the full discretion of a first-instance decisionmaker, and is subject to review only on matters of law – all within a framework that requires it to consider social and economic as well as environmental factors'.

52 Birdsong, above n 14, at 66–67.

53 Warnock, above n 47, at 513.

54 At 513, citing Ministry for the Environment *Improving our Resource Management System: A Discussion Document* (Wellington, 2013) at 13.

critics that merits review offers advantages 'we should not throw aside',[55] principally 'that it demonstrates the legitimacy of the exercise of power'.[56] Elias acknowledged that '[w]ide balancing of values not easily compared is not a method generally favoured by the courts',[57] and observed that if 'judicial involvement in primary decision-making and merits review is something we want to retain … then the better course may be to make more political effort to identify and prioritise the values the courts are to apply'.[58] Dame Sian urged the Environment Court's critics to 'think matters through' before deciding what to do.[59]

Elizabeth Fisher, Professor of Environmental Law at the University of Oxford, also encouraged more discussion. She suggested that rather than take a critical view of the debate around the RMA, a more constructive perspective comes from imagining the RMA and comparative legislation in other jurisdictions as 'constitutions' that set in motion ongoing debates about the role of law in contributing to environmental protection'.[60] Fisher argues that a constitutional model for environmental law fits with the 'hot' nature of environmental problems.[61] On this view, the debate on the RMA became 'healthy environmental constitutionalism in action'.[62]

Then, in 2017, the Supreme Court decided to apply a bottom lines approach – though not directly to s 5 – in *Environmental Defence Society Inc v Marlborough District Council* ('*King Salmon*').[63] By applying a less

---

55 Elias, above n 48, at 62.

56 At 65.

57 At 60.

58 At 62.

59 At 62.

60 Fisher, above n 7, at 64.

61 Environmental problems are 'hot' in that everything is controversial: 'the identification of intermediaries and overflow, the distribution of source and target agents, the way effects are measured. These controversies which indicate the absence of a stabilised knowledge base, usually involve a wide variety of actors. The actual list of actors, as well as their identities will fluctuate in the course of a controversy itself and the put forward mutually incompatible descriptions of future world states': Fisher, above n 7, at 67, quoting Michel Callon "An Essay on Framing and Overflowing: Economic Externalities Revisited by Sociology" in Michel Callon (ed) *The Laws of the Markets* (Blackwell, Oxford, 1998) 244 at 261. Fisher argues at 69–70 that the "hot" nature of environmental problems leads to the "hot" nature of environmental law. By this I mean that while environmental legislation is passed, environmental controversies do not dissipate and underlying questions concerning scientific uncertainty, polycentricity and normative conflict remain and raise difficult questions'.

62 At 64.

63 *Environmental Defence Society Incorporated v The New Zealand King Salmon Company Ltd* [2014] NZSC 38, [2014] 1 NZLR 593.

discretionary approach to decision-making, this case presented an opportunity to reconceptualise the role of the Environment Court.[64] The case featured a proposed plan change to the relevant regional coastal plan, that if approved would be inconsistent with a clear and direct rule in the New Zealand coastal policy statement. The Supreme Court found that if a higher order policy or plan exists that is clear and directive, it must be applied by decision-makers, including on appeal, and no overall broad judgment of the proposal should be made. Thus, a clear and directive rule in high order policy or plan can create a bottom line, and will be upheld, removing the need to resort to making a fresh judgment about whether or not the proposal promotes sustainable management. Warnock argues that this approach 'both respects the publicly inclusive policy-making process and accords with constitutional mores'.[65]

Therefore, Warnock argues that 'the greatest ramification of the case [could have been] to insulate the New Zealand Environment Court, effectively deflecting the ongoing criticisms and concerns that have called into question its continued existence'.[66] Back in 1993, Harris had argued that the vagueness of s 5 would lead to the Tribunal adopting a balancing approach and unelected judges continuing to make important policy decisions with significant social, economic and environmental effects. It is fair to say that Harris was right; the discretionary nature of overall broad judgment did lead to debate (or healthy discussion) about the constitutional role of the Environment Court. Although, as Warnock observes, *King Salmon* deflected some of this criticism, subsequent cases limited its effect to plan changes. The means that the overall broad judgment approach continues to apply to decision-making in other contexts under the RMA, such as consent applications, and the possibility of this creating challenges for the Environment Court remains.

In practical terms, *King Salmon* also emphasised the importance of having clear and distinct higher order rules in plans and showed that courts will observe the bottom lines they create. For many years, successive governments had failed to provide the necessary higher order plans and

---

64 Warnock, above n 47; Ceri Warnock "Reconceptualising Specialist Environment Courts and Tribunals" (2017) 37 LS 391; Ceri Warnock and Ole W Pedersen "Environmental Adjudication: Mapping the Spectrum and Identifying the Fulcrum" [2017] PL 643.

65 At 518.

66 At 518.

policies and this caused many issues,[67] not least of which was to compound the lack of clear priorities to guide local authorities on the meaning and implementation of sustainable management in the Act itself.[68] Once again as Harris predicted, this raised questions about the required objectivity of local authorities in rule- and decision-making and allowed some difficult environmental problems to persist.

8. IMPLICATIONS FOR LOCAL GOVERNMENT

Statutory local authorities have long played a strong role in resource management in New Zealand. It was inevitable from the outset that local government would have a major role to play under the RMA. And so it was: local authorities were asked to make policies and plans to achieve integrated resource management in regions, districts and cities,[69] and to control activities involving water, discharges to air and the coast by making rules and issuing resource consents subject only to merits appeal to the Tribunal.[70] Local authorities were also asked to perform their functions in a highly participatory way and, although diminished since 1991, public participation remains a key part of the RMA.

The overall purpose of regional and district policies and plans is to achieve the purpose of the Act by promoting sustainable management.[71] Decisions on consents are to be made 'subject to Part 2' of the RMA, which includes s 5.[72] Harris argued that the indeterminate wording of s 5 and the Tribunal's inevitable adoption of a balancing/values judgment approach, would make for a complex and difficult task for the elected law members of local authorities. As a consequence, they might make poor decisions and, given that 'discretion opens the door for arbitrariness and

67 Geoffrey Palmer "Ruminations on the Problems with the Resource Management Act" (keynote address to the Local Government Environmental Compliance Conference, Auckland, November 2015) at 15–16; "The Resource Management Act – How we got it and what Changes are Being Made to it' (paper presented to the Resource Management Law Association, New Plymouth, September 2013) at 13. This speech is published separately in two parts under the same name at [2016] NZLJ 2 and [2016] NZLJ 46.

68 Palmer "Ruminations", above n 67, at 18–19; Palmer "The Resource Management Act", above n 67, at 15.

69 Resource Management Act 1991, ss 60, 64 and 73.

70 Resource Management Act 1991, ss 68, 76 and 87.

71 Resource Management Act 1991, ss 59, 63 and 72.

72 Resource Management Act 1991, s 104.

inequality of treatment',[73] they might lack the necessary objectivity.[74] While these things have undoubtedly happened, the blame is not attributable only to Parliament. The RMA is a framework Act, and it was always envisaged that guidance over and above its words would be provided by national-level policy statements and standards. As noted above, this did not happen soon enough, and local government was left to work too many things out for itself. Speaking 22 years after the Act was enacted, Palmer (former Minister for the Environment and architect of the RMA but by now Sir Geoffrey Palmer QC) said:[75]

> Perhaps the boldest step in the RMA reforms was to give substantial power over the environmental issues to local government in the administration of the Act. Coupled with the failure of central government to live up to its responsibilities to provide the guidance provided for in the Act, many of them floundered around with injudicious use of consultants. The Councils lack capacity and skill and it took them time to develop it. …
>
> There are aspects of local government administration of the [Act] that are seriously defective. The overall performance has been unsatisfactory in many respects and inept at handling problems of complexity. …
>
> My experience is backed by the research of Jeffrey K McNeill that demonstrates that the high degree of devolution in a devolved policymaking context does not generate good environmental outcomes. It creates the opportunity for agency capture. He suggests that many regional councils are dominated by farmers which serves to explain the slow response to dairying impacts over time.

Palmer's example of dairying is telling. Dairying is both very important to the national economy, and has been carried out in ways that have contributed significantly to the degradation of water quality and habitat (with flow-on effects for endemic fish and eels), pressures on river flows (mainly from the attendant irrigation) and New Zealand's greenhouse gas emissions (in 2016, nearly half of our gross greenhouse gas emissions came from agriculture).[76] Palmer is not the only one to argue that dairying

73 Elias, above n 48, at 61.

74 Harris, above n 3, at 69–70.

75 Palmer "Ruminations" above n 67, at 20–22, citing Jeffrey Karl McNeill "The Public Value of Regional Government: How New Zealand's Regional Councils Manage the Environment" (PhD thesis, Massey University New Zealand, 2008).

76 Ministry for the Environment & Stats NZ *New Zealand's Environmental Reporting Series: Environment Aotearoa 2019* (Wellington, 2019) at 46–61, 75–81 and 94–96.

provides a good example of the 'failure to match regulatory requirements with the intensification of agriculture' that has occurred under the RMA.[77]

9. CONCLUSION: AN ABDICATION OF PARLIAMENTARY RESPONSIBILITY?

All in all, Harris's 1993 analysis accurately predicted the constitutional implications of New Zealand's attempt to enact sustainability as the overall goal of resource management. Harris's basic argument was that the indeterminacy of the RMA's definition of sustainable management would lead to the Tribunal and local government exercising a wide discretion in deciding whether or not policies, plans and proposals promote sustainable management, and that this would in turn lead to (continuing) questions about the proper function(ing) of the Planning Tribunal/Environment Court, and the quality of local government rule- and decision-making.

Unfortunately, the RMA's constitutional implications are not its most serious concern. It is an inescapable truth that the quality of the natural environment in this country has deteriorated over the life of the Act.[78] Many would, and have, argued that the RMA's environmental failures are another consequence of its indeterminately worded purpose that fails to prioritise environmental protection, coupled with the failure of executive government to step in and provide the necessary guidance through national policies and standard setting. These include Tony Randerson QC (a retired judge of the Court of Appeal, and others), who was commissioned by the government to write an independent review of the RMA in 2020.[79] Randerson proposed repealing the RMA, and replacing it with new legislation including a new Act focussed on the natural environment that aims 'to enhance the quality of the environment to support the wellbeing of present and future generations and to recognise the concept of Te Mana o te Taiao'.[80]

The sixth Labour government (2017–) has recently announced that it will seek to implement Randerson's proposals by 2023.[81] This is despite

77 Upton, above n 40, at 3.

78 At 3.

79 Resource Management Review Panel *New Directions for Resource Management in New Zealand* (Wellington, 2020) at 16–19.

80 At 23.

81 Hon David Parker (Minister for the Environment) "RMA to be Repealed and Replaced" (press release, 10 February 2021).

others – significantly including Simon Upton, once the Minister responsible for the RMA's enactment, now the Parliamentary Commissioner for the Environment, an independent watchdog on government's environmental performance – insisting that s 5 should be left alone (the RMA is 'as close as environmental law gets to having constitutional status … amendment to Part 2 should be treated with great caution') but 'supplemented with a requirement to set more precise environmental limits that will protect the natural environment and set clear norms and expectations about property rights at a national level'.[82]

Whatever eventuates, in a constitution such as New Zealand's where Parliament has law-making supremacy, failing to do *something* to arrest the on-going deterioration of the natural environment that has occurred under the RMA amounts in my opinion to a continuing and ultimate abdication of Parliament's environmental responsibility.

---

82 Upton, above n 40, at 13.

PART II

ISSUES CONCERNING THE JUDICIARY

Creativity and Pragmatism in Judicial Method

DECLARATIONS OF INCONSISTENCY AND JUDICIAL CREATIVITY

A Tale of Two *Taylors*

John Ip*

1. INTRODUCTION

As a law student who started at Auckland in the late 1990s, I received my education in public law from true titans in the field: Bruce Harris, Paul Rishworth, Mike Taggart and later Janet McLean. I would like to think that I had some sense of how lucky I was to be taught by such eminent scholars, but I suspect this would be revisionist history. As a student, one tends to have at most a superficial sense of an academic's scholarship (or even that academics do scholarship). In any case, any appreciation of an academic's scholarly reputation was secondary to what they were like as

* My thanks to Sam Bookman and Ed Willis for feedback on earlier versions of this contribution. Any errors remain my own.

a classroom teacher.[1] Some years later, I came to have the great privilege of having Bruce, Paul, Mike and Janet as colleagues. It was really only at this juncture, as a young academic starting out in the field of public law, that the full extent of the legacy I was continuing dawned upon me. At this point too, it became much clearer to me that what I had seen in the classroom as a student was just one small slice of the whole.

Universities like to talk about research-informed teaching – a synergy between one's research and teaching. For some it represents an unattainable holy grail. I do not think it was for Bruce. He taught public law at part II and honours level for many years; his scholarship covered a broad swathe of public law, as reflected by the range of contributions to this collection. While he is perhaps best known for his account of the 'third source' of executive power,[2] another focus of his scholarship was the institution of the judiciary, as exemplified by his work on remedies for judicial error and judicial accountability,[3] and his argument for a judicial commission to handle appointments, discipline and education.[4]

Bruce's interest in the judiciary extended to matters of adjudication.[5] In 2007, he published a chapter entitled 'Judicial Activism and New Zealand's Appellate Courts' for a collection edited by Brice Dickson of Queen's University Belfast.[6] Despite the title of the chapter, Bruce largely eschewed the label of judicial activism on account of its pejorative connotations, preferring instead the term judicial creativity. He argued

1 For the record, Paul was the master of wry observations, Mike was a force of nature and Bruce was the fount of avuncular assurance. Janet is (still) referred to as the goddess of public law.

2 See for example BV Harris "The 'Third Source' of Authority for Government Action" (1992) 108 LQR 626; BV Harris "The 'Third Source' of Authority for Government Action Revisited" (2007) 123 LQR 225; BV Harris "Government 'Third Source' Action and Common Law Constitutionalism" (2010) 126 LQR 373.

3 BV Harris "Remedies and Accountability for Unlawful Judicial Action in New Zealand: Could the Law Be Tidier?" [2008] NZ L Rev 483; BV Harris "The Resignation of Wilson J: A Consequent Critique of the Operation of the Judicial Conduct Commissioner and Judicial Conduct Panel Act 2004" [2011] NZ L Rev 625.

4 BV Harris "A Judicial Commission for New Zealand: A Good Idea that Must Not Be Allowed to Go Away" [2014] NZ L Rev 383.

5 See for example BV Harris "The Law-making Power of the Judiciary" in PA Joseph (ed) *Essays on the Constitution* (Brookers, Wellington, 1995) 265; BV Harris "Final Appellate Courts Overruling their Own 'Wrong' Precedents: the Ongoing Search for Principle" (2002) 118 LQR 408; BV Harris "The Continuing Struggle with the Nuanced Obligation on Judges to Provide Reasons for Their Decisions" (2016) 132 LQR 216.

6 Bruce Harris "Judicial Activism and New Zealand's Appellate Courts" in Brice Dickson (ed) *Judicial Activism in Common Law Supreme Courts* (Oxford University Press, Oxford, 2007) 273.

that New Zealand's system of government needed the courts to be creative to some degree, and that the courts had for the most part struck the right balance. One of the examples of creativity discussed in the chapter was the creation of remedies for violations of the New Zealand Bill of Rights Act 1990 ('BORA'), among them the jurisdiction to declare legislation inconsistent with the BORA.

In my contribution, I want to examine the Court of Appeal and Supreme Court's decisions in *Attorney General v Taylor*,[7] which established the jurisdiction to issue declarations of inconsistency ('DOIs'), in light of Bruce's discussion of judicial creativity. First, I argue, in keeping with Bruce's chapter, that the establishment of the DOI jurisdiction is an act of judicial creativity, and that it is a justifiable instance of it. Second, given the conventional wisdom that the decision of the Court of Appeal is manifestly more creative than that of the Supreme Court, I offer some tentative explanations for this stylistic contrast – that is, why the Court of Appeal's approach seemed to be to establish the DOI jurisdiction in the grandest way possible, while the Supreme Court's approach seemed to be the opposite.

2. JUDICIAL ACTIVISM AND NEW ZEALAND'S APPELLATE COURTS

2.1. OVERVIEW

The thesis of Bruce's chapter is that 'the optimum functioning of the New Zealand system of government not only contemplates but requires creativity from the courts, and that the appellate courts have in most cases made appropriate decisions as to when to be creative and when to be restrained'.[8] The dataset includes a few decisions of the then newly established Supreme Court, such as its decisions concerning Ahmed Zaoui,[9] as well as various decisions of the Court of Appeal when it functioned as New Zealand's de facto apex court. These include the Court of Appeal's foreshore and seabed decision,[10] and its decision concerning

7 *Attorney-General v Taylor* [2017] NZCA 215, [2017] 3 NZLR 24 [*Taylor* (CA)]; *Attorney-General v Taylor* [2018] NZSC 104, [2019] 1 NZLR 213 [*Taylor* (SC)].

8 Harris, above n 6, at 273.

9 *Zaoui v Attorney-General* [2005] 1 NZLR 577; and *Zaoui v Attorney-General (No 2)* [2005] NZSC 38, [2006] 1 NZLR 289.

10 *Attorney General v Ngati Apa* [2003] 3 NZLR 643 (CA).

the retrospective sentencing law for murders involving home invasion.[11] In order to provide a balanced assessment of the prevalence of judicial creativity in New Zealand, the chapter also considers instances of restraint on the part of the courts – with perhaps the most notable example being the Court of Appeal's decision that declined to interpret the Marriage Act 1955 to permit same-sex marriage in order to ensure consistency with the right to be free from discrimination under the BORA.[12]

The chapter also provides a survey of the debate over judicial activism in New Zealand. On Bruce's account, critics of judicial activism tend to prioritise the certainty and predictability of law, are hostile to judicial discretion and have a formalist approach to law. In the context of the BORA, they strongly adhere to the view that unelected judges should not be in the business of undoing the decisions of the democratically accountable political branches.[13]

Interestingly, there is no New Zealand judge who is identified as being the paragon of judicial restraint, a local equivalent of Oliver Wendell Holmes or Felix Frankfurter. By contrast, those identified as advocates of judicial creativity, who subscribe to the view that considerations of justice are relevant to adjudication, were all senior members of the judiciary: Lord Cooke of Thorndon, Justice Ted Thomas and Chief Justice Elias.[14]

Bruce accepts that people will have differing points of view about what constitutes appropriate and inappropriate judicial creativity.[15] But at the same time he proposes several principles as a means of distinguishing between desirable and undesirable instances of judicial creativity. First, the act of judicial creativity must be a 'a genuine and justifiable attempt to improve the law or the law's application', rather than being an act of judicial self-indulgence or self-aggrandisement.[16] Second, the court must be cognisant of the question of relative institutional competence – that is, whether the judiciary or Parliament is the 'most constitutionally appropriate and best equipped body in the structure of government to effect the innovation'.[17] Finally, the court should also 'be mindful of whether the legislature intended the court should have such freedom for innovation'.[18]

---

11 *R v Pora* [2001] 2 NZLR 37 (CA).

12 *Quilter v Attorney General* [1998] 1 NZLR 523. See also Taylor Burgess's contribution to this volume.

13 Harris, above n 6, at 284–291.

14 At 292–301.

15 At 273 and 284.

16 At 301.

17 At 301.

18 At 302.

More specifically, the legislature may be said to have 'deliberately invited judicial creativity by enacting indeterminate legislation', or to have impliedly done so 'where such innovation is necessary in order to fill a gap in legislation'.[19]

Bruce's assessment is that judicial creativity is necessary to ensure the proper functioning of the legal system. However, he states that 'New Zealand appellate courts employ their creative freedom sparingly', and that the 'overall judicial ethos ... is one of restraint'.[20] He acknowledges that the courts are 'on occasions motivated by justice considerations to be creative',[21] but in the main afford appropriate respect to the political branches. He concludes that the general perception is that New Zealand courts are striking an appropriate balance between creativity and restraint, and that 'the strident concerns of a small group of business and academic commentators' about courts run amok are accordingly overblown.[22]

2.2. JUDICIAL ACTIVISM: THE DEFINITIONAL DILEMMA

Judicial activism is a term that is implicitly value-laden, underspecified, and thus problematic. However, it is the concept at the heart of Bruce's chapter, and indeed the entire collection of which it formed a part. It is therefore necessary to outline the scholarly literature on judicial activism, and to consider Bruce's preference for the term 'judicial creativity'.

The term 'judicial activism' was first popularised by American historian Arthur Schlesinger Jr, who used it to describe the contrasting judicial philosophies of the duelling factions on the US Supreme Court in 1947. On Schlesinger's account, one group of judges, exemplified by Justices Black and Douglas, had an expansive conception of the judicial role. The other group, exemplified by Justices Frankfurter and Jackson, emphasised judicial restraint and deference to the legislature:[23]

> The Black-Douglas group believes that the Supreme Court can play an affirmative role in promoting the social welfare; the Frankfurter-Jackson group

---

19 At 302.
20 At 322.
21 At 322.
22 At 322.
23 Keenan D Kmiec "The Origin and Current Meanings of Judicial Activism" (2004) 92 Cal L Rev 1441 at 1446–1447 quoting Arthur M Schlesinger, Jr "The Supreme Court: 1947", *Fortune* (January 1947) 20.

> advocates a policy of judicial self-restraint. One group is more concerned with the employment of the judicial power for their own conception of the social good; the other with expanding the range of allowable judgment for legislatures, even if it means upholding conclusions they privately condemn. One group regards the Court as an instrument to achieve desired social results; the second as an instrument to permit the other branches of government to achieve the results the people want for better or worse.

Traces of the familiar dichotomies of the debate between judicial activism and its opposite, judicial restraint, are already evident: democratically unaccountable judges against the democratically elected political branches, obtaining desirable outcomes against maintaining principle, loose versus strict views about the binding nature of precedent, and so on.[24] But, as Keenan Kmiec observes, Schlesinger's early account 'exhibits some of the symptoms of the classic malady that has infected modern discussions of judicial activism'.[25] More specifically, it is difficult to discern what makes judicial activism activist given that Schlesinger puts forward several possible candidates for its essential characteristics. Accordingly, it is hard to know whether Schlesinger would consider flashpoint decisions such as *Bush v Gore*[26] or *Roe v Wade*[27] to be instances of judicial activism, and if so on what basis.[28] Indeed, the same can be said of that fixed star of the American constitutional firmament, *Brown v Board of Education*.[29]

But Schlesinger's pioneering effort is hardly alone in this. Mark Tushnet, writing in the same 2007 collection, observes that more recent legal scholarship is afflicted with the same issue.[30] He concludes that judicial activism lacks a clear baseline against which the activism is to be evaluated, and thus ends up being a loose term used to either lavish praise or scorn upon a judicial decision for other reasons.[31] And as Judge Frank Easterbrook observes in his trenchant critique of the concept, denunciations of judicial activism (and corresponding praise for judicial restraint) often depends upon whether liberals or conservatives form the

---

24 At 1449.
25 At 1449.
26 531 US 98 (2000).
27 410 US 113 (1973).
28 Kmiec, above n 23, at 1450.
29 *Brown v Board of Education of Topeka* 347 US 483 (1954).
30 Mark Tushnet "The United States of America" in Brice Dickson (ed) *Judicial Activism in Common Law Supreme Courts* (Oxford University Press, Oxford, 2007) at 416–417.
31 At 436.

majority on the Supreme Court.[32] Like Tushnet, Easterbrook criticises the term as being ultimately vacuous:[33]

> The term "activism" thus used is empty, a mask for a substantive position. "Activism" remains, however, a term of opprobrium. Everyone wants to appropriate and apply the word so that his favored approach is sound and its opposite "activist." Then "activism" just means Judges Behaving Badly – and each person fills in a different definition of "badly".

Even from this brief overview, we can see that there are several possible criteria for identifying instances of Judges Behaving Badly. Easterbrook's account suggests one, namely fidelity to precedent.[34] Another prominent candidate is overriding the decisions of the democratically accountable political branches. Aziz Huq, for example, defines judicial activism in terms of how often the courts declare actions of the political branches unconstitutional.[35] Of course no New Zealand court has the power to strike down legislation. Jeremy Waldron, though, defines judicial activism in terms of a broader willingness to challenge legislation, including means that are available under the BORA:[36]

> I am going to say that "judicial activist" refers to a Judge who is willing to challenge a piece of parliamentary legislation in one of the following ways: (i) by refusing to enforce it when it conflicts with what the Judge sees as fundamental rights; (ii) by denouncing it, for example in a declaration of its incompatibility with the terms of the New Zealand Bill of Rights Act 1990; or (iii) by interpreting its provisions in a way that does not correspond to what its sponsors in Parliament intended, in order to make it more just or more in accordance with fundamental rights.

Naturally, there are other candidates for signifiers of judicial activism – perhaps the most notable of these are judges imposing their personal values on

---

32 Frank H Easterbrook "Do Liberals and Conservatives Differ in Judicial Activism" (2002) 73 U Colo L Rev 1401 at 1401.

33 At 1401. See also Jane S Schacter "Putting the Politics of 'Judicial Activism' in Historical Perspective" [2017] Supreme Court Review 209 at 214.

34 See also Kmiec, above n 23, at 1466–1471.

35 Aziz Z Huq "When Was Judicial Self-Restraint" (2012) 100 Cal L Rev 579 at 581. See also Kmiec, above n 23, at 1463–1464.

36 Jeremy Waldron "Compared to What? Judicial Activism and the New Zealand Parliament" [2005] NZLJ 441 at 441.

the law,[37] and judges making law and engaging in policy-making, or legislating from the bench.[38] All of these signifiers come back, in one way or another, to some normative account of what the proper role of a judge is and what proper judging is about (and not about). The activist judge in some way falls short of what is required – by being insufficiently deferent to precedent, by too readily questioning the decisions of the political branches, by being too willing to sacrifice principle to obtain a desirable result, by making law and policy choices that are not theirs to make, and so on. Activism is, at best, a shorthand for these apparent judicial vices. But the term really does little work at all, and instead piggybacks off a particular vision of the proper judicial role, whether that be unerring fidelity to precedent, deference to decisions reached by the political branches, or limiting judicial law-making to the lacunae and interstices left by the legislature.

Given the problems identified above, and the negative connotations associated with the term, it is understandable that Bruce states at the outset of his chapter that he prefers the term judicial creativity over judicial activism.[39] But this move is not without its problems. The first is that judicial activism refuses to stay buried. Most obviously it still appears in the title of the chapter and appears from time to time in the text. Second, it introduces the additional complexity of ascertaining the relationship between judicial activism and judicial creativity. Certain passages of the chapter seem to treat the terms as synonymous. At one point, the chapter refers to differentiating between 'acceptable and unacceptable judicial creativity'.[40] At the end of the same section, the chapter refers to 'appropriate or inappropriate judicial activism'.[41] It looks as though the shift from activism to creativity is purely cosmetic; there is good and bad judicial activism, just as there is good and bad judicial creativity. It is not clear that simply rebranding activism as creativity achieves that much. The questions are simply rephrased. What makes a judicial decision creative? When is it appropriate for a court to be creative?

---

37 EW Thomas "So-Called 'Judicial Activism' and the Ascendancy of Judicial Constraints" (2005) 21 NZULR 685 at 691; Tom Campbell "Judicial Activism – Justice or Treason?" (2001) 10 Otago L Rev 307 at 312.

38 Kmiec, above n 23, at 1471; Thomas, above n 37, at 692; Campbell, above n 37, at 312; Schacter, above n 33, at 215–217.

39 Harris, above n 6, at 273. Michael Kirby does the same: see MD Kirby *Judicial Activism* (Sweet & Maxwell, London, 2004) at 76.

40 Harris, above n 6, at 301. See also at 298, referring to 'justified judicial creativity'.

41 At 302.

However, I think the best reading of the chapter is that the terms are not synonymous. As the section of Bruce's chapter entitled 'Acceptable Judicial Creativity and Unacceptable Judicial Activism' suggests,[42] judicial creativity is acceptable up to a point or under certain conditions, but at some point it can spill over into the domain of unacceptable judicial activism. This is the meaning of judicial creativity that I adopt from Bruce's chapter. There are accordingly two separate inquiries: first, whether the court has acted in a manner that can be described as creative (for example, by not strictly following precedent), and second, whether it was justified in doing so.

3. *TAYLOR v ATTORNEY GENERAL* AS AN INSTANCE OF JUDICIAL CREATIVITY

I now turn to discuss the decisions of the Court of Appeal and Supreme Court in *Attorney-General v Taylor*.[43] I first provide a brief account of these decisions and the change to the electoral legislation that led to the litigation. I then consider whether these decisions, which both held that the courts have the jurisdiction to issue DOIs, can be described as instances of judicial creativity, and, if so, whether they are examples of acceptable judicial creativity by reference to the evaluative principles set out in Bruce's chapter.

3.1. *TAYLOR*: BACKGROUND

Under the Electoral Act 1993, prisoners with sentences of preventive detention, life imprisonment or determinate sentences of three or more years of imprisonment were barred from registering to vote.[44] This position reflected the report by the Royal Commission on the Electoral System, which had recommended changing the approach of disenfranchising all prisoners, the position in New Zealand since 1956 (other than a brief

---

42 At 301.

43 *Taylor* (CA) and *Taylor* (SC), above n 7.

44 Electoral Act 1993, s 80(1)(d). See generally Greg Robins "The Rights of Prisoners to Vote: A Review of Prisoner Disenfranchisement in New Zealand" (2006) 4 NZJPIL 165.

hiatus in the mid-1970s).[45] The 1993 Act reflected a political consensus that a blanket ban on prisoner voting amounted to a breach of the right to vote in s 12 of the BORA.[46] This consensus was, however, disrupted with the enactment of the Electoral (Disqualification of Sentenced Prisoners) Amendment Act 2010. This Act, which began life as a private member's bill, amended the Electoral Act to bar any serving prisoner from registering to vote.[47]

Arthur Taylor, together with several other serving prisoners, sought a judicial declaration that the 2010 Act was inconsistent with s 12 of the BORA. It was not in dispute that the Act would remain legally operative even if a DOI were issued by a court – s 4 of the BORA says as much. There was also no dispute that the Act was an unjustified limitation on s 12 – the Attorney-General conceded as much, and at no stage during the litigation defended the Act's substance. Indeed, the Attorney-General had earlier issued a s 7 report on the bill that became the 2010 Act, which concluded that the bill was over- and under-inclusive, irrational and disproportionate, and thus was not a reasonable and justified limit on the right to vote under s 12.[48] Thus, the only issue of contention in the *Taylor* litigation was whether the courts had the jurisdiction to issue a DOI 'as a standalone remedy'.[49]

The High Court in 2015 answered this question in the affirmative, and granted the first-ever DOI, which stated that the 2010 Act was an unreasonable and unjustifiable limit on the right to vote under s 12 of the BORA.[50] The Attorney-General appealed.

The Court of Appeal affirmed the High Court's decision on the existence of the jurisdiction to issue DOIs and its decision to issue one on the facts of the case. Although the Court of Appeal did find that the text and structure of the BORA impliedly authorised the making of DOIs, this was a subsidiary justification.[51] The main basis for the judicial jurisdiction to issue DOIs, according to the Court of Appeal, lay elsewhere – namely

---

45 *Taylor* (SC), above n 7, at [9]–[11]; Janet L Hiebert and James B Kelly *Parliamentary Bills of Rights: The Experiences of New Zealand and the United Kingdom* (Cambridge University Press, Cambridge, 2015) at 159–160.

46 Hiebert and Kelly, above n 45, at 161.

47 For an account of the unfortunate background to the enactment of this legislation, see Andrew Geddis "Prisoner Voting and Rights Deliberation: How New Zealand's Parliament Failed" [2011] NZ L Rev 443.

48 *Taylor* (SC), above n 7, at [81]–[84].

49 At [73].

50 *Taylor v Attorney-General* [2015] NZHC 1706, [2015] 3 NZLR 791.

51 *Taylor* (CA), above n 7, at [109].

the courts' inherent power to state the law and resolve inconsistencies between statutes, including between rights-infringing legislation and the BORA.[52] This was the Court's response to the submission from the Attorney-General that it was 'no part of the judicial function under New Zealand's constitution to make [DOIs] absent legislation expressly authorising them'.[53] On the Court of Appeal's account, no legislative mandate was needed as making DOIs fell within the courts' common law powers of adjudication.

The higher courts' common law judicial power by definition did not depend upon legislation.[54] Rather, like the notion of Parliamentary supremacy, it derived from the post-1688 political settlement, which established not only the supremacy of Parliament over the Crown, but also the independence of the judiciary.[55] The Court of Appeal summarised the position in this way:[56]

> [J]udicial power in New Zealand can be traced through the New Zealand Constitution Act 1852 to a political settlement that distributed authority among the branches of government. The judicial function extends to answering questions of law, and as a general proposition it does not require express legislative authority. Inconsistency between statutes is a question of interpretation, and hence of law, and it lies within the province of the courts.

On the Court of Appeal's telling, Parliament and the courts are on more or less equal footing. Certainly, there is an acknowledgment of Parliament's unbounded legislative power,[57] and a disavowal of any suggestion that Parliamentary supremacy depends on the judges or the common law.[58] But at the same time, the Court of Appeal talks about the branches of government as being 'co-dependent',[59] and government as being 'a collaborative enterprise'.[60] Diceyan orthodoxy this is not.

In keeping with this view of Parliament and the courts as being co-dependent branches of government involved in the collaborative enterprise of governing, the Court of Appeal understood the rationale for

52 At [77].
53 At [41].
54 At [47].
55 At [50].
56 At [62].
57 At [77].
58 At [49].
59 At [51].
60 At [53].

DOIs in terms of dialogue. That is, even though the DOI was, in the Court's view, not a declaration of right because it 'determines no legal rights and conveys no legal consequences as between the parties',[61] it nonetheless 'expresses the court's opinion that legislation limited the plaintiff's protected right in an unjustified way'.[62] Once a DOI is issued, the initiative then shifts to the political branches, as it is they who decide whether to modify the legislation declared to be incompatible with the BORA. In this way, 'the court's opinion can be seen as part of a dialogue'.[63] In other words, a DOI strictly speaking has no legal effect – as Claudia Geiringer memorably puts it, the power to make DOIs amounts to 'a judicial power to make non-binding declarations of legal non-right'.[64] But, according to the Court of Appeal, it does create an expectation of a good faith response by the political branches: 'a [DOI], … is made in the reasonable constitutional expectation that the other branches will respond to it by reappraising the limitation and its justification'.[65]

The Attorney-General appealed once more. The Supreme Court, by a majority of three to two, dismissed the Attorney-General's appeal, holding that the lower courts were correct to declare that the 2010 Act was inconsistent with s 12 of the BORA. But the Supreme Court's reasoning differed from that of the Court of Appeal. The majority (Elias CJ, Glazebrook and Ellen France JJ) considered that the power to issue DOIs could be implied from the scheme of the BORA.[66] The majority also rejected the Attorney-General's argument that, absent legislative authorisation, a power to issue DOIs was at odds with the judicial function because it was not a declaration of right but was rather a purely advisory opinion devoid of any legal effect. Justices Glazebrook and Ellen France considered that a DOI amounted to a formal declaration about the effect of an Act on the affected person's rights, and was thus consistent with the judicial function.[67] Chief Justice Elias went further, stating that a DOI amounted to a declaration of right within the scheme of the BORA.[68] Nor was a DOI entirely without legal consequence, since it could have importance should

61 At [66].
62 At [149].
63 At [149].
64 Claudia Geiringer "The Constitutional Role of the Courts under the NZ Bill of Rights: Three Narratives from *Attorney-General v Taylor*" (2017) 48 VUWLR 547 at 551.
65 *Taylor* (CA), above n 7, at [76].
66 *Taylor* (SC), above n 7, at [50] and [117].
67 At [52]–[53].
68 At [105].

a complaint against New Zealand be made under the Optional Protocol to the International Covenant on Civil and Political Rights.[69]

The minority (William Young and O'Regan JJ) concluded that there was no jurisdiction to issue DOIs. But there are substantial areas of agreement between the majority and minority. Notably, the minority agreed that 'if such a jurisdiction exists, it flows from the Bill of Rights Act itself'.[70] However, the absence of express legislative provision for issuing DOIs counted against finding that such a jurisdiction existed.[71] Furthermore, according to the minority, implying the jurisdiction to issue DOIs from the BORA only highlighted the uncertainty as to whether a DOI ought to be understood as a remedy, or if so, whether it was an effective one. This was because the inconsistent legislation continues to apply and a DOI does not oblige 'anyone to do anything';[72] instead 'a declaration would simply hang in the air and possibly create some sort of moral obligation on the part of the legislature to reconsider'.[73] This was unlike DOIs made under the equivalent bill of rights documents in certain Australian jurisdictions, Ireland and the UK, which all have specified legal consequences.[74] The flipside of this, however, is that the minority would view the making of a DOI as being consistent with the judicial function if there were a legislatively mandated process for doing so.[75] That is, Justices William Young and O'Regan did not consider making DOIs to be inherently outside the judicial function; rather, their concern centred on the uncertain prospects of a response from the political branches.

3.2. THE ESTABLISHMENT OF THE DOI JURISDICTION AS JUDICIAL CREATIVITY

I turn to consider whether, in light of the indicia for identifying judicial activism I referred to earlier (fidelity to precedent, deference to political decision-makers and limiting judicial law-making), the establishment of a DOI jurisdiction should be seen an act of judicial creativity. First, let us consider how the DOI jurisdiction fits with the existing case law.

---

69 At [55] per Ellen France J and [101] per Elias CJ. The dissent described this as a 'relatively minor consequence': at [139].

70 At [122].

71 At [122].

72 At [134].

73 At [134].

74 At [134].

75 At [131] and [138].

As is well known, the New Zealand courts equivocated on the matter of DOIs for a considerable period of time. The Court of Appeal's decision in *Moonen* is perhaps the first watershed moment.[76] In that decision, Justice Tipping referred to:[77]

> … the Court having the power, and on occasions the duty, to indicate that although a statutory provision must be enforced according to its proper meaning, it is inconsistent with the Bill of Rights, in that it constitutes an unreasonable limitation on the relevant right or freedom which cannot be demonstrably justified in a free and democratic society.

Moonen has sometimes been understood as actually establishing the power to make DOIs. But the Court is more equivocal on the matter – it is unclear whether making a declaration referred to a declaration in the sense that term would later be used in *Taylor*, or just announcing that the court was unable to interpret the provision consistently with the BORA and was bound to apply the rights-infringing meaning as per s 4.[78] The latter has subsequently come to be known as a *Hansen* indication. It is described in this way in Justice McGrath's judgment in *R v Hansen*:[79]

> [A] New Zealand court must never shirk its responsibility to indicate, in any case where it concludes that the measure being considered is inconsistent with protected rights, that it has inquired into the possibility of there being an available rights consistent interpretation, that none could be found, and that it has been necessary for the court to revert to s 4 of the Bill of Rights Act and uphold the ordinary meaning of the other statute. Normally that will be sufficiently apparent from the court's statement of its reasoning.
>
> Articulating that reasoning serves the important function of bringing to the attention of the executive branch of government that the court is of the view that there is a measure on the statute book which infringes protected rights and freedoms, which the court has decided is not a justified limitation. It is then for the other branches of government to consider how to respond to the court's finding. While they are under no obligation to change the law and remedy the inconsistency, it is a reasonable constitutional expectation that there will

76 *Moonen v Film and Literature Board of Review* [2000] 2 NZLR 9 (CA).

77 At [20].

78 *Taylor* (SC), above n 7, at [32]. See generally Claudia Geiringer "On a Road to Nowhere: Implied Declarations of Inconsistency and the New Zealand Bill of Rights Act" (2009) 40 VUWLR 613 at 618–619.

79 *R v Hansen* [2007] NZSC 7, [2007] 3 NZLR 1 at [253]–[254].

> be a reappraisal of the objectives of the particular measure, and of the means by which they were implemented in the legislation, in light of the finding of inconsistency with these fundamental rights and freedoms …

Additionally, there were several other Court of Appeal decisions that hinted at the availability of DOIs, but for a variety of reasons declined to actually make a declaration.[80] But even though no DOI had ever been made by a New Zealand court, there was also no definitive judicial statement ruling out the possibility of a judicial power to make DOIs. In the absence of a decision ruling out the possibility of DOIs, the Court of Appeal and Supreme Court decisions in *Taylor* cannot be said to be a departure from precedent.

That said, I think that the establishment of the DOI jurisdiction does break new ground and should be understood as being an extension of the judicial statements noted above from *Moonen* and *Hansen*. More specifically, there is an important distinction to be drawn between a court stating that a statutory provision is inconsistent with the BORA with a *Hansen* indication and the DOI that was sought and granted in the *Taylor* litigation. As O'Regan J explains in his judgment in *Taylor*, a *Hansen* indication is the by-product of a court reaching a particular conclusion after undertaking the interpretative exercise contemplated by the BORA:[81]

> [*Hansen* indications] are not a remedy that can be sought in a standalone claim for a declaration of inconsistency: there needs to be a controversy that requires the court to consider whether a provision is inconsistent in the course of an interpretation dispute requiring an analysis of ss 4, 5 and 6 of the Bill of Rights Act.

Accordingly, a *Hansen* indication is only available under certain conditions. A court must conclude that certain legislation amounts to an unreasonable and unjustified limit on a BORA right, and also that the infringing legislation cannot be interpreted consistently with the BORA – with the result that the infringing meaning of the legislation prevails by virtue of s 4.[82] Accordingly, as compared to a rights-consistent

---

80 These are described by Ellen France J: see *Taylor* (SC), above n 7, at [31]–[37]. See also Geiringer, above n 78.

81 *Taylor* (SC), above n 7, at [125].

82 See also Geiringer, above n 78, at 644; Tom Hickman "Bill of Rights Reform and the Case for Going Beyond the Declaration of Incompatibility Model" [2015] NZ L Rev 35 at 40–41.

interpretation, a *Hansen* indication is very much a second-best outcome for a litigant. The facts of the *Hansen* case provide an example of this scenario. The majority of the Supreme Court concluded that the reverse onus provision in s 6(6) of the Misuse of Drugs Act 1975, whereby a person possessing more than a certain threshold amount of a controlled drug is presumed to possess it for supply unless they can prove otherwise to the balance of probabilities, was an unjustified limit on the right to be presumed innocent under s 25(c) of the BORA. However, no alternative rights-consistent interpretation of the statutory language was possible, and the originally applied meaning of s 6(6) prevailed as s 4 of the BORA requires.[83]

By contrast, a litigant seeking a DOI only claims that a statutory provision breaches a BORA right, but not that the provision can be interpreted consistently with the BORA – since otherwise there would be no need for a DOI.[84] Accordingly, the litigants in *Taylor* sought a declaration that the 2010 Act was an unjustified limit on s 12 of the BORA.[85] They did not claim that a rights-consistent interpretation was available – nor could they have done so given the language of the Act.[86]

Given this qualitative difference between a *Hansen* indication and a DOI, there is something novel about the DOI jurisdiction established in *Taylor*. Accordingly, claims that the power to issue DOIs represents merely a modest extension of that which was already accepted in the case law (namely *Hansen* indications) ought to be viewed sceptically. The Court of Appeal's *Taylor* decision implicitly relies on this claim by describing the gap between giving reasons explaining why a law is inconsistent with the BORA and a DOI as a 'seemingly short step'.[87] Chief Justice Elias's candid appraisal of the DOI power as 'constitutional innovation' is a more accurate description,[88] even if it makes potential charges of judicial activism more likely to stick.

Next, let us consider *Taylor*'s establishment of a DOI jurisdiction in terms of deference to the political branches. Recall that Jeremy Waldron's definition of judicial activism refers to challenging Parliament's legislation in a variety of ways, including by issuing a DOI. On this view, *Taylor* is

83 *Hansen*, above n 79.
84 *Taylor* (SC), above n 7, at [126].
85 At [3].
86 See Paul Rishworth "Human Rights" [2018] NZ L Rev 543 at 547 ('No interpretive argument was or could be made; the prohibition was very clear.').
87 *Taylor* (CA), above n 7, at [41].
88 *Taylor* (SC), above n 7, at [117].

straightforwardly an instance of judicial activism. The Court of Appeal and Supreme Court decisions uphold not only the jurisdiction of the courts to issue DOIs but also the particular declaration that the 2010 Act was incompatible with the right to vote under s 12 of the BORA, thereby casting constitutional aspersions upon Parliament's work.[89]

Finally, are the Court of Appeal and Supreme Court's *Taylor* decisions instances of the courts limiting their law-making to the lacunae and interstices left by the legislature? Both the Court of Appeal and Supreme Court find that the courts have the power to issue DOIs in spite of the lack of any express provision concerning remedies in the BORA itself. The original proposal for the Bill of Rights did contain a remedies provision. It stated that '[a]nyone whose rights or freedoms as guaranteed by this Bill of Rights have been infringed or denied may apply to a court of competent jurisdiction to obtain such remedy as the court considers appropriate and just in the circumstances'.[90] But this provision was not enacted. Taken in isolation, the BORA's resulting silence on the question of remedies does not mean that the courts have overridden or contradicted a decision of the political branches. After all, one possible inference from the legislative silence is that Parliament was content to leave the matter of remedies for the courts to develop as they saw fit. But this is not the only available inference from the BORA's silence on this matter.

In an article excoriating the Court of Appeal's decision in *Baigent's case*, which created a new public law remedy of damages for breaches of the BORA by the Crown,[91] John Smillie takes the position that the remedies clause was deliberately omitted because it was associated with the original supreme-law proposal for the Bill of Rights that failed to gain any political traction. On Smillie's account, the legislative history indicates that Parliament did not intend for the courts to have new powers as a result of the enactment of the BORA.[92]

A look back at the legislative debate provides support for Smillie's view. The relevant portions of *Hansard* contain mostly arguments about the need for a bill of rights, concerns about its potential transfer of power from Parliament to the courts and the watered-down nature of the bill – there are

89 At [70] and [121]; *Taylor* (CA), above n 7, at [185].

90 The text is quoted in *Simpson v Attorney General* [1994] 3 NZLR 667 at 698.

91 *Simpson v Attorney General* [1994] 3 NZLR 667.

92 JA Smillie "The Allure of Rights Talk: *Baigent's Case* in the Court of Appeal" (1994) 8 Otago L Rev 188 at 195–197. For a similar view regarding remedies under the BORA see James Allan "The Author Doth Protest Too Much, Methinks" (2003) 20 NZULR 519 at 525; Léonid Sirota "Breaking the Silence: New Zealand's Courts and Parliament after *Attorney-General v Taylor*" (2019) 30 PLR 13 at 13.

many references to a Clayton's bill of rights,[93] but precious little discussion of remedies. There is a mention of remedies from then-Prime Minister Geoffrey Palmer at the second reading of the bill, when he stressed all of the things that the bill of rights would not do: 'the Bill creates no new legal remedies for courts to grant. The judges will continue to have the same legal remedies as they have now, irrespective of whether the Bill of Rights is an issue'.[94]

One should be cautious about drawing too strong a conclusion from one piece of legislative history, and there are also difficulties in linking the Prime Minister's assurance of business as usual to Parliament's notional intent in not including a remedies clause. But even so, the Prime Minister's statement that the Bill of Rights would create no new remedies is the only clear statement on the matter in *Hansard*. Certainly, it suggests that the BORA's lack of a remedies clause was a deliberate omission on the part of Parliament rather than an inadvertent leaving of a gap for the courts to fill.

Like the Court of Appeal,[95] the majority of the Supreme Court in *Taylor* was content to rely on the foundation laid by *Baigent*. Accordingly, the BORA's lack of a remedies clause did not prove to be an obstacle to finding that the BORA included an implied power to make DOIs. Ellen France J rejected the argument that a power to make DOIs did not 'fit with the language and legislative history of the [BORA]'.[96] She cited Cooke P's statement in *Baigent* that the absence of a remedies clause in the Bill of Rights was 'probably not of much consequence'.[97] Indeed Ellen France J went so far as to state that rights are of such importance that remedies for their breach should be provided for by the courts 'unless granting such a remedy [would be] inconsistent with the statutory language'.[98]

On the Smillie view, relying on the foundation of *Baigent's case* is likely construction malpractice, since the legislative history suggests that the BORA's silence on the question of remedies is a reflection of the fact that

93 "Clayton's … (used of a poor imitation of the 'real' thing) existing in name only; not genuine, worthless: a Clayton's recovery, policy, excuse, etc.": see Tony Deverson and Graeme D Kennedy *The New Zealand Oxford Dictionary* (Oxford University Press, Oxford, 2005).

94 (14 August 1990) 510 NZPD 3450.

95 *Taylor* (CA), above n 7, at [148] (stating 'as this Court has previously remarked [in *Baigent's case*], remedies should be allowed to evolve as necessary').

96 *Taylor* (SC), above n 7, at [38]. Elias CJ expressed her agreement at [104].

97 At [39] (citing *Simpson v Attorney General* [1994] 1993 NZLR 1667, 1676). See also at [48]–[49].

98 At [41].

Parliament did not intend for the courts to have new remedial powers, whether they be DOIs or public law damages. Thus, for the courts to then create new remedies for breaches of the BORA is to resurrect what William Eskridge refers to as a rejected proposal,[99] and to undermine the intent of the legislators who enacted the BORA.

However, even if we were to accept that the legislators who enacted the BORA in 1990 did not intend for it to confer any new remedial powers on the courts, the argument that it is therefore illegitimate for the courts to then subsequently create new remedies for breaches of the BORA is incomplete. First, it could be that there are indications that subsequent legislators took a different view on the matter by ratifying or perhaps accepting a judicially created remedy.[100] Second, and quite apart from this, the argument assumes that the original intent of the legislators who enacted the BORA ought to constrain a court from developing remedies in the future. This follows, provided that one considers the correct approach to interpretation to be intentionalism. For the intentionalist, the goal of statutory interpretation is 'the retrieval of legislative intent – the resolution and desire behind the statutory text'.[101] So, when it comes to provisions in a bill of rights or constitution, the intentionalist interprets them in keeping with what the framers or ratifiers intended (in this instance, that there would be no new remedies resulting from the enactment of the bill of rights).[102]

But intentionalism is hardly the only game in town. Other interpretive approaches, such as textualism or purposivism, cast the BORA's silence on the availability of remedies in a different light.[103] For example, Ellen France J's

99 William N Eskridge "Interpreting Legislative Inaction" (1988) 87 Mich L Rev 67 at 69 (referring to the rejected proposal rule, 'which posits that proposals rejected by Congress are an indication that the statute cannot be interpreted to resemble the rejected proposals'). See also at 84–86.

100 The New Zealand Bill of Rights (Declarations of Inconsistency) Amendment Bill 2020 (230-2), if enacted, would amount to an instance of ratification. The decision to accept the Law Commission's recommendation not to legislatively override *Baigent's case* could possibly be construed as an instance of acceptance: see Mark Tushnet, *Weak Courts, Strong Rights* (Princeton University Press, Princeton, 2008) at 48.

101 Arie Rosen "Statutory Interpretation and the Many Virtues of Legislation" (2017) 37 OJLS 134 at 139.

102 Neil H Buchanan and Michael C Dorf "A Tale of Two Formalisms: How Law and Economics Mirrors Originalism and Textualism" (2021) 106 Cornell L Rev 591 at 621.

103 On these various interpretative approaches, see Michael C Dorf "The Limits of Socratic Deliberation" (1998) 112 Harv L Rev 4 at 15–18; John F Manning "Textualism and Legislative Intent" (2005) 91(2) Va L Rev 419; Buchanan and Dorf, above n 102, at 621–622.

approach in *Taylor* is probably best characterised as purposivist. She does not completely ignore legislative history, as a textualist would.[104] There are also several mentions of the BORA's purposes, such as protecting the rights and freedoms contained within the BORA and affirming New Zealand's commitment to the International Covenant on Civil and Political Rights, which includes the obligation under Article 2(3)(a) to provide those whose rights are breached an effective remedy.[105]

All of this is to say that the courts developing the DOI as a remedy is not necessarily illegitimate, even if it was not intended by Parliament in 1990. But if one adopts an intentionalist viewpoint (and the majority of the Supreme Court does not), then I think the best view is that Parliament's omission of a remedies clause reflected its intention that courts were not free to innovate with the development of new remedies. This, in turn, suggests that the development of the DOI remedy in *Taylor* is an act of judicial creativity, especially given that DOIs do represent an extension from the previous case law, and entail the courts formally questioning the legitimacy of Parliament's legislation.

3.3. ACCEPTABLE OR UNACCEPTABLE JUDICIAL CREATIVITY?

If we assume for the sake of argument that the establishment of the DOI jurisdiction in *Taylor* amounts to judicial creativity, then the next question becomes whether this development is a good thing or not. As noted earlier, Bruce's chapter offers three principles for helping us come to a conclusion about this. These are: (1) whether the judicial creativity is a genuine attempt to improve the state of the law as opposed to being an instance of judicial opportunism; (2) whether the courts or Parliament are the best placed to effect the change; and (3) whether Parliament intended for the courts to have the freedom to be creative in that particular domain.[106]

In relation to the first principle, one can confidently say that the establishment of the DOI jurisdiction is a good faith attempt to improve the effectiveness of BORA. As I have argued elsewhere, the BORA's impact on the legislative process is, at best, limited and sporadic.[107] There is no

104 See generally Dorf, above n 103, at 18; Manning, above n 103, at 420.
105 *Taylor* (SC), above n 7, at [41] and [50].
106 Harris, above n 6, at 301–302.
107 John Ip "*Attorney-General v Taylor*: A Constitutional Milestone?" [2020] NZ L Rev 35 at 43–48.

clearer illustration of this than the enactment of the 2010 Act itself. As noted earlier, the Attorney-General had issued a scathing s 7 report about the bill that became the 2010 Act. But both the report and the issues it raised about compliance with the BORA were essentially ignored during the legislative process. It is to be hoped that the establishment of the DOI jurisdiction will provide a more effective means of drawing to Parliament's attention the need to reconsider certain rights-infringing legislation, as well as greater incentive for legislators to actually engage with s 7 reports in a meaningful way.[108] My admittedly Pollyannaish hope would be that DOIs, in concert with other reforms such as the establishment of a specialist human rights committee, might lead to a more effective BORA and a Parliament more solicitous of human rights concerns.[109]

The second principle might be framed simply in terms of relative institutional competence. In abstract terms, the advantage is always with Parliament when it comes to legal reform. Legislatures invariably have a superior democratic mandate as compared to courts, and their processes enable broader input and participation. This would suggest that the courts should always exercise restraint and leave legal reform to Parliament. However, Bruce's chapter also recognises that this can mean delayed or 'perhaps even no development, if innovation is left to the legislature'.[110] Parliament has rarely ever been minded to amend the BORA. On the two occasions it has done so, it has been to tinker with the scope of certain rights such as the threshold for the right to elect trial by jury or the prohibited grounds of discrimination. And it is not as if the idea of DOIs has never been raised. Academic literature on the possibility of DOIs is almost as old as the BORA.[111] Moreover, one of the recommendations of the 2013 Constitutional Advisory Panel Report was that the government set up a process to explore how the BORA could be made more effective, including by 'giving the Judiciary powers to assess legislation for consistency with the [BORA]'.[112] Nothing concrete resulted, and in the meantime, various comparator jurisdictions have enacted weak-form, statutory bills of rights that include express provision for DOIs. Therefore, if the courts had not acted in the way they did in the *Taylor* litigation, I think it is doubtful

---

108 At 58.

109 At 67–68. The 2010 Act subject to the DOI in *Taylor* was eventually repealed by the Electoral (Registration of Sentenced Prisoners) Amendment Act 2020.

110 Harris, above n 6, at 302.

111 Ip, above n 107, at 39.

112 Constitutional Advisory Panel *New Zealand's Constitution: A Report on a Conversation* (Ministry of Justice, November 2013) at 17. See generally Hickman, above n 82.

whether the political branches would have been minded to act at all. As it turned out, before the Supreme Court heard the appeal in *Taylor*, the government announced its intention to amend the BORA to provide for a judicial power to issue DOIs,[113] although this amendment is yet to be enacted as of October 2021.[114]

The third principle requires consideration of whether Parliament intended for the courts to have freedom to innovate. On Bruce's account, the BORA is a domain where Parliament deliberately left it to the courts to fill in the gaps:[115]

> [I]n respect of the New Zealand Bill of Rights Act 1990, the legislature has deliberately left the courts to decide the relationship between sections 4, 5 and 6, the operational sections of the Act; to give content to the specified rights; and to develop remedies for breaches of those rights.

This statement is certainly true in respect of the content and definition of the rights in the BORA. It is of course simply infeasible for a legislature to do this comprehensively ex ante.[116] Thus the courts are left to give meaning to BORA rights in the context of the concrete disputes that come before them. As for remedies, Bruce observes that the courts have exhibited considerable judicial creativity here as well. They established the prima facie rule of exclusion for evidence obtained in breach of the BORA, and then replaced it with a discretionary balancing test some ten years later.[117] The Court of Appeal, as noted earlier, established a monetary remedy for breaches of the BORA in *Baigent's case*.[118] His third example, citing *Moonen*, is DOIs:[119]

> More significantly from the point of view of the relationship between the courts and the legislature, the Court of Appeal, notwithstanding the affirmation of

113 Andrew Little and David Parker "Government to provide greater protection of rights under the NZ Bill of Rights Act 1990" (26 February 2018), available at <www.beehive.govt.nz>.
114 See New Zealand Bill of Rights (Declarations of Inconsistency) Amendment Bill 2020 (230-2). At the time of writing the Bill is at second reading stage.
115 Harris, above n 6, at 304.
116 At 304.
117 *R v Butcher* [1992] 2 NZLR 257; *R v Shaheed* [2002] 2 NZLR 377. See generally Scott L Optican and Peter J Sankoff "The New Exclusionary Rule: A Preliminary Assessment of *R v Shaheed*" [2003] NZ L Rev 1.
118 *Simpson v Attorney General*, above n 91.
119 Harris, above n 6, at 305.

> Parliament's continuing law-making sovereignty in section 4, has held that it has jurisdiction to declare legislation to be inconsistent with the New Zealand Bill of Rights Act 1990. Such a declaration would not render the inconsistent legislation invalid, but it would give a clear encouragement to the legislature to reconsider the particular manifestation of its sovereign law-making powers which the court considers to be in conflict with the provisions of the Bill of Rights Act.

As discussed earlier, while the possibility of DOIs is considered in *Moonen*, it would not be until *Taylor* that the jurisdiction to issue DOIs was really established. But the more important point is that Bruce's chapter views this judicial creativity in the field of developing remedies for the BORA as an instance of the courts innovating in an area deliberately left to them by the legislature.[120] He takes the BORA's silence on the matter to be implied legislative approval for the courts to fill the gaps and fashion appropriate remedies on the theory that 'Parliament cannot have intended to create rights without remedies'.[121] Bruce's third principle is thus framed in intentionalist terms. And as will be clear from the earlier discussion regarding the BORA's lack of a remedies clause and the legislative history surrounding its enactment, I consider the conclusion that Parliament deliberately left it to the courts to develop remedies for breaches of BORA rights to be problematic from an intentionalist perspective.

In summary, the courts' establishment of the DOI jurisdiction satisfies two out of Bruce's three principles for identifying acceptable instances of judicial creativity. Moreover, the effect of this instance of judicial creativity is to augment the strength of the BORA, which, as Bruce observes, is one of the few available constitutional safeguards in a jurisdiction characterised by a 'unitary State with a unicameral legislature and a tradition of strong parliamentary sovereignty'.[122] And so, given what I have said above, and given that I am on record as saying the establishment of the DOI jurisdiction is a step in the right direction,[123] I regard the establishment of the DOI jurisdiction as an instance of acceptable, indeed justifiable, judicial creativity.

---

120 At 304.
121 At 304.
122 At 274.
123 See generally Ip, above n 107.

4. A TALE OF TWO *TAYLORS*

As noted earlier, the Court of Appeal's *Taylor* decision is primarily based upon the courts' inherent power to state the law and resolve inconsistencies between statutes, whereas the Supreme Court's *Taylor* decision relies upon the text and structure of the BORA. Their style and tone are also quite different. In the course of its decision the Court of Appeal ends up delving into constitutional history and first principles, and spelling out its vision of modern, collaborative constitutional governance. The Supreme Court, by contrast, seems content to resolve the dispute before it in a more low-key, minimalist manner, and accordingly eschews any grand theorising about the constitution.[124] In this final part of the contribution, I offer some tentative explanations for this difference between the *Taylor* decisions of the Court of Appeal and the Supreme Court, together with one clarifying qualification.

One of the clearest differences between the two decisions is their relative enthusiasm for dialogue.[125] The Court of Appeal's decision embraces the dialogue paradigm and the accompanying notions of the courts and Parliament being co-dependent branches of government acting in collaboration.[126] On this view, DOIs are a mechanism for facilitating dialogue between the courts and the legislature. In keeping with this, the Court of Appeal states that a DOI 'is made in the reasonable constitutional expectation that the other branches will respond to it by reappraising the limitation and its justification carries'.[127] Likewise, in relation to the 2010 Act, the Court reiterated a dialogic rationale for DOIs:[128]

> [T]he right to vote is a core prerogative of citizenship in a free and democratic society. The undiscriminating limitation imposed by the 2010 Act on so central a right demanded justification. None was forthcoming. The record shows that the legislature knew of the inconsistency at the time, and our attention was drawn to no developments in policy, or in other jurisdictions, that

---

124 See Sam Bookman "Decoding Declarations in *Taylor*: Constitutional Ambiguity and Reform" [2019] NZ L Rev 257 at 265–267; Sirota, above n 92, at 17; Timothy Shiels and Andrew Geddis "Tracking the Pendulum Swing on Legislative Entrenchment in New Zealand" (2019) 41 Statute L Rev 207 at 222; and Ip, above n 107, at 56.

125 For a good overview of dialogue theory, see Léonid Sirota "Constitutional Dialogue: The New Zealand Bill of Rights Act and the Noble Dream" (2017) 27 NZULR 897 at 904–905.

126 *Taylor* (CA), above n 7, at [149]–[153].

127 At [76].

128 At [185].

might lead it to reappraise the 2010 Act independently of this litigation. In these circumstances, it was not unreasonable to conclude that a DoI was the appropriate way both to convey the Court's firm opinion that the legislation needs reconsidering and to vindicate the right.

In contrast, the Supreme Court majority in *Taylor* downplay, or even disclaim, the dialogic rationale for DOIs expounded by the Court of Appeal, preferring instead a more prosaic and traditional rationale based on the vindication of rights. The Chief Justice stated that she preferred the view that a DOI was a response 'made to those whose rights are affected, rather than one to assist Parliament in its function, as the Court of Appeal suggested'.[129] Ellen France J's judgment put it more bluntly, explicitly declining to endorse the parts of the Court of Appeal's decision concerning dialogue,[130] and expressing agreement with the Chief Justice's view that a DOI is primarily concerned with vindicating a wronged person's rights.[131]

Although they really only rule out dialogue being the primary rationale for DOIs,[132] it is clear that the Supreme Court majority are less enamoured with the dialogue paradigm than the Court of Appeal. This then leads to the question of why the two courts have such differing views about the merits of the dialogic rationale for DOIs. It might simply reflect the substantive views about the BORA held by the judges on those respective courts. But it is also possible that the Supreme Court's aversion to dialogue and preference for understanding DOIs in terms of the vindication of rights reflects a strategic methodological parsimony. Let us assume that the end goal from the perspective of the judges is to have court-issued DOIs as an accepted and legitimate part of the New Zealand constitutional ecosystem. Charges of judicial activism would detract from that goal. The Court of Appeal decision, built upon its main common law foundation, requires the acceptance of more obviously contestable propositions – for example, the relationship between the courts and Parliament being co-dependent and collaborative, as well as the notion of dialogue, about which there is considerable disagreement[133] and a highly

129 *Taylor* (SC), above n 7, at [107].
130 At [66].
131 At [66], n 87.
132 Indeed Ellen France J stated that a DOI 'may also be of assistance to Parliament if the subject arises in that forum': *Taylor* (SC), above n 7, at [55] (citing *Moonen v Film and Literature Board of Review* [2000] 2 NZLR 9 at [20]).
133 Sirota, above n 125, at 905–906.

critical literature.[134] By contrast, the Supreme Court's decision, which rested upon judicial implication from the text and structure of the BORA, and relied on the venerable and longstanding notion of vindicating rights as the rationale for DOIs, provided a relatively simpler way of reaching the same goal, and one that was less vulnerable to accusations of judicial activism.

There is one additional aspect to what I have called the Supreme Court's strategic methodological parsimony. And that is that by the time the Supreme Court heard the appeal in March 2018, the government had already announced its plans to amend the BORA to provide for a judicial power to issue DOIs. Of course, one can only speculate about the impact that this might have had on how the Supreme Court judges approached the case. It is plausible, though, to suppose that the prospect of an impending legislative amendment might have reduced the incentive for any grand constitutional theorising.[135]

At this point, I should clarify that my characterising of the Court of Appeal decision as expansive and grand, and the Supreme Court decision as low-key and minimalist, pertains primarily to the respective courts' rationale for DOIs. But as Sam Bookman reminds us, we should not lose sight of the fact that the Supreme Court's *Taylor* decision, despite its unassuming appearance, lays down some important markers of its own.[136]

The first concerns the nature of the DOI itself. Compared to its excursion into constitutional fundamentals, the Court of Appeal's account of the nature of DOIs was modest. According to the Court of Appeal, a DOI is not a declaration of right,[137] but rather a purely instrumental device, whose value depends on it being able to achieve sufficient political purchase to spur the legislature into some kind of response in keeping with the dialogue paradigm. The Supreme Court majority took a different view. Ellen France J stated that:[138]

> a declaration that s 80(1)(d) is inconsistent with the Bill of Rights is a formal declaration of the law and, in particular, of the effect of the 2010 Amendment on the respondents' rights and status. It provides formal confirmation they are persons who are disqualified to vote by a provision inconsistent with their rights.

---

134 See for example Eoin Carolan "Dialogue isn't Working: the Case for Collaboration as a Model of Legislative-Judicial Relations" (2016) 36 LS 209; Aileen Kavanagh "The Lure and the Limits of Dialogue" (2016) 66 UTLJ 83.

135 Although, as noted earlier, the amendment to the BORA is still yet to be enacted.

136 Bookman, above n 124, at 267–271.

137 *Taylor* (CA), above n 7, at [66].

138 *Taylor* (SC), above n 7, at [53].

Elias CJ put things even more unequivocally:[139]

> It seems to me that the scheme of the New Zealand Bill of Rights Act makes it clear that inconsistency with rights is indeed itself a question of right for which declaratory relief may be sought. I am not able to agree with the view of the Court of Appeal … that a declaration of inconsistency "is not a declaration of right".

Second, there is the Supreme Court majority's rejection of the Crown's argument that the 2010 Act was not inconsistent with s 12 of the BORA because it impliedly altered the content of the right to the extent of the inconsistency.[140] The majority's view was that inconsistent legislation prevails (as s 4 of the BORA states that it must), but Parliament does not get to have its cake and eat it too by claiming that legislation does not breach the BORA.[141] As Ellen France J put it, 'the Bill of Rights remains as the standard or palimpsest albeit Parliament has exercised its power to legislate inconsistently with that standard'.[142] Similarly, Elias CJ stated that the BORA 'requires legislation to be given effect when it is inconsistent with the rights contained in the Act but withholds the legitimacy of compliance with those fundamental rights',[143] and further suggested that modifying the content of rights in the BORA would require legislative amendment.[144] These passages are both an important clarification of the relationship between the BORA and legislation that infringes upon it, and a robust assertion of the judicial role in determining when the BORA has been breached.[145]

5. CONCLUSION

Professor Bruce Harris has been a mainstay of public law at the University of Auckland for more than two decades (and before that at the University of Otago). He taught generations of law students, myself included. His

139 At [105].
140 See also Philip A Joseph "Declarations of Inconsistency under the New Zealand Bill of Rights Act 1990" (2019) 30 PLR 7 at 10.
141 *Taylor* (SC), above n 7, at [45]–[46], [102].
142 At [46].
143 At [102].
144 At [103].
145 See also Bookman, above n 124, at 271; Joseph, above n 140, at 10.

interests in public law ranged far and wide, making him an ideal choice to write a chapter about judicial activism in New Zealand's appellate courts.

In my contribution to this collection, I have sought to discuss Bruce's notion of judicial creativity, to apply his evaluative principles to the Court of Appeal and Supreme Court decisions in *Taylor*, and to offer some explanations for the observed contrast between the expansive and grand Court of Appeal decision and the relatively low-key and minimalist Supreme Court decision.

As for the overall question of how we should understand the Court of Appeal and Supreme Court's decisions in *Taylor* in terms of judicial creativity, I would like to think that Bruce would agree with my conclusion that their establishment of the judicial jurisdiction to issue DOIs is an instance of acceptable, indeed justifiable, judicial creativity.

JUDICIAL INNOVATION AND THE FAMILY

Taylor BURGESS*

* With my thanks to Professor Harris and to the *Festschrift* Editors.

1. INTRODUCTION

Professor Harris has urged honesty in how we talk about judicial law-making. Judges do make law and, sometimes, they should. The important questions are when and how.

In some cases, Professor Harris suggests courts will need to depart from precedent to update rules in statute or case law for a changing society. He calls this 'judicial innovation'.[1] Broadly, the judicial innovation can be broken down into two types: (1) innovation to bring the law into step with shared social values; and (2) innovation to advance the rights of a minority, notwithstanding that it may be against or in advance of the public will.

In recent cases on the meaning of the family, New Zealand courts have embraced the first kind innovation but refused to engage with the second. The refusal is centred on an idea of 'social policy'. Social policy is rarely defined or expanded upon. It is a label for the kind of rules that go to who we are as a society. Something may be a 'social policy' question because it brings up questions of shared traditions, morals or values. It is likely something on which people disagree; it may have implications for other rules and institutions.

The courts' use of social policy is unprincipled. For one, it is selective. In *Quilter v Attorney-General* and *Re AMM*, the Court of Appeal and High Court declined to engage with interpretations of 'marriage' for the issue of marriage licence under Marriage Act, or 'spouse' for the joint adoption of children, that could open eligibility to couples of the same sex.[2] Those innovations were judged to involve 'broad social policy' questions and 'challenges to the traditional family unit' that Parliament must weigh.

Yet that same court in *Re AMM* comfortably adopted a narrower extension to 'spouses' eligible for adoption: unmarried (opposite-sex) couples. Following the passage of the legislative amendments for marriage equality in 2013, the Family Court in *Re Pierney* extended that further to unmarried same-sex couples.[3] Most recently, the High Court has recognised that 'spouse' may include separated and divorced couples – it

---

1 BV Harris "The Law-making Power of the Judiciary" in Philip A Joseph (ed) *Essays on the Constitution* (Brookers, Wellington, 1995) 265 at 266 ["Law-making Power"]; and Bruce Harris "Judicial Activism and New Zealand's Appellate Courts" in Brice Dickson (ed) *Judicial Activism in Common Law Supreme Courts* (Oxford University Press, Oxford, 2007) 273 ["Judicial Activism"] at 322.

2 *Quilter v Attorney-General* [1998] 1 NZLR 523 (CA); *Re AMM & KJO* [2010] NZFLR 629 (HC).

3 *Re Pierney* [2015] NZFC 9404, [2016] NZFLR 53.

may even extend to couples who have not had a romantic relationship. These latter cases show a remarkable judge-led innovation of a 65-year-old statutory term once understood to be limited to partners in a heterosexual marriage.[4] These changes are not called social policy changes because they went with, not against, the perceived social mood.

Where raised, social policy closes consideration of judicial creativity. It is taken for granted that a social policy challenge is one to be weighed and directed by Parliament. This is an oversimplification of the law-making capabilities of Parliament and the courts. Often rules founded on policy will indeed be better formulated by Parliament. Parliament is the primary law-making body, with a direct democratic mandate of the electorate and refined law-making processes that facilitate research and community input. But as Professor Harris has so clearly catalogued, other issues can better manifest in development by the courts. Social policy should be reason to pause, not a prohibition. This is particularly important where the creativity is an available rights-consistent interpretation under the New Zealand Bill of Rights Act 1990, and where the fear of social policy is bound up in a sense that the change would be unpopular with a majority within the community.

This contribution is in five parts. First, I set out Professor Harris's arguments as to why, when and how judges might engage in creativity. Second, I summarise the key challenges to who counts as a family in New Zealand in *Quilter v Attorney-General*, *Re AMM*, *Re Pierney* and *Re Gordon & Archer*. Third, I draw out the social policy idea that marks off a different (and unacceptable) kind of judicial creativity in these challenges. Fourth, I use Professor Harris's framework to suggest a more principled approach for the courts to distinguish between leadership on individual rights creativity and deference to change sanctioned by a democratically elected Parliament in consultation with the community at large. Finally, I return to Professor Harris's proposals on how to strengthen the judiciary's practical law-making tools and encourage accountability to the community.

2. JUDICIAL CREATIVITY

In his works, including a 1995 essay "Law-Making Power" and 2007 chapter "Judicial Activism and New Zealand's Appellate Courts", Professor Harris

4 *Re Gordon & Archer* [2019] NZHC 184, [2020] 2 NZLR 436.

has built a compelling picture of how judicial creativity is both contemplated and necessary for the optimum functioning of New Zealand's system of government.[5]

Writing in 1995 Professor Harris spotlighted the reality of judge-made law.[6] New Zealand's judges do not always simply 'apply' law that has been either determined by a democratically elected legislature, or the executive.[7] Rather, judges will often be required to go further to 'make' law, for example:[8]

> The law constraining government, or protecting individual rights, may be derived from the common law, which is Judge-made and continually evolving. The precedents may be difficult to reconcile, or the particular case for decision may be novel and require the common law to be developed. Another possibility is that the common law available to regulate a situation may be out of rhythm with contemporary societal changes and require changing.
>
> Alternatively, the law … may have its origins with Parliament. The statute purporting to regulate the particular fact situation may uncomfortably fit that situation and require interpreting, perhaps imaginative stretching, in search for implied meaning. Sometimes the mood of society calls for judicial innovation in respect of statutes, ahead of action by Parliament.

Within this precis Harris brings together a spectrum of law-making occasions: from the routine, everyday interpretation of a statute or reconciliation of a precedent, to a more creative development and imaginative stretching of the law, to the bolder 'judicial innovation'.

The idea of judicial innovation is a significant part of Professor Harris's theory of functional creativity. Judicial innovation sees the courts acting as a driver of change – identifying a new direction in the law and taking the first step towards it, be it through adopting the novel interpretation or openly calling for change from the legislature.[9] The courts are acting in advance of Parliamentary will to progress issues that have been overlooked or even avoided by other branches of government.[10]

The courts may also be acting ahead of community will. As suggested at the beginning of this contribution, Harris contemplates that the courts may

5 Harris "Law-making Power", above n 1; Harris "Judicial Activism", above n 1, at 274.
6 Harris "Law-making Power", above n 1, at 266.
7 At 266.
8 At 266 (footnote omitted).
9 Harris "Judicial Activism", above n 1, at 322.
10 At 276.

innovate in time with societal norms (the example of statute or common law out of rhythm with a contemporary society) or *ahead* of social norms where necessary to protect the rights or interests of a vulnerable minority within the community.[11]

Having openly acknowledged that the courts make law, the question becomes when the courts should exercise these powers. When is it appropriate for judges to make law? When should Parliament leave an area of law indeterminate? And when should the courts take up any invitation to resolve the indeterminacy through law-making?[12]

Professor Harris approaches these questions through the rather pragmatic lens of what works best for New Zealand's system of government. From a constitutional perspective the appropriate division of law-making is critical to the legitimacy of the system. The legitimacy of the judicial branch hinges on public confidence in how the courts carry out their proper role within the system of government.[13] Accordingly, the starting point is that the law should preferably be made by elected lawmakers under the premise that Parliament is the community's primary law-making body and the most democratically accountable.[14]

The quality of the rules produced in a given area of law will often depend on who makes the law, and how the law is made. Parliament offers certain advantages for the mechanics of law-making. The parliamentary process facilitates better-researched legislative proposals. The space for lobbying of Ministers and public input through select committee hearings allows for more participatory law-making than the courts.[15] Harris suggests that rules 'founded on substantial issues of policy' will normally be best formulated with the assistance of such thorough research and participation, and accordingly should be made by an accountable Parliament.

Yet the courts bring their own strengths. Some areas may require such detail and balancing that the courts are best placed to lead incremental development as facts arise.[16] The content of the rights and freedoms affirmed in the New Zealand Bill of Rights Act is a prime example.[17] Crucially,

11 At 276 and 302.
12 Harris "Law-making Power", above n 1, at 271.
13 At 277.
14 At 271.
15 At 272.
16 At 271.
17 At 273 Professor Harris provides the example of freedom of expression.

Professor Harris argues that the governance structure of New Zealand can in fact require creativity from the courts for optimum functioning.[18] By way of example, Professor Harris suggests it is arguable that the courts' work to give content to the statutory expression 'the principles of the Treaty of Waitangi' is appropriate 'because the community is not ready for Parliament to perform this task'.[19] This kind of innovative rule-making can be an important exercise of the court's constitutional role to champion the minority interests or individual rights that may be vulnerable to the will of a democratic majority.[20]

3. INNOVATION IN THE FAMILY

This contribution takes a close look at how the New Zealand courts have taken up, and resisted, opportunities for creativity in defining the family. This part will introduce the key opportunities: (1) the call to expand who may marry a partner of their choice in *Quilter v Attorney-General*; and (2) the successive calls to open up who is considered a 'spouse' eligible to adopt children jointly across *Re AMM & KJO*, *Re Pierney* and *Re Gordon & Archer*.

These challenges test the courts' appetite for innovation. On the one hand, they bring together the prime functions of creativity identified in Professor Harris's work:

- *Updating a statute out of rhythm with contemporary society.* The Marriage and Adoption Acts were passed in 1955; a time when sexual activity between men was illegal and children born out of marriage were branded 'illegitimate'.[21] Some 40 to 60 years later, the claimants in the family recognition proceedings are calling on the courts' powers to develop the statutory anachronisms to fit a modern era where rights of LGBT community are protected,[22] increasing numbers of couples choose to live in 'de facto' relationships outside marriage,[23] and advances

18 Harris "Judicial Activism", above n 1, at 273.

19 At 272.

20 At 276.

21 See Homosexual Law Reform Act 1986; Law Commission *Adoption and Its Alternatives: A Different Approach and a New Framework* (NZLC R65, 2000) at xv.

22 Human Rights Act 1993, s 21(1)(m).

23 See, for example, New Zealand Official Yearbook 1998, available at <https://www3.stats.govt.nz/New_Zealand_Official_Yearbooks/1998/NZOYB_1998.html?_ga=2.134302129.114983764.1594991977-1571892597.1594991977#idsect1_1_36532>.

in assisted reproductive technology (ART) and surrogacy have opened up the opportunities for same-sex couples to form biological and social parenting relationships together.

- *Advancing minority rights in the face of majority apathy.* By anchoring the calls for novel interpretation in the right to freedom from discrimination, the claimants engage the court's responsibility to advance minority rights on issues that might otherwise be overlooked or deliberately avoided by a democratically elected Parliament.[24]

On the other hand, these cases are founded on so-called 'policy' issues of how the state chooses to regulate the core social institutions of marriage and adoption. The concepts of marriage and adoption are tied up in a complex mix of community values, tradition, views of morality and prejudices. The recognised status of a married spouse or parent also has significant consequences for one's benefits, rights and responsibilities in other areas of law. The resolution of deep disagreements over such issues might arguably be better left to the political branches, who can claim greater democratic legitimacy. To ask the courts to move these boundaries is to challenge judges to wade into policy-rich questions about the future of the family in New Zealand.

3.1. MARRIAGE

Quilter v Attorney-General is an example of judicial restraint.[25] In 1998, the Court of Appeal famously declined to give any other meaning to 'marriage' to allow the appellants to marry a partner of their choice. The judges deferred to Parliament and the landmark shift to embrace same-sex marriage was ultimately achieved some 15 years later through the political process, with the passage of the Marriage (Definition of Marriage) Amendment Act 2013.

The *Quilter* appellants were three lesbian couples. The Registrar of Marriages had refused to accept their notices of intended marriage under s 23 of the Marriage Act 1955 on the basis that the Marriage Act did not provide for marriage between persons of the same sex.[26] They accepted that

24 Harris "Law-making Power", above n 1, at 276.

25 *Quilter v Attorney-General*, above n 2.

26 At 526. It was understood the Registrar would similarly refuse to issue them marriage licences necessary for a valid marriage under s 24 of the Act.

when the Act was passed marriage was understood, as put by Tipping J, 'in the traditional common law sense of the union of one man and one woman'.[27] But the appellants argued that the enactment of the Bill of Rights required a modern approach to the interpretation of the word 'marriage'. Refusal of the notices constituted discrimination against same-sex couples in breach of s 19, the Act could be interpreted to include marriage between persons of the same sex, and the court was obliged to prefer this rights-consistent meaning.[28]

The sticking point for all five judges was that no other meaning of 'marriage' was possible.[29] Tipping J's judgment drew out interpretative aids to demonstrate how marriage continued to be seen in the traditional way.[30] In 1998, at the time of the appeal, there was no indication that Parliament's 'view of marriage' had changed since the 1955 Act had been passed – when speaking again in a 1995 amendment the Legislature had continued to use the gender-specific husband and wife terms.[31] In these circumstances the court considered that the New Zealand Bill of Rights Act could not be used as a 'concealed legislative tool' to rewrite the statute and thus usurp Parliament's legislative supremacy.[32] The court concluded that any change to the institution of marriage had to come from Parliament.[33]

The court split on the deeper question of whether the Act's restriction of marriage to heterosexual couples was inconsistent with the right to freedom from discrimination under s 19 of the New Zealand Bill of Rights Act. Only Thomas J accepted that the Act's use of the traditional meaning of 'marriage' discriminated on the grounds of sexual orientation.[34] The rest of the bench instead equivocated over whether the denial of the notices amounted to a breach of the New Zealand Bill of Rights Act. For Gault J, the denial of the notices did not amount to different treatment because the Registrar would have refused if the appellants had been male or if they

27 At 571.

28 At 571.

29 At 526 per Richardson P, at 526 per Gault J, at 555 per Keith J, at 581 per Tipping J and at 528 per Thomas J.

30 For example, the s 31(1) 'I take you' declaration was premised on one wife and one husband and the s 15 prohibited degrees of relationship listed a male's female relations and a woman's male relations. The reasons of Tipping J are adopted at 542 per Thomas J, at 526 per Richardson P, at 526 per Gault J and at 555 per Keith J.

31 At 580.

32 At 572 and at 542 per Thomas J.

33 At 526 per Richardson P, at 526 per Gault J, at 556–557 per Keith J, at 572 per Tipping J and at 528 per Thomas J.

34 At 528.

had been heterosexual and seeking a marriage to take advantage of civil benefits.[35] For Keith J the protection afforded by s 19 of the New Zealand Bill of Rights Act did not even reach same-sex marriages because, in his view, Parliament would not have intended such a change to the institution of marriage in the indirect manner of enacting a Bill of Rights.[36]

Within this discussion the court repeatedly voiced reservations about interfering with an institution so fundamental to society as marriage.[37] Tipping J underlined the open 'socio-legal policy' question of whether New Zealand's multicultural, secular society would wish to maintain a traditional understanding of marriage.[38] All expressed Parliament's constitutional and practical advantages in weighing such complex policy considerations to decide whether and how to change the law.[39] Thomas J took care to acknowledge the important 'democracy factors' relating to general acceptance of any extension to same-sex couples, the possible ramifications or repercussions for legislation and the timing of change.[40]

Ultimately Parliament took up the claimants' calls for innovation. In 2004, Parliament established the separate institution of a civil union, open to couples of the same or different sex.[41] This was partnered with legislation extending the rights and responsibilities of marriage to both de facto and civil union relationships.[42] The fifth Labour government emphasised that marriage would remain an institution solely available to couples of a man and a woman and its associated 'social, religious and traditional values' would continue:[43] as the Court of Appeal identified in 1998, Parliament intended to continue to limit the institution of marriage to heterosexual couples.

35 At 527.

36 At 555.

37 See at 572 per Tipping J, and at 555 per Keith J.

38 See at 572 per Tipping J, and at 542 per Thomas J.

39 At 542 per Thomas J and at 572 per Tipping J's 'socio-legal policy' description.

40 At 542.

41 Civil Union Act 2004. Under a heading 'The need for the Bill' the Bills Digest explains 'There have been several challenges to the Marriage Act 1955 aimed at establishing the right of same sex couples to have their relationships legally recognised. In *Quilter v Attorney-General* [1998] 1 NZLR 523 the Court of Appeal held that the Marriage Act 1955 applies to marriage between a man and a woman only and that this does not constitute discrimination': Civil Union Bill 2004, NZ Parliamentary Library, Bills Digest No 1111.

42 Relationships (Statutory References) Act 2005.

43 See First Reading speech of Hon David Benson-Pope, Associate Minister of Justice: (24 June 2004) 618 NZPD 13927.

Advocates of change criticised the 'different but equal' compromise and continued to argue for amendment to allow same-sex couples to marry.[44] The Campaign for Equality culminated in a 2012 private member's Bill proposing amendments to the Marriage Act to clarify that marriage 'means the union of 2 people, regardless of their sex, sexual orientation or gender identity'.[45] The Bill received considerable public attention and ultimately was passed 77–44 in early 2013 – some 15 years after the *Quilter* argument.[46]

3.2. ADOPTION

The question of who can adopt a child is a story of cautious, incremental judicial creativity. The Family Court and High Court have pursued increasingly creative interpretations of 'spouses' in s 3(2) of the Adoption Act, to open up joint adoption to de facto opposite-sex couples, de facto same-sex couples, divorced and separated former partners. Section 3(2) provides that the court may make an adoption order 'on the application of *2 spouses jointly* in respect of a child'.[47] In four short judgments the courts have transformed the key term 'spouses' from its original 'married couple' meaning to an inclusive two people in an ongoing relationship.

The first decision is *Re AMM and KJO*.[48] Appellants AM and KO had been in a settled heterosexual relationship for nearly ten years. They sought to jointly adopt the child, S, who had been conceived by AM with donor sperm. They had parented S together since he was 18 months old and wished to formally recognise KO's role as his father.

In *Re AMM and KJO*, the Attorney-General accepted that the Adoption Act discriminated against de facto couples. The question for the court was whether the court could 'do something about it'.[49] That is, whether the courts could give the term a rights-consistent meaning under the s 6 process.[50] The Full Bench of Wild and Simon France JJ found they could.

---

44 See for example Civil Union Bill 2004 (149-2) (select committee report) at 11; Miriam Bookman "Marriage (Definition of Marriage) Amendment Act 2013" (2015) 21 AULR 269 at 269–270.

45 Marriage (Definition of Marriage) Amendment Bill 2012 (39-1), cl 5.

46 Marriage (Definition of Marriage) Amendment Act 2013.

47 Marriage (Definition of Marriage) Amendment Act 2013, s 3(2) (emphasis added).

48 *Re AMM & KJO*, above n 2.

49 At [10].

50 At [10]. Interestingly, the extension had been made some 18 years earlier by a Family Court judge. In *Re Adoption of T*, Boshier J held that marriage was not a prerequisite

They reasoned that the original purpose of limiting joint adoption orders to married couples must have been to ensure that applicants 'were a man and a woman, and that they were in a committed relationship'.[51] It was not inconsistent to extend 'spouse' to a de facto relationship, provided the de facto couple was required to present other evidence of commitment and stability: the ten-year relationship and co-parenting of S sufficed.

The judges emphasised that *AMM*'s extension did not include same-sex de facto relationships. Counsel had proposed two variants on a case-stated question, one which would cover 'couples living in a relationship in the nature of marriage', and the other 'a man and a woman' unmarried but in a 'stable and committed relationship'.[52] The judges accepted that the extension to opposite-sex couples might 'open the door' for people in same-sex de facto relationships to apply, and that the present decision had broken a barrier.[53] However, that was a question for another day. In obiter, the court went further to caution that there would be formidable barriers for any application by a civil union or de facto same-sex couple as this extension would depart from the concept of a 'traditional family unit'.[54]

'Another day' came five years later. In *Re Pierney*, a couple in a same-sex de facto relationship applied to the Family Court to adopt two children.[55] Both had been conceived following artificial insemination using one applicant's sperm. The applicants had raised the children through birth, were their intended parents at the point of conception, and had always planned to apply to adopt. As the judge put it, the application was essentially to legally regulate 'a family situation which is already existent'.[56]

to the definition of 'spouse' and the court was entitled to look at the actual relationship in question to 'see whether it is of such an enduring and stable nature to warrant the title': *Re Adoption of T* (1992) 10 FRNZ 23 (FC) at 23. This wider interpretation was applied in one later recorded decision before being confined to its facts with the alarmed observation that such an extension was a policy change that would require action from Parliament: see *Re T W [adoption]* (1998) 17 FRNZ 349 (FC); and *Re R [adoption]* (1998) 17 FRNZ 498 (FC) at 512–513.

51 At [35].

52 At [6]–[7].

53 At [11] and [38].

54 At [39].

55 *Re Pierney*, above n 3.

56 At [4].

The Family Court judge reportedly accepted the applicants' argument that 'necessary societal changes' had occurred to allow 'spouse' to be extended one step further to de facto same-sex couples.[57] The applicants pointed to Parliament's recent passage of the Marriage (Definition of Marriage) Amendment Bill and the provisions within to make clear same-sex married couples could adopt going forward.[58] They also cited shifts in the field of ART – the Minister of Health had authorised the Advisory Committee to amend guidance to allow consideration of same-sex male couple applications for fertility services, and Parliament had taken steps to allow female same-sex couples to jointly register the birth of a child born via ART.[59] The judge adopted the rights-consistent wider meaning and granted the application at hand.

The next extension of 'spouses' considered the realities of parenting after separation. In the third of these decisions, *Re May*, the Family Court had accepted 'spouse' could include a separated couple who were still married but no longer living together.[60] In the fourth, and final, of these joint adoption decisions, *Re Gordon & Archer*, the High Court found that the term 'spouse' could equally include divorced partners who had remarried but remained committed to caring for their long-term foster child.[61] The judge in *Re Gordon & Archer*, Courtney J, found that a narrower meaning would discriminate on the grounds of marital status. This could not be justified when viewed against current social norms leading to the greater incidence and acceptance of the dissolution of marriage and the acceptance of differently constituted family units.[62]

Courtney J's innovation was significant in that it did away with the idea of the romantic or intimate 'couple' altogether. 'Spouse' was said to reflect an idea that it would not be safe to entrust a child's status and wellbeing to two people unless they are capable of acting jointly, of sharing responsibility and risk and acting in concert.[63] Historically we may have assumed such joint action is the domain of a married heterosexual couple. Today, we recognise that people in a range of relationships are capable of

57 At [15] and Stewart Dalley "Adoption Law Change for Same-sex De Facto Couples" (2016) 882 Law Talk 32, at 33.
58 Dalley, above n 57, at 32.
59 At 33.
60 *Re May* [2016] NZFLC 3575.
61 *Re Gordon & Archer*, above n 4, at [1].
62 At [26]–[27].
63 At [34].

providing an effective family unit.[64] Accordingly, Courtney J was satisfied that the term 'spouses' could connote 'two people who have an ongoing relationship' – not necessarily a romantic relationship, but simply one in which they are jointly committed to the role of parenting.[65]

4. QUEST FOR CONSENSUS

Across the family recognition cases the courts are wary of leading change. Courts are ready to continue change in a direction dictated by the community or by Parliament but lack the bravery to consider where else change may be needed.[66] The discomfort is reduced to a 'social policy' shorthand that hives off innovation as a matter for Parliament.

4.1. A SOCIAL POLICY SHORTHAND

Where the courts do choose to exercise creativity they follow social change. In *AMM* and *Re Gordon & Archer*, the path for recognition of opposite-sex de facto couples, and couples following separation, was smoothed by the fact that non-married couples' commitment to parenting was generally accepted within the community. Neither case gave rise to any concern about changing social understandings of a 'traditional family unit' – social norms had already evolved to embrace these family units.

Similarly, in *Re Pierney* the belated recognition of de facto same-sex couples was made simple (to the point where the Family Court leads the innovation) by the fact that it follows 'societal changes' around marriage equality and Parliament-led change to support same-sex couple adoption in the case of marriage.

Conversely, judges are slow to take up opportunities for creativity that lead change. In *Quilter*, a key part of the judges' discomfort with any wider interpretation of 'marriage' was the lack of Parliament support for change and the unclear community sentiment. Tipping J's review of other

---

64 At [34].

65 At [35].

66 See Harris "Judicial Activism", above n 1, at 298 on Dame Sian Elias's statement that the legal system requires independent judges who 'observe the discipline of the common law method, have the imagination to see when change is necessary, and the capacity to explain why in judgements that convince'.

legislation as interpretive aids produced no indication that Parliament's 'view of marriage' had changed;[67] and it was unclear how the community would receive the extension to same-sex couples or whether they would wish to maintain a traditional understanding of the institution.[68] The judges in *AMM* were careful to note the 'different arguments' that would arise if the courts were to extend 'spouse' any further to include same-sex couples in a civil union or de facto relationship.

This discomfort with innovation is expressed through a 'policy' shorthand. As noted above, *Quilter* and the 'spouse' cases are all grounded in policy questions about the nature of social institutions of marriage and adoption. But the policy content is only articulated where the courts consider it inappropriate to act for the very purpose of explaining why it is inappropriate to act. In *Quilter*, the characterisation of 'socio-legal policy', 'social policy', 'policy considerations' marked out the future of marriage as a question for Parliament to weigh.[69] In *AMM*, the court distinguished its 'predicable and limited' extension for de facto opposite-sex couples from the 'broad social policy issues' that faced the *Quilter* court and the kind of 'departure from the traditional family unit' that might arise in any future challenge by de facto same-sex couples.[70]

Where the courts are comfortable innovating policy implications pass unremarked. In *Re Gordon & Archer* counsel for the Chief Executive warned that the expansion of 'spouses' to people who were not in a relationship with each other could 'fundamentally alter the nature of who may adopt a child' – opening the door to people who had never been in a relationship, or related parties adopting together (for example two aunts jointly adopting a niece).[71] This policy shift was not central to Courtney J's reasoning. The judge essentially embraced the slippery slope potential through the reasoning that the expansion of eligibility was in tandem with changing community norms.[72]

---

67 At 580 per Tipping J.

68 At 572 per Tipping J, and at 542 per Thomas J.

69 Somewhat inconsistently, the social policy idea can also be used to diminish the concerns of those calling for change – for example Richardson P and Gault J's statements in *Quilter* in that Marriage Act wording could not be ruled unjust purely based on 'social policy implications' and 'perspectives': *Quilter v Attorney-General*, above n 2, at 526 per Richardson P and 527 per Gault J.

70 *Re AMM*, above n 2, at [39]–[40].

71 *Re Gordon & Archer*, above n 4, at [32].

72 At [26], [33] and [36].

4.2. UNPACKING THE DISCRETE CONCERNS

The judgement that some questions are too steeped in policy for the courts to intervene is important. The policy shorthand can be a convenient way to convey the assessment that the issue at hand goes beyond the judge's practical or constitutional ability to make good law. But we should be wary of allowing the shorthand to slip into a broad-brush idea that any matter of policy is for the courts not Parliament. As Professor Harris has argued, while some questions may be better addressed by Parliament with its particular strengths in research and community input, other policy issues can and should be answered in law by the courts.[73] Policy content is not the end of the matter but the opening to assess whether the court is the best body in the system of government to lead the change in question.[74]

Behind the policy concerns, we can see the courts toying with discrete factors that Professor Harris has previously canvassed on the bounds of judicial law-making. These include:

- the judges' ability to gauge what people think and do (the 'incidence' of the new social norms said to justify a creative interpretation);[75]
- what people will think (the likely 'general acceptance' of a measure and pressure on a 'toleration band');[76]
- the need to defer to Parliament's relatively stronger democratic credentials for deciding the direction of change; and
- whether the court is able to effect the required change in 'good law' that accounts for multifaceted policy implications.[77]

Open exploration of these discrete factors is particularly important in the Bill of Rights space. What people think, what people will think, and government policy on change can be bound up with the very discriminatory attitudes that a challenge such as *Quilter* aims to disrupt.[78]

73 Harris "Law-making Power", above n 1, at 272.
74 Harris "Judicial Activism", above n 1, at 301.
75 See for example Courtney J's discussion of the 'incidence and acceptance' of marriage dissolution: *Re Gordon & Archer*, above n 4, at [26].
76 See *Quilter v Attorney-General*, above n 2, at 542 per Thomas J.
77 See for example *Re AMM*, above n 2, at [41].
78 The select committee report on the Civil Union Bill recorded that most opposition to the new institution expressed personal disapproval of 'homosexuality' from a Christian or moral perspective, reflected 'an abiding fear and loathing of homosexual activity', and leaned on inaccurate claims that children raised by same-sex couples would have negative outcomes: Civil Union Bill 2004 (149-2) (select committee report) at 9–10 and 13.

I suggest we should be precise about how this kind of community sentiment is weighed in the court's decision to make law. Parliament's commitment to fundamental rights and freedoms under the New Zealand Bill of Rights Act may well require unpopular change to community institutions and it would be a failure of that Bill of Rights function to allow unpopularity to sidestep the inquiry altogether.

5. A PRINCIPLED APPROACH TO THE COURT'S INNOVATOR ROLE

This part returns to Professor Harris's work to try to unknot some of the uncertainties around appropriate law-making in the family recognition cases. I bring together principles that help make sense of the courts' struggle between bold innovation to champion individual rights, and careful deference to change sanctioned by a democratically elected Parliament in consultation with the community at large.

5.1. PUBLIC DIVISION CAN PROPERLY INFORM AVAILABLE CREATIVE INTERPRETATIONS

Public division can properly inform the courts' inquiry into available, creative interpretations and thus its decision to make law. The plaintiffs in *Quilter*, *Re AMM*, *Pierney* and *Re Gordon & Archer* asked the courts to innovate established ideas of the family unit. They challenged the courts to take on a new, creative, interpretation of an old concept – one which was fit for a new society. Such a challenge calls on the judges to inquire into what people think and what people do: is there a change in how we understand marriage, or how we conceive of committed parenting relationships, that can justify a wider interpretation of the term?

The courts are limited by the standard arsenal of interpretative tools and the scope of parties' arguments: expert evidence, publicly available reports such as census data or Law Commission reviews, or the judge's own understanding of ordinary meaning and the purpose of the enactment. Because these tools are limited, the call for innovation will be most successful where the social change is a clear new normal. In *Re Gordon & Archer*, for example, Courtney J was so confident of the changed social norms on incidence and acceptance of parenting after separation that she found grounds for the wider meaning in her own impressions of society's expectations.[79]

Where the public is divided on the change, the court's limited interpretative resources may be inadequate to find a new social understanding of the concept in question. This is the sticking point in *Quilter*. Putting aside the meaning of the non-discrimination commitment, the judges were not convinced that society had come to understand 'marriage' as including a commitment between two people of the same sex. In this situation Parliament's superior mechanisms for research and community input outlined by Professor Harris became particularly pertinent.[80] Wide, rigorous public consultation through Parliament's select committees and engagement with responsible ministers was valuable here to marshal the public's possibly divergent views on the new meaning of the institution.

Importantly, here the public division or public controversy has a narrow relevance in the court's assessment of what people do and think – not what people *would* think if the court adopted the change advanced. As argued below, the separate fears of testing the 'toleration band' for judicial change must come behind the court's responsibility under the New Zealand Bill of Rights Act.

5.2. COURTS' TOOLS TO MEASURE SOCIAL CHANGE INCLUDE EXPERTISE IN LEGAL CHANGE

Courts' tools to measure the basis for change include their clear expertise in legal change. In reflecting on where the courts are adequately equipped to determine the social basis for a new legal meaning, it is worth remembering that the relationship between the law and social policy is symbiotic. The law can reflect community values, attitudes and actions but it can also shape them. Professor Doug NeJaime, a family and constitutional law academic, has described how the US Supreme Court has itself participated in the dramatic changes to family life for same-sex couples.[81] Key decisions have responded to significant cultural shifts and contributed to further progress in the treatment of contemporary family arrangements.

---

79 See *Re Gordon & Archer*, above n 4, at [26], [34] and [35].

80 Harris "Law-making Power", above n 1, at 272.

81 Douglas NeJaime "The Constitution of Parenthood" (2020) 72 Stan L Rev 261 at 267–268 and 272.

We can see a similar link between cultural and legal changes at play in the family recognition cases. *Re Gordon & Archer* points to earlier case law to demonstrate the gradual changing social acceptance of differently constituted family units.[82] Stewart Dalley's account of *Re Pierney* (as one of the applicants in the proceeding) offers insight into how the 'societal changes' necessary to overcome the High Court's *AMM* dicta were all grounded in legal change: the decriminalisation of homosexuality, the amendments to the Marriage Act, guidance on assisted reproductive technology.[83] This is a reminder of how the assessment of a changing society can sit perfectly well within the court's usual role in reviewing a changing legal landscape of precedent and statute. It is also a reminder of the space for bravery in advancing legal change to achieve an inclusive social ideal.

5.3. 'BEST EQUIPPED' MODERATED BY LIKELIHOOD OF PARLIAMENT ADVANCING CHANGE

Writing in 2007, Professor Harris suggested that courts considering judicial creativity should 'deliberately consider whether it is the most constitutionally appropriate and best equipped body in the structure of government to effect the innovation'.[84] The judge's power to innovate is confined by the nature of the claim and the nature of the indeterminacy before the court. A change to social policy rules in this context will be an incremental expansion rather than any ground-up reconstruction of the outdated institution. There may be a concern, as in *Quilter*, about how a creative interpretation of the one statute in question will operate without related amendments across other areas of law. There may be a concern about whether the change will meet the size of the need: is the court's confined creativity a satisfactory stopgap or is that wider reconstruction necessary to remedy the injustice? Will an ad hoc extension defer the consideration of injustice elsewhere, as in the five-year lag between *AMM* and *Pierney*, and does this matter?

Judges will reasonably diverge on whether to take on the opportunity to make new law, to reluctantly plug the gap while calling on Parliament to undertake a broader legislative overhaul, or to resist creativity

82 *Re Gordon & Archer*, above n 4, at [27]–[28].
83 Dalley, above n 57, at 33.
84 Harris "Judicial Activism", above n 1, at 301.

altogether and defer development to Parliament. Within this balance, Professor Harris has suggested that the courts may properly make a practical assessment of whether the legislature is likely to include the necessary innovation in its legislative programme.[85]

This balance between what is best and what will do is pertinent to the Adoption Act innovation cases. From one point of view, Parliament would have been the best body to determine who can adopt as joint partners or, put another way, to have 'innovated'. Where the courts have been constrained by the statutory 'spouse' language and the parties seeking recognition of their relationship, Parliament would have had the opportunity to enact sweeping legislative reform. Parliament could have considered the full range of policy options for modernising the archaic statute, including the Law Commission's recommendations to remove the spousal eligibility requirement altogether and focus on the ability of the applicants in question to parent a child.[86] The processes of select committee consultation and parliamentary debate would have encouraged law-makers to grapple with the difficult questions raised in *Re Gordon & Archer* about the purpose of adoption and what it means to parent together.[87] An opportunity for comprehensive reform would have helped avoid one of the key criticisms of the Adoption Act extensions, which is that the court's attempts to resolve anomalies in an out-of-touch statute have produced new anomalies – the lag between de facto opposite- and same-sex couple adoptions and an ongoing uncertainty about whether civil union couples can jointly adopt.[88]

But short of the Parliamentary ideal, the courts have been successful in progressing a slow evolution to open up the Act's idea of the family and reduce the discriminatory impact on families outside a traditional married heterosexual norm. These achievements have been important in a context where there has been much discussion of the need for legislative reform but little action from successive governments and Parliament.[89] Perhaps perversely the scope for the court's consideration of who is 'best' or 'better placed' to achieve innovation can appropriately include the court's own advantage in securing an immediate advance to respond to

---

85 At 302.

86 Law Commission, above n 21, at 59.

87 *Re Gordon & Archer*, above n 61, at [33]–[35].

88 *Child Law* (online looseleaf ed, Thomson Reuters) at [PA2.5.07].

89 See discussion of reviews and lack of legislative reform in *Adoption Action Inc v Attorney-General* [2016] NZHRRT 9 at [4].

injustice before it versus the hope of the issue making it on to the agenda of a democratically elected Parliament in the future.

5.4. PARLIAMENTARY SILENCE, PROJECTED POSITION NO JUSTIFICATION FOR DEFERENCE

Deference to Parliament's will on matters of social change is anchored in Parliament's legislative supremacy. Where Parliament has spoken that is decisive. In the New Zealand Bill of Rights Act exercise, this means that if the rights-limiting statutory provision is capable of no other meaning, or there is no meaning that sits comfortably with the interpreted rights and freedoms in a s 5 exercise, the court is bound to give effect to the conflicting provision under s 4.[90] The court may instead consider remedies for the established breach or making a plea for Parliament to consider the need for change. Equally, where the court chooses to fill an indeterminacy with new law it is open to Parliament to overturn the innovation through fresh legislation. This kind of legislative correction may well be prompted by the public discontent and lack of acceptance that Thomas J feared in *Quilter*.[91]

Between these two opportunities for Parliament to speak on an issue there is no call to defer on what Parliament would say or why Parliament has said nothing. Speculation on Parliament's vision for change is a concerning aspect of the reasoning in *Quilter*. While the main sticking point is the unbending meaning of 'marriage', Tipping and Keith JJ explained that in any event they would be reluctant to consider an innovation to the institution of marriage when it is unlikely that Parliament could have intended such a substantial change through the indirect New Zealand Bill of Rights Act mechanism.[92] Tipping J pointed to Parliament's use of language such as 'man', 'woman', 'bride', 'bridegroom' in more recent legislation to show what 'must surely' be Parliament's unwillingness to allow same-sex marriage and its ongoing commitment to a traditional view of marriage.[93] The discussion

---

90 New Zealand Bill of Rights Act, ss 4 and 6; and Bruce Harris *New Zealand Constitution: An Analysis in Terms of Principles* (Thomson Reuters, Wellington, 2018) at [16.2.1].

91 *Quilter*, above n 2, at 542.

92 Per Tipping J at 581, Keith J at 567.

93 At 580.

blurs a line between the standard interpretative method of looking to other legislation to determine the meaning of a statutory term and a deference to what the judge perceives to be Parliament's likely position on the issue before the courts.

This question of Parliament's silence is effectively addressed by the High Court in *AMM*. Parliament had legislated in 2005 to remove numerous statutory references to marital status but had left the Adoption Act provision unchanged.[94] Counsel for the Attorney-General argued that this decision not to address adoption meant the ordinary, traditional meaning of 'spouse'. Was deliberate inaction by Parliament, or 'legislation by inaction' enough to call on s 4 of the New Zealand Bill of Rights Act?[95] The court found it was not – even though it was arguable that Parliament would wish to correct the discrimination on its own timeframe, the court's task was to alleviate the discrimination now.[96] This is a significant recognition of the court's separate role as an innovator. As Professor Harris has suggested, judicial innovation can facilitate accountability through raising issues that have been overlooked or even avoided by the other branches of government.[97] Given that Parliament's anticipated position or established inaction will likely be tied up in political popularity and the biases and prejudices underlying majority will, it would be a shame to allow these factors to detract from the court's clear mandate to uphold the New Zealand Bill of Rights Act.

5.5. DEMOCRATIC SYSTEM CONTEMPLATES, REQUIRES, INNOVATION TO ADVANCE MINORITY INTERESTS

Professor Harris has argued that the optimum functioning of New Zealand's system of government requires creativity from the courts.[98] Harris describes how creativity can act as a 'foil' to the legislature's disproportionate powers, further the development of human rights and generally foster accountability through raising issues overlooked or avoided by the other branches.[99] Harris's analysis of the constitutional

94 *Re AMM*, above n 2, at [67]–[68].
95 At [71].
96 At [72].
97 Harris "Judicial Activism", above n 1, at 276.
98 At 273.
99 At 274–276.

function of creativity illuminates that a decision to resist an innovation opportunity and defer change to Parliament is not a neutral, democratic-by-default outcome. The judicial process can also be a democratic process.[100]

The New Zealand Bill of Rights Act provides a strong platform for the kind of social changes seen in the family recognition cases. One of the difficulties identified by Professor Harris is how to maintain the court's accountability to the community as a whole.[101] Once we depart from giving effect to the will of a majority within that community, there is a question of how the court can confidently decide what is for the overall public good without falling to the risks of rule by elite and change driven by the judge's personal point of view.[102] The New Zealand Bill of Rights Act grounds change in a shared commitment to the rights and freedoms protected, affirmed by an elected legislature and with an express mandate for the courts to pursue rights-consistent interpretations of existing statute law.[103]

Further, the New Zealand Bill of Rights Act provides a clear structure to build the majority and minority interests at play into the inquiry on appropriate judicial action. Majority interests may feed into an assessment of the justified limitations on a right. Broad social norms of what people do, what people think may inform the court's assessment of available alternative interpretations of statutory terms in the way discussed in the social policy analysis above. The elected Parliament may have spoken so clearly that the courts must apply the rights-inconsistent provision, or Parliament may choose to speak again to align any New Zealand Bill of Rights Act driven innovation with community appetite for change. But outside of these openings, the court is not required to consider what people will think about the court's innovation. Where the court has found an unjustified limit on a right and an alternative rights-consistent meaning, the court's role requires such creativity in the face of any concern about the size of the change and its public reception.

---

100 See Lady Hale's remarks on judicial processes as democratic processes in Lady Hale "Law and Politics: A Reply to Reith" (Dame Frances Patterson Memorial Lecture 2019, London, 8 October 2019) at 14.

101 Harris "Law-making Power", above n 1, at 277.

102 At 277; Harris "Judicial Activism", above n 1, at 301.

103 New Zealand Bill of Rights Act 1990, s 6.

6. PROFESSOR HARRIS'S PROPOSAL FOR PRESERVING PUBLIC CONFIDENCE THROUGH JUDICIAL ACCOUNTABILITY

Professor Harris's early 'Law-Making Power' article outlined practical proposals to strengthen judicial accountability and thus maintain public confidence. As the courts were poised to take on a greater law-making role, Harris argued public confidence would only be maintained if the judiciary was clearly seen to be accountable to the community as a whole.[104] This final part of the contribution takes the opportunity to return to Harris's proposals to (1) improve transparency of judicial functioning through fuller, clearer communication of the court's role in developing the law;[105] and (2) improve the opportunities for research and community input within the court processes.

6.1. TRANSPARENCY OF JUDICIAL FUNCTIONING

Accountability requires transparency of judicial functioning. As Professor Harris emphasised, the community should be able to understand the role of the courts and see the courts carrying out that role. Where people consider the courts have carried out the role inappropriately, they should be able to respond.[106]

In the 25 years since Harris's essay, the courts have taken up a number of his proposals for helping the community *see* the courts carrying out their role. Judges abandoned wigs and gowns for everyday court business in the late 1990s. Plain English has been widely encouraged. The Institute of Judicial Studies, formed in 1998, includes good judgment writing training to simplify and streamline judgments.[107] The higher courts have taken steps to communicate on the meaning of decisions outside the formal written judgment. Media releases to 'assist in understanding' accompany all reserved judgments of the Supreme Court and Court of Appeal and High Court judgments of public interest.[108]

---

104 Harris "Law-making Power", above n 1, at 275.

105 At 285.

106 At 279.

107 See generally Institute of Judicial Studies <www.ijs.govt.nz>.

108 See Courts of New Zealand "Judgments" <www.courtsofnz.govt.nz>.

These practical steps have helped to chip away at the court's external 'mystique'. But the hard work that remains is in Professor Harris's challenge to improve transparency of the underlying judicial functioning, including how the courts are developing the law and how this fits within the court's role in the system of government. Any meaningful public scrutiny of whether the courts have exceeded, or fallen short, of their law-making function assumes a base understanding in the community of what that function entails.

One part of this transparency is judges' own appreciation of the law-making role. A shortcoming of the family cases is the courts' reluctance to describe how they are developing the law and spell out the reasons for and against the exercise of creativity. Where the courts are uncomfortable acting, this is often expressed in the 'policy' shorthand and nods to democratic processes outlined above. Where the courts are comfortable acting, the judges typically confine the reasoning to the interpretive task and avoid comment on any active decision to develop the law and resolve an issue of policy.[109] This is not a call for agreement on the exact law-making function: judges will have different views on the role for creativity and the appropriate course in a given case. It is a call for the courts to fully, openly and clearly articulate the basis for a decision to innovate or not and how this gives effect to the judge's perception of the court's role within the system of government.

An open discussion of judicial law-making in turn promotes the public understanding of the court's role. This has been important in the New Zealand Bill of Rights Act field. As suggested above, the courts' consideration of public confidence in its accountability to the community should include its vital function in upholding individual rights and freedoms. This relies on a public consciousness of the judicial branch's separate constitutional role as a champion of individual rights. Such consciousness may be fostered by the more recent high-profile New Zealand Bill of Rights Act cases, such as the *Attorney-General v Taylor* challenge to prisoner voting and *Seales* test of voluntary euthanasia, where the courts have been moved to articulate the bounds of their powers in the face of a rights breach by the executive and Legislative branches.[110]

---

109 The possible exception to this is the High Court's discussion of its separate role in ameliorating discrimination in the face of legislative inaction in *AMM*: see *Re AMM*, above n 2, at [72].

110 *Attorney-General v Taylor* [2018] NZSC 104, [2019] 1 NZLR 213; *Seales v Attorney-General* [2015] NZHC 1239, [2015] 3 NZLR 556.

6.2. FACILITATING THE LAW-MAKING ROLE

Acknowledging the courts' responsibility for making law opens up the consideration of how we can better facilitate the courts' law-making role. Improvements to the courts' processes and procedures can support a better quality of law-making and may in time expand the circumstances where judges feel appropriately placed to take up the opportunity for creativity.

Professor Harris proposed expanding the courts' opportunities for research and input into law-making decisions.[111] One option was to appoint an independent advocate to address and call evidence on the best development of the law in the circumstances.[112] This could be achieved, for example, through an extension of the amicus appointment powers, or through an extension of the role of the Law Commission.[113] Another option was to encourage all parties to the litigation to provide argument and evidence on the law-making implications, although this would raise issues of cost to the litigants for funding the law reform exercise beyond their direct interest in the litigation.[114]

An elegant new option is the intervener. It is increasingly common for the courts to permit a non-party 'intervener' to participate in proceedings in the public interest.[115] In its 2012 review of the former Judicature Act, the Law Commission described how intervention can 'provide the court with an enhanced perspective on the questions at issue in the proceedings, promote better and more informed decision-making and increase public acceptance of court decisions'.[116] This kind of public interest intervention fits neatly into the identified concerns about a court's law-making ability. It allows for interested groups to provide evidence and answer questions on the broader impact on other parts of the community and the implications of the decision beyond the direct parties to the litigation. The burden for the parties of

---

111 Harris "Law-making Power", above n 1, at 283.

112 At 283.

113 At 283.

114 At 284.

115 See Law Commission *Review of the Judicature Act 1908: Towards a New Courts Act* (NZLC R126, 2012) at [15.38]; Edward Clark "The Needs of the Many and the Needs of the Few: A New System of Public Interest Intervention for New Zealand" (2005) 36 VUWLR 71 at 72.

116 Law Commission, above n 115, at [15.39].

the extra argument can in part be addressed by the court's discretionary powers to award payment of the costs of the intervention.[117]

The public interest intervention is an exciting area of growth. While the Legislature did not take up the Law Commission's recommendation to formalise the participation of an intervener in the recent courts' legislation,[118] intervention continues at the courts' discretion. The Human Rights Commission has exercised its statutory powers to intervene in several recent significant rights decisions, including a successful challenge to the Adoption Act provisions before the Human Rights Review Tribunal and the prisoner voting litigation, and has publicly highlighted its interest in opportunities to advance its rights protection function.[119]

7. CONCLUSION

This contribution has considered Marriage Act and Adoption Act decisions as challenges for judicial creativity. The decisions show the New Zealand courts carefully and selectively employing their law-making powers to promote individual rights and keep pace with social change in the family. While they have generally reached an appropriate balance between progressive innovation and respectful deference to Parliament, the decisions underline the importance of Professor Harris's calls for an honest discussion of how the courts make law.[120] Open discussion of the law-making function is crucial to further a community understanding of the courts' distinct function in shaping rules in the good of the community and to ensure a principled approach to the courts' treatment of the controversial.

---

117 Senior Courts Act 2016, s 178.

118 Law Commission, above n 115, at [R80]. See also Senior Courts Act 2016, s 178.

119 *Adoption Action Inc v Attorney-General* [2016] NZHRRT 9; Janet Anderson-Bidois "The Human Rights Commission as Intervener in Legal Proceedings" (2017) 908 Law Talk 28. The statutory basis for intervention is found in the Human Rights Act 1993, s 5(2)(j).

120 Harris "Law-making Power", above n 1, at 267.

JUDICIAL ACTIVISM AND RESTRAINT, NEW ZEALAND STYLE

Three Case Studies in Controversy

Paul RISHWORTH

1. INTRODUCTION

For many years Bruce Harris's office shelves sported a series of boxes containing his public law materials – 'Parliamentary Supremacy', 'the executive', 'Third Source', and the like. Last box in line was 'The Future'. Less well-thumbed than the others, it was full of things yet to happen. Naturally, it was difficult to resist asking Bruce what was in it.

Then, and indeed still, talk of constitutional futures for New Zealand generally turned to well-worn conversation starters. Should there be a formal 'written constitution'? Should it include a 'higher law' bill of rights enabling judicial invalidation of inconsistent legislation? Should it contain economic and social rights and protections for the environment? Should we become a republic? What sort of constitutional reckoning with the Treaty of Waitangi will generate a consensus? Perhaps these questions never change; it is just that over time different people come to answer them. At some point political circumstances may well mean that the answers produced by that generation become the new constitutional settlement.

Bruce explored these topics in a valuable 2004 article titled "The Constitutional Future of New Zealand".[1] His focus was pragmatic and process oriented. Pointing to the difficulty of constitution-making in times of peace and harmony, he argued for a programme designed to encourage engagement by the citizenry in constitutional matters. As it transpired, in 2011 a Constitutional Advisory Panel was appointed by the National Government, producing a report in 2013 that advanced 'a way forward for future discussions about the constitution'.[2] It is fair to say that this report, like others before it, sank without trace, confirming Bruce's point that constitutional conversations are not just difficult to start but fizzle out quickly.

Numerous constitutional futures are, of course, possible. One is the continuing evolution of the so-called 'unwritten constitution' we have. This evolution already means the New Zealand constitution is not the same as it was thirty or fifty years ago. When the political climate does demand some sort of explicit constitutional reform, it will inevitably be against the backdrop of the constitutional understandings that we have reached at that stage. There may be conscious departures from some and deliberate preservation or adaptation of others. But, whatever happens, no future written constitution can be expected to capture the whole matrix of subordinate rules, principles and approaches through which constitutions (and the people and institutions within them) operate in practice. These are part of our heritage and always evolving.

My contribution seeks to explore one such 'operational' component of a constitution: the respective roles of judges and Parliament in resolving contentious moral controversies such as abortion, euthanasia and same-sex marriage – each of which involve claims of personal rights and freedoms affirmed in the New Zealand Bill of Rights Act 1990. This is a subset of the types of issues that Bruce has also examined, this time in his contribution, in 2007, to an edited collection of essays titled *Judicial Activism in Common Law Supreme Courts*.[3] As Bruce and most of the other contributors to that book pointed out, just what 'judicial activism'

1 Bruce Harris "The Constitutional Future of New Zealand" [2004] NZ L Rev 269.

2 A copy of the Panel's report can be accessed through the Ministry of Justice website at <www.justice.govt.nz/justice-sector-policy/constitutional-issues-and-human-rights/constitutional-advisory-panel/>.

3 Bruce Harris "Judicial Activism and New Zealand's Appellate Courts" in Brice Dickson (ed) *Judicial Activism in Common Law Supreme Courts* (Oxford University Press, Oxford, 2007) 273.

means is notoriously vague. The phrase is usually invoked by critics and commentators to signify vigorous disagreement with the outcome in a case – that it is illegitimate, the judicial reasoning merely a result-oriented ploy. On the other hand, judicial activism is applauded when a welcome result is reached in a creative way. (A moment's thought reveals this may be said of the same case but by different critics.) It also has to be said – and Bruce made this point strongly – that suggestions of activism are in fact advanced in only a small number of decided cases. Much judicial work involves the application of high-level laws and principles to specific facts. Judges are often required to *create* law through the process of its application, because the harsh particularities of individual cases can generate wholly unforeseen questions. This too can be called 'activism', but because of its ubiquity – indeed its necessity – Bruce preferred to speak instead of judicial 'creativity', a term somewhat less pejorative.

That said, the topic of judicial activism is famously associated with (but certainly not limited to) the US where judges interpret and enforce the constraints placed upon state and federal power – especially the individual rights set out in the Bill of Rights of 1791 and the 14th Amendment of 1865. These documents deal in vague but inspirational phrases such as the right to 'life, liberty and property' and 'equal protection of the law'. The American controversy over abortion rights is the most well-known, but then there is affirmative action, gun control, religious freedom, free speech, election funding and more besides. The period in 2020 over which this contribution was being written included President Trump's nomination of Justice Amy Coney Barrett to take the seat on the US Supreme Court formerly held by the late Justice Ruth Bader Ginsburg. That replacement was seen as enormously significant for reasons central to my topic: would it cement a 5–4 (perhaps even a 6–3) conservative majority on these questions?[4] Would incoming President Biden then consider 'packing the Court' by enlarging its size to appoint sufficient numbers of left-leaning judges to overcome that majority?[5]

---

4 It is a measure of the vagueness about the word 'activist' that it is always taken to include not only the invalidation of legislation but also the refusal to invalidate (such as where conservative judges uphold state laws restricting abortion rights because they are adjudged not to unduly burden the constitutional right to abortion affirmed in *Roe v Wade*: see further the discussion below).

5 It appears that President Biden is not inclined to do that but has commissioned a report on the matter.

These issues were well reported in New Zealand, seemingly attracting greater interest than judicial appointments to our own highest court. The reason for this is at one level quite obvious: there is no legal tradition in New Zealand whereby the outcome of moral controversies is forged by victories in court battles (as often occurs in the US). New Zealand judges do not wield the power to invalidate legislation that breaches individual rights. They cannot, therefore, place some topics beyond the reach of Parliament to regulate. Even so, I will suggest there are some substantial similarities between the judicial role in New Zealand when compared with the US and Canada, each of which have higher law constitutions involving judicial review and where the courts are seen as the forum to resolve rights claims.

First, the phenomenon of writing rights down, as occurred when the New Zealand Bill of Rights Act was enacted, has given rights in New Zealand a legal salience that they simply did not enjoy until then. Prior to 1990, it was axiomatic that New Zealanders had human rights, but these rights did not have settled names or sources. They were called 'civil liberties' or 'residual common law freedoms' – essentially all the freedom one naturally has, and which has not yet been constrained by law. But once rights and freedoms were written into the Bill of Rights in 1990, they were a Parliamentary statement of positive law, set out in some detail, against which legislation and state action was explicitly to be measured.

Second, once rights were affirmed in a legal instrument, their interpretation became a matter of law to be settled by courts. That alone joined New Zealand's courts in the same enterprise as the courts of North America. And when, in 2018, the Supreme Court affirmed that New Zealand courts have a power, sourced in the Bill of Rights, to grant 'declarations of inconsistency' it became possible to file a case solely for the purpose of eliciting such a thing – a judicial opinion on the rights-consistency of legislation.[6] True, a 'declaration of inconsistency' does not lead to legislation being invalidated (as in Canada and the US), but the litigation itself cannot meaningfully be distinguished from the judicial review deployed in jurisdictions enforcing higher law constitutions.

[6] *Attorney-General v Taylor* [2018] NZSC 109, [2019] 1 NZLR 213. See, most recently, *Make it 16 Inc v Attorney-General* [2020] NZHC 2630 where the plaintiff sought (but did not get) a declaration of inconsistency in relation to the voting age being set at 18 years by ss 74 and 3(1) of the Electoral Act 1993. The case is currently under appeal.

It is only the remedy for inconsistency that differs, with declarations being a little lower in the hierarchy than nullification.[7]

Third, and relatedly, the pronouncement of a judicial view on matters of rights and freedoms carries, it seems to me, increasing salience amongst the citizenry. Rightly or wrongly, politicians tend to be seen as venal or insufficiently responsive or hamstrung by their need to make necessary political compromises. In contrast, courts are seen as forums of principle, owing allegiance not just to the body of laws enacted by Parliament but also to the idea of law itself – to its deep principles and to the scripts of international human rights (which the anthemic language of the Bill of Rights affirms). So, a declaration of inconsistency in relation to legislation can be seen as a powerful moral judgment, even if the law is not thereby invalidated. At the same time, the reach of human rights law into issues of morality can be controversial. There can be disagreement amongst the citizenry with outcomes declared by judges in such matters, who may see such cases as going beyond the conventional determination of 'law'.

And so, for my purposes, it is enough to start here. New Zealand courts can and do get called upon to decide contested cases about rights. I will explore the indigenous phenomena of so-called judicial activism and restraint in New Zealand through the lens of some recent and contemporary moral controversies. Is there a 'New Zealand way,' a particular judicial approach, that courts take to these? I shall suggest there is, drawing on themes that Bruce nicely articulated in his 2007 piece on judicial activism. The balance of this contribution therefore explores controversies over abortion, euthanasia and sex discrimination in the US, Canada and New Zealand, enabling some conclusions in the final section about what this may mean for constitutional reform, if and when it comes to be debated.

2. ABORTION RIGHTS IN THE US AND NEW ZEALAND

The morality of abortion polarises American politics, and the Supreme Court's 1973 decision in *Roe v Wade* is the debate's centrepiece. *Roe* held

[7] And perhaps not much. The Canadian practice of declaring statutes invalid but delaying the effect of the declaration to enable a legislative response can shade into the New Zealand practice of judicial declarations that are reported to Parliament for consideration of a response. See further below.

that a woman has a constitutional right to terminate her pregnancy, grounded in the 'liberty' guaranteed by the 14th Amendment to the US Constitution, which may be taken away only by 'due process'.[8]

Even before *Roe*, it was well settled that 'liberty' denoted not just physical freedom but also a set of fundamental personal rights. None of these are set out in the Constitution; all we have is the word 'liberty' in the context of the world's oldest Bill of Rights (itself reflecting English tradition reaching back to Magna Carta in 1215). *Roe* added autonomy over abortions to the small set of rights that the Supreme Court had by then said ought not to be taken away at all, no matter how 'due' the 'process'. A law prohibiting, say, teaching one's children a foreign language is inconsistent with liberty no matter how fair any trial might be or how moderate the punishment.[9] The metaphor – oxymoron, really – of 'substantive due process' describes this phenomenon. These substantive 'liberty rights' conferred by the 14th Amendment exist in addition to those listed in the Bill of Rights (such as the freedoms of speech and religion, rights against search and seizure, bearing arms and so on).

Even so, *Roe* had its limits.[10] First, the court recognised the continuing power of a state to regulate abortion. True, it must respect a pregnant woman's decisional autonomy in respect of carrying a foetus (and focus its regulation on safety in abortions). But as a pregnancy develops, the state has a corresponding interest in the potential life of a developing foetus such that, in the final trimester abortions must generally be justified on the basis of foetal disability or threats to a woman's life or health. Second, *Roe* did not confer positive rights: while the right to liberty prevented abortions being criminalised, it did not require that they be federally funded or facilitated.[11]

---

8 *Roe v Wade* 410 US 113 (1973).

9 *Meyer v Nebraska* 262 US 390 (1923).

10 The judicial enterprise commenced in *Roe* was subjected to some searing criticisms from the start, even from the left. See, for a doctrinal critique, John Hart Ely "The Wages of Crying Wolf: A Comment on *Roe v Wade*" (1973) 82 Yale LJ 920. See also the feminist scepticism about Roe's 'paying so much attention to the views of doctors while ignoring women's stake in the matter' described in Mary Ziegler *Beyond Abortion:* Roe v Wade *and the Battle for Privacy* (Harvard University Press, Cambridge, 2018) especially at 202 and following.

11 In Canada it was the lack of facilitation – that is, the practical non-availability of consultants (in some parts of Canada, especially remote ones) who were authorised to certify the lawfulness of abortions – that led the Supreme Court of Canada to hold that Canada's abortion law impaired the rights of women to security of the person in s 7 of the Canadian Charter of Rights and Freedoms: see *R v Morgentaler* [1988] 1 SCR 30.

The post-*Roe* history of the US abortion controversy has seen attempts by many state legislatures to limit abortions by working within these features of *Roe*: that is, to impose regulatory constraints and seek to defend them from challenge in federal courts and ultimately in the Supreme Court (where *Roe* itself can be challenged). *Planned Parenthood v Casey*,[12] for example, concerned Pennsylvania laws imposing a 24-hour waiting period for abortions, requiring compulsory provision of information about foetal development and alternatives to abortion, parental consent for minors, and a requirement that married women notify husbands of planned abortions. In the Supreme Court, the Bush administration urged the Court to overturn *Roe*. But by a majority of five votes to four, the Supreme Court narrowly affirmed what it called *Roe*'s 'essential holding': that (1) a woman has a right to decide to terminate her pregnancy prior to 'viability' without 'undue' interference by the state; (2) the state has an interest throughout in regulating abortion in the interests of the health of the woman and the potential life of the foetus; and (3) a woman has the right, after foetal viability, to an abortion necessary for life or health. The court left the Pennsylvania law intact save for the requirement of notifying husbands, it alone being seen as an 'undue burden'.

What was significant about *Planned Parenthood v Casey* was that only two of the judges from *Roe* were still on the Court in 1992, and the five-judge majority was a result of their votes together with those of three new arrivals – one of whom, Justice Kennedy, had been seen as a likely vote to overrule *Roe* but voted instead with the liberal block. More recently, in a 2020 abortion case, *June Medical Services Inc v Russo*,[13] the first to come to the court after President Trump's appointment of conservative Justices Gorsuch and Kavanaugh, the Court invalidated a Louisiana law on the basis that it imposed undue restrictions on women seeking an abortion. This time a five-judge majority was procured when Chief Justice Roberts joined the liberal block only because of his view that the doctrine

---

12 *Planned Parenthood v Casey* 505 US 833 (1992).

13 *June Medical Services, LLC v Russo* 591 US __ (2020). The impugned law restricted doctors from performing abortions unless they had admitting privileges at a hospital near an abortion clinic, a measure that would have drastically limited the number of eligible doctors. A more recent bellwether of possible direction is *Food and Drug Administration v American College of Obstetricians and Gynecologists* 592 US __ (2021) (12 January 2021) where Justice Barrett joined the conservative majority to stay, pending appeal, a federal district court's ruling that had altered the regimen for access to a certain abortion drug due to the pandemic (allowing mail access instead of the statutorily required personal consultation).

of *stare decisis* so required. That focused attention therefore on whether it would be Justice Barrett's arrival that made the overturning of *Roe* possible in a future case.[14]

New Zealand's abortion law initially followed a broadly similar trajectory to that of the US but without input from the courts. Just two years after *Roe*, in 1975, a Royal Commission on Contraception, Sterilisation and Abortion was appointed. It reported in 1977,[15] and, later that year, Parliament enacted its alternative recommendation for a new abortion law. Terminating a woman's pregnancy remained generally unlawful, but not when 'continuance of the pregnancy would result in serious danger (not being danger normally attendant upon childbirth) to the life, or to the physical or mental health, of the woman or girl'.[16] Whether those conditions applied would be decided by doctors called 'certifying consultants'. These were appointed to a list maintained by the 'Abortion Supervisory Committee', which was given the power and duty of 'keep[ing] under review all the provisions of the abortion law and [its] operation and effect'.[17]

The Royal Commission report and the ensuing legislation are best read as a political settlement of the two opposing extremes in the abortion debate. It came about through a process that was deliberative: a commission of inquiry followed by extensive Parliamentary debate. The necessary compromise appears starkly from the list of criteria for appointment as a certifying consultant. The Abortion Supervisory Committee was instructed by Parliament not to appoint any doctors whose views were 'incompatible with the tenor of [the] Act'. Two incompatible views were then spelled out:[18]

(1) that an abortion should not be performed in any circumstances:
(2) that the question of whether an abortion should or should not be performed in any case is entirely a matter for the woman and a doctor to decide.

---

14 The Chief Justice's invocation of *stare decisis* rested on the case being identical to one decided four years earlier in which the court had declared the law unconstitutional. See *Whole Woman's Health v Hellerstedt* 579 US __ (2016).

15 New Zealand Royal Commission on Contraception, Sterilisation and Abortion *Contraception, Sterilisation and Abortion in New Zealand: Report of the Royal Commission of Inquiry* (1977).

16 Crimes Act 1961, s 187A, subsequently repealed by s 13 of the Abortion Legislation Act 2020.

17 Contraception, Sterilisation and Abortion Act 1977, s 14(1)(a).

18 Section 30(5).

In 2020, the Abortion Legislation Act 'de-criminalised' abortion. That is to say, it effectively enacted the second of these two 'incompatible' views. It is now lawful for a qualified health provider to provide abortion services to a person up to twenty weeks pregnant.[19] No certifying consultants need be involved, and the role no longer exists. After twenty weeks' gestation, the position is a little different: the health provider must consult one other qualified health provider and perform the abortion only if it is 'clinically appropriate'.[20] There is no definition of what is 'clinically appropriate', but the decision is to be reached after considering a woman's physical and mental health and well-being. Killing an unborn child remains an offence in the Crimes Act 1961, but the explicit exception continues for those providing abortion services under the Contraception, Sterilisation and Abortion Act 1977 – so this is the sense in which abortion is 'de-criminalised'.[21]

Intriguingly the 2020 Act also includes a provision, recommended by a majority of the Select Committee, as follows:[22]

21 Abortion for sole purpose of sex selection

(1) This Parliament opposes the performance of abortions being sought solely because of a preference for the foetus to be of a particular sex.

(2) Not later than 5 years after the commencement of this section, and then at subsequent intervals of not more than 5 years, the Director-General must—

  (a) review whether there is any evidence of abortions being sought solely because of a preference for the foetus to be of a particular sex; and

  (b) report to the Minister of Health on—

    (i) the outcome of the review; and

    (ii) if there is such evidence, any recommendations that the Director-General considers appropriate for preventing abortions being sought solely because of a preference for the foetus to be of a particular sex.

---

19 Section 10 (following amendment by Abortion Legislation Act 2020, s 8).

20 Section 11 (as amended).

21 Crimes Act 1961, s 182. See also s 183, which provides that the procurement or performance of an abortion by a person other than a health practitioner is also an offence.

22 Contraception, Sterilisation and Abortion Act 1977, s 21 (also as amended).

The provision is modelled on an equivalent section in New South Wales legislation.[23] It is an unusual use of the State's legislative power, expressing an opposition without sanctions.[24] It is Delphic, perhaps even Solomonic. The overall message is that women do not have to declare their reasons to anyone, but certain reasons would be problematic if known to exist. The actual law-bearing component of s 21 lies in sub-section (2): the Director-General's duty to review and report on whether abortions are in fact being sought for reasons of sex preference.[25] There is no explicit duty or power for the Director-General to solicit evidence about women's motivations for an abortion. And as we shall see, a case under the replaced abortion law which I shall shortly discuss suggests that gathering any such evidence would be difficult indeed.

The existence of s 21 is not, however, totally surprising. Statistics on New Zealanders' opinions about abortion suggest we are not so different from persons in the US, and that in neither country do people fall neatly into the two extreme camps suggested by the 1977 criteria for certifying consultants. A 2019 opinion poll by Ipsos Public Affairs reported 77% of New Zealanders were in favour of abortion rights with just 14% against.[26] But, importantly, the 'in favour' group comprises 51% who thought abortion should be permitted whenever a woman decides, and a remaining 25% who believe abortion 'should be permitted in certain circumstances (such as if a woman has been raped)'. We do not know whether the 'certain circumstances' that these 25% have in mind would include abortions for sex-selection purposes. But it is reasonable to think they would not approve, and that Parliament's recorded opposition in s 21(1) reflects a view likely held by these 25% and by the 14% who oppose all abortions, and likely also held by some of the 51% who support abortions in all cases but had not expressly considered abortions of otherwise-wanted children performed for discriminatory sex-selection purposes.

---

23 Abortion Law Reform Act 2019 (NSW), s 16.

24 The provision is a faint echo of s 11(1)(a) of the Human Assisted Reproductive Technology Act 2004 which makes it a criminal offence for any person to select a human embryo for implantation into a human being on the basis of the sex of the embryo. One imagines that the mechanics of implementing any such decision could make manifest the participants' 'sex-selecting' motivation. Or perhaps not; I don't know how such things are done in practice.

25 As to the phrase 'law-bearing', see David Feldman "Legislation Which Bears No Law" (2016) 37(3) Statute L Rev 212.

26 "Half of all NZers believe that abortion should be permitted if a woman wants it" (21 June 2019) <www.ipsos.com/en-nz>. The sample size was 588 and the study was conducted online.

These figures may be compared with the latest annual American Gallup poll on abortion, showing (in May 2020) that, while 79% of Americans polled were in favour of abortion rights, only 29% felt abortion should be legal in any circumstances.[27] The remaining 50% considered it should be lawful under 'certain circumstances'. Follow-up questions were then asked, disclosing that 14% considered abortion should be illegal in 'most circumstances', while 35% felt it ought to be 'legal only in a few'. One might therefore add the American Gallup figures in this way: 43% of Americans believe abortion ought to be lawful in all or most cases, and 55% believe it ought to be unlawful either completely or in all but a few cases.

Those figures ought not to surprise: they explain why abortion restrictions remain contentious in the US and why states keep passing restrictive laws. They suggest that, while we hear most from the extremes, views overall are likely more nuanced.[28] Against that background, it is interesting to consider a case from the Seventh Circuit Court of Appeals in which Justice Barrett was involved, and which involved similar legislative sentiments on sex-selection of foetuses.[29] Judge Barrett's contribution was the subject of some interest as her Supreme Court nomination proceeded.

---

27 Gallup "Americans' abortion views steady in past year" (29 June 2020) <www.gallup.com/home.aspx>. The sample size was 1,028 and the study was conducted over the telephone.

28 I recognise that some persons may be unsupportive of some or all abortions in a general sense but respect the rights of other persons to have different views and not be constrained by the law in acting upon them. Where the New Zealand Parliament sits having enacted s 21 I am not sure.

29 The phenomenon of state legislation seeking to constrain abortions by prohibiting discriminatory practices – especially sex and disability selection – is helpfully analysed by Mary Ziegler "The Disability Politics of Abortion" (2017) 3 Utah L Rev 587. Ziegler chronicles the history of abortion campaigning on both sides and how initial arguments based on the avoidance of birth defects became problematic given their association with eugenics, leading to their replacement by the claims of decisional autonomy ultimately accepted in *Roe*. For its part the pro-life movement has put disability discrimination centre-stage in arguing for restrictions, which has salience for the middle ground and especially among disability groups, albeit that there are difficulties in enforcement given that there is no way of determining the motivation of a pregnant woman who opts for abortion. In New Zealand, the possibility of disability discrimination in abortions was adverted to by the Law Commission in its Ministerial Briefing Paper but the matter was seen as outside the scope of its assigned task: see Law Commission *Alternative Approaches to Abortion Law* (NZLC MB4, 2018) at [12.21]–[12.29]. The issue was pursued by some Members of Parliament by way of Supplementary Order Papers but gained no traction in the House (See *Hansard* online (17 March 2020) at <https://www.parliament.nz/en/pb/hansard-debates/rhr/document/HansS_20200317_071850000/little-andrew>).

This case, *Planned Parenthood of Indiana and Kentucky, Inc v Commissioner of the Indiana State Department of Health*, concerned two Indiana enactments in 2016 regulating abortion, one of which made it unlawful to perform an abortion if the person knows the abortion is sought for reasons of sex selection, disability (with Down Syndrome being given as a specific example), race or colour.[30] The law was invalidated at first instance as inconsistent with *Roe v Wade*. The decision was unanimously affirmed by the Seventh Circuit (with Judge Barrett not sitting as a member). The Court's reasoning was categorical in its application of *Roe*: 'a state may not prohibit any woman from making the ultimate decision to terminate her pregnancy before viability'.[31] (Perhaps a legislative statement such as New Zealand's might have been feasible – the Court did not, obviously, traverse this[32] – but not a prohibition.)

Following its unsuccessful appeal to the Seventh Circuit, the State of Indiana then applied for 'rehearing *en banc*' – a procedure by which the whole membership of the Seventh Circuit Court of Appeals may review a decision of one of its panels if a majority of members so decides. But it transpired the whole panel was equally divided, five judges apiece. Judge Barrett was one of the five judges voting to rehear the appeal, joining an opinion of Judge Easterbrook to that effect.

The rehearing was sought in relation to the state's other enactment, which concerned the disposal of foetal remains, not in relation to the sex, race and disability ban (or, as the Easterbrook group called it, the 'eugenics statute'). This did not stop these judges, however, registering their disagreement over whether *Roe* and *Casey* required holding the ban unconstitutional. There is a difference, they said, 'between "I don't want a child" and "I want a child but only a male" or "I want only children

30 *Planned Parenthood of Indiana and Kentucky, Inc v Commissioner of the Indiana State Department of Health* 194 F Supp 3d 818 (SD Ind 2016); 265 F Supp 3d 859 (SD Ind 2017). The case concerned the Sex Selective and Disability Abortion Ban, Indiana Code ¶16-34-4, as well as an enactment concerning the mode by which foetal remains were to be disposed of after abortions (they were to be buried or cremated). Following an appeal to the Seventh Circuit – discussed above – the Commissioner petitioned the Supreme Court in September 2018 for a writ of certiorari. This was granted *per curiam* in May 2019, overturning the lower courts' injunction prohibiting the enforcement of the foetal disposal clause, but leaving the prohibition on the non-discrimination and informed consent clauses in place: see *Box v Planned Parenthood of Indiana and Kentucky, Inc* 587 US __ (2020).

31 888 F 3d 300 (7th Cir 2018) per Judge Bauer at 306.

32 I am unaware of any tradition in Indiana of legislative statements of the type in s 21(1) of the New Zealand legislation.

whose genes predict success in life"'.[33] This, they thought, was 'morally and prudentially debatable on grounds different from those that underlay the abortion restrictions at issue in *Casey*'.[34] That is presumably the same sentiment that underlies New Zealand's s 21 of the Contraception, Sterilisation and Abortion Act 1977. That is to say, the conservative view in the Indiana abortion context is not wholly different from the view apparently underlying the New Zealand Parliament's legislative statement.

What might we conclude from all this? New Zealand and the US have ended up in a broadly similar legal position on abortion – decriminalisation of abortions and their being available as a matter of right. But whereas in New Zealand it is Parliament that brought the law to that point, in the US it was the Supreme Court that did so as a matter of rights interpreted as constitutional law. The Supreme Court continues to act as the final arbiter of whether particular restrictions on abortion are permissible – meaning that the constitution is a firm 'floor' below which access to abortions may not fall. In both countries the citizenry remains divided in its views and further skirmishes around the scope of the right are evident – albeit, in New Zealand, evident only in the Parliamentary statement expressing opposition to one particular practice and a legal requirement for a review. But might there be litigation over the five-yearly reports required by s 21(2), brought by those who seek to bring judicial oversight and scrutiny to the matter of sex-selection, something Parliamentary explicitly opposes?

There has already been such litigation over the content of the reviews and reports that the Abortion Supervisory Committee was required to make under the old abortion regime – the closest we have come to a local version of *Roe*.[35] In a series of annual reports, that Committee had frequently observed that certifying consultants were applying abortion law more liberally than Parliament intended in 1977. The Committee Chair commented in 1998 that New Zealand essentially had 'abortion on demand'.[36] This attracted the attention of Right to Life New Zealand Inc, which brought proceedings against the Committee seeking a declaration

---

33 917 F 3d 532 (7th Cir 2018) per Judge Easterbrook at 536.

34 At 536.

35 See Contraception, Sterilisation and Abortion Act 1977, s 36.

36 See *Abortion Supervisory Committee v Right to Life New Zealand Inc* [2011] NZCA 246, [2012] 1 NZLR 176 at [117]–[119]. The specific quote is from CS Foster, MM Lamb and J Whittaker *Report of the Abortion Supervisory Committee for 1998* at 7–8.

that it perform its statutory functions – in particular by requesting sufficient details from consultants to determine the level of compliance and reporting accurately on what was taking place.[37]

The case essentially turned on interpretation of the Contraception, Sterilisation and Abortion Act: did it give the Committee the necessary powers to make the sorts of inquiries of consultants about individual cases that could enable it to report on the level of compliance with the Act? Or was its review and reporting to be at a high level, without descending to such details? In the High Court, Miller J agreed with Right to Life. He rejected the Committee's contention that the women's medical confidentiality precluded inquiry into the reasons for each abortion. The Court of Appeal reached the contrary conclusion,[38] Chambers and Stevens JJ ruling that nothing in the Act authorised scrutiny of individual abortions, and after-the-fact review had practical difficulties. Arnold J dissented. Agreeing with Miller J, his Honour found it difficult to see how the Abortion Supervisory Committee could discharge its statutory functions without examining how consultants performed their statutory role. And his Honour, like Miller J, pointed to the 'careful attempt to achieve the appropriate balance' whereby either of the two incompatible views on abortion precluded a doctor from being a consultant, suggesting it would be proper for a consultant's appointment to be revoked if they were in fact influenced by one of the incompatible views.[39] To this point, then, of the four judges who had heard the case, it was two votes for each side.

The Supreme Court affirmed the Court of Appeal decision by a majority of three (Elias CJ, Blanchard and Tipping JJ) to two (McGrath and William Young JJ).[40] Overall, then, nine New Zealand judges heard the case with five deciding for the Committee and four for Right to Life – evoking a comparison with the recurring five–four voting on the US Supreme Court in abortion cases.

The *Right to Life* case is not New Zealand's *Roe v Wade*. Indeed, all four judges up to Court of Appeal level rejected the more ambitious argument fielded by Right to Life – that a foetus had a "right to life"

37 *Right to Life New Zealand Inc v Abortion Supervisory Committee* [2008] 2 NZLR 825 (HC).

38 *Abortion Supervisory Committee*, above n 36.

39 Per Arnold J at [168].

40 *Right to Life New Zealand Inc v Abortion Supervisory Committee* [2012] NZSC 68, [2012] 3 NZLR 762.

under the Act which supported the case for relief against the Committee.[41] That said, *Right to Life* is a kind of analogue to the post-*Roe* cases, once it is recognised that it concerned the capacity (and inclination) of the Supervisory Committee to perform its functions under the Act. Would it, could it, dig into the statistical material to demonstrate that the Act was working as intended? The (overall) five–four outcome on what was ultimately a matter of judgment about the Committee's statutory powers shows it was a close call. I suspect the invisibility of this case in New Zealand owes much to the out-of-sight, out-of-mind nature of the abortion debate in New Zealand. The 1977 settlement was supposed to end controversy, not generate it. The overall majority in *Right to Life* did not wish to lift the lid on that debate and they adopted an interpretive approach to the Act to close it down. For its part, the Committee's candid statements about the law being applied too liberally were more in the nature of advocacy for a reform of the type we actually had in 2020 – making the liberal view in the old s 14(5) the legal view.[42]

Meanwhile the anti-sex selection provision in the new law is an important nod to the continuing moral dilemma surrounding abortion, as is Parliament's statement that it has the matter under review. Whatever the courts might have done in *Right to Life*, abortion law reform was on a trajectory controlled by the government and legislature. For myself, the minority judgments of Miller, Arnold, McGrath and William Young JJ are more convincing in legal terms, but both views were possible, and I understand the dynamics and the appeal of a result that leaves the issue to elected politicians. Was this, then, judicial creativity or activism, or both?

3. END OF LIFE ISSUES IN NEW ZEALAND, THE US AND CANADA

New Zealand's End of Life Choice Act 2019 (ELCA) came into force in 2021, after approval by a referendum held in conjunction with the 2020

---

[41] See *Abortion Supervisory Committee v Right to Life New Zealand Inc*, above n 36, at [53]–[54]. In *Roe v Wade* the Supreme Court of the US had not been prepared to recognise a foetal right to life, although the state's interest in the potential life of a foetus was recognised.

[42] That is, the section in the Contraception, Sterilisation and Abortion Act 1977 – prior to the 2020 Amendment – that set out the two opposing views that were 'incompatible with the tenor of the Act'.

election.[43] The ELCA's genesis was the court case heard in May 2015, *Seales v Attorney-General*.[44] Ms Seales suffered from terminal cancer and wished for the option of 'physician-assisted death'. She sought a High Court ruling that New Zealand's criminal law already permitted this (if interpreted as she suggested) and that, if it did not, the relevant law should be declared inconsistent with her rights in the Bill of Rights. Both these claims were rejected by the court, but the litigation made waves that led to a private member's Bill later that year. That Bill became the ELCA.

Over the years before 2015, there had been three private member's Bills seeking to legalise assisted suicide or euthanasia, but none had progressed.[45] Ms Seales's case was avowedly a mission to get traction, even if it would come too late to assist her. But the initial question was whether the High Court would go as far as the plaintiff and her advisers hoped? Would the courts rule that there is a legal right to assistance in dying, implicit in s 8 of the Bill of Rights (which affirms that 'no-one shall be deprived of life')?

Front and centre of Ms Seales's case was the Supreme Court of Canada's unanimous decision in *Carter v Canada*, delivered in February 2015.[46] The court in *Carter* had invalidated Canada's criminal prohibition of assisted suicide and euthanasia on grounds of their inconsistency with the 'right to life, liberty and security of the person' in s 7 of the Canadian Charter of Rights and Freedoms. As it often does with complex regulatory regimes, the court 'suspended' the annulment for one year to enable a legislative response to be enacted. A law allowing assisted suicide was duly passed by the Parliament, though at the time of writing there is still contention over whether the new provisions fully conform to the Supreme Court's specifications – and how much that matters.[47]

---

43 End of Life Choice Act 2019, s 2.

44 *Seales v Attorney-General* [2015] NZHC 1239, [2015] 3 NZLR 556. I should disclose my role as one of the counsel for the Attorney-General.

45 Specifically, Michael Laws's Death with Dignity Bill (defeated 61 votes to 29 in 1995), Peter Brown's Bill of the same name (defeated 60 votes to 58 in 2003) and Maryan Street's End of Life Choices Bill (never drawn from the 'biscuit tin'). This also shows the non-partisan nature of this issue: Laws was representing National at the Time, Brown was a New Zealand First MP, and Street was from Labour. See further: "Assisted Dying: New Zealand" Parliamentary Library Research Paper (December 2018).

46 *Carter v Canada (Attorney-General)* 2015 SCC 5, [2015] 1 SCR 331.

47 See: *Truchon v Attorney-General of Canada* [2019] RQJ 7750, in which the Quebec Superior Court ruled that some parts of the new law were unconstitutional. The court initially gave the government six months to pass a new law (known as 'Bill C-7'). A third extension was granted in December 2020, with the new deadline being – at the time of writing – 26 February 2021. This is the sense in which, as I suggested

The relevance of *Carter* in New Zealand was obvious because it is a matter of record that the Charter's s 7 informed the drafting of s 8 of the New Zealand Bill of Rights – the right 'not to be deprived of life' save on grounds 'consistent with the principles of fundamental justice'. The latter phrase was drawn wholesale from Canada's s 7, which in turn was inspired by the 5th and 14th Amendments to the US Constitution. The *Seales* litigation – as to the declaration of inconsistency, at least – proceeded as if the *Carter* case provided the template. If the same outcome was not to be reached in a New Zealand court, it was going to need some explaining.

What are the 'principles of fundamental justice'? That question had arisen, for Canada, in numerous cases, one of which also concerned euthanasia. In *Rodriguez v British Columbia (Attorney-General)* in 1993, all nine judges agreed that 'security of the person' was impaired by the Criminal Code's prohibition on assisted suicide, because persons might be exposed to physical and psychological pain that, despite their wishes, they cannot escape by an assisted death.[48] But, by a majority of five–four, the court held the prohibition was not contrary to 'principles of fundamental justice'. That concept was taken to denote the set of deep societal values underpinning the Anglo-Canadian justice system, which embraced both procedural and substantive guarantees of liberty and security. Looking at the subject in that light, the prohibitions on assisted suicide were well-established and long-enduring in Anglo-Canadian law and, further, they responded to individual and societal needs that remained relevant.

That in turn reflected the US' approach to the idea of 'due process' in the 14th Amendment, which – as we saw in relation to abortion – must be observed if limits are to be placed on the 'life, liberty and property' protected by the 5th and 14th Amendments. In this context, due process means substantive due process: whether there is a fundamental personal right to assisted suicide. It would appear not, for just four years after Canada's *Rodriguez* case, the US Supreme Court itself considered constitutional

earlier, a declaration of inconsistency in New Zealand has some affinity with delayed declarations of invalidity in Canada. The matter is passed to Parliament or legislature. What differs is that in Canada there will come a final date when the invalidity becomes operative. That has not happened yet, to my knowledge. In the Morgentaler decision the court annulled the abortion restrictions with immediate effect. Delayed declarations are a more recent phenomenon.

48 *Rodriguez v British Columbia (Attorney-General)* [1993] 3 SCR 519.

challenges to criminal prohibitions of assisted suicide and euthanasia in Washington[49] and New York.[50] As in Canada, both were dismissed. In *Washington v Glucksberg* the Court was unanimous in upholding the state's prohibition on assisted suicide.

But behind that unanimity lay important differences. For a majority of five, the due process challenge was answered simply (as in Canada) by the Anglo-American legal heritage which showed that a prohibition of assisted suicide had been deeply rooted in the nation's history and in English history before that. For his part, Justice Stevens was happy to agree with the five that the 'liberty' protected by the Due Process Clause does not include a categorical 'right to commit suicide which itself includes a right to assistance in doing so'.[51] But, he said, there may be circumstances where hastening death is legitimate – where an individual who is not subject to abuse or depression makes a 'rational and voluntary decision to seek assistance in dying'.[52] No such person was involved in the actual case, for it was argued by the plaintiffs as an abstract challenge to Washington's criminal code. Justice Souter, too, postulated possible deserving cases, but for him the sticking point was different. He pointed to the controversy in the legal argument before the court as to whether the (then very recent) euthanasia reforms in the Netherlands were a 'slippery slope' leading to ever more permissive laws and a devaluing of life. In his words, judicial invalidation of Washington's regulations could not be contemplated where there is 'a serious factual controversy over the feasibility of recognizing the claimed right' and the 'facts necessary to resolve the controversy are not readily ascertainable through the judicial process [but] are more readily subject to discovery through legislative fact-finding and experimentation'.[53] The Dutch law was advanced as the exemplar but, he said, 'I question whether an independent front-line investigation into the facts of a foreign country's legal administration can be soundly undertaken through American courtroom litigation'.[54]

---

49 *Washington v Glucksberg* 521 US 702 (1997).

50 *Vacco v Quill* 521 US 793 (1997).

51 *Washington v Glucksberg*, above n 49, at 741 (footnotes omitted).

52 At 747.

53 At 786–787.

54 In stark contrast, the Supreme Court of Canada was content in *Carter* to say that the first instance judge in that case had conducted an exhaustive review of the evidence placed before her about the possibility of a slippery slope, had found there was no such possibility, and that they could 'find no error' in her approach: *Carter v Canada*, above n 46, at [107] and [120].

The American approach to 'due process', focusing as it does on the nation's history and legal traditions, is both malleable and controversial. For those who view the American Bill of Rights as fundamentally a conservative document, intentionally designed to embed a set of truly foundational values against future erosion by those wielding the state's power, it is natural to measure suggested violations of due process against the foundational features of American justice – those envisaged by the founding generation. Indeed, that works pretty well for cases affecting physical liberty, for Anglo-American traditions emphasise procedural protections (as indeed is suggested by the very phrase 'due process', coming as it does from 14th-century England and a Magna Carta heritage). But for those who conceive the Constitution as a 'living instrument', a focus on history, tradition and original public meaning does not always answer modern questions. In *Bowers v Hardwick*,[55] for example, a majority held there was no 'due process right' to engage in sodomy precisely because sodomy had been unlawful since antiquity in the English and American tradition. It was only later, in *Lawrence v Texas*,[56] that a different conclusion was reached, with the majority reframing the question and finding that tradition in fact respected privacy (and thus no criminality) for intimate sexual practices of consenting couples. It was in 2015 in *Obergefell v Hodges* that a five–four majority critiqued most cogently the pitfalls – at least for living constitutionalists – of searching for liberty rights in tradition.[57] Writing for the majority, Justice Kennedy observed that 'history and tradition guide and discipline this inquiry but do not set its outer boundaries'. The appropriate inquiry 'respects our history and learns from it without allowing the past alone to rule the present'.[58]

How then did the Canadian Supreme Court handle all this in *Carter*? Recall the Court found unanimously that the prohibitions on assisted suicide and euthanasia were inconsistent with the principles of fundamental justice – overruling *Rodriguez*. Did it read the history differently, or make a fresh value judgment as in *Obergefell* and *Lawrence*? Essentially, the latter. By 2015, the approach to fundamental justice in Canada had undergone something of a metamorphosis into

55 *Bowers v Hardwick* 478 US 186 (1986).
56 *Lawrence v Texas* 539 US 558 (2003).
57 *Obergefell v Hodges* 576 US 644 (2015).
58 At 664 (page 11 of the slip opinion).

what has been described as 'instrumental rationality'.[59] That is to say, the principles of fundamental justice require that when laws restrict life, liberty or security those laws must not exhibit the substantive defects of being 'arbitrary,' 'overbroad' or 'grossly disproportionate'. And to determine whether they do, it is necessary to identify the objective of the impugned measure and the means used to attain it.

The Supreme Court accepted the trial judge's finding that the legislative objective behind laws prohibiting assisted suicide and consent to death was the protection of 'vulnerable' persons from committing suicide or agreeing to their death at a time of weakness.[60] But, it said, the law in fact impacted the choices of both the 'vulnerable' and the 'non-vulnerable'. It impacted upon their *right to life* (because the non-availability of assisted suicide might lead persons to end their own lives early while physically able, whereas its availability would enable assisted death later and so allow more life); their *liberty* (because liberty was said to include a freedom to make fundamental decisions including about one's time of death); and their *security of the person* (because non-availability of assisted death might prolong pain and suffering). The Court rejected the submission of the Attorney-General that the purpose of the law was not to protect the vulnerable, but to protect all people precisely because *all* might be vulnerable and that no administrative system could establish who was and who was not. But that argument, said the court, had 'the potential to short-circuit the analysis':[61]

> If the object of the prohibition is stated broadly as "the preservation of life", it becomes difficult to say that the means used to further it are overbroad or grossly disproportionate. The outcome is to this extent foreordained.

In other words, the Court's focus was on applying the template of instrumental rationality. The Court therefore determined that the law's objective was to protect the vulnerable. Of course, that might equally be said to have foreordained the outcome actually reached – that the law was impermissibly 'overbroad' precisely because it banned even the

59 The phrase 'failures of instrumental rationality' appears first in Hamish Stewart *Fundamental Justice: Section 7 of the Canadian Charter of Rights and Freedoms* (Irwin Law, Toronto, 2019) at 151, and was cited with approval in Peter Hogg "The Brilliant Career of Section 7 of the Charter" (2012) 58 Sup Ct L R (2d) 195 at 209. Both references were cited in *Bedford v Canada* [2013] 3 SCR 1101 at [107].

60 *Carter v Canada*, above n 46, at [74].

61 At [77].

non-vulnerable, who needed no protection, from seeking assisted death. A perfectly tailored law would protect the vulnerable and not impede the non-vulnerable.[62]

Conspicuous by its absence was the substantive inquiry: whether the prohibition of assisted suicide was itself consistent with fundamental justice – in the sense that it reflected a deep and longstanding concern of Canadian law reflecting some sort of societal consensus. The majority in *Rodriguez* had seen it that way:[63]

> While the principles of fundamental justice are concerned with more than process, reference must be made to principles which are "fundamental" in the sense they would have general acceptance among reasonable people. From the review that I have conducted above, I am unable to discern anything approaching unanimity with respect to the issue before us. ... To the extent there is a consensus, it is that human life must be respected and we must be careful not to undermine the institutions that protect it.

In short, the Supreme Court in *Carter* essentially framed the question differently from *Rodriguez*. It was not searching for a consensus among Canadians but defining the rights of individuals as a legal matter. The decisive sentence in the judgment is this: 'the law has come to recognise that, in certain circumstances, an individual's choice about the end of her life is entitled to respect'.[64] In reaching that conclusion the Court dispatched any concern about wider societal interests advanced by the law: the focus of s 7 itself was on the individual. Wider interests, said the Court, could be advanced only under s 1 (the 'reasonable limits' provision of the Charter) and formed no part of the inquiry into whether fundamental justice principles were breached in relation to the individuals before the Court. But when it came to consideration of s 1 the question became whether a law that was 'inherently flawed'[65] could ever be a reasonable limit? No, said the Court, because a less intrusive law was possible – one that regulated end-of-life decisions by requiring assessments of competence

62 For a perceptive article on the attribution of legislative purpose in Canada, see Hart Schwartz "Circularity, Tautology and Gamesmanship: 'Purpose' Based Proportionality-Correspondence Analysis in Sections 15 and 7 of the Charter" (2016) 35 Nat J Con L 105.

63 *Rodriguez v British Colombia (Attorney-General)*, above n 48, at [173].

64 *Carter v Canada*, above n 46, at [63].

65 At [95].

and voluntariness.[66] All therefore turned on the attribution of the law's purpose. A declaration of invalidity was therefore made, suspended for twelve months to allow the creation of such a regime.

Against this background, the operative reasoning in *Seales* may now be understood. First, New Zealand's s 8 contains only a right not to be deprived of life: there is no right to 'liberty' or 'security of the person'. The critical part of the *Carter* template, then, was its finding that 'life' was implicated. Here Collins J adopted a submission that 'mirror[ed] the approach taken in *Carter*' – that 'section 8 does not … require all human life be preserved in all circumstances', that 'the right to life may be engaged when the law … impose[s] an increased risk of death', and that Ms Seales was forced 'to consider taking her life earlier than she otherwise would if her general practitioner could assist her to die'. Collins J accepted these propositions without further discussion.[67]

That brought him to the principles of fundamental justice, where Collins J 'again found it helpful to resort to Canadian law'.[68] The same three aspects of Canadian fundamental justice were articulated. Obviously, it was 'overbreadth' that was of most interest since it had been the engine room of the *Carter* case. But at that point Collins J departed from *Carter*, concluding that the impugned New Zealand Crimes Act provisions were *not* overbroad. The reason lay in s 41 of the Crimes Act 1961, which says that anyone who intervenes to prevent a person committing suicide (and who might therefore be charged with assault) is 'justified' in their use of force. This, Collins J accepted, signified a legislative intention that *any* suicide can lawfully be prevented: s 41 could not be read as aimed only at irrational suicides while excluding those resulting from a rational decision to end one's life in the face of terminal illness. In short, the overall purpose of the Crimes Act was the protection of all life, not just the life of the vulnerable. On that basis, the ban on assisting suicide was not overbroad. There was therefore no 'inconsistency with the principles of fundamental justice' and no breach of s 8.

Collins J concluded thus:[69]

> The complex legal, philosophical, moral and clinical issues raised by Ms Seales' proceedings can only be addressed by Parliament passing legislation to amend

---

66 At [113].
67 *Seales v Attorney-General*, above n 44, at [166].
68 At [169].
69 At [211].

> the effect of the Crimes Act. I appreciate Parliament has shown little desire to engage in these issues ... However the fact that Parliament has not been willing to address the issues raised by Ms Seales' proceeding does not provide me with a licence to depart from the constitutional role of judges in New Zealand.

That sentiment seemed to resonate with the New Zealand media and the citizenry.[70] A decision to legalise euthanasia was not to be expected from judges. The sort of inquiry a court can make over a three-day hearing of one person's case seems no substitute for inquiries and parliamentary debates taken over a much longer period with public input. But was Collins J's decision *legally* correct? Could a suitably motivated judge have decided differently? I think so.

Recall that one is in the arena of s 8 if a life has been 'deprived' other than on grounds 'consistent with the principles of fundamental justice'. The judicial approach now common to Canada and New Zealand has been to compartmentalise these inquiries – that is, to ask, first, if life has been (or would be) deprived by operation of a law and, if so, to assess the law's consistency with fundamental justice. On that basis, and given Collins J's finding that life *was* potentially deprived by the prohibition on assisted suicide, it could just as easily have been said that the existence of s 41 did not so much *prevent* a finding of inconsistency as *add* to the reasons for it. If there is in fact a constitutional right to something (here, not to be deprived of life through being denied assistance in one's suicide), the fact that the legislation 'justifies' those who seek to impede such a suicide only makes the law's inconsistency all the more obvious. In my view, the presence of s 41 was not the 'escape hatch' from the relentless logic of the *Carter* template, even though I agree some sort of escape was needed to preserve the matter as one for Parliament. In short, the *Seales* judgment demonstrated judicial creativity in achieving judicial restraint. To be clear, the path taken by Collins J was certainly available, but another was possible, and in my view more compelling.

The real solution to the case lay in posing and answering the direct question: *is* there in fact a 'principle of fundamental justice' that rules out prohibiting assisted suicide save where a regulatory regime exists to allow assisted suicide for those found to be non-vulnerable? That is not a technical question about the instrumental rationality of any particular law, but rather a question about whether there is a societal consensus on

---

70 See Editorial "Judge unfairly targeted in Lucretia Seales right-to-die case" *Dominion Post* (Wellington, 10 June 2015).

a contested issue of morality involving numerous considerations. The American due process jurisprudence confronts this explicitly by focusing on whether there is a fundamental liberty right that should be recognised. A court may well decide that there is – and take responsibility for so deciding – as, in the context of abortion, it did in *Roe v Wade*, and in relation to same-sex marriage has since done in *Obergefell v Hodges*, but (after careful analysis) no judge in *Washington v Glucksberg* did in relation to euthanasia. Contrast that with the Supreme Court of Canada in *Carter* where the process of deeming the law's objective to be 'protecting the life of the vulnerable' (ostensibly for analytical purposes) – and then invalidating it for overbreadth because the non-vulnerable are also restrained – seemed to dress a judicial policy choice in the garb of legal technique.

The UK cases have not gone down this path, in part because the underlying right in the European Convention on Human Rights is different and the European Court's focus is not on instrument rationality but on substantive justifications for euthanasia and assisted suicide. In *R (Nicklinson) v Ministry of Justice* the plaintiffs invoked the 'right to private life' in Article 8 of the Convention,[71] which had in earlier cases been held by the European Court of Human Rights to include a right to make fundamental decisions such as how and when to end one's life – particularly to avoid a distressing and undignified end. But Article 8.2 allows the possibility of restrictions on private life, and the European Court had ruled that the need to protect the vulnerable is a legitimate reason for a *blanket* restriction on assisted suicide (that is, a prohibition with no need for a regime sorting out the non-vulnerable), and that such a law is not disproportionate (the Court does not use the Canadian expression 'overbroad').[72] That still left the UK Supreme Court to decide for itself whether it was right for the UK to have such a law, or whether (as in Canada) it should rule that a mechanism for separating the vulnerable from the non-vulnerable was a legal requirement.

The members of the Supreme Court in *Nicklinson* then went in various directions. For four (Lords Sumption, Clarke, Reed and Hughes) the question whether assisted suicide ought to be lawful belonged, in principle, to Parliament alone – due to the multiple factors involved and its moral complexity. For three (Lords Neuberger, Mance and Wilson), it was not categorically inappropriate for the courts to assess the compatibility of

71 *R (Nicklinson) v Ministry of Justice* [2014] UKSC 38, [2015] AC 657.

72 *Pretty v United Kingdom* (2002) 35 EHRR 1 (ECHR) at [76].

English law on this topic, but it was still premature to do so in advance of Parliament itself debating the matter – something scheduled to occur in the (then) near future. For their part, Lord Kerr and Lady Hale would have declared the statutory prohibitions incompatible for essentially *Carter*-type reasons.

The UK Parliament did debate euthanasia, but no legislation resulted. Subsequently, a further case has raised similar issues, but the English Court of Appeal dismissed the claim and the Supreme Court refused leave to appeal, observing:[73]

> Under the United Kingdom's constitutional arrangements only Parliament could change this law. But the Supreme Court, if it thought it right, could make a declaration that the law was incompatible with the Convention rights, leaving it to Parliament to decide what, if anything, to do about it. The questions for the court would therefore be twofold: (1) is the hard and fast rule banning all assistance to commit suicide a justified interference with the Convention rights of those who wish for such assistance? (2) If it is not, is it appropriate to make a declaration in this case? These are questions upon which the considered opinions of conscientious judges may legitimately differ. Indeed they differ among the members of this Panel.

Looking around the world, it is really only Canada that has so far deduced a fully-formed right to assisted suicide and euthanasia from its constitution, and Collins J was right to resist the siren song of the *Carter* template in New Zealand.[74] As a first instance judge striving to produce a judgment before Ms Seales passed away, he did not have the luxury of time and consideration enjoyed by the Supreme Courts of Canada, the US and the UK. But he found a path that left the matter for Parliament, even if another differently motivated judge (starting from the premise that the world is divisible into the vulnerable and non-vulnerable who simply need to be identified as such by an administrative regime) may not have been deterred by s 41 of the Crimes Act (simply adding s 41 to the list of provisions declared inconsistent). This was creativity in the service of judicial restraint, and was, I think, the right approach.

---

73 *Conway v Secretary of State for Justice United Kingdom Supreme Court* (27 November 2018) at [7]. The panel comprised Lady Hale and Lords Reed and Kerr who were, as the quoted passage says, on different sides in *Nicklinson*.

74 The approach taken by the Montana Supreme Court in *Baxter v Montana* 2009 MT 449 turned on interpretation of a provision of the state's criminal law. The same appears true in Switzerland.

4. SEX DISCRIMINATION AND SAME-SEX MARRIAGE

One of the themes of modern anti-discrimination law is its reckoning with new conceptions of identity and relationships and fitting them into established ideas about how identity and relationships are expressed in language. In New Zealand, as elsewhere, we have seen shifts in meaning of the word 'spouse' and 'marriage,' some wrought by judicial interpretation and others by legislation.

For present purposes, we can begin with *Quilter v Attorney-General*.[75] This was fought over whether the restriction of 'marriage' in the Marriage Act 1955 to marriages between men and women was discriminatory against persons seeking a same-sex marriage licence.[76] This involved deciding what marriage *is* – for it was possible to define it in a way making it apposite only for opposite-sex unions. In 2001, Canada's Supreme Court went more broadly, holding that the 'common law definition' of marriage (a union of one man and one woman) was indeed discriminatory because it excluded same-sex couples who had a legitimate claim to its benefits.[77] But in *Quilter* in 1998 the New Zealand Court of Appeal (save for Thomas J) was not prepared to go that far – albeit dividing in their reasons. Three judges gave brief explanations as to why, in their view, it was not discriminatory at all to exclude same-sex couples from marriage. These reasons rested on an established social consensus that, they said, a court simply could not disavow. Thomas J held that exclusion from marriage was indeed discriminatory; the fifth judge, Tipping J, decided he need not finally determine that question given that the Marriage Act clearly allowed only opposite-sex marriage and (as all judges agreed) that conclusion was enough to decide the case.[78]

---

75 *Quilter v Attorney-General* [1998] 1 NZLR 523 (CA).

76 The Act did not define 'marriage', but it was accepted that, at the time of its drafting, the term carried its common law meaning – that is, a union between persons of opposite sex.

77 *Reference Re Same-Sex Marriage* 2004 SCC 79, [2004] 3 SCR 79. This followed a decision by the Ontario Court of Appeal – *Halpern v Canada (Attorney-General)* [2003] OJ 2268 – that found the common law definition of marriage to violate s 15 of the Charter. The federal government chose not to appeal this, instead drafting what would become the Civil Marriage Act 2005 and referring it to the Supreme Court for an advisory opinion.

78 This was the case that contained the seeds of what blossomed into the judicial declaration of inconsistency affirmed in *Attorney-General v Taylor* [2018] NZSC 104, [2019] 1 NZLR 213.

Of present interest is the judgment of Keith J, who, like Richardson and Gault JJ, determined that the heterosexual institution of marriage was not discriminatory in terms of s 19 of the Bill of Rights. Keith J considered that neither s 19 nor the ICCPR provision on which it is based, Article 26, should be taken to 'reach' the matter of same-sex marriage. Consequently, Keith J disavowed any reliance on s 5, rejecting the idea that the Marriage Act was discriminatory but only reasonably so.[79] The same appears to be true of Richardson and Gault JJ, the latter observing that the historical definition of marriage 'should be ruled unjustifiable only by the legislature because of the social policy implications'.[80]

It is not entirely clear that there is, in fact, any textual basis for the idea that s 19 'reaches' some sorts of matters and not others.[81] Indeed, the subsequent history of s 19 suggests it is far-reaching indeed – and in any event the court's approach in *Quilter* has now been overtaken by the holding in *Ministry of Health v Atkinson* (that s 19 is infringed by different treatment based on a prohibited ground, with all questions of justification needing to be resolved under the test set out in s 5 of the Bill of Rights).[82] But Justice Keith offered the concept of 'reach' as a mode of steering the courts away from reckoning with what was then a matter of considerable social controversy. It is difficult to resist calling all these three judges' approach creative – once again in the cause of preserving an issue for Parliamentary resolution. In fact, that was to come 15 years later.[83]

The *Quilter* case may usefully be compared to two recent decisions of the Supreme Court of the US. The first is *Obergefell v Hodges*, mentioned above, where a majority of 5–4 declared that liberty in the 14th Amendment – already held to include a fundamental right to

79 *Quilter v Attorney-General*, above n 75, at 555.
80 At 527.
81 The idea of s 19 turning on its 'reach' might be said to represent a strong strain of so-called 'originalism,' often associated with conservative judging. The general idea of originalism is that interpreters seek an 'original public meaning' (how the words would be understood at the time by their intended audience). Even so, it is hard to imagine that an original audience would see in the words of s 19 any semantic basis for the non-application of s 19 to certain types of controversies, such as those that Parliament ought to decide. I would read the idea of 'reach' in Keith J's judgment as essentially a different way of putting the point that the social consensus lying behind marriage is a matter to be disturbed only by Parliament, rather like one group of Law Lords did (as to assisted suicide) in *Nicklinson*.
82 *Ministry of Health v Atkinson* [2012] NZCA 184, [2012] 3 NZLR 456.
83 Marriage (Definition of Marriage) Amendment Act 2013.

marry – included the right to marry a person of one's own sex. Such a right, said Justice Kennedy for the court, was 'inherent in the concept of individual autonomy', 'offered the hope of companionship' to everyone, met 'children's best interests', and 'contributed to social order'. That was a substantive appraisal of whether such a right existed on its merits. In New Zealand it is conceivable that, if the 2013 legislation allowing same-sex marriage had not been enacted, a court might in 2015 (the year in which *Obergefell* was decided) have reached a similar conclusion. But how? There is no right to liberty in the New Zealand Bill of Rights Act 1990. Here the second recent US case is illustrative.

In 2020, in *Bostock v Clayton County*,[84] the court considered three conjoined cases brought under the Civil Rights Act 1964, which prohibits discrimination in employment on the basis of race, colour, religion, sex or national origin. Two of the cases concerned persons claiming they were dismissed from their jobs because they were gay; the third involved a man allegedly fired because he had resolved to live and work as a woman. The issue was whether these persons had been dismissed because of their sex, or whether it was in fact their sexual orientation or transgender status (these not being explicitly included in the Act as prohibited grounds of discrimination). The court, by a majority of 6–3, found that sex was indeed the operative factor in the decisions. Justice Gorsuch, writing for the majority, said that the relevance of sex to the dismissals was inescapable: a dismissal for being gay 'penalizes a person identified as male at birth for traits or actions that it tolerates in an employee identified as female at birth',[85] and the transgendered person is dismissed for being one sex at birth and another today.[86] Coming from a conservative judge this raised eyebrows in conservative circles, as did the fact that Chief Justice Roberts also joined the majority to make (along with the four votes of the liberal block) a majority of six–three. The contrary view, put strongly by Justice Alito in dissent, was that this 'textual approach' flew in the face of expectations in 1964 about what the Civil Rights Act would cover (we might say, 'reach'). Justice Alito's view was that it was manifestly not the man's (or a woman's) sex that prevents either marrying someone of their own sex, but their sexual orientation – something proved by postulating that an employer could well dismiss or refuse to hire persons of

84 *Bostock v Clayton County* 590 US __ (2020).
85 At 10 per Gorsuch J.
86 At 19.

homosexual orientation without ever having to know what their sex was. A similar analysis could be made of the transgender ground.

Precisely these arguments had featured in *Quilter*. The 'Gorsuch approach' was accepted by Thomas J who alone would have declared the Marriage Act inconsistent with s 19 of the Bill of Rights for not allowing same sex marriage.[87] Conversely, Gault J had applied the 'Alito approach': that no ground of discrimination was involved because no different treatment here would be accorded to a person of different gender in the same situation.[88] Of the available arguments a majority in *Quilter* was minded to adopt those that steered the matter away from a judicial resolution and back to Parliament where, they felt, it belonged. I suspect it is well possible that at another time – and had the law about same sex marriage not been enacted in 2013 – a differently constituted court might have travelled the path of Justice Gorsuch.[89]

Lest it be thought that all my examples have involved judicial creativity in the service of keeping courts out of issues best resolved by Parliament, consider a recent High Court decision on the meaning of 'spouse' in the Adoption Act 1955. That Act is notoriously dated, but so far the human rights imperative has seen the word 'spouse' in s 3(2) (which requires that two persons adopting jointly must be spouses) interpreted to include de facto 'spouses'.[90] These were judgments well-capable of being labelled activist but are probably now regarded as mainstream, especially when regard is had to Parliament's instruction in s 6 of the Bill of Rights Act that courts prefer 'rights-consistent' over inconsistent interpretation of statutes. All that said, the case of *Re Gordon* in 2019 went a step further when it held that 'spouse' also includes a 'former spouse'.[91] (The two applicants had divorced and married other partners, but had continued – as separated couples often do even if in new relationships – to share the care of the

87 *Quilter v Attorney-General*, above n 75, at 535 (discrimination on the basis of sex) and 555 ('contrary to s 19 of the Bill of Rights').

88 At 527.

89 Having done so it would have been able to establish a difference in treatment based on a prohibited ground of discrimination, leaving it to the Crown to defend the 'reasonableness' (in terms of s 5 of the Bill of Rights) of the limit placed (on the right against discrimination) by the traditional concept of marriage. As *Quilter* shows it is easy to take the case in either direction from that point, so that much depends on judicial inclination to do so.

90 *Re Adoption by Paul and Hauraki* [1993] NZFLR 266, and, more recently, *Re Application by AMM and KJO to adopt* [2010] NZFLR 629 (HC). See also the somewhat contrary decision in *Adoption Action Inc v Attorney-General* [2016] NZHRRT 9.

91 *Re Gordon* [2019] NZHC 184, [2020] 2 NZLR 436.

daughter they had fostered since she was two years old and who now, at eighteen years old, wished her adoption to be completed.) *That* strikes me as judicial creativity, although it must be admitted that the case's wider implications are fairly limited, Parliament could not be expected to resolve the issue, and the outcome was happy and individually oriented. My only hesitation is that it is difficult to advise clients about the meaning of statutes when interpretive possibilities such as these may (or may not) be in play.[92]

5. SOME CONCLUSIONS

In each of the three areas of controversy – abortion, euthanasia and same-sex marriage – New Zealand courts have striven to leave space for Parliamentary resolution. In my view, they have exercised a degree of creativity to achieve that, in cases where very plausible contrary arguments were available and vigorously pressed. I would go so far as to say that there is a more or less settled tradition of deference to Parliament and the democratic process, at least in this field. There are many other areas of contentious litigation that I have not discussed, especially in the field of Māori property rights and the high-level implications of the Treaty of Waitangi, where the courts have not similarly ceded the decision-making territory to Parliament and legislation. That is not at all unexpected when regard is had to the nature of these issues concerning as they do property and similar rights not apt for legislative resolution via a Parliamentary majority. (Of course, Parliament may well *respond* to judicial declarations

92 The *Gordon* case is discussed elsewhere in this volume by Taylor Burgess, which prompts me to set out my misgivings a little more fully. The expression 'former spouse' seems to me to be the equivalent of 'not currently a spouse', and it is difficult to regard that as a 'reasonably possible' meaning of 'spouse' (which, according to the Supreme Court in *R v Hansen* [2007] NZSC 7, [2007] 3 NZLR 1, it would need to be in order to be adopted as an available meaning). In a key paragraph ([36]), Courtney J says: 'It is obvious from the previous cases that have grappled with the meaning of "spouses" in this context that conformity to a stereotypical relationship is no longer required. To be spouses for the purposes of s 3(2), so that a joint application is permitted, no longer requires applicants to be a particular sex or sexuality or even to be living together. What it requires is an actual or potential parent/child relationship in a substantive sense. Current social norms recognise that the commitment of parents to their children does not cease simply because the legal relationship between them no longer exists. Interpreting "spouses" in s 3(2) as encompassing "former spouses" does no more than recognise this.' All that is true, except perhaps the last three sentences.

of rights, and the legislative sequels to the case of *Ngati Apa v Attorney-General* concerning Māori rights over the foreshore and seabed surrounding New Zealand are good examples.[93])

The enactment of the New Zealand Bill of Rights Act 1990 was, certainly in hindsight and perhaps even at the time, the very model of the New Zealand approach. It is often said that the citizenry rejected the earlier White Paper proposal for a supreme bill of rights precisely because of its concern over social policy decisions being made by non-elected judges. But, for whatever reason, the 'New Zealand model' of a Bill of Rights, permitting judicial declarations of legislative inconsistency but not invalidation, has struck a chord also in the UK and two Australian states which adopted comparable models. The last word is left to Parliament.

Some might argue that because the last word belongs to Parliament a judicial view is quite appropriate in these cases and ought not to be withheld, since it is ultimately not dispositive and contributes to a 'dialogue' between the two branches. But the very existence of the Bill of Rights means that declarations of inconsistency with rights are formal statements of law – albeit (in some cases) law about a contentious social issue.[94] As Justice Heath said when declaring the ban on prisoner voting inconsistent, it was his obligation to 'declare the true legal position'.[95]

Yes, we certainly recognise the unceasing commitment of parents to their children endures even when a relationship no longer exists. But the Adoption Act seems to require a 'spousal' relationship between the two adopters, constituted by something other than their declared intent to 'substantively be parents' to a potential adoptee. Recall the meaning ascribed to the word 'spouse' has to work in cases where applicants have not yet engaged in being parents to the putative adoptee, who will often be a newborn baby (as the judge acknowledges by her use of the word 'potential' in the third to last sentence). For a case in which the Court of Appeal explores the overall 'fit' of a suggested meaning, and rejects it because of its broader unworkability even where it solves the immediate 'rights problem', see the majority decision (Clifford and Collins JJ) in *Fitzgerald v The Queen* [2020] NZCA 292. But the allure of a rights-consistent meaning that solves the immediate problem has to be admitted: see the judgment of Collins J in *Fitzgerald* (and subsequently, on further appeal, the Supreme Court majority in *R v Fitzgerald* [2021] SCNZ 131). Note also the creativity displayed by three members of the Court of Appeal in *R v Poumako* [2000] 2 NZLR 695 at [40] (who would have limited the objectionable retrospectivity of the law in that case to a period of 15 days, instead of indefinitely, since that was an 'available meaning'; compare Henry and Thomas JJ (at [59]–[64] and [82]–[84]) who could see no reason to adopt a meaning that Parliament clearly did not intend).

93 *Ngati Apa v Attorney-General* [2003] NZCA 117, [2003] 3 NZLR 643.

94 *Attorney-General v Taylor* [2019] NZSC 18, [2019] 1 NZLR 213 per Elias CJ at [101].

95 *Taylor v Attorney-General* [2015] NZHC 1706, [2015] 3 NZLR 791 at [70].

That is precisely why creativity is on occasion deployed to refrain from decisions where – as several Law Lords put it in *Nicklinson* – a court is invited to decide, as 'law', what is in fact a polycentric question of social policy that they are no better equipped to answer than legislators.[96] And it would have a distorting effect on moral controversies if anyone advancing a contrary view is saddled with the burden of arguing why it is necessary to breach the Bill of Rights (judges having declared it would be so). This is the burden placed on Canadian governments that seek to invoke the Charter's so-called 'notwithstanding clause' that permits legislatures to override the Charter for five-year periods. The language of overriding the Charter suggests illegitimacy, even though it might be framed as reasoned disagreement over what the Charter actually requires.

The fact that New Zealand judges have not resolved cases in these controversial areas has probably contributed to the relatively low profile of judges in the national consciousness, at least compared to the US where judges can be (relatively speaking) celebrities. And the somewhat tribal nature of American politics has translated into judges increasingly being identified with the President who appointed them, a phenomenon that has emerged much more strongly in the last twenty or so years. A recent book-length study of the partisan divisions on the US Supreme Court attributes that partisanship not to crass political affiliation, but more to the judges of both 'sides' being elites who are influenced principally by maintaining their reputations amongst those whose opinions they value.[97] These are likely persons known to judges through their (uniformly) elite law school affiliations and professional networks, and indeed their friends. These elite circles of reference mean that the judges are more responsive to 'relevant segments of the social and political elite than to the public as a whole'.[98]

I suspect that this is likely true of New Zealand judges as well, and that judges will wish their judgments to stand up to the scrutiny anticipated from those whose opinions they most respect (and with whom they are most likely to interact). The judges are sworn to do justice, and – as Bruce Harris pointed out – in some cases this will involve legitimate creativity in the cause of actively seeking a just result. But the justice that judges do is the justice of judges rather than legislators, and this can counsel restraint.

96 *Nicklinson*, above n 71.

97 Neal Devins and Laurence Baum *The Company They Keep – How Partisan Divisions Came to the Supreme Court* (Oxford University Press, Oxford, 2019).

98 At 9.

The line between these two ideas is not simple to describe, not least because the Bill of Rights positively empowers judgments about the consistency even of legislation with the rights it affirms.

Yes, the cases we have examined involve some creativity, but a creativity deployed in the cause of judicial restraint. None of the plaintiffs gained the result they sought from the judicial branch. I have suggested that, in the cases discussed, the New Zealand courts appropriately reserved significant moral controversies to the legislature for its resolution (and saw this as resonating with the judicial values to which they aspired). In *Seales* and *Quilter*, at least, the plaintiffs' arguments ultimately prevailed through the democratic process. I am less certain about the *Right to Life* case, which was essentially about the proper working of the legislated 'settlement' of the abortion controversy made by Parliament in 1977. As the overall five–four result shows, that case could have gone either way. But the abortion controversy, too, has now been superseded by legislation – albeit legislation that embraces Parliament's disapproval of sex-discriminatory abortions and the seeds of litigation to come.

THE DEVELOPMENT OF GLOBAL REGULATORY STANDARDS BY INTERNATIONAL COURTS AND TRIBUNALS

Whaling, Tobacco and Renewable Energy

Caroline E Foster*

1. INTRODUCTION

In the penultimate chapter of his book *New Zealand Constitution*, Professor Harris remarks that '[m]odern international law creates normative expectations of what the country should consider providing in domestic law in respect of large areas of generic human activity'.[1]

* Thank you to Paul Rishworth, Sam Bookman and Hanna Wilberg for their comments on this contribution in draft. Themes in this contribution are developed further in Caroline E Foster *Global Regulatory Standards in Environmental and Health Disputes: Regulatory Coherence, Due Regard, and Due Diligence* (Oxford University Press, Oxford, 2021). The case descriptions below also appear in that work with the kind agreement of both Intersentia and Oxford University Press.

1 Bruce Harris *New Zealand Constitution: An Analysis in Terms of Principles* (Thomson Reuters, Wellington, 2018) at 296.

Indeed, international law increasingly regulates matters that are central to domestic public policy. States have become answerable internationally for activity in domains such as health policy, resource management and environmental protection that were previously effectively reserved to the administration of national governments. As a result, international courts and tribunals increasingly find themselves in a position where they must address such matters of domestic public policy in order to resolve international disputes. Further, the applicable international legal rules are often lacking in specificity. The international adjudicatory response has been to engage in the formulation of standards and tests governing states' regulatory activity in finer grain.

The development of regulatory standards can notably be seen in international dispute settlement in the specialised fields of trade and investment protection, in disputes concerning riparian rights, and in the law of the sea, including specifically in areas including international health protection and the law on transboundary harm. International adjudicatory bodies' identification of regulatory standards is by nature ad hoc, and the standard articulated in each case depends on the law that is being applied. However, commonalities are becoming apparent. For instance, the standards frequently take the form of requirements for regulatory coherence, specifying that there be rational relationships between states' regulatory measures and their legitimate objectives. There is considerable debate about whether such standards should go further to incorporate requirements of proportionality between states' regulatory actions and their effects on other states' legal interests. While proportionality might in theory make for better balancing of competing interests it is doubtful that states would wish to subject themselves to the required oversight. Indeed, international law may be too far removed from the daily life of affected populations to offer the institutional mechanisms that would be needed.

International law scholars have worked hard to explain the emergence of regulatory standards, describing these standards with reference to ideas of 'standards of review' and 'methods of review', and in terms of 'deference' to domestic legal authorities.[2] This contribution refers instead to 'regulatory

2 See, for example, Caroline Henckels *Proportionality and Deference in Investor-State Arbitration: Balancing Investment Protection and Regulatory Autonomy* (Cambridge University Press, Cambridge, 2015); Lukasz Gruszczynski and Wouter Werner (eds) *Deference in International Courts and Tribunals: Standard of Review and Margin of Appreciation* (Oxford University Press, Oxford, 2014).

standards' because it takes as a starting point the premise that international courts and tribunals are setting out to resolve regulatory disputes based directly on the interpretation and application of the applicable legal rules and provisions, deriving the standards inherent in these rules and provisions by means of interpretive logic. These standards and the tests used to apply them are not merely methodological devices deployed by international courts in order to be able to address the cases before them. The standards declare the content of the law. Neither are they limited to concepts already found in domestic legal systems, such as rational connection or proportionality. There is a slowly growing jurisprudence on more novel standards such as 'due regard' standards (which oblige states to have regard to other states' legal interests), and on due diligence standards, which set out requirements for states' control of private activities that could affect the populations of other states.

In employing the terminology of regulatory 'standards', this contribution draws on the distinction between rules and standards maintained in the general legal literature, according to which any given law or legal provision may incorporate both rules and standards.[3] While the content of a rule is generally well specified, the content of a standard may need to be determined through judicial or administrative processes.[4] That process is underway in regulatory disputes in international courts and tribunals. The formal prompt for the elaboration of regulatory standards by international courts and tribunals lies in the insufficiently developed formulation of the treaty provisions and international legal rules they are often asked to apply in regulatory disputes. The content of the various standards being articulated by international adjudicatory bodies has the potential to converge over time, with global regulatory standards coming to form part of what is known as global administrative law.[5]

International courts and tribunals do not exclusively bear the burden of developing such standards. As governments come to appreciate that existing treaties are at times too bare for application without further

---

3 Neil MacCormick *Rhetoric and the Rule of Law: A Theory of Legal Reasoning* (Oxford University Press, Oxford, 2005) at 170. See also HLA Hart *The Concept of Law* (Clarendon Press, Oxford, 1961) at 127–128.

4 Duncan Kennedy "Form and Substance in Private Law Adjudication" (1976) 89 Harv L Rev 1685; Pierre Schlag "Rules and Standards" (1985) 33 UCLA L Rev 379.

5 Benedict Kingsbury, Nico Krisch and Richard B Stewart "The Emergence of Global Administrative Law" (2005) 68 LCP 15; Benedict Kingsbury "Frontiers of Global Administrative Law in the 2020s" in Jason NE Varuhas and Shona Wilson Stark (eds) *The Frontiers of Public Law* (Hart Publishing, Oxford, 2019) 41.

elaboration, they may negotiate new forms of provision. Recent trade and investment treaties provide a good illustration. As seen in the Comprehensive and Progressive Agreement for Trans-Pacific Partnership (CPTPP) governments may adopt, adapt or add to the exceptions to the multilateral rules already found in the World Trade Organization (WTO) agreements.[6] Even in the dispute settlement context, judicial development of regulatory standards is influenced by the arguments of the parties to disputes. Global regulatory standards thus develop here under the curatorship of international adjudicatory bodies but in an environment where their content is subject to considerations emphasised by the parties based on their particular case-specific and systemic interests.

The present contribution focusses on the development of regulatory standards in international courts and tribunals, offering an analysis of the interpretive and institutional dynamics involved. In order to provide a broad picture, the contribution analyses three benchmark cases from three different realms of international law: the work of the International Court of Justice, WTO dispute settlement and investment treaty arbitration. Naturally it is possible to view the developments in cases like these as relevant only in the context in which they occur but, given the number of cases involved overall, the body of regulatory standards emerging is recognisable as an important phenomenon.

This new and contemporary dimension to the international judicial role gives international adjudicators a constructive and important influence over the shaping of states' regulatory freedom and obligations across many fields of endeavour. The contribution finds that international adjudicatory bodies have been both pragmatic and creative in elaborating regulatory standards and tests to guide the application of the relevant international law. The interpretive techniques applied frequently involve supplementing textual readings with contextual reasoning and consideration of the effectiveness of the rules at issue in light of their aims. In this respect, they operate near the boundaries of the traditional international judicial role, while remaining within its formal constraints. In some situations, standards and tests are identified in the relevant treaty provisions but require adjudicatory elaboration. In other situations, the standards are

6 Comprehensive and Progressive Agreement for Trans-Pacific Partnership (CPTPP) (signed 8 March 2018, entered into force 30 December 2018), Chapter 29, and in regard to investment Chapter 9, arts 9.10(3)(d), 9.16 and Annex 9-B (Expropriation), art 3(a) and (b). Compare arts 14.11(3) and 14.13(3) relating to digital commerce.

articulated when international courts and tribunals read them into the relevant provisions in order to make these provisions function. However, the level of pragmatism and creativity is similar across both types of situation, as are the interpretive tools employed.

At the same time, international courts and tribunals are sensitive towards the desire of states to remain relatively free from international legal control while ensuring that international law demarcates their legal interests in ways that correspond to the context. Consistent with this, the dominant characteristic of the emerging standards has been their conservatism. The standards articulated by international courts and tribunals are built to accommodate domestic regulatory decision-making with relatively minimal interference by international law, helping preserve the pluralistic relationship between domestic and international legal systems.[7] However for various reasons the appropriateness of relying on international dispute settlement as the process by which such a new body of law should emerge internationally is open to question and requires further consideration. The contribution concludes by asking whether the general public should be given greater opportunity to become aware of and express views on the development of emerging global regulatory standards as an aspect of future global administrative law.

2. THE INTERNATIONAL COURT OF JUSTICE

As the principal judicial organ of the United Nations the International Court of Justice (ICJ or the Court) is a permanent and highly regarded court.[8] The court's decisions carry weight in the international legal community and are viewed as embodying authoritative pronouncements on the content of the law. Although the cases brought before the Court are often complex, they are few in number and disputes relating to environmental and health issues arise only infrequently. While the Court has expertise in dealing with law of the sea cases relating to maritime boundaries, oceans-related cases raising questions about environmental protection have generally been determined

7 James Crawford *Brownlie's Principles of Public International Law* (9th ed, Oxford University Press, Oxford, 2019) at 47; Nico Krisch *Beyond Constitutionalism: The Pluralist Structure of Postnational Law* (Oxford University Press, Oxford, 2010).

8 Malcolm N Shaw *Rosenne's Law and Practice and Practice of the International Court 1920–2015* (5th ed, Brill/Nijhoff, Leiden, 2016).

by the International Tribunal for the Law of the Sea (ITLOS) or by Annex VII arbitral tribunals operating under the United Nations Convention on the Law of the Sea (UNCLOS).[9] There are important cross-currents between these tribunals and the ICJ, especially in relation to the establishment of environmental due diligence standards.[10] However the ICJ proceedings selected as a focus for this contribution arose under the International Convention for the Regulation of Whaling 1946 (ICRW) rather than under the UNCLOS.[11] In the case of *Whaling in the Antarctic* (*Australia v Japan: New Zealand intervening*) the Court made two important contributions to the development of international legal regulatory standards.[12] The first contribution is seen in the Court's search for a reasonable relationship between the design and implementation of Japan's lethal research program and its stated objectives. The second contribution is found in the Court's identification of the obligation for parties to the ICRW to give due regard to recommendations of the International Whaling Commission (IWC).

Whaling in the Antarctic (Australia v Japan: New Zealand Intervening)

In the *Whaling in the Antarctic* case the ICJ found that special permits granted for the second Japanese Whale Research Programme under Special Permit in the Antarctic (JARPA II) did not fall within the scientific whaling provision found in Article VIII(1) of the ICRW.[13] Article VIII(1) provides that notwithstanding the other provisions of the Convention, the parties to the Convention may grant their nationals special permits authorising

---

9 United Nations Convention on the Law of the Sea 1833 UNTS 307 (opened for signature 10 December 1982, entered into force 16 November 1994). Arbitration under Annex VII is the standard form of arbitration envisaged in UNCLOS. Arbitration by technical experts is also potentially available under Annex VIII for selected categories of dispute.

10 *Case Concerning the Pulp Mills on the River Uruguay (Argentina v Uruguay)* (Judgment) [2010] ICJ Rep 14; *Responsibilities and Obligations of States Sponsoring Persons and Entities with Respect to Activities in the Area* (Advisory Opinion of 1 February 2011) ITLOS Reports 2011 at 10; *Request for an Advisory Opinion Submitted by the Sub-Regional Fisheries Commission* (Advisory Opinion of 2 April 2015) ITLOS Reports 2015 at 4.

11 International Convention for the Regulation of Whaling 161 UNTS 72 (opened for signature 2 December 1946, entered into force 10 November 1948).

12 *Whaling in the Antarctic (Australia v Japan: New Zealand intervening)* [2014] ICJ Rep 226 (hereafter *Whaling in the Antarctic*).

13 At [247(2)].

them to kill, take and treat whales 'for purposes of scientific research'.[14] The finding that Japan's programme did not fall within Article VIII(1) meant that Japan was obliged to comply with the other obligations imposed by the Convention to refrain from taking whales in the Southern Ocean Whale Sanctuary, to observe a zero-catch limit on commercial whaling, and to comply with a factory ship moratorium. In permitting JARPA II's whaling Japan had acted inconsistently with these obligations.[15]

Rather than looking at the meaning of the term 'scientific', the Court reached the conclusion that the Japanese whaling programme did not fall within the scientific whaling provision in Article VIII(1) instead by applying a test oriented around certain objective characteristics of the programme's design. Specifically, the standard applied by the Court for determining whether Japan's scientific whaling programme was 'for purposes of scientific research' asked whether 'in the use of lethal methods, the programme's design and implementation are reasonable in relation to achieving its stated objectives'.[16] This was consistent with Australia's pleadings,[17] and Japan, too, had discussed JARPA II's operational design in defending it as a scientific whaling programme.[18]

The Court found that JARPA II failed the test.[19] It had not been established that in the use of lethal methods JARPA II's design and implementation were reasonable in relation to achieving its stated objectives.[20] The four main reasons given by the Court for this conclusion included Japan's failure to have analysed the availability of non-lethal sampling methods in the light of advances over the past twenty years[21]

---

14 Article VIII(1) provides that: 'Notwithstanding anything contained in this Convention any Contracting Government may grant to any of its nationals a special permit authorizing that national to kill, take and treat whales for purposes of scientific research subject to such restrictions as to number and subject to such other conditions as the Contracting Government thinks fit, and the killing, taking, and treating of whales in accordance with the provisions of this Article shall be exempt from the operation of this Convention …'.

15 *Whaling in the Antarctic*, above n 12, at [247(3)]–[247(5)].

16 At [67] and [88].

17 *Whaling in the Antarctic (Australia v Japan) Memorial of Australia* (in English, 9 May 2011) 206 at 215.

18 *Whaling in the Antarctic (Australia v Japan: New Zealand intervening)* Verbatim Record (Original Language, 4 July 2013 at 3pm) 22, at 25–88, Professor Iwasawa for Japan, discussing the programme's use of random sampling, investment of effort in non-lethal methods, and vessel tracklines.

19 *Whaling in the Antarctic*, above n 12, at [98]–[227].

20 At [227].

21 At [128]–[144].

and the scale of lethal sampling,[22] as well as the way in which Japan had determined sample sizes[23] and the difference between planned sample sizes and actual take.[24] Additional factors included the programme's open-ended timeframe, its limited scientific output, and the low level of cooperation with other research institutions.[25] On one additional point the Court found in favour of Japan, holding that Japan had complied with its obligations under paragraph 30 of the Schedule to the Convention to notify the IWC Secretary of proposed permits to enable review and comment by the Scientific Committee.[26]

Onlookers might have expected the decision in this case to hinge more closely on the interpretation of Article VIII rather than on a newly identified regulatory coherence test. For instance, the Court could have grounded its decision in the interpretation of the term 'scientific' in the context of the provision and the Convention. However, the Court did not seek closely to interpret the text of the Whaling Convention.[27] The Court began by indicating that Article VIII would be read in context and in light of the Convention's object and purpose.[28] It noted the parties' disagreement on whether conservation or sustainable exploitation were the purposes to be emphasised,[29] but the Court's interpretive process essentially halted here. The judgment turned almost directly to the standard it intended to apply in reviewing Japan's permitting as above.[30] Various of the Separate and Dissenting Opinions criticise the Court for insufficient attention to the interpretation and application of the relevant treaty provisions.[31] A number of judges considered that there was important scope for recognition within an interpretive process of shifts in societal values concerning the use of lethal methods in whale research and in favour of conservation.[32]

---

22 At [145]–[156].

23 At [157]–[198].

24 At [199]–[212].

25 At [213]–[222].

26 At [247(6)].

27 Margaret A Young and Sebastián Rioseco Sullivan "Evolution through the Duty to Cooperate: Implications of the Whaling Case at the International Court of Justice" (2015) 16 Melbourne Journal of International Law 311 at 332.

28 *Whaling in the Antarctic*, above n 12, at [55].

29 At [56]–[58].

30 At [62].

31 Dissenting Opinion of Judge Yusuf at [3]–[4]; Dissenting Opinion of Judge Bennouna at 1, 3 and 5; Dissenting Opinion of Judge Owada at [4]–[12].

32 Dissenting Opinion of Judge Yusuf at [25]–[28], [46]–[47] and [60]; Separate Opinion of Judge Xue at [2]; Separate Opinion of Judge ad hoc Charlesworth at [3]–[5];

The Court's methodological approach was thus the subject of differing views within the Court. Judge Keith endorsed the approach. He underlined that together with other features of the case the contracting parties' common interest in the Convention indicated real limits on the Article VIII permitting power. However he would have reformulated the Court's task to ask whether a contracting government's decision to award a special permit was objectively justifiable in the sense that the decision was supported by coherent scientific reasoning.[33] Judge Abraham had difficulty following the court's reasoning.[34] Judge Yusuf considered the Court's test an extraneous, undefined, obscure and debatable standard of review,[35] resort to which was unexplained and which appeared ungrounded in law and in the practice of the Court.[36]

The Court's reasoning responded closely to the pleadings in the case in a variety of ways. On the core matter of the reasonableness test applied by the Court, the judgment referenced Japan's espousal during pleadings of the idea that a decision should have to be 'supported by coherent reasoning and respectable scientific evidence and to be in this sense objectively justifiable'.[37] This was drawn from the WTO test for assessing whether a WTO Member's measures to protect human, animal and plant life and health are based on a risk assessment under the Agreement on Sanitary and Phytosanitary Measures. The WTO jurisprudence requires a rational or objective relationship between the scientific evidence, the risk assessment and the defending state's trade measures.[38] The Court's reasonableness test bore considerable similarity to the WTO jurisprudence. However, Japan perhaps did not expect the Court to employ the notion of reasonableness

---

and Separate Opinion of Judge Cançado Trindade at [24]–[71]. See also Separate Opinion of Judge ad hoc Charlesworth at [6]–[10] on the reinforcing influence of the precautionary approach.

33 Declaration of Judge Keith at [8].

34 Dissenting Opinion of Judge Abraham at [32]–[33].

35 Dissenting Opinion of Judge Yusuf at [3]–[4], [24] and [27]–[28].

36 At [12]–[16].

37 *Whaling in the Antarctic*, above n 12, at [66]; Verbatim Record (Original Language, 15 July 2013 at 3pm) 60, Mr Lowe for Japan. See also the formulation in Declaration of Judge Keith at [8], who would have articulated the test as requiring the Contracting Government's decision to award a special permit to be objectively justifiable in the sense that the decision is supported by coherent scientific reasoning, and Separate Opinion of Judge Xue at [16].

38 *United States – Continued Suspension of Obligations in the EC – Hormones Dispute, Report of the Appellate Body* (16 October 2008) WT/DS320/AB/R, DSR 2008:X, 3507 at [590]; *Australia – Measures Affecting the Importation of Apples from New Zealand, Report of the Appellate Body* (29 November 2010) WT/DS367/AB/R, DSR 2010:V, 2175 at [204]–[231] and [249]–[262].

in quite the way that it did. Japan had emphasised that in its view the Court might assess the reasonableness of Japan's permitting decision in terms of its having been made in good faith, and being neither arbitrary nor capricious,[39] nor manifestly unreasonable.[40] These criteria are all rather more general than the test on which the Court ultimately settled. Judge Owada considered the Court to have taken Japan's remarks out of context and grossly to have misrepresented what the parties were prepared to accept as common ground.[41]

Australia had from the beginning emphasised that compliance with the ICRW in good faith implied reasonableness, requiring the exercise of a right in a way that was appropriate and necessary for the purpose of the right.[42] Australia considered the design and implementation of the whaling program was driven by non-scientific purposes and urged the Court to consider a number of ways in which this was so.[43] Good faith obliged the parties to apply treaty provisions in a reasonable way and such that their purposes could be realised. This had been recognised in the ICJ decision concerning the River Danube in the *Gabčikovo-Nagymaros* case.[44] Australia further directed much of this argument to the idea that, due to its characteristics, Japan's whaling could not be considered 'scientific'.[45]

New Zealand for its part as intervenor had urged the possibility and importance of employing an objective approach in assessing permitting

39 *Whaling in the Antarctic*, above n 12, at [65]; Counter-Memorial of Japan (in English, 9 March 2012) at 411–412; Verbatim Record (Original Language, 4 July 2013 at 10am) at 17–18, Mr Lowe for Japan.

40 *Whaling in the Antarctic*, above n 12, at [65]. See also Verbatim Record (Original Language, 15 July 2013 at 10am) at 24, Mr Akhavan for Japan.

41 Dissenting Opinion of Judge Owada [29]–[38].

42 Memorial of Australia (in English, 9 May 2011) at 163. See also Written Observations of New Zealand (in English, 4 April 2013) at 23–24.

43 Memorial of Australia (in English, 9 May 2011) at 3, 77–86, 113–114, 206–252, 257–259 and 261–270. See also Verbatim Record (Original Language, 26 June 2013 at 3pm) at 53, Professor Crawford for Australia; Verbatim Record (Original Language, 27 June 2013 at 3pm) at 41, 48–49 and 53–55, Professor Crawford for Australia.

44 Verbatim Record (Original Language, 26 June 2013 at 3pm) at 31, Professor Crawford for Australia, citing *Gabčikovo-Nagymaros Project (Hungary v Slovakia) (Judgment)* [1997] ICJ Rep 7 at [142]. See also Verbatim Record (Original Language, 8 July 2013 at 10am) at 21, Mr Finlayson for New Zealand, and at 41–42 Dr Ridings for New Zealand invoking the court's remarks in *Certain Questions of Mutual Assistance in Criminal Matters (Djibouti v France) (Judgment)* [2008] ICJ Rep 177 at 229 as well as the *Dispute Regarding Navigational Rights (Costa Rica v Nicaragua) (Judgment)* [2009] ICJ Rep 213 to the effect that a discretion must be exercised in good faith and according to the specific purpose for which it is given.

45 See, for example, Memorial of Australia (in English, 9 May 2011) at 206–243.

decisions to see whether they constituted a proper exercise of the Article VIII discretion.[46] The Court could evaluate a permitting decision with reference to a programme's objective features, including by examining its methodology, design and characteristics.[47] Relevant aspects of a programme included its scale, structure, the manner in which it was conducted, and its results.[48] New Zealand referred to WTO Appellate Body guidance on how an objective determination could be made of whether a trade-inhibiting measure was being applied so as to afford domestic economic protection, and specifically outlined how this could be applied in the context of Article VIII.[49] Ultimately, as we have seen, this was the course adopted by the Court, demonstrating the significance of third-party submissions in international dispute settlement.

The additional feature of the judgment in *Whaling in the Antarctic* of significance in this contribution is the reliance it places on the concept of due regard. Specifically the Court considered that states party to the ICRW had an obligation to give 'due regard' to IWC recommendations calling for assessment of the feasibility of non-lethal alternatives, founded on a duty to cooperate with the Commission and its Scientific Committee.[50] The concept of cooperation was one on which New Zealand had placed some weight in its pleadings, emphasising the importance of meaningful cooperation, incorporating a commitment to take into account the views of others and potentially to modify one's own approach.[51]

The concept of due regard for the views of the IWC had been floated by Australia.[52] Australia considered that due regard was required as a

---

46 Declaration of Intervention by New Zealand (20 November 2012) at 16; Written Observations of New Zealand (4 April 2013) at 28–30. See also e.g., Memorial of Australia (9 May 2011) at 152.

47 Declaration of Intervention by New Zealand (in English, 20 November 2012) 16–18; Written Observations of New Zealand (in English, 4 April 2013) at 2, 28–30, 33–35, 63 and 65.

48 Written Observations of New Zealand (in English, 4 April 2013) at 35, 63 and 65; Verbatim Record (Original Language, 8 July 2013 at 10am) at 48, Dr Ridings for New Zealand.

49 Written Observations of New Zealand (in English, 4 April 2013) at 33–34 quoting *Japan – Taxes on Alcoholic Beverages*, Report of the Appellate Body (4 October 1996) WT/DS8/AB/R, WT/DS10/AB/R, WT/DS11/AB/R, DSR 1996:I at 97, 29. See also *Whaling in the Antarctic* (*Australia v Japan: New Zealand intervening*) Verbatim Record (Original Language, 8 July 2013 at 10am) at 30, Mr Finlayson for New Zealand.

50 *Whaling in the Antarctic*, above n 12, at [78] and [83].

51 Written Observations of New Zealand (in English, 4 April 2013) at 53, 55, 61 and 62; Verbatim Record (Original Language, 8 July 2013 at 10am) at 43–47, Dr Ridings for New Zealand.

52 Memorial of Australia (in English, 9 May 2011) at 255.

matter of good faith and flowed from the duty to cooperate in achieving the object and purpose of the Whaling Convention.[53] The Court recorded that Japan had accepted that there was a duty to give due consideration to the relevant recommendations while emphasising that they were not binding.[54] The Court reasoned that due regard implies that a permitting state will have carried out analysis to ascertain that lethal sampling is not being used more than necessary in relation to achieving the programme's stated research objectives.[55] The unexplained lack of such analysis and the difficulty in reconciling this with Japan's due regard obligations constituted one of the main reasons why the Court concluded that JARPA II's design and implementation were not reasonable in light of its stated research objectives and thus that the programme was not 'for purposes of scientific research'.[56] It is meaningful that the Court looked for evidence of such analysis from Japan.[57] Dissenting judges were concerned that the Court's approach might be considered to have converted non-binding IWC recommendations into obligations.[58] However, this does not seem to be the case, as the pivotal point in the Court's decision against Japan was not the use of lethal methods per se but the absence of analysis supporting the decision to employ them and of an explanation for this.[59] In this respect the requirement for due regard is reminiscent of the obligation to take adverse interests into consideration when engaged in good faith negotiation, as identified in the *Lac Lanoux* arbitration in 1957.[60]

'Due regard' standards, which may take various forms, potentially operate as an important discipline on state regulatory freedom. In law of the sea disputes, the text of UNCLOS may point tribunals directly to the need to elaborate due regard standards, while in a context such as the *Whaling in*

53 Verbatim Record (Original Language, 26 June 2013 at 3pm) at 53–54, Professor Crawford for Australia.

54 *Whaling in the Antarctic*, above n 12, at [80]. See for instance Counter-Memorial of Japan (in English, 9 March 2012) at 375 and 413. The Court added at [83] that this does not establish a requirement that lethal methods be used only when other methods were unavailable.

55 *Whaling in the Antarctic*, above n 12, at [137].

56 At [138]–[141], [144] and [212].

57 As the Chagos Marine Protected Area Tribunal was to do from the UK in 2015. *Chagos Marine Protected Area (Republic of Mauritius v United Kingdom) (Award)* (2015) 162 ILR 1. See further Caroline E Foster *Science and the Precautionary Principle in International Courts and Tribunals: Expert Evidence, Burden of Proof and Finality* (Cambridge University Press, Cambridge, 2011).

58 *Whaling in the Antarctic*, above n 12, Dissenting Opinion of Judge Abraham at [38]; and Dissenting Opinion of Judge Bennouna at [3].

59 *Whaling in the Antarctic*, above n 12, at [135], [137] and [141].

60 *Lake Lanoux Arbitration (France v Spain)* (1957) 24 ILR 101 at 141.

the Antarctic case they may be encouraged to do so through pleadings and submissions. In contradistinction with the *Whaling in the Antarctic* case, in the majority of cases alluding to due regard requirements due regard is to be paid to the international legal interests of another state, rather than to the views of a collective entity such as the IWC. The diversity of cases in which aspects of due regard are beginning to arise indicates its potential. Read into international law more widely, due regard standards could make an important contribution to international legal relations and could take the pressure off the debate over the need for substantive proportionality testing, and thus avoid the need for international tribunals – removed from the ordinary politics of domestic systems – to determine sensitive substantive policy issues.

In summary, both the Court's reliance on the expectation that a scientific whaling program be reasonable in relation to its stated objectives and its reliance on the concept of due regard were novel. Yet arguably each was grounded in the innate logic and the operation of the ICRW and enabled the Convention's provision on scientific whaling to be applied consistently with the treaty's object and purpose.

3. WORLD TRADE ORGANIZATION DISPUTE SETTLEMENT

The conclusion of the Uruguay Round of multilateral trade negotiations and the establishment of the WTO in 1995 brought to international trade a more judicialised dispute settlement system than that previously relied upon in the General Agreement on Tariffs and Trade (GATT) era, now equipped with a standing Appellate Body. Review of that new dispute settlement system was subsequently mandated in 2001 as part of the agenda for the Doha round of trade negotiations. WTO Members' discontent with various aspects of the system's functioning have meantime culminated in US actions paralysing the Appellate Body's operation through the refusal to make new appointments. Until the impasse can be resolved a number of WTO Members have agreed *inter se* to rely on a Multiparty Interim Appeal-Arbitration Arrangement (MPIA) operating under Article 25 of the WTO Dispute Settlement Undertaking (DSU).[61] It is expected that

---

61 Statement On A Mechanism For Developing, Documenting And Sharing Practices And Procedures In The Conduct Of WTO Disputes – Addendum (30 April 2020) JOB/DSB/1/Add.12 <https://docs.wto.org/>. See also Joost Pauwelyn "WTO Dispute Settlement Post 2019: What to Expect?" (2019) 22 JIEL 297.

reliance will continue to be placed on the previous jurisprudence of the Appellate Body.

The Appellate Body has been a careful and strategic decision-maker in the environment and health arena. It has been sensitive to WTO Members' needs. It has been aware, too, of generalised public concerns that the multinational international trade regime insufficiently or ineptly addresses certain pressing developmental and social needs, human rights and sustainability demands.[62] However, true to its judicial mandate, the Appellate Body applied itself in a focused and judicious way to the disputes that came before it. This said, the lack of specificity in various of the WTO treaty provisions requiring to be applied placed the Appellate Body in a difficult position. Article 3.2 of the DSU states that WTO dispute settlement recommendations and rulings 'cannot add to or diminish the rights and obligations provided in the covered agreements'. At the same time, Article 3.2 describes the dispute settlement system as serving to 'clarify the existing provisions of those agreements in accordance with customary rules of interpretation of public international law'.[63] The reality is that the task of producing the standards and the detail in the law needed to enable the accommodation of competing interests has been left to the dispute settlement system,[64] yet this has had to be done in a manner that as far as possible would not arouse complaint about failure to stay within the bounds of the law as negotiated. The challenge for tribunals in navigating this balance can be seen in the Appellate Body's approach to interpreting the 'necessity' tests found in certain WTO provisions.

The concept of necessity is a pivotal term found in WTO provisions including the 'general exceptions' in Article XX of the GATT and XIV

---

62 Sarah Joseph *Blame it on the WTO? A Human Rights Critique* (Oxford University Press, Oxford, 2011); Robert Howse "The Legitimacy of the World Trade Organization" in Jean-Marc Coicaud and Veijo Heiskanen (eds) *The Legitimacy of International Organizations* (United Nations University Press, New York, 2001) 355; Andrew Lang *World Trade Law after Neoliberalism: Reimagining the Global Economic Order* (Oxford University Press, Oxford, 2011); Gillian Moon and Lisa Toohey (eds) *The Future of International Economic Integration: The Embedded Liberalism Compromise Revisited* (Cambridge University Press, Cambridge, 2018).

63 Article 3.2 reads: 'The dispute settlement system of the WTO is a central element in providing security and predictability to the multilateral trading system. The Members recognize that it serves to preserve the rights and obligations of Members under the covered agreements, and to clarify the existing provisions of those agreements in accordance with customary rules of interpretation of public international law. Recommendations and rulings of the DSB cannot add to or diminish the rights and obligations provided in the covered agreements'.

64 Tomer Broude *International Governance in the WTO: Judicial Boundaries and Political Capitulation* (Cameron May, London, 2004).

of the General Agreement on Trade in Services (GATS). Regulatory measures must be necessary to the regulatory purpose at hand if they are to fall within these exceptions. The Agreement on Technical Barriers to Trade (TBT Agreement),[65] and the Agreement on the Application of Sanitary and Phytosanitary Measures (SPS Agreement),[66] both incorporate requirements that regulatory measures be no more trade restrictive than necessary.

Historically, the Article XX necessity formula was developed in the context of Korea's attempt to rely on one of the subparagraphs of the GATT general exceptions, Article XX(d), in the *Korea – Beef* case.[67] In that case the Appellate Body upheld the Panel's rejection of Korea's assertion that its dual retail system requiring domestic and imported beef to be sold in separate stores was necessary in order to combat the fraudulent and deceptive practice of passing off domestic beef as imported beef in order to secure higher prices. The Panel found, and the Appellate Body agreed, that Korea could instead have adopted targeted control mechanisms employing routine investigation and enforcement practices.

The elaboration of the necessity test in *Korea – Beef* can be understood as a product of interaction between interpretive principles of contextualism and effectiveness, the Appellate Body drawing on and giving effect to

65 Agreement on Technical Barriers to Trade 1994 1868 UNTS 120, LT/UR/A-1A/10, art 2.2: 'Members shall ensure that technical regulations are not prepared, adopted or applied with a view to or with the effect of creating unnecessary obstacles to international trade. For this purpose, technical regulations shall not be more trade-restrictive than necessary to fulfil a legitimate objective, taking account of the risks non-fulfilment would create. Such legitimate objectives are, inter alia: national security requirements; the prevention of deceptive practices; protection of human health or safety, animal or plant life or health, or the environment. In assessing such risks, relevant elements of consideration are, inter alia: available scientific and technical information, related processing technology or intended end-uses of products'.

66 Agreement on the Application of Sanitary and Phytosanitary Measures 1867 UNTS 493, WTO Doc LT/UR/A-1A/12, art 2.2: 'Members shall ensure that any sanitary or phytosanitary measure is applied only to the extent necessary to protect human, animal or plant life or health, is based on scientific principles and is not maintained without sufficient scientific evidence, except as provided for in paragraph 7 of Article 5.' Agreement on the Application of Sanitary and Phytosanitary Measures, art 5.6: 'Without prejudice to paragraph 2 of Article 3, when establishing or maintaining sanitary or phytosanitary measures to achieve the appropriate level of sanitary or phytosanitary protection, Members shall ensure that such measures are not more trade-restrictive than required to achieve their appropriate level of sanitary or phytosanitary protection, taking into account technical and economic feasibility'.

67 *Korea – Measures Affecting Imports of Fresh, Chilled and Frozen Beef*, Appellate Body Report (11 December 2000) WT/DS161/AB/R, DSR 2001:I at 5.

WTO treaty values as it understood them to be.[68] The text of Article XX(d) permits regulatory measures 'necessary to secure compliance with laws or regulations which are not inconsistent with the provisions of this Agreement …'.[69] The Appellate Body's initial reasoning on necessity in *Korea – Beef* encased itself in the language of a classic interpretation: 'we look first to the ordinary meaning of the word 'necessary', in its context and in the light of the object and purpose of Article XX, in accordance with Article 31(1) of the Vienna Convention'. *The New Shorter Oxford English Dictionary* suggested that the word 'necessary' normally denoted something 'that cannot be dispensed with or done without, requisite, essential, needful'.[70] However, a standard law dictionary cautioned that the word 'necessary' had to be considered in the connection in which it was used, that it was a word susceptible of various meanings. It might import absolute physical necessity or inevitability, or it might import that which was only convenient, useful, appropriate, suitable, proper, or conducive to the end sought. It was an adjective expressing degrees and might express 'mere convenience or that which is indispensable or an absolute physical necessity'.[71]

The Appellate Body famously reached the view that, as used in the context of Article XX(d), the reach of the word 'necessary' was not limited to that which was 'indispensable' or 'of absolute necessity' or 'inevitable'. Rather it referred to a range of degrees of necessity. At one end of the continuum lay 'necessary' in the sense of 'indispensability' while at the other end 'necessity' was to be understood as 'making a contribution to'. The Appellate Body went on to reason that, under Article XX(d), 'necessity' was significantly closer to 'indispensability' than to the opposite pole of simply 'making a contribution to'.[72] Article XX(d) protected measures that were necessary to ensure compliance with a potentially wide variety of laws and regulations. Giving further thought to this context, the Appellate

---

68 Isabelle Van Damme *Treaty Interpretation by the WTO Appellate Body* (Oxford University Press, Oxford, 2009) at 298. See also Ingo Venzke *How Interpretation Makes International Law: On Semantic Change and Normative Twists* (Oxford University Press, Oxford, 2012) at 184.

69 Article XX(d) allows for measures 'necessary to secure compliance with laws or regulations which are not inconsistent with the provisions of this Agreement, including those relating to customs enforcement, the enforcement of monopolies operated under paragraph 4 of Article II and Article XVII, the protection of patents, trademarks and copyrights, and the prevention of deceptive practices'.

70 *Korea – Beef*, Appellate Body Report, above n 67, at [159]–[160] citing *The New Shorter Oxford English Dictionary* (Clarendon Press, Oxford, 1993) vol II at 1895.

71 At [160] citing *Black's Law Dictionary* (West Publishing, Eagan, 1995) at 1029.

72 At [161].

Body commented that in respect of Article XX(d) a treaty interpreter might in appropriate cases take into account the relative importance of the interests or values that the law or regulation to be enforced was intended to protect: 'The more vital or important those common interests or values are, the easier it would be to accept as "necessary" a measure designed as an enforcement instrument'.[73]

The Appellate Body reasoned that further aspects of an enforcement measure to be considered in evaluating the necessity of the measure included the extent to which the measure contributes to the realisation of the end pursued, i.e., the securing of compliance with the law or regulation at issue. The more the measure contributed to this end, the more easily might the measure be considered 'necessary'.[74] Recalling the preamble to the GATT 1994,[75] the Appellate Body observed that it was important also to consider the extent to which the compliance measure produced restrictive effects on international commerce – in a case like the present one, restrictive effects on imported goods that were inconsistent with Article III:4. A less trade-restrictive measure with a relatively slight impact might more easily be considered as 'necessary' than a measure with intense or broader restrictive effects.[76]

Combining the above, the Appellate Body now elaborated the Article XX(d) necessity formula. As set out in *Korea – Beef* and applied consistently since, the necessity formula holds that:[77]

> In sum, determination of whether a measure, which is not 'indispensable', may nevertheless be 'necessary' within the contemplation of Article XX(d), involves in every case a process of weighing and balancing a series of factors which prominently include the contribution made by the compliance measure to the enforcement of the law or regulation at issue, the importance of the common interests or values protected by that law or regulation, and the accompanying impact of the law or regulation on imports or exports.

The Appellate Body stated clearly that the process outlined here formed part of a comparison between the challenged measure and reasonably

73 At [162].
74 At [163].
75 The last paragraph of the Preamble of the GATT of 1994 reads as follows: 'Being desirous of contributing to these objectives by entering into reciprocal and mutually advantageous arrangements directed to the substantial reduction of tariffs and other barriers to trade and to the elimination of discriminatory treatment in international commerce.'
76 *Korea – Beef*, Appellate Body Report, above n 67, at [163].
77 At [164].

available less trade-restrictive alternatives, as employed in pre-WTO GATT Article XX(d) dispute settlement.[78] This distinguishes the Appellate Body's necessity test from proportionality testing.[79] Decisions resting on the reasonable availability of alternative measures may incorporate a weighing and balancing, but there is a cap on this in WTO law as those measures must always be capable of ensuring a WTO Member's chosen level of protection against a given risk.

All the elements of the *Korea – Beef* necessity formula are represented similarly in later embodiments of the formula articulated under other relevant WTO provisions, including the public morals cases considered under the general exceptions in Article XX(a) of GATT and Article XIV(a) of GATS, and the human, animal and plant life or health cases considered under the general exceptions in Article XX(b) of GATT and Article XIV(b) of GATS. Naturally, an evaluation of the reasonable availability of alternatives may not be necessary where it is found that a measure is not trade restrictive or makes no contribution to the objective at hand. In such cases these factors may be determinative on their own.[80] There is widespread acceptance that the necessity formula developed under Article XX of the GATT applies also under Article 2.2 of the TBT Agreement.[81]

The multifaceted necessity formula stands in stark contradistinction with the bare textual provisions on which it is based. Although the Appellate Body's initial articulation of the formula in *Korea – Beef* began with a textual analysis, this rapidly evolved into a more deductive explication of how a measure's necessity to the purpose of hand is to be determined. WTO Members have consistently relied on the necessity formula in their pleadings, though there has been some objection to aspects of the formula that the US is concerned could license the ranking by degree of importance of the various policies pursued by Members.[82] Among the

---

78 At [166]–[167].

79 Peter Van Den Bossche "Looking for Proportionality in WTO Law" (2008) 35(3) LIEI 283.

80 *United States – Measures Concerning the Importation, Marketing, and Sale of Tuna and Tuna Products*, Report of the Appellate Body (16 May 2012) WT/DS381/AB/R, DSR 2012:IV at 1837 [321], fn 647.

81 As evidenced for instance in the pleadings of geographically diverse WTO members in *Australia – Certain Measures Concerning Trademarks, Geographical Indications and Other Plain Packaging Requirements Applicable to Tobacco Products*, Reports of the Panels (28 June 2018) WT/DS435/R, WT/DS441/R WT/DS458/R, WT/DS467/R, Addendum.

82 See for instance WTO (Dispute Settlement Body), "Minutes of Meeting held on 17 December 2007" (15 February 2007) WT/DSB/M/243, [55]–[70], 'Brazil – Measures affecting imports of retreaded tyres' at [66]–[67].

instances of the necessity formula's application that have been particularly pertinent for New Zealand are the proceedings in the *Australia – Plain Packaging* dispute.[83] The New Zealand legislation parallels in content the plain packaging policies introduced by Australia, and New Zealand made third-party submissions in these proceedings.[84]

Australia – Plain Packaging

The *Australia – Plain Packaging* case illustrates well how the WTO necessity test, as a regulatory standard, accommodates domestic decision-making. It is important here to appreciate that the weighing and balancing that takes place in the formula's application occurs in the context of determining the reasonable availability of alternative measures. Any alternative measure would only count as such if it would achieve the same level of protection against the risk in question as the disputed regulatory measures. It is in this respect that the Panel's approach in this case differs clearly from the proportionality testing seen for instance in EU Law.

The *Australia – Plain Packaging* case involved complaints by Honduras, the Dominican Republic, Cuba and Indonesia about requirements for plain packaging of tobacco products found in Australia's Tobacco Plain Packaging Act 2011, accompanying regulations, and amendments to the Australian trademarks legislation.[85] As set down in the Australian Act, the measure's objective was to improve public health by discouraging people from taking up smoking or using tobacco products, encouraging people to give up smoking and to stop using tobacco products, discouraging people who had given up smoking or stopped using tobacco products from relapsing, and reducing people's exposure to smoke from tobacco products.[86] Tobacco products were to comply with the Act's retail packaging requirements, which envisaged uniform plain packaging in a

---

83 *Australia – Certain Measures Concerning Trademarks, Geographical Indications and Other Plain Packaging Requirements Applicable to Tobacco Products*, Reports of the Panels (28 June 2018) WT/DS435/R, WT/DS441/R WT/DS458/R, WT/DS467/R (hereafter *Australia – Plain Packaging*, Panel Reports); *Australia – Certain Measures Concerning Trademarks, Geographical Indications and Other Plain Packaging Requirements Applicable to Tobacco Products*, Reports of the Appellate Body (9 June 2020) WT/DS435/AB/R, WT/DS441/AB/R at [7.14]–[7.15] (hereafter *Australia – Plain Packaging*, Appellate Body Reports).

84 Smoke-free Environments (Tobacco Standardised Packaging) Amendment Act 2016.

85 *Australia – Plain Packaging*, Panel Reports, above n 83.

86 Tobacco Plain Packaging Act 2011 (Cth), s 3(1). *Australia – Plain Packaging*, Panel Reports, above n 83, at [2.15].

drab dark brown colour. Brand names and company names were to appear in a specified location and orientation, printed in a specified font, typeface and colour. With this exception, the appearance of trademarks was generally prohibited. The appearance of tobacco products themselves was also regulated and requirements set down for cigars as well as cigarettes. Especially when combined with an increase in the size of graphic health warnings, the visual effect was dramatic. The *Australia – Plain Packaging* complainants asserted unsuccessfully that Australia's measures were inconsistent with its WTO commitments, including centrally Australia's obligations under Articles 2.1 and 2.2 of the TBT Agreement and Articles 16.1 and 20 of Agreement on Trade-Related Aspects of Intellectual Property Rights (TRIPS).[87] The Appellate Body rejected appeals by Honduras and the Dominican Republic.[88]

Under Article 2.2 of the TBT Agreement, the Panel found that the objective of Australia's plain packaging measures was the legitimate objective of improving public health by reducing the use of, and exposure to, tobacco products. Accordingly, the *Australia – Plain Packaging* Panel set out to conduct a relational analysis of the public health contribution made by the Australian plain packaging regime, the measure's trade restrictiveness, and the nature of the risks at issue. This application of the necessity test was combined with consideration of the gravity of the consequences that would arise from Australia's non-fulfilment of the regime's objective as required under the TBT agreement.[89] This analysis then informed the comparative analysis of possible reasonably available less trade restrictive alternatives that would potentially have made an equivalent contribution to Australia's public health objectives.

The Panel moved first to assess the extent to which the measures contributed to this objective, beginning with a general review of the scientific literature relating to the effectiveness of plain packaging, which stood up well to complainants' critiques.[90] Looking at the evidence, the Panel was unpersuaded by arguments from the complainants that the measures would be incapable of contributing to Australia's objective.[91] The Panel came then to evidence relating to the application of the measures.

87 At [8.1].

88 *Australia – Plain Packaging*, Appellate Body Reports, above n 83, at [7.14]–[7.15].

89 *Australia – Plain Packaging*, Panel Reports, above n 83, at [7.31]–[7.32], [7.184]–[7.185], and [7.1724]; as endorsed by the Appellate Body in *Australia – Plain Packaging*, Appellate Body Reports, above n 83, at [6.157].

90 *Australia – Plain Packaging*, Panel Reports, above n 83, at [7.423] and [7.541]–[7.645].

91 At [7.929]–[7.1034].

This was not straightforward as Australia had put in place requirements for enlarged graphic health warnings at the same time as its plain packaging requirements. Nevertheless the evidence was consistent with the hypothesis that Australia's plain packaging measures had had an impact on actual smoking behaviours, even though some of the outcomes sought could only be expected to manifest themselves over a longer period of time.[92] Overall, on the matter of the Australian measure's contribution to their objectives the Panel found that the evidence in its totality supported the view that the plain packaging measures, in combination with other tobacco-control measures maintained by Australia, were apt to and did in fact contribute meaningfully to Australia's objective of reducing the use of, and exposure to, tobacco products. In making this determination, the Panel remained mindful that the impact of the Australian measures might evolve over time.[93] The Appellate Body rejected challenges to this finding.[94]

The Panel then came to the Australian measure's trade-restrictiveness, and the nature and gravity of the risks that would be generated by non-fulfilment of Australia's health objectives. The Panel concluded that insofar as Australia's measures reduced the volume of imported tobacco products on the market they had a limiting effect on trade, and that they might in future reduce the value of imported tobacco products.[95] The Appellate Body likewise rejected a challenge on this point.[96] Reviewing the statistics on morbidity and mortality associated with tobacco use, the Panel found the public health consequences of use of and exposure to tobacco 'particularly grave',[97] with especially grave consequences for youth.[98] It had gone undisputed that there was no safe level of tobacco use or exposure to tobacco smoke, and Australia considered the interests at stake to be of the utmost importance.[99]

Focussing on the possibility that there might be reasonably available less trade restrictive alternatives, the Panel assessed four proposed alternative measures. The Panel found that the complainants had not

---

92 At [7.932]–[7.986].

93 At [7.1025], [7.1043], [7.1725] and [7.1044].

94 *Australia – Plain Packaging*, Appellate Body Reports, above n 83, at [7.2].

95 *Australia – Plain Packaging*, Panel Reports, above n 83, at [7.1255], [7.1207]–[7.1208] and [7.1725].

96 *Australia – Plain Packaging*, Appellate Body Reports, above n 83, at [7.3].

97 *Australia – Plain Packaging*, Panel Reports, above n 83, at [7.1310], [7.1322] and [7.1725].

98 At [7.1317], noting also Australian remarks concerning the disproportionate effects of tobacco use on Aboriginal and Torres Strait Islander peoples at [7.1318].

99 At [7.1319].

demonstrated that any of these alternatives would make a contribution to Australia's objective that was equivalent to that made by the Australian plain packaging measures as part of Australia's regulatory framework for tobacco control, even if they were less trade restrictive, of which the Panel remained unpersuaded. Neither would they do so if combined.[100] The four proposed alternatives comprised: an increase in the minimum legal age for smoking,[101] increased taxation of tobacco products,[102] making more use of social marketing campaigns,[103] and a system that would pre-vet all proposed tobacco product packaging individually.[104] The Appellate Body upheld this conclusion.[105]

The *Australia – Plain Packaging* Panel refrained from conclusively weighing and balancing the factors at play within the necessity formula under the TBT Agreement.[106] The Panel simply reiterated its conclusions that, although they were trade restrictive to the extent they resulted in a reduction in total volume of imports, plain packaging requirements made a meaningful contribution to Australia's public health objectives, and the consequences of non-fulfilment of Australia's objective were particularly grave, while none of the proposed alternative measures had been shown to constitute a less trade restrictive alternative that would make an equivalent contribution to Australia's objective.[107] The Panel emphasised that, as reflected in the sixth recital of the TBT Agreement, no WTO Member should be prevented from taking measures necessary for the protection of human, animal or plant life or health or the environment.[108]

The formula later articulated by the Panel for determining whether plain packaging requirements constituted an unjustifiable encumbrance on trademark use under Article 20 of TRIPS was akin to the necessity formula and was applied in a way that mirrored the Panel's analysis under Article 2.2 of the TBT Agreement, although the Panel may have come a little closer, in its TRIPS analysis, to the determinative weighing and balancing of competing interests. The Panel framed its task as assessing the public health concerns underlying the plain packaging rules against

100 At [7.1721], [7.1725] and [7.1726].
101 At [7.1468]–[7.1471].
102 At [7.1542]–[7.1545].
103 At [7.1620]–[7.1624].
104 At [7.1713]–[7.1716].
105 *Australia – Plain Packaging*, Appellate Body Reports, above n 83, at [7.6].
106 *Australia – Plain Packaging*, Panel Reports, above n 83, at [7.1724]–[7.1732].
107 At [7.1725]–[7.1726].
108 At [7.1731].

their implications for trademark use.[109] The Panel then reiterated the undisputed and exceptionally grave domestic and global health problem involved in tobacco use together with the fact that the Australian plain packaging measures had in fact contributed to its public health objective. The Panel's overall conclusion was simply that it was not persuaded that the complainant had demonstrated that Australia had acted beyond the bounds of its latitude under Article 20 of TRIPS.[110] The Appellate Body found no error in the Panel's conclusion.[111]

In summary, under the WTO general exceptions jurisprudence and under the corresponding text in Article 2.2 of the TBT Agreement, the WTO Appellate Body and panels have relied on interpretations of necessity grounded in principles of contextualism and effectiveness. The necessity formula is a pragmatic and creative response to the need for WTO Members' regulatory policy to balance trade and non-trade considerations. Whether the approach under the TRIPS will remain similar or evolve on its own trajectory is an open question.

4. INVESTMENT TREATY ARBITRATION

Investment treaty arbitration is a relative newcomer to the international adjudicatory scene, and has been controversial for the way in which small ad hoc tribunals have the power to make rulings potentially delineating states' regulatory freedom or awarding large sums to foreign investors who have privileged access to this form of dispute settlement.[112] Moves to stabilise investor-state dispute settlement by setting up an appeals mechanism or an investment court are currently under discussion in a process established by the United Nations Commission on International Trade Law (UNCITRAL).[113] The EU has recently made provision for such arrangements in the bilateral context, including in its free trade agreement with Canada, the Comprehensive Economic and Trade Agreement

109 At [7.2591].

110 At [7.2592] and [7.2604].

111 *Australia – Plain Packaging*, Appellate Body Reports, above n 83, at [7.12]–[7.13].

112 Kate Miles *The Origins of International Investment Law: Empire, Environment, and the Safeguarding of Capital* (Cambridge University Press, Cambridge, 2013).

113 For developments in the UNCITRAL Working Group tasked with considering reform see <http://www.uncitral.org/uncitral/en/commission/working_groups/3Investor_State.html>.

(CETA).[114] The importance of acknowledging and evaluating the regulatory standards that are emerging from investment treaty arbitration increases in light of the development of this institutional machinery, which is likely to entrench certain understandings of international investment law, especially if multilateralised.

Investment treaties commonly incorporate a suite of requirements concerning the treatment that host states are required to afford investors in addition to provisions governing the expropriation of foreign investments. The guarantee of fair and equitable treatment is central; frequently it is accompanied by a guarantee of full protection and security. Then there are the non-discrimination disciplines including the national treatment requirement as well as the requirement for most favoured nation treatment.[115] Most difficult for investment tribunals to determine has been compliance with the fair and equitable treatment guarantee. The determination of whether treatment of an investor is fair and equitable will take into account, as an overarching consideration, the need to preserve scope for regulatory activity on the part of host states.[116] It appears clear that substantive unfairness will arise where administrative decisions are arbitrary or unreasonable, or in circumstances where there is unfair discrimination, coercion, harassment or bad faith.[117]

The general concept of fair and equitable treatment can still be difficult to pin down operationally. According to descriptions of arbitral methodology in existing scholarship, one way that investment tribunals approach this task is to develop a line of reasoning that works out the essential elements of the guarantee by employing abstract reasoning.[118] For instance, the influential award in *Saluka v Czech Republic* viewed the fair and equitable treatment guarantee as requiring that a host state refrain from acting

114 Canada-European Union (EU) Comprehensive Economic and Trade Agreement (CETA) (signed 30 October 2016, entered into force provisionally 21 September 2017). See also Opinion 1/17 (2019) EU:C:2019:341, at [148]–[161].

115 Campbell McLachlan, Laurence Shore and Matthew Weiniger *International Investment Arbitration: Substantive Principles* (2nd ed, Oxford University Press, Oxford, 2017) at [7.01]. The national treatment discipline requires foreign investors to be treated no less favourably than national investors, while the most favoured nation discipline requires them to be treated no less favourably than investors from other countries.

116 At [7.24], [7.178] and [7.228].

117 At [7.208].

118 Rudolf Dolzer and Christoph Schreuer *Principles of International Investment Law* (2nd ed, Oxford University Press, Oxford, 2012) at 141; Stephan Schill "Fair and Equitable Treatment, the Rule of Law, and Comparative Public Law" in Stephan Schill (ed) *International Investment Law and Comparative Public Law* (Oxford University Press, Oxford, 2010) 153 at 157.

in a way that is 'manifestly inconsistent, non-transparent, unreasonable (that is, unrelated to some rational policy), or discriminatory (that is, based on unjustifiable distinctions)'.[119] Pleadings are not available and the *Saluka* Tribunal does not cite direct authority for its dictum, and so it is difficult to understand the formal derivation of the test, but later cases commonly cite to *Saluka* for the point. The *Saluka* case concerned the effects of the imposition of a forced administration on Saluka's shareholding in a state-owned commercial bank and the bank's exclusion from state aid in response to a systemic debt problem.

Given the significance of moves to renewable energy in the context of the fight against climate change, it seems appropriate to investigate the evolution in investment treaty law of the regulatory standard requiring reasonable relationships to rational policies with reference to a renewable energy case. *Mesa Power v Canada* demonstrates how this standard is brought into the evaluation of host state conduct by an investment tribunal and relied upon to make pivotal findings, in this instance favouring the host state.[120]

Mesa Power v Canada

Mesa Power v Canada was a dispute under the North American Free Trade Agreement (NAFTA).[121] The *Mesa v Canada* dispute arose when companies owned ultimately by the Mesa Power Group LLC, registered in the US, all failed to secure contracts for the supply of renewable energy to Ontario. Mesa was unsuccessful in its claims against Canada. Mesa's claim that it had not received fair and equitable treatment in accordance with Article 1105(1) of NAFTA was rejected based on tests embodying the need for a reasonable relationship to rational policies, which had been emphasised by the claimant itself in pleadings.[122] Mesa's claims of discrimination under

---

119 *Saluka Investments BV v Czech Republic PCA*, Partial Award, 17 March 2006 (Arthur Watts, L Yves Fortier and Peter Behrens) at [309] (hereafter *Saluka*). See also at [307].

120 *Mesa Power Group, LLC v Canada*, PCA Case No 2012-17, Award, 24 March 2016 (Gabrielle Kaufmann-Kohler, Charles N Brower and Toby Landau) (hereafter *Mesa Power Group, LLC v Canada*).

121 North American Free Trade Agreement (signed 17 December 1992, entered into force 1 January 1994).

122 *Mesa Power Group, LLC v Canada Memorial of the Investor* (20 November 2013) at [357], [359], citing *Saluka* together with academic commentary, Kenneth J Vandervelde *Bilateral Investment Treaties, History, Policy, and Interpretation* (Oxford University Press, Oxford, 2010). Investor's Reply Memorial and Rejoinder on Jurisdiction (30 April 2014) at [528] citing *Saluka*.

NAFTA Articles 1102 and 1103 were also dismissed, on the basis that the Ontario FIT program constituted government procurement.

In 1980 the Government of Ontario had created by legislation the Ontario Power Authority (OPA) with responsibility for long-term planning, procurement of new power generation through long-term purchase agreements, and for promoting diversification in Ontario's power supply with particular emphasis on renewable energy.[123] In 2009 the Minister of Energy of the government was authorised by legislation to direct the OPA to develop a feed-in tariff program (the FIT program) to promote renewable energy generation and consumption in Ontario. This took place under the Green Energy and Green Economy Act 2009, a piece of legislation enacted to build a green economy. The FIT program would be administered by the OPA which would set prices and administer contracts.[124] The government received a high number of applications to participate in the FIT program.[125] Those were scored and ranked to determine which projects would be awarded contracts, based on the available transmission capacity,[126] and contracts began to be awarded in successive rounds from April 2010.[127] Contracts were offered only where the transmission capacity for connecting the project to the grid was available. This was determined using a Transmission Availability Test. Where capacity was not available the OPA was to determine the economic and technical feasibility of upgrading the transmission system through an Economic Connection Test (ECT).[128]

Mesa's projects faced transmission difficulties because they were in the Bruce Region of Ontario.[129] Connection of projects in the Bruce Region required construction of a new high-voltage transmission line, the Bruce to Milton line.[130] Meantime the FIT's success was already bringing Ontario close to target for renewable energy supply (the target of a 10,700 MW capacity by 2018) and Ontario needed to slow the pace of its renewable energy procurement.[131] In this context, the Minister of Energy directed in

---

123 *Mesa Power Group, LLC v Canada*, above n 120, at [9].
124 At [11].
125 At [16].
126 At [17].
127 At [28].
128 At [24] and [621].
129 At [26] and [28].
130 At [623].
131 At [33] and [624].

2011 that a discrete regional process take place.[132] The OPA was to award contracts for the supply of 750 MW in the Bruce Region. Applicants were given a five-day window, publicised in advance, to change their projects' connection points by selecting a new point outside the Bruce Region and building themselves the transmission lines from their generation facilities to this point.[133] Contracts were then awarded.[134] No province-wide ECT was conducted.[135] A full ECT would likely have led to excess procurement.[136]

The Tribunal describes separately in its Award the process of discussion that had been taking place in the interim between the government of Ontario and a consortium comprising two Korean companies (Samsung C & T Corporation and Korea Electric Power Corporation). These discussions involved a Memorandum of Understanding signed in December 2008[137] and a January 2010 Green Energy Investment Agreement (GEIA) providing for what Canada described as the largest investment in renewable electricity generation in the province's history.[138] The Korean consortium was to establish and operate manufacturing facilities for wind and solar generation equipment in the province while in exchange it was guaranteed priority access to 2,500 MW of transmission capacity to be phased in over five years,[139] with a higher price for its electricity than that given to FIT producers.[140] Ontario provided for the Korean consortium's priority access by holding transmission capacity in reserve in a number of regions, including 500 MW of transmission capacity in the Bruce Region, by direction of the Minister of Energy.[141]

Mesa contended that the GEIA with the Korean consortium led to the failure of Mesa group companies to secure FIT contracts.[142] The Tribunal dismissed Mesa's Article 1105 claim[143] on the basis that Mesa had not made out the required facts and Canadian conduct did not reach 'the high threshold needed to establish a violation of Article 1105'.[144] In relation to

132 At [34]–[35] and [626].
133 At [34]–[35].
134 At [36].
135 At [614].
136 At [625].
137 At [38].
138 At [39].
139 At [40].
140 At [555].
141 At [41].
142 At [42].
143 At [682] and [706(iv)].
144 At [512].

Mesa's argument that the conclusion of the GEIA constituted unjustifiable preferential treatment for the Korean consortium, the Tribunal was not prepared to intervene in the Ontario government's decision to pursue the GEIA, where *there was a reasonable relationship between the justification given for the GEIA and the terms of the GEIA*.[145] The Tribunal identified a fourfold rationale for the GEIA. The GEIA provided a committed 'anchor tenant' to help ensure the government could achieve its renewable energy goals; it provided substantial amounts of green energy; it would attract manufacturing plants to Ontario; and it would create jobs in the wake of the global economic crisis.[146] The Tribunal added that so long as the conclusion of the GEIA was pursuant to a bona fide policy decision by the Ontario government at the time it was not relevant whether or not the GEIA actually succeeded in its objectives.[147] The Canadian action was acceptable even if, for instance, the need for an anchor tenant could have been questioned by January 2010 and the government could have decided not to go ahead with the GEIA.[148] The same applied in relation to the Ontario government's decision on the process applied to allocate capacity on the Bruce to Milton line.[149]

Consistent with this, in relation to Mesa's argument that allocation of capacity in the Bruce region had benefitted particular FIT applicants the Tribunal found that the Minister's direction '*was based on rational considerations* responding to the situation prevailing at the time in Ontario' and if it favoured a few applicants that was the outcome of this 'rational policy'.[150] Allegations of the exertion of influence over officials,[151] and of a quid pro quo for political donations[152] went unsubstantiated. All this said, in reaching the conclusion there had been no violation of Article 1105(1) the Tribunal criticised the government's decision 'to run two renewable energy programs in parallel' without clearly articulating the relationship between them or their interaction in the event of changes in the electricity market.[153]

Arbitrator Brower's dissenting views highlight the contrast between the Tribunal's reasoning concerning the GEIA and the conclusions it

145 At [579].
146 At [565].
147 At [573].
148 At [579].
149 At [632].
150 At [672] (emphasis added).
151 At [676]–[678].
152 At [680].
153 At [682]. See also [607].

might alternatively have reached. Arbitrator Brower considered that the government of Ontario had acted 'arbitrarily, grossly, unfairly, unjustly, idiosyncratically, discriminated against the FIT applicants and in favour of the Korean Consortium, and acted with a complete lack of transparency and candor'.[154] At the nub of the matter was the fact that at the time the government of Ontario decided to go ahead and conclude the GEIA it was already known that the FIT program could supply the desired power.[155] Yet the government went ahead. This enabled FIT applicants ranked far lower down the list than the claimants to capitalise on their 'otherwise doomed investments' by selling them to the Korean Consortium while the claimant missed out on any allocation of capacity despite the high ranking of its top projects.[156] Arbitrator Brower considered this 'grotesque' and viewed the GEIA as standing the FIT program on its head,[157] making a mockery of it,[158] and pulling the rug out from under it.[159] This 'misconduct' could not be 'excused' 'by noting that a sovereign is to be given a certain degree of deference' or that regulatory change remained permissible.[160]

Mesa Power v Canada provides a strong example of the approach seen in *Saluka v Czech Republic*, whereby the question of whether an investor has been accorded fair and equitable treatment has been analysed with reference to regulatory standards calling for the existence of a rational or legitimate policy and the reasonableness of the act of the relevant state in relation to the policy. For those with an interest in tobacco control, it may be noted that the reasoning in the investment proceedings in *Phillip Morris v Uruguay* is similar, and defeated Philip Morris's expropriation claim as well as its claim for breach of the fair and equitable treatment guarantee.[161]

The development of rational relationship testing is a further instance of pragmatic and creative traditional method in international dispute settlement relating to domestic regulatory freedom and obligations. Formally, the derivation of the rational relationship test in investment treaty arbitration remains under-articulated, but in many respects the test is a helpful contribution to investment treaty law. The test is a response to the need to be able to apply general or vaguely worded international

154 Concurring and Dissenting Opinion of Judge Charles N Brower at [4] and [22].
155 At [22].
156 At [14]–[16], [20] and [22].
157 At [4].
158 At [5].
159 At [16].
160 At [17].
161 *Philip Morris Brands Sàrl and ors v Uruguay* ICSID Case No ARB/10/7, Award, 8 July 2016 (Piero Bernardini, Gary Born and James Crawford).

legal provisions in specific contexts. It is notable that the test is paralleled in non-discrimination jurisprudence both in international investment law and under the WTO general exceptions.[162]

5. CONCLUSION

This contribution has considered international disputes arising in relation to states' legislative and administrative activity in domains including environmental protection, health policy, and domestic infrastructure and resource management. Regulating this type of subject matter is core to the work of any government and was until recently essentially a matter for states to determine for themselves, subject to international human rights considerations. However, through their adherence to various far-reaching treaties over recent decades, in the field of international economic law in particular, states have created a situation where, from time to time, disputes are likely to arise calling for scrutiny of their domestic regulatory activity, including permitting decisions for offshore activities. In order to determine these cases, international courts and tribunals increasingly find themselves identifying regulatory standards and tests in applicable legal provisions and rules. Commonalities in the decisions of international adjudicatory bodies suggest that global regulatory standards are emerging.

The contribution has looked primarily at three selected examples as they appear in three cases from three distinct realms of international law. In all three settings we can see the pragmatic and creative approaches taken by the relevant adjudicatory bodies as they articulate and apply differing tests requiring distinct forms of coherence between regulatory measures and their objectives. In the *Whaling in the Antarctic* case the ICJ found Japan's research program was not 'for scientific purposes' as required by Article VIII(1) of the ICRW on the basis that, in the use of lethal methods, Japan had not shown that the programme's design and implementation were reasonable in relation to achieving its stated objectives.[163] This avoided the need for closer scrutiny of Japan's permitting decision, or the reasons for its programme. In *Australia-Plain Packaging* the WTO Panel charged with the case applied the creative but now institutionally accepted WTO

---

162 For further discussion see Caroline E Foster *Global Regulatory Standards in Environmental and Health Disputes: Regulatory Coherence, Due Regard, and Due Diligence* (Oxford University Press, Oxford, 2021).

163 *Whaling in the Antarctic*, above n 12, at [67] and [88].

necessity test, which imposes a certain discipline on regulating states but also affords them an important latitude. Finally in the investment dispute in *Mesa Power v Canada* the Tribunal pragmatically applied the rational relationship tests that have emerged from earlier investment arbitration. This simultaneously allowed that a government in Ontario's position might enjoy considerable policy room and gave a boost to states working to ensure the success of renewable energy schemes.

Each of these decisions demonstrates that international courts' and tribunals' selection and elaboration of the regulatory standards and tests they choose to employ in the application of relevant treaty provisions is informed by the parties' pleadings, while also reflecting respect for domestic governments' decision-making authority. The cases show also that practice is beginning to coalesce around potentially central tenets, including the rational or reasonable relationship of means to ends, and may in due course give rise to recognisable global regulatory standards. However, knowledge and understanding of these developments remains largely confined to certain professional circles. It is difficult to regard the emergence of new dimensions of global administrative law as legitimate in the absence of broader public awareness and the opportunity for discussion about these standards, including in relation to the deference they often afford to states in the light of contemporary global challenges and imperatives.

PART II

ISSUES CONCERNING THE JUDICIARY

Judicial Appointment and Accountability

BV HARRIS'S PROMOTION OF A JUDICIAL COMMISSION FOR NEW ZEALAND

EW Thomas

1. THE IMMENSE POWER OF JUDGES

In approaching the question whether a judicial commission should be established in New Zealand, Bruce Harris begins by emphasising the immense power judges exercise. Judges decide, inter alia, whether citizens should be imprisoned, whether contracts exist and should be enforced, and whether decisions of Ministers should be rendered valid or invalid. It follows, in Harris's thinking, that society should ensure the best possible processes are in place for judicial appointments, judicial discipline and continuing professional development.

I propose to focus on Harris's proposal that a judicial commission should be established to monitor judicial appointments.[1] Harris's writings on this topic reflect his capacity to approach a practical issue with academic discipline.

Harris's emphasis on the vast power judges exercise is undoubtedly the correct starting point. In a democracy, power is not permitted to go unrestrained. Those who exercise that power must be held accountable. The conflict or tension which Harris then confronts is the need to maintain the independence of the judiciary, on the one hand, while at the same time holding judges accountable, on the other. This tension necessitates a more formal process than that which is now in place. The present system, he argues, is unsatisfactory when tested against constitutional principle and when contrasted with the successful experience of judicial commissions overseas.

2. THE INDEPENDENCE OF THE JUDICIARY

The main constitutional principle that supports the adoption of a judicial commission is 'the furthering of the actual and perceived independence of the judiciary'. Harris contends that the 'foundational principle' is that the judiciary needs to be in both reality and perception independent from the legislature, the executive and all other organisations and individuals within the community. This foundational principle is the basic theme in Harris's advocacy for the creation of a judicial commission.

I consider that Harris is correct to emphasise that the principle embraces the 'perceived' and not just the 'factual' independence of the judiciary. For the public to have confidence in the judiciary, the perception is probably as important as the reality. A formal process for the appointment of judges can only strengthen the perception the judiciary is independent.

---

1 Harris has written a number of articles on, or touching upon, the establishment of a judicial commission, including the following; "The New Supreme Court" [2003] NZLJ 15; "Employment Changes for Judges", *Employment Today*, April/May 2003; "Judicial Activism and New Zealand's Appellate Courts" (Oxford University Press, Oxford, 2007) at 273; "Remedies and Accountability for Unlawful Judicial Action in New Zealand: Could the Law Be Tidier?" [2008] NZ L Rev 483; and "A Judicial Commission for New Zealand: A Good Idea that Must not be Allowed to go Away" [2014] NZ L Rev 383 ("A Judicial Commission for New Zealand"). The latter article provides a useful outline of Harris's thinking. Any quotations in this contribution are taken from that article.

3. THE NEED FOR WIDE CONSULTATION

The second foundational principle that Harris posits in influencing the design of a judicial appointments process is the need for the decision-making person or body to have access to and consider the views of a range of appropriate persons as to the suitability of any proposed appointee. Those consulted, he suggests, need to be both within and without the judiciary. Harris is undoubtedly correct. There can be no gainsaying the fact that the person or body responsible for a judicial appointment should have access to and consider the views of a range of persons able to contribute to the process of determining the suitability of a candidate for appointment.

4. THE CURRENT PROCESS

In examining the current process for the appointment of judges, Harris begins with the fact that all judges are appointed by the executive, that is, by the Attorney-General. In a system of governance which values the separation of powers, the fact appointments to the bench are made by the executive is, in itself, a cause for concern. In effect, judges are required to be independent of the branch that is responsible for their appointment and promotion. A judicial commission for the appointment of judges, in Harris's view, which I readily endorse, would minimise this conflict.

Harris recognises that the present system is a democratic model that facilitates ministerial responsibility for all decisions related to judicial appointments. Judges are formally appointed by the Governor-General who by convention acts on the advice of the Attorney-General.[2] Thus, the decision as to who to appoint is effectively made by the Attorney-General in respect of all judges, except for the Chief Justice and the judges of the Māori Land Court.[3]

Harris is fully cognizant of the argument that the present system gives 'democratic legitimacy' to judicial appointments and allows political accountability for the decisions made. The Attorney-General may be called upon to account by his or her fellow ministers and by Parliament should a judicial appointment turn out to be inappropriate or otherwise

2 Crown Law Office, *Judicial Appointments Protocol* (21 May 2014).

3 In accordance with the Senior Courts Act 2016 s 100(2) the Chief Justice is appointed by the Governor-General on the advice of the Prime Minister. The ultimate power to appoint judges to the Maori Land Court effectively rests with the Minister of Maori Affairs.

warranting criticism. In theory, the Attorney-General's decision can be tested or questioned in the debating chamber of Parliament or before one of Parliament's select committees. Harris points out, however, that there have been no calls for the Attorney-General to account to Parliament and the public for the appointment of a judge in the history of this country. I would add that, in reality, any questions raised in the House are likely to be of a political nature.[4]

Harris traverses the differences in the processes for the appointment of District Court judges and High Court judges. The basis for appointment in both cases is 'merit' and the publicly listed criteria for appointment include 'legal ability, qualities of character, personal and technical skills and reflection of society'.[5]

The 'flexible' process presently followed for High Court judges requires the Attorney-General to settle a shortlist of not more than three possible appointees. They are required to obtain the agreement of the Chief Justice to the shortlist.[6] The Attorney-General selects one candidate from the shortlist and notifies Cabinet of his or her pending appointment. The appointment is formally made by the Governor-General but, notwithstanding these requirements, Harris is correct in emphasising that the effective power to decide who is appointed remains with the Attorney-General.

5. THE LAW COMMISSION REPORT

Before moving to a detailed exposition of the process he prefers, Harris deals with the report of the Law Commission.[7] The Law Commission concluded that the current process is 'sound'[8] and expressly stated it would 'not reconsider the basic tenet of the current process whereby ultimate appointments are proposed by a member of the executive'.[9] Nor did it think the Attorney-General should change the consultation processes

---

4 My appointment as an Acting Judge of the Supreme Court in 2005 was questioned in the House by a Member of the Act Party as I was, at the time, a member of the Board of the Reserve Bank. But it was well known that the Member did not like my 'liberal' approach to the law.

5 *Judicial Appointments Protocol*, above n 2.

6 Ibid, n. 2.

7 *Law Commission Review of the Judicature Act 1908: Towards a New Courts Act* (NCLR 126, 2012)

8 At [3.14] and [3.16].

9 At [3.4] and [3.19].

or selection criteria which were currently employed. It concluded, however, that the system lacked 'transparency' in respect of those who are consulted and the criteria applied to decide on an appointment.[10] The Law Commission recognised that the list of those whom it should be obligatory for the Attorney-General to consult should be prescribed by statute. In the result, the Minister of Justice advised Cabinet that the recommendation there be greater transparency should be accepted, but advised it should not be incorporated in legislation.[11]

Harris accepts that an obligation to publish the process would lead to greater transparency and facilitate the Attorney-General's political responsibility for the decision-making. It would also ensure that the public maintained confidence in the appointment process. But, as Harris rightly notes, the real power of appointment would remain with a member of the executive, the Attorney-General.

The Law Commission's Report discouraged the government from taking any steps directed at establishing a judicial appointments body. The Law Commission did not think a more formal structure and process would be viable in New Zealand where there are approximately a dozen judicial appointments each year. It contrasted this minimal number with the 700 or more judicial appointments made on the recommendation of the UK Judicial Appointments Commission each year.[12]

Harris's criticism of the Law Commission's Report is telling. First, he points out that the need to maintain the independence of the judiciary appears to be compromised by retaining the real power of appointment in the Attorney-General. A judicial appointments commission would address this concern. Secondly, Harris refuses to accept that it is not possible to design a judicial commission, including a judicial appointments committee, which is 'tailored' to New Zealand's needs. I agree that this must be so. Harris could well have added that, in addition to new appointments, the Attorney-General is responsible for the promotion of judges from one court to a higher court and, thus, the number of decisions the Attorney-General is required to make is significantly greater than the number of judges appointed each year.

---

10 At [3.22].

11 Cabinet Social Policy Committee, "Government Response to the Law Commission's report: *Review of the Judicature Act 1908: towards a new Courts Act*" (April 2013) at [30].

12 Above n 7.

6. HARRIS'S CRITICISM OF THE CURRENT SYSTEM

Harris sets about designing a judicial commission 'tailored' to New Zealand's needs. But before doing so he reiterates his argument that, although the Attorney-General acting as the First Law Officer of the Crown, may by constitutional convention be expected to exercise the judicial appointment function apolitically and independently of his or her fellow ministers, only advising, but not consulting Cabinet, the Attorney-General nevertheless remains a Minister performing an executive governmental function.

What immediately follows in Harris's thesis is, I believe, a realistic perception of the Attorney-General's role. He points out that the Attorney-General may hold other portfolios and may be perceived to be committed to the general ideology of the government and party of which he is a member. It is, says Harris, naïve to think that the Attorney-General is not influenced subconsciously, if not overtly, by his or her political disposition and the party-political environment in which they work on a daily basis. Harris refers again to the perception of at least a large section of the public that the Attorney-General is a member of the government. He cites Sir Geoffrey Palmer's acknowledgment that there may be, in some circumstances, neither actual nor apparent independence of the Attorney-General's decision-making from the executive branch of government. Non-promotion, he adds, may provide better evidence of subtle political considerations than fresh appointments.

In addition, Harris confirms that the individual preferences of Attorneys-General can play an important role in their decision-making. This must be right. It is inconceivable that an Attorney-General, who is also a politician and member of the government, will not endeavour to 'put a stamp on the judiciary'.[13]

Harris endorses the notion that modern society accepts that group decision-making in respect of public matters is often likely to produce better outcomes than individual decision-making. He points out that group decision-making ameliorates the inevitable subjectivity that has the potential to influence decisions and also allows a broader range of considerations to be brought to bear on any decision.

---

13 Geoffrey Palmer "Judicial Selection and Accountability: Can the New Zealand System Survive?" in BD Gray and RB McClintock (eds) *Courts and Policy: Checking the Balance* (Brookers, Wellington, 1995) 11 at 81–84.

One of the persons who is, and will inevitably be, consulted pending a judicial appointment is the Solicitor-General. Harris endorses Sir Geoffrey Palmer's point that consulting the Solicitor-General has the 'appearance' of a threat to the independence of the judiciary.[14] There is the potential for the Solicitor-General to have an influence on the judicial appointment process when they will be appearing as counsel for the Crown before the judges who are appointed. Harris observes that Sir Geoffrey Palmer balances this concern against the value of the Solicitor-General's likely knowledge of what is expected of judges and the qualities particular applicants will be likely to bring to the position.

Harris, however, expresses a further concern about consulting the Solicitor-General. There is a history of Solicitors-General being appointed direct to the Court of Appeal. Knowing of the possibility that he or she will be appointed to that court, Harris contends, it is inappropriate that they should have the opportunity to influence who may or may not be their future colleagues on the bench, particularly as such persons, when appointed as judges may themselves be able to influence whether the Solicitor-General should eventually be appointed to the bench.

I accept that these reservations are theoretically correct. But, for myself, I would not be persuaded to place great weight on them if the arguments in favour of a judicial appointments commission otherwise obtained acceptance.

Harris necessarily refers to the experience of other jurisdictions in which bodies independent of the executive recommend persons suitable for judicial appointment. In such jurisdictions, however, a minister in the executive retains the decision as to who is to be appointed to a judicial vacancy after being presented with one recommended appointee or a list of recommended appointees. Generally speaking, it is open to the Minister to reject a recommended appointee or all the recommended appointees and ask the judicial appointments body to make a further recommendation or recommendations.

Harris undertakes a thorough examination of the constitution and operation of such bodies in England and Wales. He notes that the ongoing concern in both England and Wales is to obtain greater gender and ethnic diversity with the objective of maintaining the confidence of the community.

---

14 At 52.

7. HARRIS'S DETAILED PROPOSAL

Based on his view that the current system in this country does not meet the community's expectations of judicial independence from the executive and his consideration of the models which exist in other jurisdictions, Harris sets out in considerable detail the model which he contends would better facilitate the actual and perceived independence of the judiciary from the executive in this country.

Harris contemplates establishing three interlinked statutory bodies; one a judicial commission, another a judicial appointments committee, and a third, a judicial disciplinary committee. The executive would appoint the judicial commission and determine the size and nature of the commission's membership and the process that would be adopted for appointing its members. Like the Ombudsman and the Auditor-General, the members appointed to the judicial commission would be responsible to Parliament. He anticipates that the legislature could be trusted to act apolitically in appointing the judicial commission.

Harris proposes that both the judicial commission and the appointments committee would be constituted and empowered by statute. The appointments committee would, he suggests, solicit and receive applications for appointment to the bench, collect information in respect of those being considered for appointment, and consult an extensive list of relevant 'stakeholders' both inside and outside government, along with others at its discretion. After considering all the information which had been collected, the appointments committee would decide who should be recommended for appointment.

As between a model in which the commission or appointments committee would make direct appointments and a model in which the commission or committee would be restricted to recommending appointments, Harris clearly favours the latter. But he nevertheless insists that the Attorney-General should be obliged by convention to follow the advice he or she receives without any discretion.

Harris does not satisfactorily confront the obvious criticism that in adhering to such a convention, the critical decision is, in effect, being made by the appointments committee, as the Attorney-General lacks a realistically exercisable discretion. Further, Harris notes that, as the Attorney-General's compliance with the wishes of the committee would be a matter of convention, it would be incapable of judicial enforcement. He points out that, as a result, a determined Attorney-General could legally choose to breach the convention and risk any consequential political and wider community criticism.

Harris, therefore, proposes an alternative model in which the commission or appointments committee would provide the Attorney-General with a number of names of persons considered to be suitable for appointment. The Attorney-General would exercise a choice as to which one he or she would recommend to the Governor-General for appointment. In this way, the principle of political accountability would be preserved, at least theoretically, but the Attorney-General's discretion would be restricted.

As already indicated, Harris considers that the judicial commission and judicial appointments committee should be prescribed by statute. The judicial commission, he suggests by way of example, would be required to appoint a judicial appointments committee consisting of three judges, two lawyers and two lay people.[15] The three judges would be a judge from the Supreme Court, a judge from either the Court of Appeal or the High Court and a District Court judge.

Harris considers that the appointments committee would be more likely to be impartial than the Attorney-General acting informally as at present. The impartiality of the committee would follow from the established impartiality of those appointed to the committee and the impartiality of the persons appointed to the commission. He argues that, ultimately, impartiality is a state of mind, the responsibility for which must rest with each individual member of the appointments committee.

Harris confronts the argument that such a committee, as a group, may be more inclined than the Attorney-General to appoint persons who are unlikely to 'push boundaries' with the risk of being regarded as overreaching. But this reservation, he considers, can be met by the qualities of those persons appointed to the commission. I doubt that this response adequately meets the criticism that a committee would be more unlikely than the Attorney-General to appoint persons who would 'push boundaries'. Relying on the 'qualities' of the persons appointed to the commission is not a sound framework for a commission assuming constitutional importance.

---

15 The writer can testify to the value of lay people. When Chairperson of the New Zealand Law Practitioners Disciplinary Tribunal from 1984 to 1989, the Law Practitioners Act 1982 required two members of the Tribunal to be lay persons. Over that period the lay persons proved their worth time and time again.

Based on the composition of judicial commissions overseas, Harris suggests that certain existing office holders could be appointed to the commission; the Chief Justice, the Chief High Court Judge, the Chief District Court Judge, the President of the New Zealand Law Society and the President of New Zealand Bar Association. With the addition of two lay members appointed by Parliament for fixed but staggered terms of four years, the judicial commission would total seven members.

8. THE ACCOUNTABILITY OF THE JUDICIAL COMMISSION

No doubt because he is critical of the accountability of the Attorney-General for judicial appointments under the current system, Harris is concerned to establish that the judicial appointments committee would not lack accountability. He accepts that the decisions of the judicial appointments committee recommending judicial appointments will be independent from the executive, but considers that, as with equivalent statutory bodies, the committee will be vulnerable to judicial review by the High Court on traditional procedural grounds. However, he rightly acknowledges the difficulties in having the High Court review a body on which judges, including senior judges, will sit. He does not consider, however, that this factor should rule out judicial review.

The main accountability path put forward by Harris would be to have the decision-making of the judicial appointments committee subject to review by a bipartisan select committee of Parliament constituted under the Standing Orders of the House of Representatives. The Select Committee would report annually to Parliament but would not revisit particular judicial appointment decisions. Rather, it would provide oversight of the administration of broad issues such as the appropriateness of the processes employed by the judicial appointments committee or the appropriateness of the gender and ethnic composition of the different courts. Harris does not doubt that the select committee's report would be taken into account by the judicial appointments committee.

No doubt appreciating that such an arrangement could be problematic, Harris suggests a 'further accountability path'.[16] This path would

16 "A Judicial Commission for New Zealand", supra n 1, at 405–406.

entail establishing a sui generis statutory body to facilitate substantive accountability for the decisions of the judicial appointments committee. Harris acknowledges that such an alternative would be cumbersome and cause yet another public body to be put in place at taxpayers' expense. I would add that having a second body review and, in effect, second guess the recommendation of the judicial appointments committee would be procedurally highly unsatisfactory. It would necessarily tend to undermine the work of the judicial appointments committee. Nothing would be more likely to impair public confidence in the appointments committee than having the committee's recommendations qualified, or even vetoed, by such a sui generis body. Moreover, it would be prohibitively awkward for nominees if the process had advanced to the stage where a recommendation had been made.

9. HARRIS'S SUMMARY

It is appropriate to quote Harris's own summary of the model he advances:[17]

> To summarise, a judicial appointments committee under the umbrella of a judicial commission could enhance the quality of the judicial appointment process in New Zealand. Most importantly, the committee could assume the primary decision-making role in respect of judicial appointments. This would relieve the Attorney-General of the task and establish the clear independence of the process from the executive branch of government. Accountability for the decision-making would no longer be possible through the Attorney-General's ministerial responsibility to Parliament. The quality of the judicial appointment decision-making process would rather be maintained by the quality and appropriateness of appointments to the judicial commission, which will in turn ensure the quality and appropriateness of appointments to the judicial appointments committee. Both the commission and the committee would be vulnerable to supervision of the quality of their procedures through judicial review. Review of the merits of particular judicial appointments is unlikely other than indirectly through the processes of the Judicial Conduct Commissioner and the Judicial Conduct Panel Act 2004. The administration by the judicial appointments committee of broader issues to do with judicial appointments may be susceptible to review by a select committee of Parliament.

---

17 Above at 405–406.

10. THE DISCIPLINARY PROCESS

Once a Judicial Commission is established it follows in Harris's view that the Commission should be responsible for the disciplinary process of judges. It would replace the present system provided in the Judicial Conduct Commissioner and Judicial Conduct Panel Act 2004. Harris makes out a compelling case. I have focused on Harris's arguments in support of a judicial commission for the appointment of judges and do not need to dwell on this aspect. Suffice to say, Harris would remove the Attorney-General, and therefore the executive, from any decision-making role in respect of judicial discipline. The judicial commission would appoint a judicial conduct commissioner or a small panel of commissioners to screen complaints against judges and decide which matters should be referred to a judicial disciplinary committee. The committee would decide whether or not a judge would be removed from office. If it decided a full hearing was required, it would conduct the hearing. A right of appeal would lie to a sui generis appeal body.

Once again, the importance of Harris's argument is the principle and not the detail of his proposal. In my view, once it is accepted that there should be a judicial commission it is logical to vest the disciplinary process relating to judges in that body.

11. CONTINUING JUDICIAL EDUCATION

Harris also proposes that the judicial commission should assume responsibility for judicial independence and continuing judicial education. Two principles are advanced for the provision of professional development; the first is that such development has to be provided consistently and preserve the independence of the judiciary; the second is the need for a strong involvement of the judges themselves.

I would part company with Harris on this point. I consider the task or process of educating members of the judiciary is essentially different from the functions of appointing judges and disciplining judges. It is a function that can be left largely to the judiciary and the Institute of Judicial Studies as at present. The danger of executive interference compromising the independence of the judiciary is so minimal as to be of little consequence in this context. The present system already involves the judges themselves. Moreover, apart from the educational function being essentially different in kind from the functions of appointing and disciplining judges, it would be unwise to divert the judicial commission's attention from these core responsibilities.

12. A FINAL APPRAISAL

I admit to having been vaguely neutral about the need for a judicial commission to determine or recommend the appointment of judges. Harris, however, has made out a compelling case for the establishment of a judicial appointments body and I am now of the view that such a body should be established.

One cannot fault Harris's starting point; that is, the extent of the judicial function. The power of the judiciary in carrying out the judicial function is too great to leave the appointment of judges to an informal system.

As indicated, for the judiciary to retain the confidence of the community the perception is as important as the reality. Citizens within the community must perceive the judiciary as being fully deserving of their confidence. That perception, I would think, necessarily requires them to be confident that the integrity of the process by which judges are appointed is beyond question. At present it is not, and cannot be, beyond question that judges are independent of the executive, when it is the executive that appoints them in the first place and that is then responsible for their promotion within the court hierarchy.

Although it is not without value, I consider that Harris probably weakens his overall case by providing an overly detailed formula for the establishment and composition of a judicial commission and judicial appointments committee. The detail invites scrutiny and disputation. While having been brought to the view that there needs to be a formal process, I have reservations about any number of aspects of the process Harris has suggested. It would be more productive, I would think, to establish the principle that there needs to be a formal appointments process and leave the detail to be worked out in the legislative process. Interested parties would undoubtedly be consulted – or, if not consulted, insist on having their say. Once the principle has been accepted it can be assuredly anticipated that much discourse would ensue as to the form the appointments body should take. I suspect that the outcome would be a compromise adopting some of Harris's suggestions but rejecting others.

I believe that anyone approaching the question whether there should be a formal appointments process with indifference or reservations will undergo the same change in thinking as I have, as they read and reflect on

Harris's proposal. Ultimately, the important task and power of the judiciary is too far reaching and too important to the community to leave to the vagaries and potential mishaps inherent in the present informal process. Ultimately, Harris's case is compelling.

Harris has written on this subject with his customary analytical and logical clarity. It is a joy to read his work. And, most importantly, his proposal for a judicial appointments body needs to be revisited.

THE CONSTITUTIONAL STATUS OF THE SENIOR JUDICIARY AND THE COURTS IN NEW ZEALAND

A Sketch

ATH Smith

1. INTRODUCTION

Sir Geoffrey Palmer has expressed the view that 'the New Zealand judiciary is an understudied institution'.[1] I agree with that evaluation, and am very pleased to have this opportunity to add incrementally to judiciary studies as part of this tribute to the career and work of Bruce Harris. The invitation to contribute also affords an opportunity to respond, however belatedly, to the plea of the Hon Justice John Priestley in the Henry Harkness Lecture,[2] when he said:

> As a group, the New Zealand judiciary find it difficult to explain or defend its constitutional role and its importance. Occasional champions are needed. Who better than the legal profession, *legal academics*, and (rarely I fear) a well-informed media.

As my title of this contribution suggests, I am concerned here with the position of the courts as well as the status of the judiciary. The two topics are interrelated in rather complicated ways, but my thesis of this contribution is that because of this interconnection, the judges are quite widely perceived as being, without more, a species of civil servant. This chimes with the remarks of the former Chief Justice, Dame Sian Elias, who expressed related sentiments concerning the status of the courts:[3]

> the courts ... are not seen as standing apart from the whole of government effort. They are not seen as a separate institution of government

What Dame Sian complains of, in effect, is that the separation of powers, the set of common law constitutional principles that seeks to treat the legislature, the executive and the judiciary as separate institutions, is not being fully respected in the New Zealand context, at least so far as the judges are concerned. Justice Priestley made a similar complaint, referring to an incident when he was identified on a

---

1 Geoffrey Palmer "The Judiciary as an Institution" (2015) 46 VUWLR 257 at 257. The article introduces a series of studies conducted by honours students as contributions to the general topic.

2 John Priestley "Chipping Away at the Judicial Arm?" (2009) 17 Waikato L Rev 1 at 1. The emphasis is mine. I confess that I am not entirely sure how best to offer my support to the judiciary, but the spirit is willing.

3 Sian Elias "Managing Criminal Justice", Address given at the Criminal Bar Association Conference, 5 August 2017.

name-plate at a seminar as 'Justice John Priestley from the Ministry of Justice'. His point was that 'a judge is … part of an arm of government, independent, and performing a vital constitutional role', rather than a civil servant, which his maladroit labelling implied if not asserted.[4] The significance of the point is, in the words of Professor Aileen Kavanagh that:[5]

> The independence of the courts ensures that they will not become the mere instrument of the executive or legislative branch when adjudicating disputes about what the law requires. It enables them to resist pressure from those other branches, thus strengthening their ability to uphold the rule of law.

The independence of the judiciary is implemented through a number of constitutional safeguards[6] regulating, in particular, appointment, remuneration and removal or dismissal. The constitutional guarantees surrounding these aspects of the judicial role, and especially the laws regulating dismissal are, I would argue, somewhat stronger than mere aspirations – they are more or less absolute values.

It is perhaps worth pausing to remark at the outset that no British monarch has been asked to exercise the power of dismissal, at least against English judges,[7] in the three hundred and twenty plus years since the Act of Settlement (Eng) was passed in 1700.[8] The procedure set out in that Act, involving as it does the participation of both Houses of Parliament was clearly intended to constitute a solemn and weighty process, not to be undertaken without serious prior deliberation.

A possible candidate for the application of the full weight of this procedure in the UK was Sir Peter Smith J, whose quixotic misconduct was referred to the Judicial Conduct Investigations Office (JCIO) in July 2015.[9] The conduct included the canvassing of some of the leading firms of solicitors for a partnership with a view to standing down from the bench,

---

4 Priestley, above n 2, at 2.

5 Aileen Kavanagh "The Constitutional Separation of Powers", in David Dyzenhaus and Malcolm Thorburn (eds) *Philosophical Foundations of Constitutional Law* (Oxford University Press, Oxford, 2016) 221 at 231.

6 See further below at n. 14.

7 An Irish judge of the Admiralty Court, Sir Jonah Barrington, is said to have been removed by William IV after an address by both Houses of Parliament in 1830, but there is some uncertainty surrounding this incident.

8 The Judicial Conduct Investigations Office was established in 2013 by the Constitutional Reform Act 2005 (UK) to replace the Office for Judicial Complaints.

9 See Barrie Lawrence Nathan "'Ain't Misbehavin': Judicial Conduct and Misconduct" (2020) 2 Amicus Curiae 8.

in the expectation of a large income.[10] Whilst still a High Court judge, he decided to sit in a case involving British Airways, with which he had been having heated exchanges about the loss of his luggage on a recent trip to Italy. At the beginning of the hearing, his first question to counsel for the airline was as to the whereabouts of his luggage, and he lost his temper with counsel who pointed out that the court had not been convened to consider that matter.[11]

In May 2016, the judge agreed to refrain from sitting, although he continued to be paid a full salary. In July 2017 the Lord Chief Justice, Lord Phillips made a further reference involving Smith J to the JCIO on a different matter. After investigation, the Lord Chief Justice issued a reprimand to the judge, which is the most severe form of discipline under the Constitutional Reform Act 2005, s 108(3). In October 2017, in the face of an impending investigation by the JCIO, the judge retired on full pension.

Sir Jeremiah Harman was another possible candidate after the strong criticism of him by the Court of Appeal for failing to produce a judgment until twenty months after the relevant proceedings were heard. His obituary in *The Times* said that 'in 1998, he was left with little option but to resign after an unprecedented attack from the Court of Appeal'.[12]

Transposed into the New Zealand landscape, the 1700 Act and its successors have had to be altered over the intervening years, to take account of local circumstances as they have evolved to meet New Zealand's changing constitutional needs. The abolition of the Upper House, the Legislative Assembly, in 1950 was one development that clearly necessitated change, so that the address in New Zealand now requires only an address by the House of Representatives.[13]

The 'safeguards'[14] are supplemented by a number of practices and constraints whose observance by individual members of the judiciary in turn guarantees that practical, day-to-day independence is maintained. They consist in practice of a number of areas of self-denial which exclude judges from the exercise of certain aspects of citizenship, and they are articulated in the Guidelines for Judicial Conduct 2019.[15] These require,

10 Lord David Pannick "A Case About Luggage with a Great Deal of Judicial Baggage" *The Times* (3 September 2015).

11 There was considerable evidence to the effect that the judge treated others to intemperate outbursts. See Nathan, above n 9.

12 "Sir Jeremiah Harman obituary" *The Times* (United Kingdom, 13 March 2021).

13 Constitution Act 1986, s 23. This is discussed further below.

14 Outlined above at n 6.

15 The original Guidelines were dated 2003, but they were not published on the Courts of New Zealand website until 2007.

for example, that judges must exercise restraint relating to membership of political organisations, voting, making submissions to Parliamentary Select Committees, participating in public debate, and so forth.

So far as the practical realities of the concept of the independence of the judiciary are concerned, a sombre note was struck in a lecture[16] by Sir Geoffrey Vos, then Chancellor of the British High Court:[17]

> No judiciary is completely independent of its government. The justice system has to be financed by the government, and judicial leadership must in practice co-operate with government if the justice system is to operate properly alongside other state structures to deliver efficient high-quality justice.

This chimes with Dame Sian's remarks, cited above,[18] which had in turn prompted Dr David McGee, a former Clerk of the House of Representatives and editor of *Parliamentary Practice in New Zealand* to suggest that 'The solution to the problem raised by the Chief Justice is surely recognition of a separate judicial branch assuming many of the functions now done by the Ministry of Justice. Its parliamentary link would be the Attorney-General. In this way the judiciary would be fully responsible (and accountable) for all judicial services in this country'.[19]

To date, that suggestion has not borne fruit, but the value of its insight should perhaps merit a fresh consideration.[20] There has been, since 2018, a 'Statement of Principles' on the Courts of New Zealand website, which is said to record '... the respective responsibilities and obligations of the Ministry of Justice and Judiciary relating to the administration of the courts and how these are appropriately discharged'.[21]

---

16 Delivered at the Victoria University of Wellington, "Limits of and threats to Judicial Independence" (Wellington, 19 October 2017). I record my gratitude to Sir Geoffrey for making a transcript available to me.

17 Sir Geoffrey took up office as the Master of the Rolls on 11 January 2021.

18 See Elias, above n 3.

19 Letter to *The Dominion Post* (New Zealand, 29 August 2017).

20 The courts are now dealt with administratively by the Ministry of Justice. Formerly, from October 1995 to October 2001, there was a separate Department for the Courts, and there is still a Minister for Courts, but the Ministry of Justice provides administrative support for the courts.

21 Courts of New Zealand "Statement of Principles" <www.courtsofnz.govt.nz/about-the-judiciary/statement-of-principles/>. In the original version, capitals were not used in relation to the Judiciary. This reinforces the complaints of Dame Sian and Justice Priestley already mentioned above. It may also be observed that judicial email addresses were for a time in the form Justice.surname@justice.govt.nz, but have now reverted to using '@courts' rather than '@justice'.

That may indeed represent a tidy administrative solution, but it would not solve the difficulty to which Sir Geoffrey Vos alludes,[22] namely that the courts ultimately remain in some measure at the mercy of the executive in matters of finance.

Public servants who interact with the senior members of the judiciary on a regular and routine basis probably have a slightly better understanding than most people of the subtle constitutional considerations at work. It is an almost universal source of tension that the civil servants have the power of the purse on their side in their dealings with the judiciary when the matter of resourcing the judicial branch is under discussion.[23] It is in the latter situation, I suspect, that the 'independence of the judiciary' is most at threat.[24] To quote Justice Priestley again: 'The judicial arm of government in New Zealand, although respected, is often sidelined or downgraded. There are constitutional risks in this phenomenon'.[25]

2. GENERAL PUBLIC PERCEPTIONS OF THE JUDICIAL ROLE

An underlying premise of my contribution to this tribute to Bruce Harris is that the complex, nuanced, constitutional position of the New Zealand judiciary is not particularly well understood: not by the media,[26] or by

22 See Vos, above n 17.

23 See Vos, above n 17.

24 This is a theme that ran through the account of the situation, following the implementation of the David Beattie *Report of the Royal Commission on the Courts* (Wellington, 1978) in Thomas Eichelbaum "The Courts: An Era of Change" in Ian Barker (ed) *Law Stories: Essays on the New Zealand Legal Profession 1969-2003* (LexisNexis NZ, Wellington, 2003) at 1. See also Thomas Eichelbaum "The Inaugural Neil Williamson Memorial Lecture: Judicial Independence Revisited" (1997) 6 Canterbury L Rev 421; Sian Elias "The Next Re-Visit: Judicial Independence 7 Years On" (2004) 10 Canterbury L Rev 217. It is also implicit in the remarks of Sir Geoffrey Vos cited above at n 16.

25 I rather suspect that, had the naming of the recently-built structure in Christchurch been left to the judiciary, it would not have been labelled as the 'Justice and Emergency Services Precinct'. No fewer than nineteen courts are accommodated in the new complex.

26 The financial resources of the New Zealand media generally are in a parlous state. See Mel Bunce *The Broken Estate: Journalism and Democracy in a Post-Truth World* (Bridget Williams Books, Wellington, 2019). They are such that specialist legal correspondents are rare, unlike better resourced jurisdictions such as the British and US presses. A number of academics do, however, comment on topical items of legal

parliamentarians,[27] or even by Ministers,[28] and not by the general public.[29] Even amongst lawyers, there appears to be little profound awareness or acute consciousness of New Zealand's constitutional heritage that places the judiciary in a special, but not privileged position.

In an effort to counter this misunderstood profile, the Judicial Office for Senior Courts recently 'produced a multi-lingual video explaining the role of the Courts and the key principles on which New Zealand's legal system is based'.[30] The audience at which this product is largely addressed is not made clear, but the sentiment behind it is surely to be applauded, and the accompanying 'Media Statement' noted that: 'Since her appointment as head of the judiciary, (Chief) Justice Winkelmann has emphasised the importance of making the courts and the law itself more accessible, and better understood, by all New Zealanders'.[31]

One of these 'risks' to which Justice Priestley alludes is arguably that the security of judicial tenure could be undermined as a result of this attitude to the judiciary. The unfortunate events surrounding the resignation of Justice Bill Wilson in 2010, discussed below,[32] are something of a bellwether.

---

interest on their own blogs and websites, and are willing to appear on radio, television and in the written press.

27 Guy Chapman "Criticism of Judges, Courts and Judicial Decisions, Especially by Politicians" [1995] NZLJ 267.

28 The relationship between ministers and the judges is dealt with in the *Cabinet Manual* at [4-12]–[4-16] and in the *Guidelines for Judicial Conduct 2019*. At the time of Wilson J's resignation, the Guidelines were dated 2003, but they were not published on the Courts of New Zealand website until 2007, and Justice Wilson indicated that he had not been made aware of them at the time of his appointment. See the Report of the Judicial Conduct Commissioner *Decision of the Judicial Conduct Commissioner as to Three Complaints Concerning Justice Wilson* (7 May 2010) at [96].

29 See the remarks of Matthew Palmer cited below at n 40. Relatively few New Zealanders are likely to have any first-hand legal dealings with the Senior Judiciary. Most of the routine legal disputes in New Zealand are litigated in the District Courts.

30 Judicial Office for Senior Courts "'Our Courts' a new video" (press release, 12 November 2019).

31 Above n 30. The Chief Justice is reported as stating that 'The independence of our judiciary is constitutionally important in New Zealand, but it is not well understood. It is essential for the judiciary to be independent to fulfil the role of checking the exercise of public power and upholding the rule of law'.

32 A detailed account of the proceedings leading up to Justice Wilson's decision to resign is contained in *Judicial Conduct Commissioner*, above n 28. The Report, dated 7 May 2010, is signed by Sir David Gascoigne KNZM, who succeeded Mr Ian Haynes as the Judicial Conduct Commissioner on 3 August 2009. The first complaint in relation to the Justice Wilson case was lodged on 16 May 2008. No immediate action was taken on that complaint by the new Commissioner, because there were proceedings pending on the matter in the Supreme Court.

I readily admit to being in the category of those who were made 'uncomfortable' by that incident,[33] but I wish to edge away from that starting point to ask some questions about public attitudes towards the institution of the judiciary in New Zealand more generally. In sum, there seems to be a general lack of understanding of the part that the judges play in New Zealand's legal and constitutional arrangements.

There would seem to be several reasons that contribute to this lack of understanding of the role of the judiciary. One explanation is that the position and roles of the judiciary are not static, even if they are reasonably stable. Their position can alter in ways that can be described as kaleidoscopic, as a result of changes made elsewhere in the body politic. For example, legislation designed to enhance the judicial protection of rights, such as the New Zealand Bill of Rights Act 1990 was bound to make some change to the judicial role, though it was difficult to predict at the time of enactment precisely what further alterations this might engender in the role of the judiciary. It is altogether likely that the constitutional relationship will alter further if the Declaration of Inconsistency Bill (2019) should become law.[34]

Similarly, in *New Zealand Māori Council v Attorney-General*,[35] s 9 of the State-Owned Enterprises Act 1986 was agreed by the judges of the Court of Appeal to be 'a firm declaration by Parliament that nothing in that Act shall permit the Crown to act inconsistently with the "principles of the Treaty of Waitangi" and overrides the rest of the Act'. This was a recipe for difficulty and was very likely to give rise to public disquiet about the judicial role in the interpretation of the Treaty of Waitangi Act 1975. At the end of his judgment, Cooke P states that: 'If the judiciary has been able to play a role to some extent creative, that is because the legislature has given it the opportunity'.[36]

Richardson J expressed his disquiet somewhat differently:[37]

> much of the contemporary focus is on the spirit rather than the letter of the Treaty, and on adherence to the principles rather than the terms of the Treaty.

---

33 See the words of Professor Harris quoted below at n 78.

34 See also the decision of the Supreme Court in *Attorney-General v Taylor* [2018] NZSC 104, [2019] NZLR 213, where the court held by a 3–2 majority that the court enjoyed a jurisdiction to make a declaration that legislation was inconsistent with the New Zealand Bill of Rights Act 1990.

35 *New Zealand Māori Council v Attorney-General* [1987] 1 NZLR 641 (HC and CA).

36 At 668.

37 At 672–673.

> Regrettably, but reflecting the limited dialogue there has been on the Treaty, it cannot yet be said that there is broad general agreement as to what those principles are.

A second possible explanation for the lack of understanding about the constitutional position of the judiciary is that some of the concepts and terminology regularly employed to explain the significance of the standing of the judiciary are themselves difficult to comprehend. They are expressed in terms of 'principles' which is in itself a mode of thought that is not easily grasped. Non-lawyers might well struggle to find access to clear and readily intelligible explanations of some of the key concepts underlying our constitutional arrangements. What exactly is meant by 'the Rule of Law',[38] and what *is* 'judicial independence'?[39] Independent of whom and what? What could amount to improper pressures from government figures?[40]

A third and slightly different explanation for local lack of knowledge (or indeed public interest in) the role of the judiciary is perhaps camouflaged to a certain extent by the fact that New Zealand is an aggressively egalitarian society.[41] In the face of that widespread social attitude, it can be difficult to maintain the argument that judges do and must occupy a special position in New Zealand's constitutional arrangements. This claim, when publicly articulated,[42] can readily give rise to the counter that, because judges are paid from the public purse, they are, or should be, in much the same position as civil servants so far as tenure of office and public

---

38 One of the best expositions of the concept is to be found in the book by Brian Tamahana *On the Rule of Law: History, Politics, Theory* (Cambridge University Press, Cambridge, 2004), who states in the prefatory section that he had his non-lawyer father in mind as the audience when he wrote. In 2015, uncertainty as to its place in legislation was evident when it was dropped from the Judicature Modernisation Bill 2013 without explanation. The incident was made the subject of public comment by Sir John McGrath at his final sitting, and the reference to the rule of law was reinstated later in the Parliamentary proceedings that ultimately became the Senior Courts Act 2016.

39 See Robert Stevens *The Independence of the Judiciary: A View from the Lord Chancellor's Office* (Clarendon Press, Oxford, 1993).

40 Matthew Palmer "Open The Doors and Where are the People" in Claire Charters and Dean R Knight (eds) *We the People(s): Participation in Governance* (Victoria University Press, Wellington, 2011) 50 at 63 says that 'I worry about this norm. Its meaning is not well understood either in theory or in practice. And I doubt it is well entrenched in our national psyche or by any cultural attitude'.

41 That is, for me, part of Aotearoa's charm. But see the editorial comment on the award of honours discussed below.

42 See the quote from Dame Sian Elias below at n 44.

accountability is concerned.[43] As the former Chief Justice, Dame Sian Elias once put it:[44]

> It needs to be acknowledged that the distinct place of the judiciary is not a popular notion. Politicians in my country tend to become indignant at the idea, pointing to their own meager (sic) retirement benefits and there is no widespread understanding that there is public interest in the separate treatment of judges. Indeed such notions tend to be resented as elitist.

Traces of the same themes can be discerned in the recent discussions as to whether or not the contempt law of scandalising should be abolished without replacement by Parliament, following the example of the UK.[45]

This attitude fails to give adequate weight to the constitutional history and the contemporaneous context that supports the independence of the judiciary, which is in turn a bulwark of the way in which the rule of law operates, at least in common law countries. The clamour that arises from time to time in the media about judicial salaries and pensions frequently contains a considerable amount of misinformed comment, much of it overlooking centuries of the history that gave rise to, and still lie behind, the protections that guarantee the independence of the judiciary.

3. APPOINTMENTS

Originally, appointments to the New Zealand judiciary were made in the UK under the Supreme Court Ordinance 1841, 5 Vict 1 (an Act of the Legislative Council), which established the Supreme Court of New Zealand.[46] The power to appoint judges was conferred upon the

---

43 Other public offices that are afforded comparable protection in New Zealand are the Parliamentary Ombudsman, and office of the Auditor General. Mr Martin Matthews resigned as Auditor-General on 4 August 2017 as a result of a decision of the Officers of Parliament Committee of the House of Representatives. See Geoffrey Palmer "A Constitutional Moment" [2017] NZLJ 382. Mr Matthews has appealed to Parliament to re-open the matter, and the proceedings are ongoing.

44 Sian Elias "Judicial Retirement Benefits: Superannuation" Judicial Conference of Australian professional Association of Judges and Magistrates (paper presented to Judicial Conference of Australian professional Association of Judges and Magistrates, 2004).

45 See further the discussion of this issue below, section 6.

46 See J Hight and HD Bamford *The Constitutional History and Law of New Zealand* (Whitcombe and Tombs Limited, Christchurch, 1914) at 360–361. There is a full

Crown and the Governor acting separately from one another, according to the needs of the circumstances. Twelve men were appointed permanently to the Supreme Court of the colony in the nineteenth century. All were born in the UK and most received their legal education and qualified there.[47]

Historically, considerable secrecy surrounded the various processes relating to the judiciary, and in particular the appointments processes. In the words of Professor Philip Joseph, prior to 1999 'the appointments criteria were not publicised, judicial vacancies were not advertised, expressions of interest were not called for, candidates were not interviewed and consultation procedures were ad hoc and uncertain'.[48]

Sir Thomas Eichelbaum acknowledged that, when he was appointed to the office of Chief Justice, 'there was insistent public and media criticism of the judicial appointments process to the effect that it was the preserve of an 'old boy's network' perfected by a mysterious process known as shoulder tapping'. Not perhaps surprisingly, Sir Thomas was quick to point out that 'this was not … how more than 40 Court of Appeal and High Court vacancies were filled while he was in office'.[49]

Over the years, there have been calls for a more publicly accessible and formal process,[50] suggesting that there should be an institutionalised procedure such as the establishment of a Judicial Commission for dealing with this extremely important exercise. These suggestions would have been expensive and difficult to implement, the proposal was opposed by the existing judiciary,[51] and the preference was to leave the matters in the hands of successive Attorneys-General.[52] The figure of the

account of the early developments of the courts and the judiciary in Peter Spiller "The Courts and the Judiciary" in Peter Spiller, Jeremy Finn and Richard Boast (eds) *A New Zealand Legal History* (2nd ed, Brookers, Wellington, 2001) at 187–249. See also Robin Cooke *Portrait of a Profession: The Centennial Book of the New Zealand Law Society* (Reed, Wellington, 1969) at ch 4 and 5 for details of the personalities.

47 At 47.

48 Philip A Joseph *Constitutional and Administrative Law* (5th ed, Thomson Reuters, Wellington, 2021) at 872.

49 Eichelbaum, above n 24. Sir Thomas was Chief Justice for the years 1989–1999.

50 AAT Ellis "Do we Need a Judicial Commission?" [1983] NZLJ 206, and the reply by Kenneth Keith "A Judicial Commission? Some Comments on the Independence of the Judiciary" [1983] NZLJ 239.

51 See Philip A Joseph "Appointment, Discipline and Removal of Judges in New Zealand" in HP Lee (ed) *Judiciaries in Comparative Perspective* (Cambridge University Press, Cambridge, 2011) 66.

52 *Judicial Appointments, Report to the Cabinet Strategy Committee*, STO (98) 245, 12 October 1998; *Judicial Appointments: Office of the High Court Judge*, Attorney-General's Department, Wellington 1999.

Attorney-General in New Zealand has a central role to play in the appointments process.[53] Given that the holder of that office is not required to be a qualified lawyer, there may be some residual doubts as to the wisdom of such a course,[54] even though there is now a consultation process that the Attorney-General is required to pursue. The Attorney is a member of the Cabinet,[55] but the Office that handles the appointments, the Judicial Appointments Unit is located as part of the Ministry of Justice.

In line with international practices,[56] the process has become increasingly formal, and has an eye to the inclusion of sections of the public that were hitherto overlooked or even systematically excluded.

Some rigour was provided when, in April 2013, the Crown Law Office published a *Judicial Protocol*, which describes in some detail the procedures and processes involved in appointments to the judicial positions. The obligation to proceed with greater openness than hitherto is now recognised in legislation, namely the Senior Courts Act 2016, s 93 of which provides that:

> The Attorney-General must publish information explaining his or her process for—
>
> (a) seeking expressions of interest for the appointment of Judges and Associate Judges; and
> (b) recommending persons for appointment as a Judge or an Associate Judge.

Critics will still say that the consultation process is still deficient in the appointment of the Chief Justice, because of a certain lack of transparency.[57]

53 See further below, section 6.

54 Sir Michael Cullen, who held the office from February until October 2005, was one such. Those looking for a parallel in the UK might point to the abolition of the office of Lord High Chancellor (one of the most ancient offices in the UK), who was until the enactment of the Constitutional Reform Act 2005 the Head of the Judiciary. Now the holder of the replacement office (Lord Chancellor) need not be a lawyer, and the Head of the Judiciary (as in New Zealand) is the Chief Justice.

55 Unlike the situation in the UK, where the Attorney has operated outside the Cabinet since 1924. For the background, see J Ll J Edwards *The Law Officers of the Crown* (Sweet & Maxwell, London, 1964) at ch 11.

56 See United Nations *Commentary on the Bangalore Principles of Judicial Conduct* (2007).

57 Matthew Hooton "Jacinda Ardern's most important decision as Prime Minister" *The New Zealand Herald* (New Zealand, 9 November 2019).

There is an extensive consultation process, which Professor Joseph describes as follows:[58]

> For High Court appointments, the Attorney-General and Solicitor-General each consult a range of persons representative of the professional legal community. These include the Chief Justice, the President of the Court of Appeal, such other judges as the Attorney-General or Solicitor-General choose to consult and the presidents of the New Zealand Law Society and the New Zealand Bar Association. Recent Attorneys-General have also consulted the opposition shadow Attorney-General, as symbolic endorsement of the apolitical nature of appointments.
>
> In consultation with the Solicitor-General, the Chief Justice and the President of the Court of Appeal produce a 'long list' of potential candidates, from which a 'short list' is drawn up when vacancies arise. ... The shortlist is presented to the Attorney-General, who makes the final decision.

Historically, positions on the higher courts were reserved for men. No women were appointed to the judiciary until 1993 when the dam was broken by the appointment of Dame Silvia Cartwright.[59] Dame Sian Elias was made a Justice of the High Court in 1995, and she became the first female Chief Justice of New Zealand (the most senior member of the country's judiciary) in 1999, being replaced by Dame Helen Winkelman in March 2019. In a recent lecture,[60] the new Chief Justice has made it plain that she would like to see a judiciary that is more representative of the people whom it serves. At some risk of being thought complacent about the fulfilment of this aspiration, it may be suggested the extensive consultation processes that must now precede judicial appointments[61] should ensure that this objective is more likely to be accomplished than at any time in the development of the nation's legal system. The appointment of Justice Joe Williams to the Supreme Court as the first Māori person is surely a harbinger of better things to come, and the fact that he was awarded a knighthood in December 2019 for his services to the judiciary

58 Joseph, above n 51, at 68–69. In the case of the appointment of the Chief Justice, the Prime Minister makes the recommendation to the Governor-General.

59 Having been made the first female Chief District Court judge in 1989, she became New Zealand's second female Governor-General in 2001.

60 Helen Winkelmann "What Right do We have? Securing Legitimacy in Changing Times" [2020] NZ L Rev 175.

61 Described above, section 3.

is a recognition of the different perspective that the judge has been able to bring to bear on the development of New Zealand law.

To return briefly to the claim made earlier that public misunderstanding of the judicial role may have their origins in New Zealanders' strong attachment to egalitarianism, one can point to the common public reactions to the granting of honours to judges. Unlike the situation in the UK, where knighthoods and dameships are conferred automatically upon appointment, in New Zealand any later elevation will be awarded according to the 'merit' of the judge in question. Any topic better calculated to provoke indignant and egalitarian letters to the editor it is difficult to imagine. An editorial in *The Dominion Post*,[62] having noted that 'Judges in the upper echelons of the court system still usually get a nod' went on to comment:

> It is a notion that some find odd in a society that prides itself on its egalitarianism ... For some, a system that included knights and dames was redolent of a society of aristocratic privilege, and hierarchies inappropriate to a small democracy on the cusp of the 21st century.

This appears to be both an objection to having an honours system at all, and to the fact that members of the judiciary are not infrequently the beneficiaries of it. It is not possible to counter both of these propositions in the course of a contribution such as this one. Suffice it to say that I believe the egalitarianism is misplaced when deployed against the members of the judiciary.

4. SECURITY OF JUDICIAL TENURE, REMUNERATION AND DISMISSAL FROM OFFICE

As described earlier, one of the constitutional legacies bequeathed to New Zealand by its historical British origins was a series of laws and practices which regulated (in part) the status of the New Zealand judges. The formal arrangements for security of tenure of office in the UK were to be found in the Act of Settlement 1700, which provided that no judge

62 "Honours from Her Majesty" *The Dominion Post* (New Zealand, 5 June 2007).

could be dismissed by any authority other than the monarch,[63] who could act to dismiss only if there was an address to the monarch by *both* Houses of Parliament.

The original judges appointed in New Zealand were not, initially, protected by the Act of Settlement 1700, so during the period 1840 to 1858, the judges held office at pleasure.[64] It was not until the enactment of the Supreme Court Judges Act 1858, which was modelled upon the Act of Settlement 1700, that the protections guaranteed by that statute were extended to the New Zealand judges. The general spirit of the Act of Settlement is now preserved in the Constitution Act 1986, s 23 of which provides that:[65]

> A Judge of the High Court shall not be removed from office except by the Sovereign or Governor-General, acting upon an address of the House of Representatives, which address may be moved only on the grounds of that Judge's misbehaviour or of that Judge's incapacity to discharge the functions of that Judge's office.

4.1. REMUNERATION

So far as remuneration is concerned, the salaries of the judges were originally fixed by statute, and were thus not subject to annual appropriation. The Constitution Act 1852, s 65, repeated in the Judicature Act 1908, made provision to the effect that salaries were not to be diminished during continuance in office. That situation is now preserved in the Constitution Act 1986, s 24 of which now provides that:

> The salary of a Judge of the High Court shall not be reduced during the continuance of the Judge's commission.

---

63 At that time, appointments were made by the monarch, and the judges held office at the Crown's pleasure. The Judges and the Demise of the Crown Act 1760 ceased the practice whereby judicial appointments lapsed upon the death of the monarch, but s II of the Act reiterated that the power to dismiss judges was to be retained in the monarch 'upon the address of both houses of parliament'.

64 See Philip A Joseph *Constitutional and Administrative Law in New Zealand* (5th ed, Thomson Reuters, Wellington, 2021) at 849.

65 Note that 'incapacity' was not a ground specified in the Act of Settlement 1700.

More comprehensive treatment of the matter is to be found in the Senior Courts Act 2016, s 135, which now provides:

> **Remuneration of Judges**
>
> (1) Judges must be paid, out of public money, without further appropriation than this section,—
> (a) salaries at such rates as the Remuneration Authority from time to time determines; and
> (b) such allowances as the Remuneration Authority from time to time determines; and
> (c) such additional allowances, being travelling allowances or other incidental or minor allowances, as the Governor-General may from time to time determine.

That this situation can cause mild irritation in some circles is illustrated in an article by Claire Trevitt,[66] who quotes then Prime Minister John Key as saying, shortly after MPs in Parliament had resolved to ask the Remuneration Authority not to raise MPs' wages in the light of the poor state of the New Zealand economy:

> I'm sure judges and the like will take a similar view and I'm sure the Remuneration Authority, in reaching their conclusion, will take into consideration that this is a time of restraint and it's important that we, as well-paid New Zealanders, show leadership.

It is difficult to know whether the Prime Minister was aware that he was treading on rather dangerous constitutional ground.

4.2. THE JUDICIAL CONDUCT COMMISSIONER AND JUDICIAL CONDUCT PANEL ACT 2004

After guaranteeing security of tenure by the enactment of the Supreme Court Judges Act 1858, no formal procedure had ever been put in place for bringing an 'address' before Parliament for the removal of a judge. At first the Constitution Act 1986, s 23 of which carried over the protections for the judicial security of tenure, was likewise not seen to require any

---

66 "Key Gives Judges a Pay Hint" *The New Zealand Herald* (New Zealand, 11 February 2009).

special implementation process. This was seen to be unsatisfactory to the Attorney-General, the Hon Margaret Wilson, who took the view that current practice (or rather, lack of it) did not adhere to New Zealand's commitment to the United Nations' Basic Principles on the Independence of the Judiciary,[67] Article 17 of which requires that:

> … a charge or complaint made against a judge in his/her judicial and professional capacity shall be processed expeditiously and fairly under an appropriate procedure. The judge shall have the right to a fair hearing. The examination of the matter at its initial stage shall be kept confidential, unless otherwise requested by the judge.

Largely in pursuance of that obligation, Parliament enacted the Judicial Conduct Commissioner and Judicial Conduct Panel Act 2004, which established a completely new framework for addressing and regulating judicial misbehaviour, and ultimately dismissal.

The purposes identified in the Act are uncontroversial enough. Section 4 provides that:

> **4 Purpose**
>
> The purpose of this Act is to enhance public confidence in, and to protect the impartiality and integrity of, the judicial system by—
>
> (a) providing a robust investigation process to enable informed decisions to be made about the removal of Judges from office:
> (b) establishing an office for the receipt and assessment of complaints about the conduct of Judges:
> (c) providing a fair process that recognises and protects the requirements of judicial independence and natural justice.

4.3. THE REGIME IMPLEMENTED BY THE JUDICIAL CONDUCT PANEL ACT

Where a complaint is made to the Judicial Conduct Commissioner about inappropriate behaviour by a member of the judiciary, the Commissioner has a number of options. The Commissioner may after investigation dismiss

[67] (13 May 2004) 617 NZPD 12934.

the complaint or recommend that the Attorney-General[68] should appoint a Judicial Conduct Panel to conduct further inquiries. The Panel is to be held in public, subject to a discretion in the Panel to proceed in private, and there is a power to prevent the publication of the Panel's deliberations. In the *Wilson* case, the Minister of Justice (Judith Collins)[69] acting for the then Attorney-General made a recommendation that a Panel should be appointed.[70] Justice Wilson sought judicial review of this determination, which was unsuccessful in the High Court,[71] but an appeal was allowed on further appeal to the Court of Appeal. Before any further legal proceedings could be commenced, however, Justice Wilson resigned. The worry that these events generated is that, were similar circumstances to recur, almost any judge is likely to prefer to resign rather than face a public Panel with wide-ranging powers to investigate the surrounding circumstances in search of evidence of 'misbehaviour' sufficient to warrant dismissal. As Professor Joseph put it in 2011,[72] this was generally taken to require some sort of 'moral turpitude' which distinguishes misbehaviour in this context from other conduct that would not justify removal. Shortly after Professor Joseph had published, however, in *Wilson v Attorney-General*, a full High Court found that 'moral turpitude, while determinative where it can be established, is not a necessary element of misbehaviour'.[73]

4.4. THE BACKGROUND TO THE RESIGNATION OF WILSON J

In the course of litigation before the Court of Appeal,[74] complaint was made by counsel for one of the parties that Justice Wilson had not disclosed to

---

68 Judicial Conduct Commissioner and Judicial Conduct Panel Act 2004, s 15(5). It is perhaps a matter of some concern in this context that the role of the Attorney-General in New Zealand is not required to be held by a qualified lawyer, although in those circumstances, it is likely that advice would be sought from senior counsel in the Crown Law Office.

69 There was a potential conflict of interest at work, since the Attorney-General, the Hon Christopher Finlayson and Justice Wilson had formerly been partners in a legal practice.

70 *Judicial Conduct Commissioner*, above n 28.

71 *Wilson v Attorney-General* [2011] 1 NZLR 399 (HC).

72 Joseph, above n 51, at 84–85. The language used to characterise misbehaviour has included 'corruption or corrupt motive, dishonest motive, perversion of justice, abuse of power, badness of heart and corrupt intention, partial and oppressive behaviour, partisan political bias, moral delinquency and corruption or moral turpitude'.

73 Joseph, above n 51, at 85.

74 *Wool Board Disestablishment Co Ltd v Saxmere Co Ltd* [2007] NZCA 349.

the other parties to the proceedings that he was in a business arrangement with counsel to one of the parties to the proceedings, nor to his colleagues on the court. When complaint was made by one of the parties to the proceedings[75] pursuant to the new legislation, the Commissioner decided to recommend to the Attorney-General[76] that a Panel should be convened to inquire into the conduct of the Honourable Justice Wilson.

Aspects of the way in which events developed thereafter were unfortunate. The existence of the recommendation to establish a Panel became public knowledge, and the judge took judicial review proceedings in the High Court to quash the decision.[77] That application to a full bench was unsuccessful, but leave to appeal from the High Court decision was given. In the circumstances, the judge decided in 2010 that he was compelled to resign from the Supreme Court. The honorand of this collection, Professor Bruce Harris summarised the general response as being that 'both participants and members of the wider community were left feeling uncomfortable by the exercise'.[78]

There have been some real concerns that recent experience shows just how easy it might now be to dislodge a judge from office. The issue is a sensitive one, following the resignation of Justice Bill Wilson from the Supreme Court Bench on 5 November 2010, and I address it with some circumspection. The topic has been comprehensively addressed by Professor Harris in his writings.[79] I am not at all sure that it is generally understood, even now, just how much damage to our constitutional arrangements might have been done by the events surrounding Justice Wilson's resignation.

After a trio of complaints had been made by separate complainants, the process by which events developed appear to have taken on a life of

75 The first of the three complainants was Mr PE Radford who was the sole shareholder and director of Saxmere Co Ltd, one of the parties to the proceedings that gave rise to the later proceedings. He took the view that Justice Wilson should have recused himself and that the attempted disclosure of the conflict of interest was inadequate.

76 As it happens, there was an acting Attorney-General in place at the critical time, Ms Judith Collins, because Justice Wilson was a former partner of Christopher Finlayson, who held the post at the time, and this was thought to give rise to a conflict of interest. It was she who took the decision to appoint a Panel to hear and determine the matter.

77 *Wilson v Attorney-General* [2011] 1 NZLR 399 (HC).

78 See Bruce Harris "The Resignation of Wilson J: A Consequent Critique of the Operation of the Judicial Conduct Commissioner and Judicial Conduct Panel Act 2004" [2011] NZ L Rev 625 at 626.

79 Harris, above n 78. See also Grant Illingworth "The Judicial Conduct Commissioner" [2011] NZLJ 35.

their own, and, once initiated, they proceeded with the inevitability of a classical tragedy. In brief, it was alleged that Justice Wilson, who had been designated to hear an appeal as a member of the Court of Appeal,[80] failed adequately to disclose the extent to which he was in a business relationship with counsel to one of the parties. There was a complaint that the judge should have recused himself at the outset of the case.[81] When the matter went to the Supreme Court, the court, not knowing the full extent of the business relationship between the judge and counsel, dismissed the appellant's claim. On a further hearing, however, the judge was required to disclose the details and extent of the business relationship in the course of three further statements that he subsequently made to the Supreme Court. As a result, the Supreme Court recalled its earlier judgment, and the Court of Appeal was directed to hear afresh the original appeal.[82]

There was very little public clamour amongst non-lawyers, and even lawyers who did know something of what was afoot were somewhat muted in their reactions. Were something similar to occur in the future, can we really be sure that the lessons learned from the Wilson proceedings will not be repeated? When we contrast what has happened in New Zealand with the counterpart arrangements in the UK,[83] something seems to be out of proportion.

4.5. A LESSON LEARNT

Questions may perhaps be asked as to whether or not the requirements of United Nations' Basic Principles (and in particular the requirement that 'the examination of the matter at its initial stage shall be kept confidential') were adequately respected in the Wilson scenario.

According to the Annual Report of the Judicial Conduct Commissioner for the year to 31 July 2020, one Panel has been established in the course of the year under review, but no details that would enable the identification of the individual who is currently the object of the process are provided.

---

80 *Wool Board Disestablishment Co Ltd v Saxmere Co Ltd* [2007] NZCA 349.

81 [2009] NZSC 72, [2010] 1 NZLR 35.

82 *Wool Board Disestablishment Co Ltd v Saxmere Co Ltd* [2010] NZCA 513, [2011] 2 NZLR 442.

83 Discussed above, n 7.

5. THE JUDICIARY, POLITICS, POLICY AND THE PROTECTION OF RIGHTS

Judges are by strong constitutional convention obliged to be politically neutral.[84] This is a fundamental principle underpinning judicial independence. Individual political preferences should play no part in judicial appointments, and no part in their decision-making. Historically, there were no doubt some difficulties about maintaining such a principled and pristine stance in the small jurisdiction of New Zealand.[85]

The courts provide the forum in which disputes between citizens *inter se* and between citizens and the state can be legally settled, in accordance with the rules and principles of the established laws. That is, in one obvious sense, their constitutional function. Where the dispute takes the form of a criminal prosecution, the courts will use the jury system in serious cases to assist in the settlement of questions of guilt or innocence. In the field of public law, they may also be called upon to settle disputes between citizens and the state, often by way of judicial review of administrative action. Perceived overuse of this judicial check on the executive could incite a governmental reaction.[86] It is at this point that the independence of the judiciary becomes one of high constitutional importance. It may be said that, in New Zealand, the device is used with some sensitivity.[87]

5.1. NEW ZEALAND BILL OF RIGHTS ACT 1990

One of the principal difficulties with the New Zealand Bill of Rights Act 1990 (BORA) was that it was not entirely clear how it was intended by Parliament to fit within the New Zealand constitutional and jurisprudential

84 See Joseph, above n 48, at 800. A classic study of this subject in the UK is found in the five editions of JAG Griffiths *The Politics of the Judiciary* (1977–1997). See also David Feldman (ed) *Law in Politics, Politics in Law* (Hart Publishing, Oxford, 2013).

85 In the course of his long career, Sir Robert Stout held the offices of Chief Justice and Prime Minister. It is possible that party politics were not then as tribal and partisan as they have subsequently become.

86 The UK government has established a Commission, under the supervision of a former Minister Edwards Faulks, to inquire into the use that is currently being made of this powerful remedy, which has its origins in the ancient common law.

87 See generally Dean R Knight *Vigilance and Restraint in the Common Law of Judicial Review* (Cambridge University Press, Cambridge, 2018).

framework so far as the judges were concerned.[88] The BORA did not provide any mechanism for the enforcement of its own provisions, which left it to the courts to implement, and it was not at all clear what they were expected to do.

Professor James Allan has long taken the view that the presence of a Bill of Rights within the common law jurisdictions represents the starting point along a road to government by the judiciary.[89] I have argued elsewhere that it has provided a mechanism in which the rights identified in the Act (such as the right to freedom of expression) had now to be brought into the judicial evaluation of marginal decisions such as the meaning of 'disorderly' in public order cases.[90] That is, it was a significant aid to interpretation.

Unlike the UK's Human Rights Act 1998, which made express provision for making declarations of incompatibility,[91] with the attendant legal consequences being carefully spelled out, there was an ambivalence about whether or not it might be open to the New Zealand courts to take a comparable step. The lack of clarity about this may have contributed to the fact that the BORA was initially regarded with some scepticism by the local legal professions.

5.2. DECLARATIONS OF INCONSISTENCY

Thirty years after the Bill of Rights Act came into force, and after a certain amount of hesitation,[92] the Supreme Court took the step in

---

88 See James Allan "The Effect of a Statutory Bill of Rights where Parliament is Sovereign: The Lessons of New Zealand" in Tom Campbell, KD Ewing and Adam Tomkins (eds) *Sceptical Essays on Human Rights* (Oxford University Press, Oxford, 2001) 375. For a view from the bench, see Patrick Elias "Reflections on Judicial Power and Human Rights" in Alan Bogg, Jacob Rowbottom and Alison L Young (eds) *The Constitution of Social Democracy: Essays in Honour of Keith Ewing* (Hart Publishing, Oxford, 2020) 1.

89 See "Bills of Rights and Judicial Power – A Liberal's Quandary" (1996) 16 OJLS 337; "Turning Clark Kent into Superman: The New Zealand Bill of Rights Act 1990" (2000) 9 Otago L Rev 613. It is a view that Professor Allan regularly airs in the Australian edition of *The Spectator* magazine.

90 ATH Smith "The Criminal Law and the Constitution" in Bruce Robertson (ed) *Essays on Criminal Law: A Tribute to Professor Gerald Orchard* (Brookers, Wellington, 2004) 119; ATH Smith "The Interpretation of Criminal Statutes" in Jeremy Finn and Stephen Todd (eds) *Law, Liberty and Legislation: Essays in Honour of John Burrows QC* (LexisNexis, Wellington, 2008) 25.

91 See ATH Smith "The Human Rights Act and the Criminal Lawyer: The Constitutional Context" [1999] Crim L Rev 251.

92 Claudia Geiringer "On a Road to Nowhere: Implied Declarations of Inconsistency and the New Zealand Bill of Rights Act" (2009) 40 VUWLR 613.

Attorney-General v Taylor[93] of confirming that there is a power in the courts to make a declaration of inconsistency.[94] That is, the courts would be empowered henceforth to state that legislation coming before them could be found to be incompatible with the provisions of the BORA. There was something to be said in favour of this development. Not least, it would resolve an issue that had been simmering for some years as to whether the courts already possess such a power as part of their general jurisdiction to grant declarations.[95] Clarity and certainty on important constitutional issues such as this is obviously highly desirable, and the present confusion is correspondingly undesirable.

Almost perversely, on 26 February 2018, the government announced that it intended to introduce legislation to create a power in the courts to grant declarations of inconsistency. A Bill to implement that step is currently before Parliament.[96] The step is not perhaps as great a constitutional innovation as it might at first sight appear – it had been a feature of the UK's Human Rights Act 1998[97] from the outset, and is used regularly within that jurisdiction without giving rise to much antagonistic comment. The significant feature of that legislation is that both the UK Act and the New Zealand Bill provide mechanisms through which the executive is given the power to alter the law to bring it in to line with the law with which it has been declared to be inconsistent.

The development in New Zealand is one that I welcome. But one purpose of this contribution is to issue the warning, I hope still timely, that we 'should be careful what we wish for'. Such a development would, in my view, potentially carry with it a number of risks that might give rise to unintended constitutional consequences. The principal of these is that

---

93 *Attorney-General v Taylor* [2018] NZSC 104, [2019] 1 NZLR 213. For a discussion of the case in the Court of Appeal, see Claudia Geiringer "The Constitutional Role of the Courts under the NZ Bill of Rights: Three Narratives from *Attorney-General v Taylor*" (2017) 48 VUWLR 547; John Ip "*Attorney-General v Taylor*: A Constitutional Milestone?" [2020] NZ L Rev 35.

94 See generally Nicolas Petrie "Indications of Inconsistency" (2019) 78 CLJ 612.

95 See the articles cited in notes 92 and 93 for detailed discussion.

96 The New Zealand Bill of Rights (Declaration of Inconsistency) Amendment Bill 2020 is currently before Parliament. The closing date for submissions was 11 August 2020. It is clear that the suggested remedies proposed in the Bill, would put the initiative for remedial action squarely in the hands of the political branch following a ruling of inconsistency.

97 The Act came into force on 1st October 2000, following an intense educational programme directed at those who were destined to have the most extensive (and intensive) dealings with the operation of the Act; in particular, the judiciary and the legal professions.

it might affect the constitutional, non-political nature of the New Zealand judiciary. The extent to which the New Zealand judiciary might already be politicised is, in itself, a contested area. Professor James Allan claims that the courts are inevitably dragged into this by non-democratic Bills of Rights.[98] This is not a view that I share. Where I think we should be able to find common agreement in this area is that, ideally, the judiciary should be as politically neutral as it is possible to be when they are confronted by contested areas of social policy.

An example of this might have been found in the decision of Collins J relating to the legality of assisted suicide in *Seales v Attorney-General*.[99] After an exhaustive analysis of the relevant provisions of the Crimes Act 1961, Collins J declined to grant a declaration to the effect that the provisions of the Crimes Act 1961 prohibiting euthanasia were in contravention of various sections of the Bill of Rights Act, indicating in effect that he had no power to make such a declaration.[100] It is likely that, if he had done as he was urged to do, there would have been a public outcry of the 'High Court Judge declares euthanasia lawful' kind. As it is, Parliament enacted the End of Life Choice Act 2019, and in consequence, a binding referendum on the issue as to whether or not the law should be implemented was conducted in parallel with the general election of October 2020. The result of the referendum was 65.2% in favour of change.

6. CONTEMPT OF COURT – THE ABOLITION AND REPLACEMENT OF 'SCANDALISING'

Much of the law of contempt of court is designed to protect and promote the administration of justice, whether that be by preventing the disruption of court business, preventing interference with the fairness of trials and/or compelling compliance with court orders.[101] In the course of administering these complex processes, individual judges are not infrequently made the subject of personalised attacks and criticisms by participants in the process. There is an ancient common law form of contempt, known as

98 See the articles cited at notes 90 and 91.

99 [2015] NZHC 1239, [2015] 3 NZLR 556.

100 At [210].

101 See *Arlidge, Eady and Smith on Contempt* (5th ed, Sweet & Maxwell, London, 2017) at [5-211]–[5-310] and *Supplement* (2019).

'scandalising the court'.[102] The terminology is clearly antiquated, and a number of jurisdictions, the UK in particular,[103] have recently dispensed with this form of contempt without replacement. Its use in New Zealand is very rare.[104]

6.1. THE KIWISFIRST WEBSITE

Before proceeding further with this topic, it is necessary to describe a website known as (and easily accessible as) 'KiwisFirst'. The entries consist of a list of, at the time of writing, nearly 100 members of the judiciary listed according to a 'rating' system. Some of the judges mentioned (and 'rated') have retired, and in a few cases are no longer alive. Much of the material is defamatory and would be actionable as such, and much of it gratuitously offensive to the judges and the members of their families and associates. It is not easy to ascertain when the website was first created, and it is possible that it has been in existence for many years. There was no reference to it in the seminal article written by John Caldwell.[105]

There is little doubt that the contents of this list are capable of doing considerable damage to the institution of the New Zealand judiciary, and to the reputations of the individuals depicted. One example may suffice. In 2006/7, Justice Dame Lowell Goddard[106] was invited to chair a Commission

102 In Scotland, 'murmering': see *Arlidge, Eady and Smith on Contempt*, above n [102], at [16-70].

103 Crime and Courts Act 2013 (UK), s 33. The leaders in this initiative were Lords Pannick and the late Lord Lester. The former was the author of "'We do not Fear Criticism, nor do we Resent it': Abolition of the Offence of Scandalising the Judiciary" [2014] PL 5.

104 A case that arguably falls into this category is *Solicitor-General v Smith* [2004] 2 NZLR 540 (HC), where a Member of Parliament, in the course of a family law litigation under active consideration in the court, contacted the opponent of one of his constituents and sought to persuade her to take a course of action that would be in favour of his constituent. In the course of a phone call, Dr Smith said that 'he was a Member of Parliament which was the highest Court in the land and that everyone is answerable to Parliament' (at [50]). The Court held that Dr Smith was in Contempt of Court.

105 JL Caldwell "Is Scandalising the Court A Scandal?" [1994] NZLJ 442. See also Priestley, above n 2.

106 Dame Lowell Goddard, who in 1988 was one of the first two women appointed Queen's Counsel, and who is thought to be the first person of Māori ancestry appointed to the High Court, where she served as a judge from 1995 to 2015. As at the time of writing, the website is still in existence. The webpage is headed with the following statement. 'Section 22 *of the* CONTEMPT OF COURT ACT 2019 makes it an imprisonable criminal offence to publish false statements about New Zealand judges or courts.

of Inquiry in the UK into historical child sex abuse in various institutions. It was a tribunal that had already proved very difficult for several chairs, and the decision was clearly intended to find a fresh face from another jurisdiction. Simply by typing her name in to Google, a number of my legal contacts in the UK had discovered KiwisFirst, and contacted me to ask about the credentials of the website and its assessments. As it happens, Dame Lowell was placed at the bottom of the list of judges on the KiwisFirst website. The damage done to New Zealand's judiciary generally is palpable and obvious. Dame Lowell had already agreed to accept the nomination before her name was made public, and she had little option but to proceed as agreed. In the result, she resigned after some three months of taking up the poisoned chalice, and it is not far-fetched to surmise that KiwisFirst had some hand in this outcome.

For the reasons articulated by the former Chief Justice Dame Sian Elias in her evidence to Parliament,[107] it is quite 'unrealistic and in any event undesirable' to expect the judges to take private action against these unfair and unjust barbs, by bringing proceedings in their own time and at their own expense for defamation or harassment.[108] Anybody who has been involved in such proceedings will know how time consuming and physically draining they can be.

6.2. THE CONTEMPT OF COURT ACT 2019

The recently enacted Contempt of Court Act 2019 is a comprehensive codification of most of the common law relating to this complicated area of the law.[109] Section 26(5)(f) abolishes the common law form of contempt by 'scandalising the court'. It is replaced with a separate offence of publishing a statement about a judge or court that is false, and the person publishing knew that it was false. In addition, it has to be shown that there

---

You can trust kiwisfirst.com to provide accurate information on New Zealand judges, having published information which brought down two high ranking NZ judges (Bill Wilson and Lowell Goddard) for breaching their oaths and having never been prosecuted for an alleged false statement since its launch in 2005'.

107 Sian Elias "Submissions to the Justice Committee on the Administration of Justice (Reform of Contempt of Court Bill 2018" (26 June 2018) at [18].

108 But see *Foskett v Ezeugo* [2018] EWHC 3694 (QB) where three judges brought successful proceedings under the Protection from Harassment Act 1997 (UK) against a defendant who was engaged in a social media and email campaign against them.

109 Law Commission *Reforming the Law of Contempt of Court: A Modern Statute* (NZLC R140, 2017). The author served as one of the 'independent reviewers' for this project.

is a real risk that the statement could undermine public confidence in the independence, integrity, impartiality or authority of the judiciary or a court.[110] There is a further mens rea requirement that the publisher ought reasonably to have known that the statement could undermine public confidence in the independence, integrity, impartiality, or authority of the judiciary or a court.

There is an associated power to make take down orders,[111] failure to comply with which is met by various punishments that include, ultimately, imprisonment.[112] It is a measure of the seriousness with which the offence is viewed, and sensitivity to the fact that these orders may interfere with the legitimate exercise of the right to freedom of expression, that s 23(1) provides that a charging document for an offence under s 22(1) may be filed only with the consent of the Solicitor-General, and s 23(2) provides that proceedings must be transferred from the District Court to the High Court.

Despite these precautions, and the degree of sensitivity with which these apparent restrictions upon freedom of expression are viewed, it seems altogether likely that the ambit of the statute will be challenged as being in breach of the freedom of speech guaranteed in the Bill of Rights Act. This was anticipated by the Law Commission, which addressed the point in its Final Report:[113]

> It is also important to emphasise that this contempt is not designed to prevent or deter legitimate criticism of court decisions or the views of judges expressed in those decisions or in papers or speeches. The right to freedom of expression, now affirmed by the New Zealand Bill of Rights Act 1990 (NZBORA), extends to criticism of judges and courts. The New Zealand Court of Appeal has always recognised the right of the media and the public to criticise courts and their work.

This effectively reflects the state of the common law, as explained by North P in *Re Wiseman*:[114]

> … we wish to make it perfectly clear that Judges and Courts are alike open to criticism and if reasonable argument or expostulation is offered against any

110 Section 22(1).
111 Section 24.
112 Section 16.
113 Law Commission, above n 109, at [6.3].
114 *Re Wiseman* [1969] NZLR 55 (CA) at 58. See Michael Taggart "Vexing the Establishment: Jack Wiseman of Murrays Bay" [2007] NZ L Rev 271.

> judicial act as contrary to law or the public good, no Court could or would treat that as contempt of Court. No wrong is committed by any member of the public who exercises the ordinary right of criticising, in good faith, in private or public, public acts done in the seat of justice.

Powers are conferred upon the High Court to make take-down orders on application by the Solicitor-General.

Now that the Contempt of Court Act is in place,[115] it may be hoped that the Solicitor-General will be moved to find the time and resource to deal with the blot that is much of the KiwisFirst website. It is a standing reproach to New Zealand's public affairs that this situation has been permitted to continue for so long. That is not to criticise those who have found themselves without the legal powers to tackle the admitted problem. The New Zealand public must be free to comment upon the judges and their handiwork. But the law should not permit comment that is manifestly false, or that impugns without reason or evidence the good faith or integrity of the judges and those who appoint them.

7. CONCLUDING REMARKS

As Sir Geoffrey's comment cited at the beginning of this contribution acknowledges, the New Zealand judiciary encapsulates and presents a topic that bears further and deeper study. What strikes me particularly is that the position of the judiciary is somewhat kaleidoscopic. A shake to the prism through which our judges are viewed can change the constitutional perspective. What will be the details of the role that the judges will perform when they grant declarations of inconsistency, for example. As yet, the fine detail has not been set, and we have to wait and see how far the judicial role may be altered, perhaps subtly in the initial phases, to meet the changing circumstances.

Finally, reverting to the plea of Justice Priestley that academics might be willing to support the courts rather more than they do,[116] I trust that my continued support for the Law Commission in its work on the law of Contempt to rectify this longstanding problem can be treated as being, in part, the support of Justice Priestley's 'occasional champions'.

---

115 The Act came into force on 26 August 2019.

116 Priestly, above n 2.

PART III

THE NATURE OF UNWRITTEN CONSTITUTIONS AND THEIR FUTURE

DWORKIN AND THE TREATY OF WAITANGI AS A LEGAL PRINCIPLE

John DAWSON

1. INTRODUCTION

This contribution concerns the status of the Treaty of Waitangi ('the Treaty') in New Zealand law.[1] It is stimulated by reading Bruce Harris's excellent recent book, in which he analyses the New Zealand constitution 'in terms of principles'.[2] Bruce's analysis of the constitution in that book is as clear and comprehensive as I remember his classes to be, when I had the good fortune to have him as my teacher, of both contract law and administrative law, at the Otago law faculty, in the 1970s. Subsequently, Bruce has had a long and distinguished career – as teacher, scholar and dean – at both the Universities of Auckland and Otago. I salute his achievements. It was a pleasure to have him as my teacher and later as a colleague. I am delighted to have the chance to honour him in this book.

1 For the official texts of the Treaty, in Māori and English, see Treaty of Waitangi Act 1975, Schedule 1.

2 Bruce Harris *New Zealand Constitution: An Analysis in Terms of Principles* (Thomson Reuters, Wellington, 2018).

Chapter three of Bruce's recent book concerns 'The Principle of Legislative, Executive and Judicial Respect for the Treaty of Waitangi'.[3] I propose to consider how this principle relates to concepts of law. First, I discuss the traditional – positivist and dualist – account of the circumstances in which the Treaty is recognised by the courts as part of the law of New Zealand. Next, I canvass two, related, alternative concepts of law, drawn from the work of Ronald Dworkin and Mayo Moran respectively. I suggest that these alternative concepts of law provide a better foundation for an explanation of how the courts use the Treaty in their reasoning than that provided by a strictly positivist concept of law. I conclude, drawing on these alternative concepts of law, that – contrary to the traditional view – the Treaty 'itself' is part of New Zealand law.

2. THE LEGAL STATUS OF THE TREATY

The traditional view (as I will call it) of the legal status of the Treaty in New Zealand is the one expounded by the Privy Council, in 1941, in *Hoani Te Heu Heu Tukino's* case.[4] On that view, the Treaty is not part of New Zealand law unless 'incorporated' into the relevant field of domestic law by legislation. This view reflects, firstly, the notion that a proposition will only count as law when 'positively' incorporated into a source of law recognised and enforced in the courts. And, secondly, it reflects the dualist conception of the relationship between international and national (or domestic) sources of law. On this dualist account, treaties are generated on the plane of international law and only enter the national legal system when actively brought within it by legislation enacted by the domestic parliament.[5] This dualist approach seeks to avoid the 'democratic deficit' that would otherwise arise if the executive (or 'Crown') could, simply by entering a treaty, change domestic law without consent of Parliament.

These propositions about dualism, in particular, and the need for the Treaty to be incorporated into New Zealand law, have never been explicitly repudiated by New Zealand courts, despite the extraordinary consequences.

---

3 See also Bruce Harris "The Treaty of Waitangi and the Constitutional Future of New Zealand" [2005] NZ L Rev 189.

4 *Hoani Te Heu Heu Tukino v Aotea District Māori Land Board* [1941] AC 308 (PC).

5 On the debate whether the Treaty of Waitangi meets the tests for qualification as a treaty under international law, see Matthew Palmer *The Treaty of Waitangi in New Zealand's Law and Constitution* (Victoria University Press, Wellington, 2008) at 154–168.

Those consequences include the fact that the Treaty, solemnly entered into between the British Crown and some 500 Māori leaders, in 1840, at many ceremonies and locations, would be viewed by the British as a sufficient foundation for their declaration of sovereignty over New Zealand, bringing these islands within the British Empire. And yet the courts of that Empire, that began to operate in New Zealand, would not view the promises made to Māori in the Treaty – to protect 'full, exclusive and undisturbed possession of their lands and estates, forests, fisheries', for instance (in the English version)[6] – as guarantees protected by law (a consequence that produced the famous Māori political slogan of the 1970s, 'The Treaty is a fraud').

Harris accurately summarises the traditional view when he writes: 'The starting point is acceptance of the negative principle that the Treaty by itself is not part of New Zealand justiciable law'.[7] Relying on that view, one might think that, if the Treaty had not been incorporated into the relevant field of domestic law, it would play no significant role in the reasoning of New Zealand courts, or, if it did, the courts would be mistaken: they would be acting contrary to the view of the Privy Council in *Tukino's case* that a litigant 'cannot rest his claim on the Treaty of Waitangi' unless he can 'refer the court to some statutory recognition of the right claimed'.[8]

Nevertheless, the leading texts all agree that, even when the Treaty is not incorporated into the relevant field of law, it can play a significant role in the reasoning of New Zealand courts.[9] It can significantly influence statutory interpretation.[10] It can generate mandatory relevant considerations that must be taken into account by public sector decision-makers, even when not mentioned in the statute governing the relevant power.[11] It can affect

6 Treaty of Waitangi, Article 2.

7 Harris *New Zealand Constitution*, above n 2, at 30. Philip A Joseph *Constitutional and Administrative Law in New Zealand* (4th ed, Thomson Reuters, Wellington, 2014) at 82 writes: 'The *Lands* case affirmed the status of the Treaty as a non-justiciable instrument' citing Richardson J in *New Zealand Māori Council v Attorney-General* [1987] 1 NZLR 641 (CA) at 672.

8 *Hoani Te Heu Heu Tukino*, above n 4, at 325.

9 Harris *New Zealand Constitution*, above n 2, at 32–34; Palmer *The Treaty of Waitangi in New Zealand's Law and Constitution*, above n 5, at 203–215; Ross Carter *Burrows and Carter on Statute Law in New Zealand* (5th ed, LexisNexis, Wellington, 2015) at 519–522.

10 *Huakina Development Trust v Waikato Valley Authority* [1987] 2 NZLR 188 (HC); *Barton-Prescott v Director-General of Social Welfare* [1997] 3 NZLR 179 (HC).

11 *Attorney-General v New Zealand Māori Council* [1991] 2 NZLR 129 (CA); *New Zealand Māori Council v Attorney-General* [2007] NZCA 269, [2007] 1 NZLR 318.

judicial discretion in public law remedies.[12] Its content can overlap with common law rules concerning Māori entitlements, that are progressively being developed by the courts.[13] And it may be stimulating the courts to recognise certain principles of tikanga Māori (Māori customary law)[14] as part of New Zealand common law (even in preference to rules drawn from English common law).[15]

None of the leading texts suggests that the courts are making a mistake in permitting the Treaty to have such influence on their reasoning, or that these developments constitute 'backdoor incorporation' of the Treaty into domestic law.[16] Yet these texts continue to assert that New Zealand courts adhere to the dualist approach: that the Treaty is not an enforceable part of our domestic law until incorporated into the relevant field by legislation.[17]

---

12 See *Ngai Tahu Māori Trust Board v Attorney-General* HC Wellington CP 559/87, 2 November 1987 in discussion of the appropriate remedy. This important but unreported decision, halting implementation of the Quota Management System for commercial fishing due to inconsistency with the statutory protection of 'Māori fishing rights', is attached to Law Commission *The Treaty of Waitangi and Māori Fisheries* (NZLC PP9, 1989) at Appendix F.

13 *Te Weehi v Regional Fisheries Officer* [1986] 1 NZLR 680 (HC); *Ngati Apa v Attorney-General* [2003] NZCA 117, [2003] 3 NZLR 643.

14 Law Commission *Māori Custom and Values in New Zealand Law* (NZLC SP9, 2001); Joseph Williams "Lex Aotearoa: An Heroic Attempt to Map the Māori Dimension in Modern New Zealand Law" (2013) 21 Waikato L Rev 1; Richard Benton, Alex Frame and Paul Meredith *Te Mātāpunenga: A Compendium of References to the Concepts and Institutions of Māori Customary Law* (Victoria University Press, Wellington, 2013); Māmari Stephens "Māori Law and Hart: a Brief Analysis" (2001) 32 VUWLR 853. On incorporation of Māori customary law into the legal education curriculum, see *Inspiring National Indigenous Legal Education for Aotearoa New Zealand's Bachelor of Laws Degree* (Michael and Suzanne Borrin Foundation, 2020). On certain barriers to recognition, see John Dawson "The Resistance of the New Zealand Legal System to Recognition of Māori Customary Law" (2008) 12 JSPL 56. The role of Māori customary law within the New Zealand legal system may soon be addressed by the New Zealand Supreme Court, which has granted leave to appeal in *Ellis v R* [2019] NZSC 83.

15 *Ngati Apa v Attorney-General*, above n 13; *Takamore v Clarke* [2012] NZSC 116, [2013] 2 NZLR 733; *Proprietors of Wakatū v Attorney-General* [2017] NZSC 17, [2017] 1 NZLR 423; *Ngāti Whātua Ōrākei Trust v Attorney-General* [2018] NZSC 84; *Trans-Tasman Resources Ltd v Taranaki-Whanganui Conservation Board* [2020] NZCA 86; Natalie Coates "The Recognition of Tikanga in the Common Law of New Zealand" [2015] NZ L Rev 1.

16 A broadly similar approach is taken to international law generally, and to fundamental common law rights, in New Zealand courts: see Claudia Geiringer "*Tavita* and All That: Confronting the Confusion Surrounding Unincorporated Treaties and Administrative Law" (2004) 21 NZULR 66; Claudia Geiringer "International Law through the Lens of *Zaoui*: Where is New Zealand at?" (2006) 17 PLR 300; Philip A Joseph "Constitutional Review Now" [1998] NZ L Rev 85.

17 Harris writes: '… New Zealand takes a dualist approach to international law. A dualist, as opposed to a monist approach, requires a treaty's contents to be adopted in a statute

3. IS THE TREATY 'ITSELF' PART OF NEW ZEALAND LAW?

What, then, is the position? Is the Treaty – unincorporated – part of New Zealand law or not? In particular, the question I pose is this: if the courts adhere to all these propositions simultaneously – dualism in relations between international and national law; the unincorporated Treaty not being part of New Zealand law; the Treaty nevertheless having significant impact on the courts' reasoning; and none of this is a mistake – what concept of law can they be relying upon? Could all these propositions be based on a single, coherent theory of law?

Dualist theory seems to take a binary approach to what counts as law. A proposition that starts life on the international plane will either be incorporated into a state's law by legislation, and then be embedded in a recognised source,[18] or it will not be incorporated, and will not become part of its law. On this view, incorporation is a sort of on-off switch to a proposition's status as justiciable domestic law. But how could that approach be consistent with the idea that a treaty is still influential, on occasion, in the reasoning of domestic courts, even when not incorporated into the relevant field of law?

In New Zealand courts, the unincorporated Treaty might even have mandatory force, of a certain kind. As mentioned, it might bear on contested matters of interpretation,[19] or factors to be considered in the exercise of a governmental discretion,[20] or the exercise of the court's own discretion as to a remedy. In such cases, the court might, first, be obliged to consider the bearing of the Treaty on the problem, and then it might have to justify, in its reasoning, the impact of the Treaty on the result. How could such implications of the Treaty for a court be understood if it were

before they become enforceable as domestic law. The Treaty of Waitangi thus has to find its legal force through a variety of statutory routes': *New Zealand Constitution*, above n 2, at 30–31; see also, Joseph, above n 7, at 71; Palmer, above n 5, at 168.

18 See the discussion below of HLA Hart's ideas concerning courts' recognition of positive sources of law.

19 'When legislation is ambiguous, an approach consistent with the Treaty is to be preferred': Sian Elias "Māori and the New Zealand Legal System" (2002) 76 ALJ 620 at 626, citing *New Zealand Māori Council v Attorney-General* above n 7 at 656 per Cooke P.

20 'Perhaps most importantly, the Treaty impacts upon the exercise of discretions conferred as a matter of statute or prerogative. It is here that a real revolution in attitude to the Treaty can be seen', above n 19, at 626.

not part of New Zealand law? It would surely be strange to say that a court must take something into account, for such purposes, when it is not part of the law.

Perhaps the key to identifying the dominant concept of law underpinning the traditional view of the Treaty's legal status is the frequent use of certain terms: terms such as 'directly', 'enforceable', 'justiciable' law, that 'determines' 'claims of right'. Perhaps the use of these terms suggests that the name of domestic law should only apply to propositions that can be directly relied upon in national courts to enforce or determine claims of right, or that only when litigants can put their 'cause of action' 'directly' on the Treaty should it be viewed as part of New Zealand law.

But is this the right concept of law to deploy, if it cannot adequately explain certain less direct but still significant (and perhaps even mandatory) roles that the Treaty is playing in the courts' reasoning, and we do not think the courts, in this regard, are making a mistake? For a better explanation, do we need a different concept of law?

The remainder of this contribution explores two alternative concepts that might provide a more coherent foundation for such an understanding. One of these comes from the work of Ronald Dworkin, who argues that legal principles, as well as more determinative legal rules, are part of the law. The other comes from the work of Mayo Moran, a Canadian scholar. She argues that 'influential authority' is an important part of the law.

4. RONALD DWORKIN'S CONCEPT OF LAW

One way to argue that the Treaty is part of domestic law is to say that it functions as a legal principle in New Zealand courts even when not incorporated by legislation into a directly applicable legal rule, and that, in this sense, it is part of our law.

Dworkin argues that the law is composed of both legal principles and legal rules. To make this case, first he distinguishes legal principles from legal rules. Then he claims that both should be treated as part of the law.[21] Legal principles, for Dworkin, are general standards expressing propositions of 'political morality' that are embedded in the law. Nevertheless, they are distinguishable from legal rules, particularly because different methods

---

21 See, especially, Ronald Dworkin "The Model of Rules I" and "Hard Cases" in *Taking Rights Seriously* (Harvard University Press, Cambridge, 1978) at ch 2 and ch 4; Ronald Dworkin *Law's Empire* (Harvard University Press, Cambridge, 1986).

are required for their identification and they function differently in legal argument.

As is well known, Dworkin developed his ideas in response to the positivist legal philosophy of HLA Hart. Hart had argued in *The Concept of Law* that, in a developed legal system, law consists of special social rules derived from specific sources that are recognised as authoritative and binding by the courts (or other officials) of that legal system.[22] These social rules meet the tests for law set by the 'rules of recognition' (to use Hart's famous term) that are followed by the courts of that legal system.[23]

The courts will generally apply the rules, derived from the recognised sources, in some established, hierarchical order: rules higher in the order trumping those lower in the order, and so on. In addition, on the positivist account (though Hart does not make much of this point), the rules will generally be organised into distinct compartments (or fields) of law – crime, property, company, family, tax, and so on. And these compartments will usually be viewed as fairly tightly sealed. So, it would not be permissible to 'drag' a rule from one compartment to another, wherein it does not 'strictly apply'.

This vertical and horizontal ordering of the rules drawn from particular, recognised sources of law is of course designed to permit *legal* rules to be distinguished from rules drawn from other spheres of social life: morality, religion, politics, culture, and so on. Rules drawn from those spheres will count as *legal*, on this view, only when incorporated into a recognised source of law. The aim is to establish clarity and certainty as to what counts as law, permitting people to identify, and know, the content of the norms with which they must comply.

How, then, does Dworkin's position differ? In constructing his concept of law, Dworkin accepts much of this positivist case. But he takes the view that Hart's account of how the courts recognise (or identify) law seriously underestimates the range of resources that courts actually use to resolve disputes (especially in 'hard cases'), particularly the extent to which the courts use certain moral and political propositions in their reasoning without any apparent need to go beyond the law. These weaknesses in Hart's account are particularly evident, says Dworkin, when Hart fails to recognise the role being played by legal principles in the courts' reasoning.

---

22 HLA Hart *The Concept of Law* (Clarendon, Oxford, 1961).

23 At 100–107.

As said, legal principles, for Dworkin, are broad standards that express propositions of political morality embedded in the law – propositions about rights, justice, fairness, the conduct of good government, and so on. But crucially, these principles cannot always be identified by reference to any formal rule of recognition, developed by the courts, that sets the test for law in that legal system. A principle might not fit the rule of recognition, either because it does not have the right standing within the structure of legal norms, or because it does not come from the right compartment of law. This is the difficulty with the Treaty when not incorporated by legislation into the relevant field: it seems to stand outside the recognised sources of law.

Dworkin nevertheless argues that principles can be viewed as part of the law – even when not coming from sources with the right standing in the structure of norms, or from the right compartment of law. He therefore parts company here with the positivist account of law.

4.1. HOW LEGAL PRINCIPLES ARE TO BE IDENTIFIED

Principles can be identified, says Dworkin, by a distinct process of inference. They are immanent in the law. Courts can infer them from diverse sets of materials, drawn from across the legal system as a whole. Principles can be inferred from networks of legal rules, both statutory and common law. They can even be inferred from rules that might be thought to belong in the 'wrong' compartment so not 'directly' relevant to the current legal problem. Principles of political morality can be identified that the rules in those other compartments 'presuppose by way of justification'.[24] Or, putting it another way, authoritative values can be found, embedded in those other compartments' rules. These authoritative values are part of the law as a whole. They can therefore be legitimately used by courts in their reasoning.

Principles can also be inferred from the design of legal institutions. They are immanent, for instance, from the separation of powers deliberately established between different branches of the government, and

---

24 'Rights and responsibilities flow from past decisions [of courts and legislatures] and so count as legal, not just when they are explicit in these decisions but also when they follow from the principles of personal and political morality the explicit decisions presuppose by way of justification': Dworkin *Law's Empire*, above n 21, at 96.

in the allocation of certain roles, to judge, jury and witness, in the criminal trial. They can be seen in judicial conventions and practices: in patterns of judicial deference, for instance, to other branches of government.

These principles express certain values that have been installed within the legal system's network of rules, or within its institutions and judicial practices, by decisions made in the past – by the Crown, Parliament, courts, institutional designers, and so on, in the construction of the legal order. Their content can be identified with tolerable clarity, even if they have never been stated in a rule with the right pedigree – even, perhaps, if they have never previously been reduced to a verbal formulation at all. Finding principles in this way is standard judicial practice, says Dworkin, and there is no good reason to think that the norms so identified fall outside the law.

Drawing inferences as to these authoritative values will require the courts to engage in 'interpretation' of the normative fabric of the law. That engagement can be controversial, and the courts will be forced to make difficult judgments – about the precise principles to identify, and the exact weight (or importance) they will carry in different contexts. To perform those tasks, the courts will have to grapple with the actual content of the values the principles express. That cannot be a purely formal exercise. But it is necessary, if the courts are to give consistent expression to the values already found within the law.

4.2. HOW PRINCIPLES FUNCTION IN LEGAL REASONING

None of this means that principles, so identified and weighed, necessarily function in the same way in courts' reasoning as clearly formulated rules that have been laid down in the right source and are found in the right compartment. Principles can (and do) function differently than rules in legal argument – though this need not stop us calling them law.

Generally, in courts' reasoning, says Dworkin, a principle – unlike a directly applicable rule – will not 'determine' the case. Instead, it will exert a certain force, or pressure, on the argument, depending on the weight it carries, in this context. It will influence the argument, not determine it. Furthermore, the weight of any counter-principle, that points in another direction, must also be assessed.

Then, having identified and weighed the relevant principles, the court must state the reasons for its judgment, explaining how and why certain principles support its decision. The quality of those reasons is critical. How convincing is the court's explanation? Do the reasons given best fit the full set of legal materials, and best elaborate, in the current context, the values found within the law?

In this mode, principles can resolve conflicts between rules, settle the interpretation of rules, or fill the spaces between rules. A principle can bear on the exercise of discretion. It can intensify the judicial gaze. It can even 'crystallise', on occasion, into a new rule – when necessary to give that principle proper effect within the legal order, and no more important principle stands in the way.

The normative power of a principle might even cause a court to refuse to follow a clearly applicable legal rule. Those occasions will be rare, because one powerful principle of the legal system is that clear legal rules should be applied, and that principle will usually win. In that case, the force of the principle and the application of the rule will coincide. But even this 'clear rules should be applied' principle is not absolute: it can be set aside, on occasion, by an even more powerful counter-principle – by the idea, for instance, that the government should be kept within the rule of law.[25]

In effect, Dworkin is asking: if principles can be identified in this manner, and do play such an important role in courts' reasoning, why not call them law – even if they function differently in argument than directly applicable legal rules?

Finally, Dworkin argues, if principles are law, then their use is not optional for a court. The court must identify and apply them, if it is to make proper use of all available law – as the litigants are entitled to expect.

5. THE TREATY AS A SOURCE OF LEGAL PRINCIPLE

Such a graduated concept of law would seem to provide a better foundation for an understanding of the role played by the Treaty in the reasoning of New Zealand courts.

The precise character of the Treaty principle to be identified is obviously open to debate. We might infer that the Treaty now forms the foundation for a powerful principle of political morality within the New Zealand legal system that imposes a duty on the state to respect the authority, rights and culture of Māori, within a national system of government.[26]

---

25 *Anisminic v Foreign Compensation Commission* [1969] 2 AC 147 (HL).

26 When Chief Justice, Dame Sian Elias wrote extra-judicially: 'The "kawanatanga" [governance] ceded to the Queen was effective to cede territorial sovereignty but it

We can readily see the range of resources from which such a principle can be drawn via the process of inference that Dworkin describes.[27] It can be drawn from the extensive network of New Zealand statutes that incorporate references to the Treaty (or its 'principles') into specific fields of law: statutes governing state-owned lands, fisheries, conservation, resource management, the environment, education, health, science, and so on. Such a principle can also be drawn from the dozens of statutes enacted to give effect to 'Treaty settlements' entered between the New Zealand Crown and specific Māori descent groups, with a view to quietening their grievances concerning breach of the Treaty regarding their authority, assets and interests.[28] The features of these Treaty settlement statutes include establishing complex co-management regimes between Māori collectives and public authorities over aspects of the environment. These statutes also recognise that specific Māori descent groups hold mana whenua (customary authority) over certain regions of the country or features of the environment. They refer to Māori customary law concepts. And they record apologies that state the Crown's intention to atone, through the Treaty settlement, for the wrongs of the past, and its intention to establish a new relationship with the group based on respect for the Treaty's guarantees.[29] Would we really say that these Treaty-related statutes as a whole exert no gravitational force on legal argument in other compartments of law?

We can see Treaty values in the design of certain major institutions of New Zealand's government and legal system. They are immanent in the existence of the Māori seats in Parliament, that ensure there is always some Māori representation in the House.[30] They are present in the current functions of the Māori Land Court – ensuring the retention of Māori land.[31] We see them in the functions of the Waitangi Tribunal, which

---

preserved as much autonomy or rangatiratanga to Māori as did not imperil the overall objective. The Treaty was … a blueprint for future development, and a foundation of obligations and rights recognisable in a working legal system': in "Māori and the New Zealand Legal System", above n 19, at 625.

27 See Williams, above n 14.

28 Nicola Wheen and Janine Hayward (eds) *Treaty of Waitangi Settlements* (Bridget Williams Books, Wellington, 2012); Alan Ward *An Unsettled History: Treaty Claims in New Zealand Today* (Bridget Williams Books, Wellington, 1999).

29 For example, Waikato Raupatu Claims Settlement Act 1995, s 4; Ngai Tahu Claims Settlement Act 1998, s 4; Maureen Hickey "Apologies in Treaty settlements" in Wheen and Hayward, above n 28, 79. See how clauses 22.2 and 22.3 of the statement of claim were pitched by the applicants in *Ngāti Whātua Ōrākei Trust v Attorney-General*, above n 15, at [23].

30 Electoral Act 1993, ss 45 and 76–79.

31 Te Ture Whenua Māori Act 1993/Māori Land Act 1993.

conducts inquiries into Crown breaches of Treaty principles and makes recommendations for redress.[32] And we see them in the authority conferred by statute on agencies such as Te Ohu Kai Moana, which manages and distributes collectively owned Māori commercial fishing assets.[33] Parallel expressions of principle can be found in developments in the common law of aboriginal peoples' rights and concerning the fiduciary obligations of the Crown.

Without difficulty, powerful principles of political morality can be inferred from these statutory, common law and institutional arrangements as a whole, principles reinforced on the international plane by the United Nations Declaration on the Rights of Indigenous Peoples, issued by the General Assembly,[34] that New Zealand has endorsed.

Clearly, principles of such power exert significant pressure on legal argument, even in fields where Treaty values have not been incorporated into a directly applicable legal rule. Under Dworkin's concept of law, when the courts respond to such pressure, they are simply giving proper weight to a central principle of political morality that has been woven – mainly by actions taken by Parliament – into the texture of New Zealand law.

6. MAYO MORAN ON 'INFLUENTIAL AUTHORITY'

Using very similar ideas to those of Dworkin (as she acknowledges), Moran draws attention to the role in contemporary legal reasoning of what she calls 'influential authority': that is, authority that is less than strictly binding on a court, but more than merely persuasive.[35] The unincorporated Treaty could also be described in these terms.

Moran has written on the role of unincorporated treaties (or conventions) in domestic law, and the role of constitutional bills of rights in litigation between private parties (when a bill of rights usually applies directly only to state action, or the exercise of public functions, not the actions of private parties).[36] In both situations, Moran argues, the relevant

---

32 Treaty of Waitangi Act 1975.

33 Māori Fisheries Act 2004, Part 2.

34 United Nations Declaration on the Rights of Indigenous Peoples GA Res 61/295 (2007).

35 Building on H Patrick Glenn "Persuasive Authority" (1987) 32 McGill LJ 261.

36 For example, Mayo Moran "Authority, Influence and Persuasion: *Baker*, Charter Values and the Puzzle of Method" in David Dyzenhaus (ed) *The Unity of Public Law* (Hart, Oxford, 2004) at 389.

legal instruments are 'influential' in the courts' reasoning. On their own, these instruments may not establish a cause of action or grant substantive legal rights.[37] Nevertheless, they can have mandatory consequences for the courts' reasoning. First, the court must take them into account, when relevant, and assess their weight, in the context of the case. Then the court must justify its decision on those aspects of the case, as part of its duty to give reasons.[38]

Nevertheless, in these situations, Moran says, it is not the text or precise rules (or 'rights') included in the international convention or constitutional instrument that exert the influence on the reasoning. It is the values for which the whole instrument stands. When the Canadian Charter is invoked in private litigation, for instance, the courts talk of 'Charter values' as carrying the influence, not 'The Charter' or its 'rights'. When, in such situations, the instrument is not directly applicable, it functions in a different way, as a source of general standards of political morality that, due to infusion in the instrument, are part of the legal order as a whole. In short, the instrument acts, in this context, as a source of principle, not rules. Using this terminology in New Zealand, we could say that the Treaty of Waitangi functions as a form of influential authority in adjudication, even when not directly incorporated into the relevant field of law.

Moran writes:[39]

> I particularly want to draw attention to the role of mandatory values in adjudication ... These values exert a certain kind of demand that gives them something in common with binding rules – they do not simply persuade, they compel.

They compel in the sense that they must be considered by a court, and that they must be accounted for in the court's justification of its decision.[40]

---

37 The Supreme Court of Canada has said of the analogous constitutional doctrine of the honour of the Crown, in Canada, that it '... is not a cause of action in itself; rather it speaks to how obligations that attract it must be fulfilled': *Manitoba Métis Federation v Canada* 2013 SCC 14, [2013] 1 SCR 623 at [73].

38 Dame Sian Elias CJ has referred to 'a climate of justification which has transformed public power': "Fundamentals: A Constitutional Conversation" (2011) 19 Waikato L Rev 1 at 10. See also David Dyzenhaus "Law as Justification: Etienne Mureinik's Conception of Legal Culture" (1998) 14 South African Journal on Human Rights 11; John Ip "*Attorney-General v Taylor*: A Constitutional Milestone?" [2020] NZ L Rev 25.

39 Mayo Moran "Influential Authority and the Estoppel-like Effect of International Law" in Hilary Charlesworth and others (eds) *The Fluid State: International Law and National Legal Systems* (The Federation Press, Sydney, 2005) 156 at 159.

40 Similarly, it has been suggested that 'the Māori legal system ... was fundamentally values based, not rules oriented': Edward Durie "Will the Settlers Settle? Cultural

7. CONCLUSION

This contribution has inquired into the concept of law that underpins the New Zealand courts' approach to the unincorporated Treaty, in their reasoning. My conclusion is that a concept of law that considers the Treaty part of New Zealand law only when incorporated into a directly applicable legal rule cannot explain the sophistication of the courts' practices. Those practices are better explained by viewing the law as composed of either directly applicable rules *and* those principles of political morality that are immanent in the legal order as a whole; or as a spectrum of authoritative sources, from strictly binding, through influential, to persuasive. If certain propositions consistently influence judicial reasoning in a manner considered legitimate, why not call them law?

In the current context, use of such an expanded concept of law has many advantages. It permits us to see that the Treaty – even when not directly incorporated into the relevant field – is part of New Zealand law. It suggests that blunt statements to the effect that the Treaty is not part of 'justiciable' or 'enforceable' law should not be taken at face value. Those statements might be accurate if based on a concept of law that included within its compass only legal rules that 'directly ground claims of right', or something of that kind.[41] But, why should we accept such a narrow concept of law, if it does not adequately explain the complexity of the phenomena? Such a concept does not help us understand that the Treaty is an important source of legal principle that can powerfully (even if 'indirectly') influence legal argument. Nor does it indicate that the unincorporated Treaty can have mandatory effects, expressing authoritative values that must be accounted for in the justification of a court's decision.

On this view, for the courts to be influenced by the Treaty as a principle would not take them beyond the law, or beyond their legitimate role, especially when it is Parliamentary action, above all, that has brought the Treaty within the fabric of New Zealand law. Even the courts' crystallisation of new rules to give better effect to the Treaty principle, including

Conciliation and Law" (1996) 8 Otago L Rev 449 at 455; Carwyn Jones *New Treaty, New Tradition: Reconciling New Zealand and Māori Law* (UBC Press, Vancouver, 2016) at ch 2. It has also been suggested that it is the values of Māori customary law that will be recognised as part of New Zealand common law: *Takamore v Clarke* [2011] NZCA 587, [2012] 1 NZLR 573; *Takamore v Clarke*, above n 15; Coates, above n 15.

41 Carter *Statute Law in New Zealand*, above n 9, at 519, summarises the traditional view in close to this form when he says: 'The traditional view is that the Treaty of Waitangi … creates no rights directly enforceable in our courts'.

development of new common law rules, need not be viewed as taking the courts beyond existing law.

Using such a concept reveals the rolling system of principle of which our law is partly composed. It shows why the courts are bound to be influenced by the gravitational force of the Treaty principle, as it becomes imprinted in the fabric of the law. It shows that further legal developments are likely, including the courts issuing declarations of incompatibility between legislation and the Treaty principle,[42] and the courts even declaring legislation invalid when they find it contrary to that principle (whether or not they express it in that way).[43]

There are of course many other powerful principles of political morality that influence the reasoning of New Zealand courts, not least the principle of parliamentary democracy that stands behind the force of statute. Nevertheless, New Zealand law seems to be moving towards a position in which the courts will need to justify a decision to give that parliamentary democracy principle more weight than the Treaty principle, on important occasions.

---

42 As canvassed by Hanna Wilberg "Judicial Remedies for the Original Breach?" [2007] NZ L Rev 713; *Kiwi Party v Attorney-General* [2020] NZCA 80 at [50]: 'In an appropriate case it may be possible to argue that there is a similar jurisdiction to that recognised in *Taylor* for the courts to declare legislation inconsistent with the Treaty of Waitangi'.

43 A different kind of development would be the establishment of a Treaty of Waitangi select committee of Parliament.

WRITTEN AND UNWRITTEN CONSTITUTIONS

The Modality of Change

Paul Craig

1. INTRODUCTION

Written constitutions are the norm, unwritten constitutions the rare exception. There is much that can be said as to the commonalities and differences between them. There are, nonetheless, two principal variables that underscore the respective forms of constitution, which in turn impact on the modality of change: the extent to which the constitution is committed to writing, and the extent which the constitution is perceived to be separate from, and superior to, ordinary law.

These twin variables are commonly perceived to be linked. There is empirical warrant for this assumption. The paradigmatic written constitution, which contains the principal constitutional norms in a single document, will commonly also enshrine, expressly or impliedly, constitutional review through which courts subject ordinary statute to review for constitutional compliance; the constitutional norms of the paradigmatic unwritten constitution will normally be found in a plethora of sources, and ordinary statute will customarily have pride of place in the constitutional schema.

There is, however, no a priori normative reason why these twin variables should be linked in this manner. The embodiment of constitutional norms in a canonical document does not predetermine the content of the constitution, nor does it impel the conclusion that constitutional review exercised by a court must be part of the resulting schema. This is exemplified, as will be seen below, by the UK, where some suggestions for the shift to a written constitution are premised on the assumption that parliamentary sovereignty remains a cornerstone of the constitutional ordering. It is, by parity of reason, equally possible in principle to think of an unwritten constitution, the central features of which are markedly similar to those of the paradigmatic written constitution, such that it is accepted by all relevant players that ordinary legislative power is bounded by certain structural and rights-based precepts that are enforced, inter alia, by the courts. The manner through which this might occur will be considered more fully below.

It follows from the foregoing that while the extent to which constitutional norms are committed to writing is of significance in distinguishing the two forms of constitution, the second variable is more important in normative terms, and shapes the way in which change is effectuated. The contrast in this respect is sharp. The foundational starting point of the standard written constitution is the distinction between law-making through ordinary politics and the constitution; the latter circumscribes the former, such that the terrain of ordinary politics is bounded by the constitution. The foundational starting point of the UK unwritten constitution is that parliamentary sovereignty is the principal constitutional principle; the terrain of ordinary politics is boundless and parliamentary sovereignty instantiates and elevates ordinary statute as the vehicle for its delivery.

This contribution in honour of Bruce Harris explores the foregoing ideas and their implication for the modality of constitutional change.

Issues of constitutional change within the unwritten constitution have been one of the main themes in Harris's scholarship.[1]

The discussion of written constitutions begins with certain preliminaries as to the origins of the modern constitutional form. It is followed by consideration of constitutional content, distinguishing between the horizontal, vertical and structural features generally found in written constitutions, and includes discussion of over- and under-constitutionalisation. The analysis concludes with brief reflection on the manner of constitutional change.

The focus then turns to the UK unwritten constitution. It begins with certain preliminaries as to historical origins. The ensuing discussion considers the horizontal, vertical and structural provisions of the UK unwritten constitution and the way in which they are shaped by parliamentary sovereignty. The analysis includes the emergence of parliamentary sovereignty in the UK constitutional order, the parallel historical discourse concerning fundamental law, the resultant centrality of parliamentary sovereignty and the ways in which this was justified over time. The inquiry concludes with the modality and frame for constitutional change in the UK.

2. WRITTEN CONSTITUTIONS

2.1. PRELIMINARIES

Constitutions have existed for a very long time. This is a trite proposition. The relative provenance of the 'modern' written constitution is, however, contested, as are the criteria that should count in this respect, and the cause of its emergence. This is not the place for exegesis on this issue, which could well occupy an article or book. Some sense of the argumentation is, nonetheless, helpful for the ensuing analysis. Dieter Grimm's account is helpful in this regard.[2]

---

1 See, for example, BV Harris "The Constitutional Future of New Zealand" [2004] NZ L Rev 269; BV Harris "Constitutional Change" in Raymond Miller (ed) *New Zealand Government and Politics* (4th ed, Oxford University Press, Melbourne, 2006) 115.

2 Dieter Grimm *Constitutionalism, Past, Present and Future* (Oxford University Press, Oxford, 2016).

He argues that the modern written constitution should be dated from the American and French revolutions, and the subsequent constitutional settlements. The term 'constitution' can be found earlier, but it generally denoted 'the condition or situation of a state', as shaped by 'historical development, natural features and legal order'.[3] In this sense 'every state was in a certain "constitution", and where no constitution could be identified, no state existed'.[4] This older conception of the constitution was thus principally empirical, by way of comparison to the modern constitution that was normative, insofar as it prescribed how state power should be established. The modern constitution thus 'constituted' rule, it was 'comprehensive' in the sense of regulating the entirety of rule, and also 'universal' in that it benefited all persons subject to rule.[5] For Grimm, the distinguishing feature of the American and French revolutionaries was that their discontent was 'not limited to the person of the ruler, but encompassed the system of rule'.[6] The forces that shaped the modern constitution appear from the following passage.[7]

> Historically, constitutions are a product of the conflict between the liberal bourgeoisie and the absolute monarchy. The bourgeoisie was seeking to emancipate the production and commercial sphere from hierarchical direction and to guarantee the predictability of state power. To this end, it demanded the limitation of princely competence to questions of security and order as well as participation in state decision-making concerning issues of freedom and property. These demands were justified on the basis of natural law and were to be secured through positive law. The means was the constitution, which regardless of how it came to be in each individual case had a contractual character. It typically contained basic rights to re-define the social sphere of freedom, on the one hand, and rules regulating the holders and modalities of the exercise of state power on the other. In particular, it provided for representational bodies to communicate civic interests to the state, a guarantee that the state complied with the decisions of these bodies, together with the establishment of independent courts as a complementary safeguard.

For Dieter Grimm, the single biggest challenge to this conception of the constitution has been the changing nature of state obligations, principally, albeit not exclusively, through the emerging conception of the social state,

---

3 At 44.
4 At 44.
5 At 43.
6 At 6.
7 At 128–129.

with the consequence that the 'constitution can no longer restrict itself to organizing the state apparatus and limiting state power', but must 'order not only the state, but society as well'.[8]

2.2. CONTENT: HORIZONTAL, VERTICAL AND STRUCTURAL

Constitutions vary significantly in terms of the topics covered, and the depth of the coverage. This is an issue that will be addressed below when considering over-constitutionalisation. This heterogeneity should not, however, conceal the commonality of subject-matter as between written constitutions, and this is so notwithstanding the obvious fact that different polities may choose to address such issues in different ways. The common core consists of constitutional provisions that are horizontal, vertical and structural in nature.

The horizontal dimension speaks to the procedural and substantive rules that establish and regulate the principal organs of government, their constitution and powers. These rules classically relate to the legislature, executive and judiciary. They will identify the respective organs, and specify their powers. Procedural norms will, for example, specify how legislation is to be passed, whether special majorities are required and the like. Substantive norms will, for example, denominate the legislature and the nature of its power, the same being true for the executive and the judiciary. There can be difficulties in defining the institutions that exercise certain types of power, and there can also be difficulties in deciding on the precise powers that a certain institution should have. This is especially so in relation to executive power. Constitutions are, in general, not good at defining the executive, or the scope of its powers.[9] This is so for a concatenation of reasons, a principal cause being the duality in the meaning of the term executive. It can mean the body charged with developing policy and the legislative agenda; it can also connote the body charged with implementing legislation. The increased use of agencies that exercise executive powers, and operate outside the strict confines of departmental structures, has exacerbated the difficulties in identification of the executive and the delineation of its powers. Constitutional uncertainty concerning

---

8 At 135.

9 See Paul Craig and Adam Tomkins (eds) *The Executive and Public Law: Power and Accountability in Comparative Perspective* (Oxford University Press, Oxford, 2005).

the location and scope of executive power then generates rival theories that give diverse answers to these issues, which play out not just in law review exchanges, but in high-level politics.

The vertical dimension of the constitution traditionally captures constitutional rules that regulate the interrelationship between citizen and state. The paradigm situation is rights-based constraints on government action, through a Bill of Rights enshrined in the Constitution. This may form part of the initial constitution, as is commonly the case with constitutions created after 1945. It may be added later through constitutional amendment, as with the US Constitution. There will then be a range of second order issues that fall to be resolved, most prominently the rights to be included in the constitutional document. There is significant choice in this respect, ranging from the traditional focus on civil and political rights, to more expansive documents that also include social and economic rights, such as the EU Charter of Rights. The other central issue concerns the reach of the Bill of Rights, whether it operates only on a vertical plane, or whether it also has a horizontal impact as between private parties. This choice may be made explicitly in the Bill of Rights, but where there is uncertainty, it falls to the courts to make the interpretive choice.

The structural dimension of the constitution in nation states that are federal is concerned with the division of power between the federal and state level. A written constitution may also contain analogous provisions that demarcate the boundaries between central power and that of regions where there is a measure of devolution. The constitutional criteria used for such division or demarcation of power are varied, including specification of subject matter and impact across intra-state territorial boundaries. The criteria often lack pristine clarity, thereby sowing the seeds for contestation as to the boundaries of power that fall to be resolved in the courts. This uncertainty can impact diverse issues, including the allocation of regulatory authority as between the federal and state level, and the federal constraints on state rules concerning who can vote in federal elections.

There will, however, always be an unwritten element in all written constitutions, even those that are more detailed. There may be issues that were never addressed in the constitution, because they were never thought about by those who drafted the document. There may be certain constitutional provisions, whether horizontal or vertical, which are set at a high level of abstraction, thereby requiring further specification through legislation, judicial interpretation or administrative practice, or an admixture of all three.

2.3. CONTENT: OVER- AND UNDER-CONSTITUTIONALISATION

Constitutions vary significantly when judged by a plethora of criteria. A significant factor in this respect is the constitution's relative breadth or narrowness, as judged by the range of its coverage and the detail thereof. To put the point more starkly, constitutions can be relatively fat or thin. There is no a priori reason to prefer one over the other. The choice betwixt the two can be the result of conscious constitutional design, or adventitious historical circumstance flowing from the founding constituent moment. A range of considerations may well play into the option thus selected. The choice will perforce have consequences. Thus, other things being equal, the greater the constitutional coverage, the more issues are taken off the agenda of normal politics, or the normal political process is circumscribed. This in turn prompts inquiry into the problem of over-constitutionalisation.

This can be exemplified by discourse in the EU, most notably by Dieter Grimm.[10] His central thesis is that the EU Treaties are over-constitutionalised, with the consequence that issues are thereby taken off the agenda of normal politics, notwithstanding the fact that they might be regarded as within the province of ordinary law in Member States: 'in the EU the crucial difference between the rules for political decisions and the decisions themselves is to a large extent levelled'.[11] It is inherent in the nature of constitutions that they function as the framework for political decisions, with the consequence that elections 'do not matter as far as constitutional law extends'.[12] There may be too little constitutionalism, but there may also be too much, with the consequence that the democratic process is fettered.[13] While there are no universally applicable principles for determining the content of a constitution, the 'function of constitutions is to legitimise and to limit political power, not to replace it',[14] with the consequence that constitutions are a 'framework for politics, not the blueprint for all political decisions'.[15]

For Grimm, the EU Treaties fulfil many functions of national constitutions, specifying matters such as the inter-institutional distribution of power, the

10 Dieter Grimm "The Democratic Costs of Constitutionalisation: The European Case" (2015) 21 ELJ 460.
11 At 470.
12 At 463.
13 At 464.
14 At 464.
15 At 464.

mode of law-making, and the respective competence of the EU and Member States. They also go significantly beyond the remit of national constitutions, with the consequence that a wide range of matters becomes constitutionalised and taken off the agenda of normal politics. The effect of this is further enhanced by the constitutional doctrines of direct effect and supremacy, which transformed the four economic freedoms from 'objective principles for legislation into subjective rights of the market participants who could claim them against the Member States before the national courts'.[16]

This then meant that there were two modes of EU integration. The Treaty precepts could be advanced through legislation enacted by the EU institutions, or they could be taken forward through judicial decisions, which were imbued with considerable force through direct effect and supremacy.[17] Member States had limited influence over the latter, and this was particularly important since the lack of differentiation between the constitutional law level and the ordinary law level meant that the 'constitutionalization of the treaties immunizes the Commission and particularly the ECJ against any attempt by the democratically responsible institutions of the EU to react to the Court's jurisprudence by changing the law'.[18] For Grimm, the remedy was to limit the EU Treaties to their truly constitutional elements and downgrade other Treaty provisions that were not constitutional nature to the status of secondary law.

2.4. CHANGE: MODALITY AND FRAME

This brief excursus into written constitutions ends with consideration of the modality and frame though which constitutional change occurs. There are four principal modes in this respect.

The most obvious is perforce formal constitutional amendment,[19] the catalyst for which varies.[20] In some instances, it is the realisation that the

---

16 At 467.

17 JHH Weiler "The Community System: The Dual Character of Supranationalism" (1981) 1 YBEL 267 and "The Transformation of Europe" (1991) 100 Yale LJ 2403 at 2412–2431; PP Craig "Once Upon a Time in the West: Direct Effect and the Federalization of EEC Law" (1992) 12 OJLS 453.

18 Grimm, above n 10, at 471.

19 Richard Albert *Constitutional Amendments, Making, Breaking and Changing Constitutions* (Oxford University Press, New York, 2019); Yaniv Roznai *Unconstitutional Constitutional Amendments: The Limits of Amendment Powers* (Oxford University Press, Oxford, 2017).

20 Compilation of Venice Commission Opinions concerning Constitutional Provisions for Amending the Constitution, CDL-PI (2015) 023; Venice Commission, Report on Constitutional Amendment, CDL-AD (2010) 001.

initial constitutional design is imperfect; in others it is the result of new political configurations that wish to re-shape the country's institutional and constitutional architecture; in yet other instances, the motives may be darker, such that current majorities seek to reinforce their power through constitutional amendment designed, for example, to limit the power of the judiciary.[21]

The second impulse for constitutional change is judicial interpretation. This language is, however, inherently tendentious, since it is based on assumptions as to how courts do and should interpret the constitution. The very idea that the constitution has or has not been changed depends, inter alia, on the theory of constitutional adjudication accepted by that legal order or espoused by academic commentary. This is the site of well-known battles, including that between constitutional originalists, and those who subscribe to a more Dworkinian view of constitutional interpretation. Matters are rendered more complex by the plethora of very different theories of what constitutional originalism means, and by similar variation in the latitude afforded by non-originalist theories.[22] This is quite apart from the small matter as to whether court decisions over time can be said to subscribe to any consistent view within a particular jurisdiction.

The third driver of constitutional change is constitutional legislation, which is somewhat less obvious, but equally important. It is normatively and pragmatically mistaken to draw a rigid line between the constitution and legislation that is designed to fill out the meaning of its provisions, and it is misguided to elide the existence of the same provision in many constitutions with equivalence of application. Constitutional legislation is in many respects the lifeblood of the constitution. Other things being equal, the thinner the constitution and the more abstract its provisions, the greater the role for constitutional legislation and adjudication to imbue the terms

---

21 Kim Lane Scheppele "Autocracy under Cover of the Transnational Legal Order" in Gregory C Shaffer, Tom Ginsburg and Terence C Halliday (eds) *Constitution-Making and Transnational Legal Order* (Cambridge University Press, Cambridge, 2019) ch 7.

22 See, for example, Jeffrey Goldsworthy "Constitutional Interpretation: Originalism" (2009) 4 Philosophy Compass 682; Keith E Whittington "Originalism: A Critical Introduction" (2013) 82 Fordham Law Review 375; Symposium on Originalism in (2019) 37(3) Law and History Review; John Hart Ely *Democracy and Distrust: A Theory of Judicial Review* (Harvard University Press, Cambridge, 1980); Ronald Dworkin *Taking Rights Seriously* (Harvard University Press, Cambridge, 1978).

with more concrete meaning. Such legislation is nonetheless important in all constitutions, although its incidence may vary. The constitution may contain noble provisions concerning free and fair elections, but the reality can only be tested by examination of the detailed electoral legislation that puts flesh on these constitutional bones. It is powerfully attested to by recent legislation in some states of the US, which has placed increased barriers on people's ability to vote in state and federal elections. There may be laudable constitutional guarantees for political parties, only for these to be heavily circumscribed by legislation that defines the qualifications for a political party to appear on the ballot. The force of constitutional protections for free speech may be qualified by legislative rules related to association. The need to be mindful of the link between constitutional terms and consequent legislation is important in relation to many other issues commonly found in constitutions, such as principles concerning equality, the judiciary and the like, which are then articulated in more detail in, or affected by, legislation.

The final factor in this respect is constitutional practice, which may take various forms. There may be institutional conventions, or perceptions of the constitution by the people. There may be practice by the relevant players, which either undermines the formal constitutional norms, or imbues them with greater force than they would otherwise have as judged by their formal text. There may be events that test the ambit of formal constitutional provisions, with the resolution of the contestation casting the constitutional norms in a somewhat different light than hitherto.

3. UNWRITTEN CONSTITUTIONS

3.1. PRELIMINARIES

Most current constitutions are written. Unwritten constitutions are the exception. This, like the proposition that began the previous section, is trite. However, in common with that discussion, matters rapidly become more complex and contestable when we move beyond this simple terrain. This is more especially so, if the inquiry is as to why a particular polity chose to buck the trend, and to stick with an unwritten constitution. The answer will perforce depend, inter alia, on an admixture of historical, social and economic circumstance. These issues are beyond the remit of the present contribution and would require an article or book to do justice to the topic. Nor is the intent to engage in the debate as to whether the UK should have a written constitution.[23]

This preliminary foray is limited to making a simple conceptual point, which will be developed hereafter. The content of unwritten constitutions can, in principle, vary significantly. There is, moreover, no a priori reason why a state might not choose to stick with an unwritten constitution for an admixture of historical, social and economic circumstance, and yet still replicate, in unwritten form, many features commonly found in a written constitution. It might limit the remit of ordinary statute in accord with constraints typically found in written constitutions, and these rules might be accepted as obligations by the key political and legal players. The net effect might be a constitutional order that is similar to, and equally efficacious as, its written constitutional cousin.

There can, however, also be an unwritten constitution, such as that in the UK, where the animating constitutional principle is that of parliamentary sovereignty. This constitutional choice is premised on normative assumptions that are very different from those that underpin written constitutions, and the alternative unwritten constitution sketched above. This in turn affects the modality and scope for constitutional change. It should, moreover, be recognised that if a polity decides to shift from an unwritten to a written constitution it has considerable choice as to its content. Thus, an interesting consideration in the context of the present discussion is that many of the proposals for a written constitution in the UK are predicated on preservation of parliamentary sovereignty, or something closely akin thereto.[24]

3.2. CONTENT: PARLIAMENTARY SOVEREIGNTY, THE HORIZONTAL, VERTICAL AND STRUCTURAL

There can, as noted above, be difficulties in determining the more particular content of written constitutions. Difficulties are, however, relative by

---

23 The principal proposals for a written constitution can be found in Jo Eric Khushal Murkens "A Written Constitution: A Case not Made" (2021) 41 OJLS 1. See also, Vernon Bogdanor and Stefan Vogenauer "Enacting a British Constitution: Some Problems" [2008] PL 38; Nick Barber "Against a Written Constitution" [2008] PL 11; Political and Constitutional Reform Committee *A New Magna Carta?* (House of Commons, 463, July 2014); Vernon Bogdanor *Beyond Brexit: Towards a British Constitution* (Hart, Oxford, 2019).

24 Murkens, above n 23, at 6–8.

nature, and they are greater when trying to determine the content of an unwritten constitution, such as the UK. We can, nonetheless, make progress in this respect. The basic taxonomy of horizontal, vertical and structural constitutional provisions is equally pertinent to an unwritten constitution as to the more common written version.

There is no doubt that the UK unwritten constitution contains rules that speak to the horizontal, vertical and structural features commonly found in written constitutions. Thus, there are a number of statutes dealing with the horizontal dimension, insofar as this connotes the powers vested in the legislative, executive and judicial branches of government, including, inter alia, the Bill of Rights 1689, Act of Settlement 1700, Parliament Acts 1911 and 1949, Ministers of the Crown Act 1975, and hitherto the European Communities Act 1972. The statutes that address the vertical features of a constitution include the Bill of Rights 1689 and the Human Rights Act 1998. The structural constitutional dimension is exemplified by the legislation relating to devolution, the modern incarnation of which began with the Scotland Act 1998 and the Government of Wales Act 1998. This legislation has been held by the courts to have constitutional status, which has, as will be seen below, implications for the manner of change.[25]

There are, in addition, important constitutional precepts such as the rule of law. This is not the place for exegesis on the meaning of the rule of law, and its significance within the UK unwritten constitutional order. Suffice it to say that it is of considerable importance, as manifest in principles of judicial interpretation whereby statutes that limit access to courts will be narrowly construed, as will legislation that limits human rights. The rule of law also shapes the legislative process, through the importance attached to ensuring that statutory provisions are clear and prospective, and it underpins judicial review, such that power accorded to ministers and agencies is held to account. There are, nonetheless, abiding difficulties concerning the scope and source of executive power, which is a powerful theme in Bruce Harris's work.[26]

It is, nonetheless, necessary to confront the centrality of parliamentary sovereignty in the UK unwritten constitution. It is the dominant occupant of this conceptual terrain. The orthodox reading of parliamentary sovereignty is that Parliament is omnipotent, and thus can be subject to no

25 *R (HS2 Action Alliance Ltd) v Secretary of State for Transport* [2014] UKSC 3.

26 See, for example, BV Harris "The 'Third Source' of Authority for Government Action" (1992) 108 LQR 626; "The 'Third Source' of Authority for Government Action Revisited" (2007) 123 LQR 225; "Government 'Third Source' Action and Common Law Constitutionalism" (2010) 126 LQR 373.

substantive or procedural limits. This precept is subject to one exception, which is that Parliament cannot bind its successors. The thesis is thus one of continuing parliamentary sovereignty, such that each successive Parliament is invested with the same omnipotence as its forbears, thereby reflecting the normative claim that each Parliament is entitled to the same authority flowing from the fact that it has equal democratic pedigree to the Parliaments that preceded it.

The possible twin qualifications to this proposition are well known and do not warrant detailed explication here. They relate to the possibility of procedural constraints on sovereignty, whereby Parliament would be bound by manner and form provisions contained in earlier legislation, unless and until they are altered; and to the possibility that the courts might, in extreme circumstances, refuse to apply legislation that is deeply problematic in terms of substance.

These possible qualifications should not mask the centrality of parliamentary sovereignty to the UK unwritten constitution, or the contrast with the basic precepts of written constitutions. The foundational starting point of written constitutions is the distinction between ordinary politics and the constitution; the latter circumscribes the former, such that the terrain of ordinary politics is bounded by the constitution. The foundational starting point of the UK unwritten constitution is that parliamentary sovereignty is the principal constitutional principle; the terrain of ordinary politics is boundless and parliamentary sovereignty instantiates and elevates ordinary statute as the vehicle for its delivery.

This in turn leads to the following irony. Written constitutions have an inherent weakness, insofar as they do not have the same enforcement mechanism as ordinary statute. There are to be sure methods of enforcement through constitutional courts and the like, but this does not dispel the preceding concern. An unwritten constitution grounded on parliamentary sovereignty obviates this problem, by the very fact that ordinary statute, cloaked with the mantle of parliamentary sovereignty, is constitutional centre-stage, and partakes of enforcement mechanisms attendant on normal legislation.

This naturally invites inquiry as to why the UK opted for an unwritten constitution with parliamentary sovereignty as its central component, given that the latter is not a pre-ordained component of the former. The reasons are assuredly eclectic and linked.[27] They reside in part in

---

27 Christopher Hill *The World Turned Upside Down, Radical Ideas During the English Revolution* (Penguin, 1972) ch 7; Donald Veall *The Popular Movement for Law Reform,*

historical circumstance.[28] The Bill of Rights 1689 was only a partial constitutional settlement. It did, however, circumscribe monarchical power, and bolster that of Parliament. The nobility and the middle class did not feel the imperative for a formal written constitution to safeguard their rights, and the flipside of this same coin was that they did not wish for limits on the powers of a Parliament over which they had control. The emergence of parliamentary sovereignty was, moreover, influenced at various junctures by Parliament's status as the highest court, as well as the legislature.[29] It was also affected by the writings of Hobbes[30] and Filmer,[31] who lent credence to the idea that there had to be a locus of undiminished power. The dispatch of the Stuarts and the post-1689 settlement laid to rest the remnants of previous debate about the possessor of sovereign power. Sovereignty resided in the King-in-Parliament, in the sense that it was the King acting in conjunction with the Commons and Lords which possessed all-embracing power.

The gradual emergence of parliamentary sovereignty in something akin to its modern form by the end of the 17th century should not, however, lead to neglect of the concept of fundamental law, or the relationship between fundamental law and the constitution, to which reference was made throughout the century and beyond. English scholars of the Tudor age used Aristotelian ideas of 'politeia' but did not speak of an English constitution.[32] Recourse to the term 'constitution' in connection with forms of government began in the 17th century. Its roots lay, in part, in analogies between nature and politics, as epitomised in the ideal of a healthy body and a healthy body politic; and in part in development from the Latin term '*constitutio*', which was used in Roman law to connote imperial decrees, and by the mid-17th century was employed to capture the fundamental constitution of the kingdom.[33] It is, nonetheless, clear

1640–1660 (Oxford University Press, Oxford, 1970); Stephen Sedley and Lawrence Kaplan (eds) *A Spark in the Ashes, The Pamphlets of John Warr* (Verso, London, 1992).

28 See Jeffrey Goldsworthy *Parliamentary Sovereignty: Contemporary Debates* (Cambridge University Press, New York, 2010) for detailed discussion of contending views as to the nature of parliamentary sovereignty in the 17th century.

29 JW Gough *Fundamental Law in English Constitutional History* (Clarendon Press, Oxford, 1955) at 82–84 and 171–173.

30 Thomas Hobbes *Leviathan* (WG Pogson Smith, Clarendon Press, Oxford, 1909).

31 Peter Laslett (ed) *Patriarcha and other works of Sir Robert Filmer* (Garland, New York, 1984).

32 Gerald Stourzh *Fundamental Laws and Individual Rights in the 18th Century Constitution* (Claremont Institute, Bicentennial Essay Number 5, 1984) at 2–3.

33 At 3–6.

that the concept of fundamental law bore various meanings, but did not generally connote the idea of a constitution policed through courts and judicial review,[34] notwithstanding that writers drew on the work of Coke in support of such developments in the US.[35] In England, it was used to capture a plethora of ideas, including the social contractarian nature of the bond between the people and their representatives; the existence of certain liberties and rights that should be protected; that politics was subordinate to moral obligation; and that there should be constraints against arbitrary power, inter alia, by ensuring that there were checks and balances within government broadly conceived. There was resort to fundamental law by all sides in the 17th-century conflicts, and unsurprisingly the meaning accorded to it shifted depending on the position of the particular party.[36]

Recourse to ideas of fundamental law waned as conceptions of parliamentary sovereignty gained traction. However, as John Gough duly notes, this coincided with more detailed attempts to justify the emerging constitutional order, to show that the omnipotence was defensible and would not jeopardise rights and liberties valued by the people.[37] This was readily apparent from discourse in the 18th, 19th and 20th centuries, wherein different arguments were advanced for the constitutional centrality of parliamentary sovereignty and ordinary law.

Blackstone furnished the principal argument in the 18th century. He followed Coke and affirmed that the power and jurisdiction of Parliament was so transcendent and absolute, that it could not be confined, either for causes or persons, within any bounds, nor could it be controlled by an external body.[38] The existence of this power was, however, premised on a political theory of balanced constitutionalism expounded by Blackstone, whose reasoning echoed earlier discourse, most notably that of Harrington and the republican tradition.[39]

34 Gough, above n 29, at 2–3 and 206–207.

35 See, for example, Edward S Corwin "The 'Higher Law' Background of American Constitutional Law" (1928) 42 Harv L Rev 149 at 365.

36 Gough, above n 29, 162–163.

37 At 173; Stourzh, above n 32, at 8–9.

38 William Blackstone *Commentaries on the Law of England* (16th ed, Cadell and Butterworth, London, 1825), Vol I, Bk 2, at 160–61.

39 James Harrington "The Commonwealth of Oceana" in JGA Pocock (ed) *The Political Works of James Harrington* (Cambridge University Press, Cambridge, 1977); JL de Lolme *The Constitution of England, or an Account of the English Government* (Robinson, 1796 ed). See generally JGA Pocock *The Machiavellian Moment: Florentine Political Thought and the Atlantic Republican Tradition* (Princeton University Press, Princeton, 1975); Corinne Weston *English Constitutional Theory and the House of Lords 1556–1832* (Routledge and Kegan Paul, London, 1965).

The famous Blackstonian quotation appeared at the end of a long chapter, in which he described how Parliament functioned. Tyrannical governments were, said Blackstone, those in which the power of making and enforcing laws was vested in the same person. Things were different where the legislative and executive authority were in different hands, since 'the former will take care not to entrust the latter with so large a power as may tend to the subversion of its own independence, and therewith the liberty of the subject'.[40] In England power was thus divided. The legislative branch was the Parliament, which consisted of the King, Lords and Commons; the executive branch consisted of the King alone.[41] The relationship between them was vital:[42]

> It is highly necessary for preserving the balance of the constitution, that the executive power should be a branch, but not the whole, of the legislative. The total union of them, we have seen, would be productive of tyranny; the total disjunction of them, for the present, would in the end produce the same effects, by causing that union against which it seems to provide. The legislature would soon become tyrannical, by making continual encroachments, and gradually assuming to itself the rights of the executive power.

For Blackstone the 'true excellence' of English government was that all parts operated as a mutual check upon each other. In the legislature, the people were a check on the nobility, and the nobility a check upon the people, through 'the mutual privilege of rejecting what the other has resolved'.[43] The King was a check upon both, which preserved the executive power from encroachments. The executive power itself was checked and kept within due bounds by the two houses, through the privilege of inquiring into, impeaching, and punishing the conduct, not of the King or Queen since this would destroy their constitutional independence, but of 'evil and pernicious counsellors'.[44] The two houses of Parliament naturally represented different interests, and the Crown yet another. They mutually kept each other from exceeding their proper limits. It is only after this discourse that the quotation about parliamentary omnipotence appears, and the body 'thus united' is the body functioning in the manner described above.

---

40 Blackstone, above n 38, at 146.
41 At 146–7.
42 At 153–4.
43 At 154–5.
44 At 155.

Dicey furnished the leading reaffirmation of parliamentary sovereignty in the 19th century, drawing on Coke and Blackstone. However, the normative justification for this ascription of parliamentary power differed.[45] He recognised that he could not simply draw on the Blackstonian normative argument, since it would not have been applicable, without substantial modifications, to the changed conditions of the 19th century. Dicey, therefore, constructed an alternative normative argument to justify the parliamentary sovereignty that he had empirically described.

The essence of the argument was that a Parliament, duly elected on the extended franchise, represented the most authoritative expression of the will of the nation. The Parliament thereby elected should therefore be able to carry out any action. Dicey believed that Parliament would control the executive and that MPs would not pass legislation contrary to the interests of those who elected them. Constitutional protections against the exercise of parliamentary power were not therefore required, since 'the permanent wishes of the representative portion of Parliament can hardly in the long run differ from the wishes of the English people, or at any rate of the electors; that which the majority of the House of Commons command, the majority of English people usually desire'.[46] The normative argument was, therefore, apparently simple. UK democracy was founded upon a channel of authority flowing from the bottom upwards. The expanded electorate chose representatives. The Parliament thus chosen had legitimacy because of the extended franchise and should therefore have all embracing powers. The elected MPs articulated the views of those who had chosen them, and they controlled the executive. Legislation that was constitutionally questionable would not, therefore, be passed, or would be repealed expeditiously. Parliamentary sovereignty would not place the rights of individual citizens in jeopardy. The defects in this mode of argument have been examined elsewhere.[47] Suffice it to say for the present that our system of democracy never really operated in this self-correcting way, and this vision of the relationship between electors, Parliament and the executive certainly does not accord with present reality.

The 20th-century normative argument for parliamentary sovereignty as the cornerstone of the UK constitutional order differs yet again from the Blackstonian and Diceyan antecedents, in part at least because the ideals

45 Paul Craig *Public Law and Democracy in the United Kingdom and the United States of America* (Clarendon Press, Oxford, 1990) ch 2.

46 AV Dicey *An Introduction to the Study of the Law of the Constitution* (10th ed, Macmillan, London, 1959) at 83.

47 Craig, above n 45, at ch 2.

of balanced constitution and self-correcting democracy no longer have purchase. The 20th-century claim is therefore commonly grounded on two complementary arguments. There is the contention that a Parliament duly elected on a full democratic franchise has legitimacy and thus should have such sovereign authority. This is complemented by the argument that it should not be subject to limits such as constitutional review, whereby the court can invalidate legislation. This reasoning underpins much political constitutionalist thought. Waldron[48] and Bellamy[49] are the leading opponents of rights-based constitutional review of statute.[50] Waldron is a court-sceptic, but not a rights-sceptic. Bellamy's position is more complex. He is certainly a court-sceptic, and is also more sceptical about rights, insofar as he believes that citizenship should not be equated with a narrow concept of individuals being rights-holders against the state, but comprises a 'continuously reflexive process, with citizens reinterpreting the basis of their collective life in new ways that correspond to their evolving needs and ideals'.[51] There is, nonetheless, much common ground in the reasons for their court-scepticism. Thus, the central premise to Waldron and Bellamy's argument is the prevalence of disagreement concerning the rights that should be included in a Bill of Rights and their interpretation. For both writers such disagreement pervades the very foundational ideas of justice on which society is grounded. They maintain therefore that whether viewed in terms of process, or in terms of outcome, it is preferable for such matters to be decided ultimately by the political and not the legal process.

3.3. CONTENT: OVER- AND UNDER-CONSTITUTIONALISATION

The preceding analysis considered the issue of over- and under-constitutionalisation in the context of written constitutions. The issue

48 Jeremy Waldron *Law and Disagreement* (Oxford University Press, New York, 1999) and "The Core of the Case against Judicial Review" (2006) 115 Yale LJ 1346.

49 Richard Bellamy *Political Constitutionalism: A Republican Defence of the Constitutionality of Democracy* (Cambridge University Press, Cambridge, 2007).

50 See also, Mark Tushnet *Taking the Constitution away from the Courts* (Princeton University Press, Princeton, 1999); Larry Kramer, *The People Themselves: Popular Constitutionalism and Judicial Review* (Oxford University Press, New York, 2004).

51 Richard Bellamy "Constitutive Citizenship versus Constitutional Rights: Republican Reflections on the EU Charter and the Human Rights Act" in Tom Campbell, Keith Ewing and Adam Tomkins (eds) *Sceptical Essays on Human Rights* (Oxford University Press, Oxford, 2001) 15.

is also relevant for unwritten constitutions, and the answer will depend on the relative breadth and depth of its coverage. It is possible in theory for an unwritten constitution to be relatively dense in terms of the mesh of rules that speak to constitutional issues. The empirical reality tends to the contrary, such that the constitutional frame is more skeletal in this respect. This is more especially so where the dominant constitutional principle is parliamentary sovereignty, which, as seen above, weakens the binding force of other constitutional constraints. There is then a greater danger of under-constitutionalisation. Whether this would be alleviated by a written constitution depends in large part on the content thereof, and its animating principles. Thus, a UK written constitution crafted on the bedrock of parliamentary sovereignty could still be under-constitutionalised. Having said this, it should be acknowledged that the very ascription of the label under-constitutionalised to such a putative written constitution is predicated on certain normative assumptions, the principal one being that Parliament should not have such legal omnipotence. This assumption is normatively contestable, but so too is the contrary assumption. The under-constitutionalised nature of the UK unwritten constitution can, nonetheless, be exemplified by experience with Brexit.

Take by way of example the way in which the devolved regions were treated in the Brexit process. They were denied effective voice in the shaping of the Brexit process, ever more so the longer it went on; and their substantive preferences received scant attention.[52] Whether matters would have been different if we had a written constitution would depend very markedly on its terms. It is possible to imagine a UK written constitution that embodied the legal status quo, in which case the position of the devolved regions would be no better than at present. It is, by way of contrast, possible to imagine a very different form of constitutional ordering, which gave greater procedural protection to regional voice, invested the Sewel convention, namely that the Westminster Parliament cannot normally legislate on a matter within devolved competence without the consent of the devolved legislatures,[53] with binding constitutional force, and made constitutional provision for protection of the regions' substantive political preferences, within the areas that fell within their scope of authority.

Take by way of another example the balance between prime ministerial, executive and legislative power revealed by Brexit. The executive, and increasingly the Prime Minister, dominated the Brexit process. Whether

52 P Craig "Brexit, A Drama: The Interregnum" [2017] Yearbook of European Law 1.
53 Scotland Act 2016, s 2.

a written constitution would have made any difference would depend on its terms. This is more especially so, since constitutions do not have a good track record at identifying the nature of executive power and the boundaries thereof.[54] Nor are they particularly good at specifying the more granular detail of relations between the executive and the legislature. However, if the UK had a written constitution, then it is likely that UK membership of the EU would have been enshrined therein. It would have had constitutional status, the corollary being that it could only be changed by the process for constitutional amendment. Whatsoever such requirements for change might be, the reality is that a referendum, followed by an ordinary statute, would almost certainly not suffice to change the constitution.

3.4. CHANGE: MODALITY AND FRAME

There can assuredly be change in unwritten constitutions. The ability to adapt is indeed said to be a virtue of this constitutional form. There is some truth in this. The claim is nonetheless commonly overplayed, insofar as it fails to distinguish between the ability of a system to adapt existing constitutional rules to novel circumstance, and its capacity to meet change because there are no constitutional rules that govern the matter. The focal point of the ensuing discussion is, however, somewhat different. It concerns two related issues: the way in which constitutional change can occur in a system premised on parliamentary sovereignty; and the way in which parliamentary sovereignty frames this process. They will be considered in turn.

3.4.1. Modality

The key to an understanding of the way in which constitutional change can occur is that the orthodox proposition concerning parliamentary sovereignty is empirical, not a priori. It is dynamic and not static and hence can alter over time. The rule concerning parliamentary sovereignty, as set out above, can be regarded as the rule of recognition of the UK system, in the sense that it is the ultimate rule of the legal system, to which the validity of all other legal rules can be traced. Its validity is not, however, dependent on the rules that constitute its content at any point in time,

54 Craig and Tomkins, above n 9.

since that would be bootstrapping. It is rather dependent upon social acceptance by those within the polity.[55]

The proposition that statutes duly enacted have the force of law, and that subject to this so too do judicial decisions, constitutes the core of the rule of recognition because it is accepted by those within the system, including the legislature and the courts. The enactment of a statute attesting to this fact could not itself invest statute with this status. A statute cannot, therefore, in itself, alter the rule of recognition, but it can act as the catalyst for a shift in the social acceptance on which the rule of recognition depends.

It follows that the rule of recognition is inherently dynamic, not static. The version we currently operate with, that Parliament can do whatsoever it likes through statute duly enacted by simple majority, has not always been so. It was certainly not the ultimate test of legal validity prior to the latter part of the 17th century, and it is over-simplistic to imagine that Parliament's status thereafter was secured in the manner that it is commonly regarded now. The dynamic nature of the concept means, moreover, that the rule might change and having done so it might revert in the future to the status quo ante, as the result of developments that trigger shifts in the social acceptance that underpin the concept.[56] The initial catalyst for change might come from Parliament, the executive or the courts. Change in the rule of recognition will, however, normally require acceptance from all such key players.

This can be exemplified by the accommodation of EU law prior to Brexit, as evidenced by the leading UK decisions.[57] The UK courts held that the relationship between EU law and national law in terms of supremacy was to be decided by the UK courts as a matter of UK constitutional law, taking account of any statutes enacted by Parliament. They also held that the concept of *implied repeal*, or *implied disapplication*, under which inconsistencies between later and earlier norms were resolved in favour of the former, would generally not apply to clashes concerning EU and national law, with the consequence that if Parliament wished to derogate from its EU obligations, then it would have to do so *expressly and unequivocally*. The reaction of our national courts to such an eventuality was never tested. The courts might have chosen to follow the latest will

---

55 HLA Hart *The Concept of Law* (Oxford University Press, Oxford, 1961) at 97–107.

56 At 144–150.

57 *R v Secretary of State for Transport, ex p Factortame Ltd (No 2)* [1991] 1 AC 603; *R v Secretary of State for Employment, ex p Equal Opportunities Commission* [1995] 1 AC 1; *Thoburn v Sunderland City Council* [2003] QB 151; *HS2*, above n 25.

of Parliament, or they might have decided that it was not open to the legislature to pick and choose which obligations to subscribe to while still remaining within the EU.

This still left open the way in which this change should be conceptualised. There were suggestions that this could be achieved through statutory construction. This was, however, problematic. While all would agree that if a statute could be reconciled with an EU norm through construing the statutory words without unduly distorting them then this should be done. However, the species of statutory construction considered here was more far-reaching, because the rule of 'construction' was more akin to a 'priority' rule, whereby inconsistencies *would* be resolved in favour of the EU law, *unless* Parliament indicated clearly and ambiguously that it intended to derogate from EU law. The degree of linguistic inconsistency between the statute and the EU norm was not the essential point of the inquiry.

An alternative explanation could, however, be cast in terms of change to the rule of recognition, through a technical legal revolution. On this view, the case law considered above, combined with acceptance by the leading political players, brought about modification of the rule of recognition. An accurate rendition of the ultimate legal principle during the pendency of UK membership of the EU would then have been as follows: Parliament can do anything that it wishes through statute enacted by simple majority, including implied repeal or amendment, except in the areas covered by EU law where Parliament would have to legislate expressly and unequivocally in order to derogate from EU law. This modification of the top rule of the system was, as noted above, not immutable. The rule of recognition could have been recast, so as not to include the preceding qualification. This might have occurred if the UK courts had changed their legal position concerning the relationship between UK and EU law while the UK was still a Member State, and the other organs of government accepted the change. The fact of Brexit, *ex hypothesi*, did recast the rule of recognition, since the very rationale for accommodating EU law had been removed. However, the legal Brexit arrangements attest to the continuing force of the preceding reasoning, since Parliament, pursuant to its sovereignty, decided to continue to accord authority to EU law in certain respects, which has been accepted by the courts.[58]

The modality of change in the rule of recognition, and the limits thereto, can be further exemplified by devolution. The enactment of

58 European Union (Withdrawal) Act 2018, ss 5–6.

devolution legislation by the Labour government in the late 1990s, the Scotland Act 1998 and the Government of Wales Act 1998, was significant in political terms, through the very grant of autonomy over the devolved issues. This was further enhanced through subsequent legislation, notably the Government of Wales Act 2006, the Wales Act 2014 and the Scotland Act 2016, which further augmented their respective powers.

There is little doubt that the enactment of this legislation might have had implications for the rule of recognition. It would not, for the reasons given above, have effectuated this change in itself, but could have been the catalyst for alteration in the social acceptance that underpins the rule of recognition. The reality is that any such change has been relatively minor. This is in part because of the terms of the enabling legislation, which make clear that the Westminster Parliament can still make laws for Scotland and Wales.[59] It is in part because of political considerations. The UK government is opposed to the Scottish National Party's separatist ambitions and opposed also to the holding of a referendum to determine the wishes of the Scottish people. This has played out in constitutional terms, with the UK government emphasising the sovereignty of the Westminster Parliament and the fact that its consent is a condition precedent to the holding of a referendum. The limits to any change in the rule of recognition also flow in part from judicial decisions. Courts interpret legislation and not infrequently make choices as to the consequences that should flow from statutory amendments. This is readily apparent from the judicial reaction to the change in the Sewel Convention, which established that the Westminster Parliament would not legislate on devolved matters without the consent of the Scottish Parliament. The Convention was embodied in the Scotland Act 1998[60] as a result of the Scotland Act 2016. However, in *Miller* the Supreme Court held that this legislative amendment did not render the Sewel Convention legally enforceable.[61] Courts of law 'cannot enforce a political convention'.[62] Judges were 'neither the parents nor the guardians of political conventions; they are merely observers'.[63] The fact that the Sewel Convention had been enshrined in legislation by s 2 of the Scotland Act 2016 did not thereby render a political convention legally enforceable.

59 Scotland Act 1998, s 28(7).
60 Section 28(8).
61 *R (Miller) v Secretary of State for Exiting the European Union* [2017] UKSC 5 at [136]–[137].
62 At [141].
63 At [146].

The devolution legislation has, therefore, not been the trigger for significant change in the rule of recognition so far as Scotland, Wales and Northern Ireland are concerned. It would, however, be misguided to assume that it has had no such effect. Consider in this respect the constitutional reaction to wholesale repeal of this devolution legislation, such that all matters without exception were run from the Westminster Parliament, with the consequence that the principal devolved political institutions were dissolved. Whatsoever the judicial response to such legislation might be, it would almost certainly be regarded as a constitutional revolution. This reaction would be premised on the assumption that post-1998 the constitutional settlement in the UK was one in which Scotland, Wales and Northern Ireland should have some considerable authority over their own affairs. This, in turn, would be reflected in the rule of recognition, which would, in essence, have read that while Parliament could do anything that it wished by simple majority, it would not generally do so in the devolved areas without securing their assent through their respective political institutions. Repeal of the devolution legislation would thus be regarded as a re-orientation of the rule of recognition.

3.4.2. Frame

Change in the rule of recognition is, therefore, perfectly possible. Parliamentary sovereignty, conceptualised in terms of the absence of substantive and procedural limits as to what can be done through ordinary legislation, nonetheless frames this process. This is manifest in at least four ways.

First, there is the flipside of the point in the previous section, which is also salient here. Thus, while limits on parliamentary sovereignty might develop through change in the social acceptance that constitutes the rule of recognition, the assumed starting point is that there are no substantive and procedural limits as to what can be done through ordinary legislation, the corollary of which is that social acceptance as manifest by the key institutional players might revert back to this position, even if there has been movement therefrom.

Secondly, elevation of the traditional conception of parliamentary sovereignty as the key constitutional principle has implications for any limits placed thereon. Consider in this respect the way in which we conceptualise constitutional statutes.[64] The recognition afforded to this concept is to be

[64] *Thoburn*, above n 57 at [59]–[63]; *McWhirter v Secretary of State for Foreign and Commonwealth Affairs* [2003] EWCA Civ 384 at [14]; *H v Lord Advocate* [2012] UKSC 24;

welcomed. It is, nonetheless, acknowledged that the ascription of this status is limited in terms of consequences. It is still open to Parliament, in accord with its sovereignty, to repeal or amend any statutes commonly included on this list, subject to the injunction that it must do so expressly and unequivocally, with only very limited, if any, room for implied change. Consider further in this respect the way in which we think of the principle of legality. It captures the idea that Parliament can do anything it likes by statute duly enacted, subject to the interpretive precept that the courts will not read general statutory words so as to interfere with fundamental rights. Parliament must, as Lord Hoffmann stated,[65] pay the political cost of its action, which meant that if it wished to limit such rights it would have to do so clearly and unequivocally through language that revealed that Parliament understood what it was doing. It is, however, still open to Parliament to take such action and any challenge based on the Human Rights Act 1998 is bounded by s 4, which limits the court to a declaration of incompatibility, while leaving the validity of the legislation unaffected.

Thirdly, the traditional conception of parliamentary sovereignty frames government thinking and reform initiatives in the public law context. This is exemplified by Ministry of Justice initiatives concerning judicial review,[66] and the HRA.[67] These initiatives have been fuelled prominently, albeit not exclusively, by claims of judicial overreach, the allegation being that the courts have trespassed too far on terrain that is properly the preserve of the legislature and/or the executive. The terms of reference for the HRA review are motivated by similar considerations, as evident in questions as to whether the courts have been too intrusive in their interpretation of s 3 of the HRA. The claims of systemic judicial overreach do not withstand examination,[68] and the argument that the courts have overstepped proper bounds in the context of the HRA has been rejected by the Joint Committee on Human Rights.[69] The apposite point for present purposes is that a particular conception of parliamentary sovereignty frames these inquiries and the current executive's approach to them.

HS2, above n 25; David Feldman "The Nature and Significance of 'Constitutional' Legislation" (2013) 129 LQR 343; PP Craig "Constitutionalizing Constitutional Law: *HS2*" [2014] PL 373; Farrah Ahmed and Adam Perry "Constitutional Statutes" (2017) 37 OJLS 461.

65 *R v Secretary of State for the Home Department, ex p Simms* [2000] 2 AC 115.

66 *Independent Review of Administrative Law* (CP 407, 2021).

67 *Independent Human Rights Act Review* (IHRAR, 2021).

68 PP Craig "Judicial Review, Methodology and Reform" [2022] PL 19.

69 Joint Committee on Human Rights *The Government's Independent Review of the Human Rights Act* (HC 89, HL Paper 31, 8 July 2021).

Finally, there is a second order dimension to the way in which parliamentary sovereignty frames UK constitutional discourse. This connotes the way in which the concept underpins, or influences, other constitutional doctrine. Consider, by way of example, the law relating to parliamentary privilege, and judicial strictures that courts should not look beyond the parliamentary roll. There are assuredly multiple purposes served by doctrines of parliamentary privilege, and they are not logically dependent on parliamentary sovereignty. This can be accepted. There is, nonetheless, a sense in which the overall contours of such doctrine are shaped by parliamentary sovereignty. The primacy accorded to ordinary statute grounded in Parliament's electoral legitimacy is external in its orientation. The privilege afforded to Parliament in the conduct of its own proceedings is an internal manifestation of Parliament's sovereign position, a recognition that it should be master of its internal domain.

4. CONCLUSION

There are, to draw on a common metaphor, many views of the cathedral. This very fact is enriching, since it can thereby furnish fresh perspectives on oft-discussed issues. This contribution does not claim such novelty in this respect. It has, nonetheless, sought to highlight the significance of the difference between the normative precepts that underpin the standard written constitution and the unwritten constitution that has parliamentary sovereignty as its centrepiece. The normative rationale for the ascription of parliamentary sovereignty has, as we have seen, altered over time and it continues to shape the modality and frame for constitutional change in the UK.

CONSTITUTIONAL SCHOLARS AND THE UNWRITTEN CONSTITUTION

Interpreters, Reformers, Communicators

Sam BOOKMAN*

* Thank you to Elisabeth Perham, Rosalind Dixon, Adrienne Stone, and all the participants at the Comparative Constitutional Law Roundtable held at the Gilbert and Tobin Centre for Public Law at the University of New South Wales, 8–11 December 2020. Thanks also to the reviewers, Ed Willis and Max Harris, for their careful critiques and suggestions. All errors are my own.

1. INTRODUCTION

One of the hallmarks of the 'unwritten' constitution is its resistance to precise definition. The unwritten constitution is sometimes ascribed an almost esoteric quality, divinable only to a priestly caste of experts. Sir Geoffrey Palmer has compared New Zealand's constitution to the elusive 'Snark' in Lewis Carroll's nonsense poem, *The Hunting of the Snark*: constitutional interpretation is like searching for a monster that is both elusive and imaginary.[1] Whatever its merits, the unwritten constitution poses difficulties in matters of academic interpretation, practical application and education.

Enter Bruce Harris. In a vast and distinguished body of work, his latest contribution may be his most impactful. In *New Zealand Constitution: An Analysis in Terms of Principles*, Professor Harris offers a summary of the New Zealand constitution that is remarkable in its simplicity and readability.[2] The text's central conceit is that the New Zealand constitution can be succinctly systematised in 16 principles, each of which is neatly set out and analysed. The book provides a uniquely accessible advanced introduction to the New Zealand constitution.[3] But it is more than a restatement. It is simultaneously an interpretation of New Zealand's constitutional arrangements; a prescription for reform; and an educational tool.

Efforts such as Harris's *New Zealand Constitution* raise questions about the role that scholars play in New Zealand's constitutional arrangements. This contribution argues that the academy is part of the interpretive community which produces New Zealand's constitution. Yet the constitutional role of academics has seldom been examined. In Section 2, I make the case for treatment of the academy as a constitutional institution. In doing so, I draw on recent scholarly analysis which recognises the constitutional role of public officials,[4] integrity

---

1 Geoffrey Palmer *Reform: A Memoir* (Victoria University Press, Wellington, 2013). See further Lewis Carroll, "The Hunting of the Snark", Poetry Foundation <www.poetryfoundation.org> (original poem published in 1876).

2 Bruce Harris *New Zealand Constitution: An Analysis in Terms of Principles* (Thomson Reuters, Wellington, 2018).

3 For reviews of the book, see Margaret A Wilson "Book Review: Bruce Harris 'New Zealand Constitution: An Analysis in Terms of Principles'" [2019] NZLJ 303; Edward Willis "Book Review: New Zealand Constitution: An Analysis in Terms of Principles" (2019) 16 Otago L Rev 247.

4 See, for example, Matthew SR Palmer "What is New Zealand's Constitution and Who Interprets it? Constitutional Realism and the Importance of Public Office-holders" (2006) 17 PLR 133.

agencies[5] and 'knowledge institutions'.[6] In Section 3, I set out the constitutional functions carried out by law teachers. Academics perform three functions: interpretive/descriptive, evaluative/normative and educational/ communicational. Different academic roles and strategies can be assumed within these functions. For example, the evaluative/normative function could involve radical critique and deconstruction, challenging the very foundations of public law or the postcolonial liberal state; from this standpoint, a scholar may prescribe transformational change,[7] or adopt the role of an external critic.[8] Alternatively (and perhaps more commonly), the evaluative/normative function offers prescription for reform. This reformist mode, in which the scholar offers prescription for change that fits within existing constitutional structures, is one which Bruce Harris has often adopted, and is the primary focus of this contribution. Finally, in Section 4 I consider the implications of this dynamic for the role that academics play in New Zealand's constitutional system.

Throughout this contribution, the terms 'scholar', 'academic' and 'law teacher' are used interchangeably. Rather than having any technical meaning, these terms are used broadly to refer to those whose professional vocation is the study and teaching of fields of law which can be broadly considered 'constitutional' in character. Such scholars may not always be lawyers or affiliated to law schools: many scholars have performed important functions in New Zealand's constitutional system from institutions other than law schools.[9]

---

5 See, for example, James Spigelman "The Integrity Branch of Government" (2004) 78 ALJ 724; Bruce Ackerman "The New Separation of Powers" (2000) 113 Harv L Rev 633.

6 See, for example, Vicki C Jackson "Knowledge Institutions in Constitutional Democracies: Of Objectivity and Decentralization" (29 August 2019) Harvard Law Review Blog <blog.harvardlawreview.org>; Vicki C Jackson "Legal Scholarship and Knowledge Institutions in Constitutional Democracy" (Summer 2019) AALS Newsletter 1.

7 See, for example, Margaret Mutu "'To Honour the Treaty we must First Settle Colonization': the Long Road from Colonial Devastation to Balance, Peace and Harmony" (2019) 49 Journal of the Royal Society of New Zealand 4.

8 See for example much of the work of Moana Jackson, which calls for 'the formation of a different Māori polity that necessarily questions the legitimacy of the colonising one': Moana Jackson "The face behind the law" (2005) 8(2) Yearbook of New Zealand Jurisprudence 10 at 30. For further discussion of the strategies available to a radical constitutional scholar, see Aziz Rana "Freedom Struggles and the Limits of Constitutional Continuity" (2012) 71 Maryland L Rev 1015.

9 Perhaps the most prominent may be Moana Jackson, a lecturer at Te Wānanga o Raukawa for many years.

2. BROADENING THE SUBJECTS OF CONSTITUTIONAL ANALYSIS

Constitutional scholarship has historically focused attention on legislators, judges, and senior government politicians. Over time, the focus has expanded. The burgeoning of the administrative state has led to greater attention being paid to the ways in which the practices of bureaucrats and officials shape the constitution.[10] Attention has also turned to the constitutional roles of 'integrity' institutions. Both bureaucracies and integrity institutions have been referred to as the 'fourth branch' of government.[11] More recently, attention has also turned to the roles played by non-governmental institutions, including the concept of 'knowledge institutions' as constitutional actors.[12] This part offers a brief survey of these developments, and situates the role of legal scholars within this widening conception of constitutional actors.

Central to this analysis is a functional conception of the unwritten constitution: that is, the constitution includes those elements and actors who practically shape the norms, limits and future directions of the exercise of public power.[13] This analysis eschews formal categories and definitions of 'the constitution' and its institutions. The framework of 'constitutional realism' developed by Matthew Palmer, and Bruce Harris's pragmatic approach in *New Zealand Constitution*, are both examples of functional approaches.[14] The central claim in this part is that constitutional scholars are constitutional actors because they exercise crucial functions in defining

---

10 See, for example, Janet McLean and Mark Tushnet "Administrative Bureaucracy" in Mark Tushnet, Thomas Fleiner and Cheryl Saunders (eds) *Routledge Handbook of Constitutional Law* (Routledge, Abingdon, 2013) 121.

11 See, for example, Peter L Strauss "The Place of Agencies in Government: Separation of Powers and the Fourth Branch" (1984) 84 Colum L Rev 573; WMC Gummow "A Fourth Branch of Government?" (2012) 70 AIAL Forum 19; Ackerman, above n 5.

12 Jackson "Knowledge Institutions", above n 6.

13 For further discussion and critique of the functional approach in comparative perspective, see the seminal work of Konrad Zweigert and Hein Kotz *Introduction to Comparative Law* (3rd ed, trans Tony Weir, Oxford University Press, Oxford, 1998), and discussion in Ralf Michaels "The Functional Method of Comparative Law" in Mathias Reimann and Reinhard Zimmerman (eds) *The Oxford Handbook of Comparative Law* (Oxford University Press, Oxford, 2006) 340.

14 See in particular Palmer, above n 4, at 138: 'An analysis of constitutional elements should be undertaken in light of their function in defining the generic exercise of public power'. For further discussion of the similarities and differences between Harris and Palmer's approaches, see Edward Willis's contribution to this volume.

and developing the unwritten constitution, despite the fact that scholars have no formal authority to do so.[15]

2.1. PUBLIC OFFICIALS

A functional approach reveals that many actors beyond judges and politicians shape the constitution. This includes public officials such as government lawyers and public sector managers. The constitutional role of public officials fits within Matthew Palmer's account of 'constitutional realism'.[16] Palmer argues that the essence of any constitution goes beyond its formal text. It is instead 'about public power and how it is exercised', including 'the structures, processes, principles, rules, conventions and even culture that *constitute* the ways in which government power is exercised'.[17] Palmer suggests that not only the instruments of each branch of government, but also the interpretations of each branch, form part of the constitution itself.[18] These interpretations create 'bodies of precedent or practice that have less formal but still normatively persuasive constitutional effect'.[19] In Palmer's realist scheme, public officials play an important role as members of an 'interpretive community', who – through a 'complicated and iterative interaction' between advisers and decisionmakers – offer interpretations that are '*authoritative in practice* ... as applied to a particular instance of doubt or dispute. ... advice on the interpretation of a constitutional element by an experienced official with a deserved reputation for giving good advice will almost always be followed'.[20] Palmer offers several examples of this dynamic, including Cabinet's regular reliance on advice sought and offered by New Zealand's Solicitor-General.[21]

---

15 In doing so, this contribution goes further than Matthew Palmer's realist approach, whose primary focus is on actors whose constitutional interpretation is 'authoritative in practice': see Palmer, above n 4, at 149.

16 One need not be a functionalist or realist to recognise the influential constitutional role of public officials: see, for example, Janet McLean "The Unwritten Political Constitution and its Enemies" (2016) 14 Int'l J Const L 119.

17 Palmer, above n 4, at 135. Palmer draws on the political constitutional tradition, citing AV Dicey *Introduction to the Study of the Law of the Constitution* (10th ed, MacMillan, London, 1960) at 23, and Ivor Jennings *The Law and the Constitution* (3rd ed, University of London Press, London, 1943) at xv.

18 At 138.

19 At 139.

20 At 148–150 (emphasis in the original).

21 Palmer, above n 4, at 150, citing John McGrath "The Crown, Parliament, and the Government" (1999) 7 Waikato L Rev 1 at 5, 7–11 and 14–19.

As Edward Willis demonstrates elsewhere in this volume, Palmer's scheme of 'constitutional realism' is not without its critics.[22] Palmer's approach can underplay the role of normative analysis and principles, reducing New Zealand's constitution to a messy 'adhocracy'. But it has the strength of accurately capturing the day-to-day workings of the constitution in practice and establishes how public officials play a vital role as part of the constitution's 'interpretive community'.[23] In this sense, it is an effective functional approach which identifies the institutions that interpret and shape New Zealand's constitution.

2.2. INTEGRITY INSTITUTIONS

Palmer's work identifies a widening array of constitutional actors. Another example is the focus on 'integrity' institutions. These are public institutions designed to facilitate accountability of executive government and 'further help ensure the quality of executive decision-making'.[24] New Zealand examples include the Ombudsmen and Auditor-General, both of whom scrutinise executive action and offer citizens formal (but non-judicial) processes for holding their government to account. The place of these institutions in New Zealand's constitutional system is now widely recognised.[25] Among the 16 principles summarised in *New Zealand Constitution*, Harris includes 'the principle that the executive government is accountable through the integrity branch of government'.[26] He cites as examples Ombudsmen,[27] the Controller and Auditor-General,[28] Human Rights Commission,[29] Children's Commissioner[30] and Independent Police

22 See Edward Willis's contribution to this volume.

23 Palmer, above n 4, at 148, citing William S Blatt "Interpretive Communities: The Missing Element in Statutory Interpretation" (2001) 95 Northwest U L Rev 629. See also Philip A Joseph and Gordon R Walker "A Theory of Constitutional Change" (1987) 7(2) OJLS 155 at 166–167.

24 Harris, above n 2, at 229.

25 See, for example, recognition of the Ombudsmen Act 1975, Official Information Act 1982, and Public Finance Act 1989 as sources of New Zealand's constitution in the introduction to the 2017 Cabinet Manual: New Zealand Cabinet Office, *Cabinet Manual 2017*, at 2.

26 Harris, above n 3, at 229.

27 Ombudsmen Act 1975; Official Information Act 1982.

28 Public Audit Act 2001.

29 Human Rights Act 1993.

30 Children's Commissioner Act 2003.

Conduct Authority.[31] All these institutions have in common the goal of maintaining governmental integrity, 'ensuring that powers are exercised for the purposes and in the manner envisaged.[32]

As with Palmer's discussion of public officials, the recognition that these institutions are 'constitutional' in nature reflects a pragmatic, functional approach. No positive law instrument confers constitutional status on these bodies, and they are instead created by ordinary statutes. However, scrutinising the exercise of power – including oversight of transparency, human rights and police conduct – raises the familiar constitutional issues of rights and democratic structures. Integrity branch institutions are routinely included in written constitutions in other jurisdictions.[33] Within New Zealand's unwritten structure, the legislation which creates these institutions can be considered components of New Zealand's constitution, and the interpretations and determinations issued by these bodies form a part of New Zealand's constitutional canon.[34]

2.3. THE CONSTITUTIONAL ACADEMY AS A KNOWLEDGE INSTITUTION

A functional account of New Zealand's constitution is concerned with the actors and institutions who shape New Zealand's constitution. It is less concerned with the formal status of those actors: thus, non-governmental institutions may be considered constitutional actors. In the comparative context, scholars such as Vicki Jackson have argued that non-governmental institutions – including the press, academy and civil society – form a coherent category which together can 'contribut[e] to a

31 Independent Police Conduct Authority 1988.

32 Spigelman, above n 5, at 737.

33 Data from the Constitute Project records 34 constitutions which provide for a 'counter corruption commission', 49 constitutions which provide for a 'human rights commission', and 88 constitutions which provide for ombudsmen. See "Constitute Project" <www.constituteproject.org>.

34 See Palmer, above n 4, at 153–162; Harris, above n 2, at 229; *Cabinet Manual*, above n 25, at 2. Note that Palmer's list of integrity institutions that comprise elements of the constitution is shorter than Harris's – Palmer, for example, does not include the Office of the Children's Commissioner. This likely reflects a difference in focus of the functions considered: while Palmer is concerned with the accountability of *officials* who exercise general public powers, Harris is more broadly concerned with actors who hold the government to account on an *institutional* level.

sound epistemic base for representative democracy … working together, as part of a knowledge ecosystem'.[35] Although such bodies are not formal branches of 'constitutional *government*' (unlike public officials and integrity institutions), these institutions are 'necessary organ[s] of constitutional democracy'.[36] These 'knowledge institutions' provide citizens with necessary information to participate in governance through the democratic process as voters, deliberators and scrutinisers of government action.[37]

Jackson argues that law schools hold a 'special role' in this knowledge ecosystem.[38] This role includes the training of lawyers, and legal scholarship which shifts public policy and influences judicial decisions.[39] Liora Lazarus builds on this idea by arguing that constitutional law professors are 'analogous to integrity institutions'.[40] Constitutional scholars hold judges to account by scrutinising the reasons for their decisions.[41] Scholars evaluate whether the reasons given by judges are plausible interpretations of constitutional law and may offer critiques where judgments fall short. This position is enhanced by the relative independence of academics, who – unlike practising lawyers – do not have the same incentives to avoid judicial censure. Indeed, New Zealand universities have a statutory *duty* to act as the 'critic and conscience of society'.[42]

Furthermore, like integrity institutions, legal academics scrutinise 'claims to the constitutionality of political action' – that is, actions and justifications offered by the legislative and executive branches.[43] Most constitutional questions do not reach the attention of courts: they play out in the everyday world of ordinary politics, where politicians address their arguments to the general public. Scholars have questioned the

35 Jackson "Knowledge Institutions", above n 6.
36 Above n 6 (emphasis in the original).
37 Above n 6.
38 Above n 6.
39 Above n 6.
40 Liora Lazarus "Constitutional Scholars as Constitutional Actors" (2020) 48 Federal Law Review 483 at 495.
41 At 487–489, citing Mark Tushnet "Preserving Judicial Independence in Dominant Party States" (2015) 60 NYLS L Rev 107 at 108; Tarunabh Khaitan, "*Koushal v Naz*: Judges Vote to Recriminalize Homosexuality" (2015) 78 MLR 672 at 678.
42 Education and Training Act 2020, s 268(2)(d)(E).
43 Lazarus, above n 40, at 490.

constitutionality of government action ranging from the development of the New Zealand Convention Centre,[44] the failure to recognise Māori property rights in the foreshore and seabed[45] and the passage of legislation which consolidated executive powers following the Christchurch Earthquakes.[46] Furthermore, the legal arguments developed by constitutional scholars contribute to constitutional texts and doctrines, and 'facilitate robust constitutional debate' as to the legal validity and desirability of certain actions.[47] Lazarus illustrates this claim with specific examples of how the competing interpretations of constitutionality of prorogation shaped the legal arguments presented in, and the elite and public reaction to, the UK Supreme Court's decision in *Miller/Cherry*.[48] John Finnis's defence of prorogation was prominently cited by conservative media,[49] while the scholarship of Jeff King, Nick Barber and Tom Hickman contributed to legal argument presented to (and adopted by) the Supreme Court.[50] In the US, the testimony of constitutional law professors was widely cited in support of (and opposition to) efforts to impeach President Donald Trump.[51] On a more general level, Lazarus also cites examples of constitutional scholarship which has led to sweeping law reform, such as Francesca Klug's critical role in securing the passage of the UK Human Rights Act 1998.[52] New Zealand examples could include

44 McLean, above n 16, at 129–135.

45 See Moana Jackson and Claire Charters "Te Ahi Kaa 17 Haratua (May) 2009" (17 May 2009) RNZ <https://www.rnz.co.nz/national/programmes/teahikaa/audio/1946187/te-ahi-kaa-17-haratua-may-2009>.

46 See Stuart Anderson and others "Legal Expert: Quake Law a Worrying Precedent" (28 September 2010) New Zealand Herald <https://www.nzherald.co.nz/nz/ilegal-expertsi-quake-law-change-a-worrying-precedent/2HXPQA4SA7DAJQX643V5ZCTHWI/>.

47 Lazarus, above n 40, at 491.

48 At 490, citing *R (Miller) v Prime Minister* [2020] AC 373.

49 At 490. Lazarus cites a front-page article in *The Telegraph* which directly referenced John Finnis as "an eminent Oxford Professor". Charles Moore "Fixing the Supreme Court Should be Boris Johnson's Constitutional Priority" (7 February 2020) The Telegraph <www.telegraph.co.uk>.

50 At 491, citing "UCL Laws Academics Praised for the Argument that Led Gina Miller to Victory" (2 February 2020) UCL Faculty of Laws <www.ucl.ac.uk>.

51 At 492. This influence reached new heights after the testimony of four law professors before the House Judiciary Committee. See Amy Davidson Sorkin "What the Law Professors Brought to the Trump Impeachment Hearings" (5 December 2019) The New Yorker <www.newyorker.com>.

52 At 491.

the advocacy-scholarship of Sir Geoffrey Palmer in laying the groundwork for the New Zealand Bill of Rights Act 1990 and moves towards proportional representation,[53] as well as the long-run impacts of Moana Jackson's landmark 1987 criminal justice report, *He Whaipaanga Hou*.[54]

Jackson and Lazarus's arguments about 'knowledge institutions' are not without faults. In particular, Jackson's objective and uncontroversial conception of knowledge production grates against prevailing social science epistemology. Knowledge is rarely uncontested: even an agreed set of facts or observations may give rise to different meanings, depending on the standpoint or 'paradigm' of the scholar or observer.[55] No institution can claim a pure monopoly as a source of knowledge, and institutions must contend with the fact of disagreement. Scholars do communicate a core of basic (and more-or-less objective) information about how the constitution operates. But for the most part, it might be more accurate to acknowledge constitutional scholars as engaged in an ongoing struggle in which they communicate competing interpretations, critiques and prescriptions, bounded by the discourse of constitutional law. Over time this may produce some knowledge which commands universal agreement; but what is certain is that – as discussed below – the interpretations and prescriptions offered by scholars are a form of knowledge production with significant implications for the evolution (or unsettling) of the unwritten constitution and the ways in which governmental actors are held to account.

Notwithstanding these criticisms, the 'knowledge institution' concept is helpful in drawing attention to the dependence of constitutional systems on an underlying body of knowledge, even if it downplays the extent to which that body of knowledge is contested. Knowledge production is a constitutional function, and production institutions are constitutional actors. As Matthew Palmer observes, the sources of the unwritten

53 See, for example, Geoffrey Palmer *Unbridled Power* (1st ed, Oxford University Press, 1979). The example is complicated by the fact that Palmer's intervention as a legislator and Cabinet Minister (rather than academic) was ultimately decisive in securing these innovations.

54 Moana Jackson, *He Whaipaanga Hou* (1987) available online at <https://safeandeffectivejustice.govt.nz/research/a-new-perspective-part-1/>.

55 This is not to say that objective truth is impossible, but rather that Jackson's account underplays the difficulty in arriving at any such truths. For a canonical account of the subjectivity of knowledge production, see discussion of non-linearity and "paradigm shifts" in Thomas S Kuhn *The Structure of Scientific Revolutions* (University of Chicago Press, Chicago, 1962). In Jackson's defence, she does concede that objectivity is often an aspiration rather than a reality. See Jackson, "Knowledge Institutions", above n 6.

constitution include the community of actors who discipline the way that public power is exercised.[56] Lazarus's analysis demonstrates that constitutional law scholars are undoubtedly part of that community. As Lazarus emphatically concludes:[57]

> … whether indirectly – through teaching and training of future lawyers (and politicians), publishing research, writing textbooks, practitioner handbooks and constitutional commentaries – or directly through active public engagement – constitutional scholars facilitate robust constitutional debate and shape the constitution. They are part of the formation and development of constitutional texts, doctrine, interpretation of doctrine and conventions, evaluation of judicial pronouncements on doctrine and constitutional arguments before courts. Their diverse contributions constitute part of the constitutional accountability fabric and shape the environment in which constitutions are formed.

3. INTERPRETERS, REFORMERS, COMMUNICATORS

Having established that academics are constitutional actors, this part explores *how* scholars discharge their constitutional role in New Zealand. This part focuses on three functions, all of which are typically included in an academic's 'job description'. First, academics perform an interpretive or descriptive function. Academics analyse the practices and statements of other constitutional actors and interpret how they do (or do not) make sense in New Zealand's constitutional framework, or how they might affect or amend the unwritten constitution. Defining the unwritten constitution is a key component of this function. Secondly, academics perform an evaluative or normative function. In doing so, scholars can adopt a range of different standpoints, including the outsider critic, revolutionary or reformer. In all these standpoints, the scholar evaluates aspects of the unwritten constitution (including recent developments) and offers a prescription or critique. Finally, academics are communicators and educators. They communicate knowledge to constitutional elites, future lawyers and the general voting public.

---

56 See further Palmer, above n 4, at 148–49.

57 Lazarus, above n 40, at 491.

In what follows in this section, I elaborate further on each of these functions, drawing on examples from New Zealand scholars (including Harris). Furthermore, I argue that while each function can be independently identified and described, the boundaries between them are fuzzy: the three functions are inherently interconnected. An exercise of one function will often simultaneously perform at least one of the other two.

3.1. INTERPRETATION

In legal theory, 'interpretation' is a loaded term. In most discussions it relates to the role of judges in applying legal rules or – in other jurisdictions – constitutional texts.[58] That is not the meaning that concerns me here. Instead, in the context of the unwritten constitution I argue that a core constitutional function involves defining what the constitution *is*. In the absence of an authoritative written document, this will often be a matter of interpreting how different practices or instruments fit within the constitutional framework, explaining how the constitution enables (or is enabled by) certain practices or ideas, or explaining how recent practices or decisions by other institutions have changed the constitution.[59]

Interpretation is a core function of legal research. Academics engage with the products of constitutional practice (legislation, judicial decisions, administrative practices) and purport to make sense of it all. This could include an attempt to find coherence and principle within the unwritten constitution, presenting it as a cogent and ordered system.[60] But interpreters may also reject the coherence of the constitutional order, contesting it as unprincipled or incoherent.[61] Classic archetypes of interpretive approaches include doctrinal restatement, recasting projects, critical projects and

58 For examples in the US context, see John Hart Ely *Democracy and Distrust: A Theory of Judicial Review* (Harvard University Press, Cambridge, 1980); Ronald Dworkin *Freedom's Law: The Moral Reading of the American Constitution* (Harvard University Press, Cambridge, 1996).

59 I thus use 'interpretation' in a different sense to that employed by Palmer, above n 4, at 1481–1449. Palmer is concerned with the 'authoritative in practice' determinations of how legal rules apply in particular fact situations.

60 This view is strongly influenced by the ideas of Ronald Dworkin: see, for example, Dworkin, above n 58.

61 See, for example, Mutu, above n 7; Jackson, above n 8.

comparative and historical inquiries.[62] The need for interpretation reflects the law's unavoidable tensions and ambiguities. New Zealand's constitution depends on interpretation to identify principles which can make sense of seemingly conflicting or random practice, or predict how authoritative constitutional actors (judges, legislators and public officials) might act in the future.[63] Alternatively, it is vulnerable to more radical critiques which may expose its incoherence or need for reconstruction.

New Zealand's constitutional framework presents a double ambiguity, in which academics must interpret both the content and the sources of the constitution. Scholars in all countries face challenges in defining 'the constitution'. Even in jurisdictions with codified constitutional texts, the broader framework of the 'small-c' constitution includes legislation,[64] judicial precedents,[65] as well as practices and conventions.[66] In New Zealand, this ambiguity is particularly explicit: there is no defined textual starting point from which to begin the interpretive task. Often the interpreter attempts to explain how a recent development coheres with existing constitutional principles, or whether elements of the constitution have changed. The unwritten constitution thus offers opportunities for academic creativity while also acting as an organising principle. Through the process of interpretation, academics take part in drawing and critiquing the boundaries of the constitution, as well as filling in the details.

Interpretation is also bounded by academic institutions: the language, logic and conventions of academic argument. To state the obvious,

62 See Martha Minow "Archetypal Legal Scholarship: A Field Guide" (2013) 63 Journal of Legal Education 65.

63 Interpretation can therefore serve functions identified by both Dworkin's vision of law as 'integrity', and by Oliver Wendell Holmes's injunction that the law is 'the prophecies of what the courts will do in fact, and nothing more pretentious'. See respectively Ronald Dworkin *Law's Empire* (Harvard University Press, Cambridge, 1986) at 176–275; Oliver Wendell Holmes "The Path of the Law" (1897) 10 Harv L Rev 457 at 461.

64 See, for example, William N Eskridge and John Ferejohn "Super-Statutes" (2001) 50 Duke LJ 1215; Richard Albert and Joel Colon-Rios (eds) *Quasi-Constitutionality and Constitutional Statutes: Forms, Functions and Applications* (Routledge, New York, 2019).

65 See, for example, Akhil Amar *America's Unwritten Constitution: The Precedents and Principles We Live By* (Basic Books, New York, 2012), which discusses the issue of judicial precedents among other sources of the US Constitution.

66 See, for example, Rosalind Dixon and Adrienne Stone (eds) *The Invisible Constitution in Comparative Perspective* (Cambridge University Press, Cambridge, 2018); Keith E Whittington "The Status of Unwritten Constitutional Conventions in the United States" (2013) 5 U Ill L Rev 1847; Farrah Ahmed, Richard Albert and Adam Perry "Judging Constitutional Conventions" (2019) 17 Int'l J Const L 787.

constitutional scholars are usually (but not always) socialised in the same institutions as practising lawyers.[67] Most of the time they speak the language of legal practitioners. They are trained to interpret based on precedent and legal reasoning, presenting arguments which would be taken seriously in court. The most prestigious acts of interpretation – publication in legal journals – are further disciplined by the process of peer-review, and the intended audience of fellow experts and practitioners.

The role of scholarly interpretation can be illustrated with reference to one recent example: the academic response to judicial decisions concerning the 'declaration of inconsistency' remedy. This remedy was recognised by the High Court in *Taylor v Attorney-General* and subsequently upheld by the Court of Appeal and Supreme Court.[68] The remedy allows the High Court to formally declare primary legislation to be inconsistent with rights enumerated in the New Zealand Bill of Rights Act 1990 (NZBORA). The declaration does not invalidate the legislation. It leaves significant ambiguity as to the remedy's constitutional significance, and how it fits with existing principles and doctrines. In *New Zealand Constitution*, Harris interprets the remedy as a manifestation of the principle that 'all aspects of the New Zealand system of government are subject to the expectation of compliance with the Bill of Rights Act', while expressing concern that the remedy has an uneasy relationship with the competing principle of comity.[69] In one of the first academic responses to the Court of Appeal's *Taylor* decision, Claudia Geiringer offers an example of interpretation which searches for coherence and principle.[70] Geiringer offers three possible interpretations of the Court's decision, each one grounded in a different 'narrative' based on a particular interpretive standpoint and academic tradition. In each case, the narrative explains how the *Taylor* decision fits (or does not fit) with New Zealand's constitution, and questions how it might change (or fail to change) future judicial practice. Geiringer's analysis has set the scene for subsequent

67 See further David Fontana "What Do Constitutional Law Professors Do?" [2020] Wisc L Rev 317 at 319 and 328.

68 *Taylor v Attorney-General* [2015] NZHC 1706, [2015] 3 NZLR 791 (*Taylor NZHC*), affirmed in *Attorney-General v Taylor* [2017] NZCA 215, [2017] 3 NZLR 24 (*Taylor NZCA*); *Attorney-General v Taylor* [2018] NZSC 104, [2019] 1 NZLR 213 (*Taylor NZSC*).

69 Harris, above n 2, at 288–292.

70 Claudia Geiringer "The Constitutional Role of the Courts under the NZ Bill of Rights: Three Narratives from *Attorney General v Taylor*" (2017) 48 VUWLR 547.

interpretation of the decision, which over time may coalesce around a single dominant narrative for understanding this remedy.[71]

Interpretation is a constitutional function for several reasons. First, it produces legal knowledge and arguments which can be taken up by lawyers and advisers in authoritative adjudicative contexts. Arguments drawn from scholarly interpretation are frequently cited in court or in governmental legal advice. Although not as authoritative as formal judicial precedents, scholarly arguments are often cited as authority for particular statements: Geiringer's analysis was cited by the Supreme Court when considering the Attorney-General's appeal in *Taylor*.[72] Second, interpretations can shape the views of other constitutional actors. Thus, even in in the absence of any formal process, interpretation will often set the framework for what is taught in law schools and assumes orthodoxy. Academics pay attention to one another's writings and to emerging scholarly consensus. This shapes the content of constitutional syllabi, influencing what future lawyers understand to be the content of the unwritten constitution. Finally, as discussed below, the interpretive function often informs normative positions, both reforming and radical.

3.2. REFORM

3.2.1. The Reforming Function

Academics can take a range of normative standpoints in relation to the unwritten constitution. Some may take what could be called a 'radical' standpoint, viewing the constitution as incoherent or unjust. They may prescribe possibilities for reconstruction, transformation or revolution, or simply offer radical critiques from outside of the dominant constitutional paradigm.[73] The work of the Matike Mai Aotearoa working group offers a

---

71 See Nicholas Petrie "Indications of Inconsistency" (2019) 78 Cambridge LJ 612; Sam Bookman "Decoding Declarations in *Taylor*: Constitutional Ambiguity and Reform" [2019] NZ L Rev 257; John Ip "*Attorney-General v Taylor*: A Constitutional Milestone?" [2020] NZ L Rev 35.

72 *Taylor NZSC* above n 68, at [134].

73 For examples, see Mutu, above n 7; Jackson, above n 8. See also Jane Kelsey *Rolling Back the State* (Bridget Williams Books, Wellington, 1993); Jane Kelsey *The New Zealand Experiment* (Bridget Williams Books, Wellington, 1997). While some radical projects offer prescription for change, others expose the shortcomings of the existing order. This may include engaging in what some refer to as 'trashing' existing ideologies or doctrines. See Mark G Kelman "Trashing" (1984) 36 Stan L Rev 293.

powerful example of a project aimed at constitutional transformation.[74] More commonly, constitutional scholars work within existing paradigms, prescribing opportunities for change. I describe this standpoint as one of 'reform', and it is the primary focus of this section. It is also the standpoint most frequently adopted by Bruce Harris. While the difference between 'reform' and other standpoints is not capable of precise definition, there is something distinctive about a standpoint which accepts the value of existing constitutional structures, ideas and principles, even as it offers prescription to change or fine-tune some of those features.

In the absence of formal amendment procedures, constitutional changes in New Zealand come about in a variety of ways, including judicial decisions (such as the decision in *Taylor v Attorney-General*), ordinary legislation (such as the enactment of the Constitution Act 1986 and the New Zealand Bill of Rights Act 1990), or simply changes in practice, conventions, or prevailing norms of propriety (such as the development of the 'caretaker convention' in the aftermath of the 1984 election).[75]

The fluidity of constitutional change offers academics an opportunity to take part. Academics directly prescribe changes: scholars do not merely purport to *interpret* the constitution, but to *change* it, calling on other actors – parliamentarians, judges, executive officials and voters – to take action. In this mode, scholars take on the role of advocate, drawing on their particular institutional capacities to promote change. This is to say nothing of the roles that academics have formally played as Royal Commissioners, Law Commissioners, consultants and periods as legislative, executive and judicial officeholders.

Scholars have unique institutional capacity to spur change. First, scholars are experts. They are hired on the basis of their qualifications, experience and publications. They face constant incentives to maintain their expert status, including peer review, professional prestige, and the need to maintain current legal knowledge to teach emerging lawyers. They have relatively high levels of public trust,[76] and are one of the 'few sources of

---

74 *The Report of Matike Mai Aotearoa – The Independent Working Group on Constitutional Transformation*, 2016, retrieved at <https://web.archive.org/web/20181218055650/http://www.converge.org.nz/pma/MatikeMaiAotearoaReport.pdf>.

75 For further discussion on this convention, see the *Cabinet Manual 2017*, above n 25, at [6.21]–[6.40]; Harris, above n 2, at 195–197.

76 The 2019 edition of the Victoria University Wellington Trust Survey reports that universities have a 32% 'net trust' rating (percentage of people who trust universities minus those who distrust), which has increased from 23% over the previous two years. See "Latest trust survey explores link to political leanings" (13 June 2019) Victoria University Wellington <www.wgtn.ac.nz>.

authority to guide [the public] in coherently distinguishing between what is constitutional and what is not'.[77] Secondly, New Zealand scholars have a high degree of independence. Unlike practising lawyers, scholars owe no obligations to clients and their salaries are not conditional on presenting particular arguments or points of view. Instead, they are protected by the principle of academic freedom. This allows for more independent appraisals of constitutional problems and reduces the potential for capture by special interests. Thirdly (and relatedly), scholars can make law reform part of their core work. Advocacy efforts can be folded into legal research and publications: expressly normative scholarship is regularly accepted by New Zealand law journals. Research agendas can be built around reform projects. Opportunities for law reform activities may also arise in the 'service' component of the academic job description.[78] This contrasts with practising lawyers, whose first duty is to their clients: any law reform activities must therefore either be done on behalf of clients (and are not independent) or carried out in a lawyer's 'spare time'.

These institutional features may explain why New Zealand academia has a distinguished record of spurring constitutional change.[79] Scholars have utilised books, journal articles, affidavits and public advocacy to harness public opinion, sway judges, and develop arguments that have been taken forward by legislators and executive officials. The best-known example may be Sir Geoffrey Palmer's 1979 work, *Unbridled Power*.[80] *Unbridled Power* received widespread public attention and ran to three editions, the most recent of which was published in 2004.[81] Palmer's advocacy of constraints on the Executive laid the groundwork for the constitutional reforms of the fourth Labour government (which he helped to usher in as Attorney-General and Minister of Justice), and electoral reforms in the 1990s. Since his retirement from politics, Palmer has continued his attempts at constitutional reform by campaigning for a written New Zealand constitution as a public intellectual and commentator.[82]

---

77 Palmer, above n 4, at 141.

78 As John Ip discusses in his contribution to this volume, the standard division of academic labour is 40% research, 40% teaching and 20% service.

79 For further examples see McLean, above n 16, at 124–126.

80 See Geoffrey Palmer, above n 53.

81 GWR Palmer and Matthew Palmer *Bridled Power* (3rd ed, Oxford University Press, Auckland, 2004).

82 GWR Palmer and Andrew Butler *A Constitution for Aotearoa New Zealand* (Victoria University Press, Wellington, 2016); GWR Palmer and Andrew Butler *Towards Democratic Renewal* (Victoria University Press, Wellington, 2018).

Other prominent examples of scholarly involvement in constitutional reform include: the affidavits of Sir Hugh Kāwharu, extensively cited by the Court of Appeal in the *State-Owned Enterprises Case*;[83] and an extensive range of scholars cited in the select committee report on the Supreme Court Bill (later the Supreme Court Act 2003), which established New Zealand's Supreme Court.[84] The Supreme Court was also shepherded through Parliament by another law-professor-turned-Attorney-General, Dame Margaret Wilson.[85] Examples of expressly prescriptive scholarship can also be found in Harris's work, who has issued practical calls for greater accountability for judges,[86] the need for recognition of the Treaty of Waitangi in New Zealand's constitutional future,[87] and reform of the office of Governor-General.[88] Many of these ideas are brought together in *New Zealand Constitution*.[89]

3.2.2. *The Relationship between Interpretation and Prescription*

Interpretation and prescription are closely related activities. On one level, interpretation may be a primarily *descriptive* act: it makes sense of constitutional practice by describing how it fits (or does not fit) with other principles, or how it might shift the contours of the unwritten constitution. But no act of description is free of normative implications. This is particularly so in the fuzzy world of the New Zealand constitution. Interpretation contributes to prescription in two ways.

The first is straightforward and explicit. Works of interpretation typically include overt recommendations for reform.[90] Harris's *New Zealand Constitution* is a classic example: after interpreting and defining New Zealand's constitution in 16 principles, a final chapter

83 *New Zealand Maori Council v Attorney-General* [1987] 1 NZLR 641 (HC and CA) at 662, 681–682 and 713.

84 Supreme Court Bill 2003 (16–2) (select committee report) at 6–8, 11, 23, 27 and 32.

85 See further Margaret Wilson "From Privy Council to Supreme Court: A Rite of Passage for New Zealand's Legal System" (2010) 18 Waikato L Rev 1.

86 Bruce Harris "The Resignation of Wilson J: A Consequent Critique of the Operation of the Judicial Conduct Commissioner and Judicial Conduct Panel Act 2004" [2011] NZ L Rev 625.

87 Bruce Harris "The Constitutional Future of New Zealand" [2004] NZ L Rev 269; Bruce Harris "Treaty of Waitangi and the Constitutional Future of New Zealand" [2005] NZ L Rev 189.

88 Bruce Harris, "The Irish President, the New Zealand Governor-General and the Head of State in a Future New Zealand Republic" [2009] NZ L Rev 605.

89 Harris, above n 2, at ch 18.

90 At the risk of sounding self-referential, the present contribution offers one such example.

considers opportunities for change.[91] For many, this is the primary motivation in producing legal scholarship. Conversely, a prescriptive argument will simply lack persuasiveness without a solid grounding in descriptive interpretation. A typical structure for an academic argument is to diagnose a problem, and then propose a solution. It is very hard to explain what the constitution *should be* without first explaining what it *is*. Thus, the scholar who advocates a particular reform must first explain what it is she is reforming.

The second link between interpretation and prescription is more subtle. The unwritten constitution is constantly being made and remade through the practice of constitutional law,[92] as well as discursive contestation which 'locates the constitution and gives it meaning'.[93] Neither the content nor boundaries of the constitution are set by a codified written text, and many norms are enforced by conventions rather than authoritative rules. The relative lack of authoritative constitutional sources leaves uncertainty as to the content of constitutional norms and conventions. Nevertheless, many constitutional actors – legislators, judge, and officials – are committed to constitutional compliance and propriety.[94] In this context, the mere act of *describing* the constitution and its content often becomes an act of creation and prescription.[95] 'Constitutional' is a weighty term.

---

91 Harris, above n 2, at ch 18.

92 This dynamic is not unique to the unwritten constitution, as the burgeoning US scholarship on 'small-c' constitutionalism and constitutional conventions demonstrates: see, for example, Amar, above n 65.

93 See further Joseph and Walker, above n 23, at 172–181. Joseph and Walker argue that dominant paradigms of constitutional law are established and changed by 'interpretive communities' of individuals and institutions whose discourse 'locates the constitution and gives it meaning'. On this view, discourses compete to translate 'constitutional experiences of facts' into dominant narratives of constitutional change. As new constitutional facts and practices render an earlier paradigm incoherent or contradictory, a new paradigm emerges, bringing with it a new way to make sense of constitutional practices. These paradigms simultaneously offer an *interpretation* of constitutional facts, and also a means for *guiding future practice* within the boundaries set by the dominant paradigm. As Joseph and Walker acknowledge, this conception owes much to the epistemology of Thomas Kuhn, above n 55.

94 To put this in Hartian terms, such actors adopt an 'internal perspective' in their search for reasons to justify future conduct: see HLA Hart *The Concept of Law* (Clarendon Press, Oxford, 1961) at 85–92.

95 This role bears some similarity to the effect of 'restatements' produced in the US and many civil law countries: see, for example, Herbert Weschler "Restatements and Legal Change" (1968) 13 Saint Louis U LJ 185. The closest text to a restatement of New Zealand constitutional law is Philip A Joseph *Constitutional and Administrative Law in New Zealand* (4th ed, Thomson Reuters, Wellington, 2014), which is frequently cited as a source of authority.

It signifies that a rule or norm is foundational in the New Zealand legal order, deserving special scrutiny and protection.[96] Over time, scholarly interpretation of what the constitution is may have the effect of guiding the actions of other constitutional actors, especially if academic consensus emerges on particular issues. In these cases, scholarly interpretations take on a conduct-guiding function and become 'constitutive of the legal order itself'.[97] This dynamic underscores the constitutional role the scholars play through their interpretive function. Scholarly interpretations of constitutional propriety may not be formally authoritative, but they often carry significant normative weight as actors strive to comply with the constitution. Interpretations can guide politicians' and officials' sense of constitutional propriety. This dynamic is heightened by the close-knit nature of New Zealand's legal community, whereby academics frequently share ideas in conferences and informal networks with lawyers, politicians and judges. Bruce Harris observes that many positive law rules have been enacted in order to give effect to prevailing norms of propriety.[98] Matthew Palmer – a former high-ranking public official, former scholar and now High Court Justice – has observed how the very labelling of an action as 'constitutional':

> … can instantly elevate the political stakes, especially if used by a respected independent political commentator. The odd politician has used the constitutional label to advantage and effect in political debate. Almost all Ministers and Members of Parliament and all officials, with whom I advised or interacted with as a senior public figure, would behave differently if clearly advised against, or in favour, of a course of action on the grounds of its constitutional propriety.[99]

A similar dynamic exists between the academy and judiciary. Academics help frame the parameters of arguments that will be considered by judges in court. Scholarly interpretations are often couched in the language of legal logic and argumentation. Scholars hold judges to account in their fidelity to 'the law' by defining what the 'law' is.[100] Furthermore, the

---

96 See further Palmer, above n 4, at 152.

97 Lazarus, above n 40, at 490.

98 Harris, *New Zealand Constitution*, above n 2, at 306.

99 Palmer, above n 4, at 141.

100 See further Mark Tushnet "Judicial Accountability in Comparative Perspective" in Nicholas Bamforth and Peter Leyland (eds) *Accountability in the Contemporary Constitution* (Oxford University Press, Oxford, 2013), cited in Lazarus, above n 40, at 489.

prestige and reputation carried by legal scholars gives weight to academic interpretations. These interpretations confer weight and power on arguments presented in court, while academic critiques may discipline the boundaries of which arguments are likely to be accepted by judges. Fontana puts it well when he observes that 'constitutional law professors are shaping the Overton Window for Justices by shaping what arguments are correct or incorrect, or simply plausible or implausible in the first place'.[101] Fontana describes this as the 'production role' of law professors.[102] Conversely, academics play the role of gatekeepers: they determine which arguments are inappropriate or too 'radical' to gain acceptance within the legal orthodoxy, ruling out particular ideas or modes of reasoning.[103] Interpretive scholarship which describes (for example, by stating which norms are 'constitutional') thus serves a prescriptive function in elevating the importance of those norms amongst the legislature, executive and judiciary. It directs the exercise of power.

Interpretive argumentation therefore has important prescriptive consequences. The relationship also flows in the opposite direction: interpretive arguments produced by legal scholars will often be guided by the scholar's own normative standpoint. The philosophy of science has long explored the ways in which the process of descriptive observation depends on a prior theory of the world.[104] The relatively high degree of ambiguity in New Zealand's constitution means that practices can often be interpreted in a number of different ways. In the absence of formal legal guideposts, scholars must necessarily reach for normative principles to guide their interpretations. While some of these may be internal to the constitutional tradition (for example, searching for coherence in judicial decisions and executive practices), in many cases those principles will be located external to law. The scholar's normative standpoint, as well as the disciplining force of prevailing legal norms, will affect how they interpret a set of legal practices and texts.[105] In *New Zealand*

101 Fontana, above n 67, at 318.

102 Fontana, above n 67. The 'Overton Window' is a term widely used in public policy literature to refer to 'the spectrum of ideas on public policy and social issues considered acceptable by the general public at a given time': see further Lexico: Powered by Oxford <https://www.lexico.com/en/definition/overton_window>.

103 See further David Pozen and Adam M Samaha "Anti-Modalities" (2021) 119 Mich L Rev 729.

104 See, for example, Imre Lakatos "Falsification and the Methodology of Scientific Research Programmes" in Imre Lakatos and Alan Musgrave (eds) *Criticism and the Growth of Knowledge* (Cambridge University Press, Cambridge, 1970).

105 See Kuhn, above n 55; Lakatos, above n 103.

Constitution, Harris acknowledges the role of normative political theory as a source of New Zealand's constitution, and part of what enables the constitution to act as what he perceives as an 'integrated system'.[106] He offers the instructive example of separation of powers, which relies on Locke and Montesquieu's normative theories about human nature and the need for checks and balances.[107] Harris freely acknowledges that these normative ideas shape not only positive law, but also conventions (such as the apolitical nature of judicial appointments) and their accompanying scholarly interpretation.[108] The relationship between interpretation and prescription is thus bidirectional: interpretation provides a normative guide for action, while normative beliefs guide acts of constitutional interpretation.

The concept of the 'third source of authority for government action' developed by Bruce Harris illustrates many of the dynamics discussed in this Part. Through an extensive body of scholarship,[109] Harris has argued that, in addition to executive powers conferred by statute or prerogative, there exists a 'residuary freedom which the government has to act where not legally prohibited'.[110] The concept has been developed with reference to legal interpretation. Harris has argued that the existence of the concept is a necessary prerequisite of effective constitutional government, and can be *interpreted* from judicial decisions.[111] Harris also makes a prescriptive case for *reform*, arguing for formal recognition of the 'third source' so as to place limits on its exercise so that it is consistent with the rule of law (arguing, for example, that it should be limited to 'conventional exercise' of executive powers,[112] or that such powers be subject to judicial review on irrationality grounds).[113] In addition to explicit calls for reform, Harris's

106 Harris, above n 2, at 1. See also the discussion at 6–7 and 305–306.

107 At 7.

108 At 6–7. As an illustration, Harris cites his own scholarship: BV Harris "A Judicial Commission for New Zealand: A Good Idea that Must Not Be Allowed to Go Away" [2014] NZ L Rev 383 at 393–394.

109 Harris's work on this concept dates back to at least 1992. See BV Harris "The 'Third Source' of Authority for Government Action" (1992) 108 LQR 626.

110 BV Harris "The 'Third Source' of Authority for Government Action Revisited" (2007) 123 LQR 226 at 226.

111 At 230–236. See also Harris, above n 108, at 627–630; BV Harris, "Recent Judicial Recognition of the Third Source of Authority for Government Action" (2014) 26 NZULR 260.

112 At 249–250.

113 BV Harris "A Call to Maintain and Evolve the Third Source of Executive Authority for Government Action" (2017) 27 NZULR 853.

work carries implicit normative consequences. The existence of a 'third source' of executive authority could be interpreted by other actors as a basis for expanding the scope of executive powers, and the concept has been adopted by government lawyers as the basis for such an argument.[114] Finally, Harris freely acknowledges that his own normative standpoint has influenced his interpretive arguments in favour of the third source's recognition. Harris argues that third source powers are necessary to meet the 'practical day-to-day needs of government. The government is able to respond quickly, flexibly, and relatively unhindered with the action it considers to be appropriate to meet, sometimes unexpected, societal needs'.[115] Harris thus acknowledges that his concept emerges from a normative belief in nimble responsive government as a force for good: its need for unenumerated powers flows from that belief.

3.3. EDUCATION

3.3.1. The Educative Function

Scholars are educators. They educate students, other constitutional actors, the media and the general public. Scholars transmit knowledge about the constitution and work to enhance others' understandings of constitutional institutions and processes. In doing so, scholars perform a constitutional function by equipping others with the knowledge necessary to take part in the exercise and scrutiny of public power.

The educative functions take place across a range of audiences. In some instances, scholars communicate with constitutional elites, such as politicians, public lawyers and judges. This education is often complex and specialised, occurring through media such as handbooks, guides and formal training (such as judicial training coordinated by the New Zealand Institute of Judicial Studies).[116] One particularly influential manifestation of this function is the introduction to the New Zealand Cabinet Manual entitled "On the Constitution of New Zealand: An Introduction to the

---

114 See the arguments presented in *Quake Outcasts v Minister for Canterbury Earthquake Recovery* [2015] NZSC 27 at [86]–[107], contrasting the Crown's arguments based on 'common law powers' with the appellants' submissions that such powers were extinguished by statute. See also arguments advanced in *Hamed v R* [2011] NZSC 101.

115 Harris, above n 110, at 237.

116 See, for example, "IJS Schedule of Programs" Institute of Judicial Studies <ijs.govt.nz>.

Foundations of the Current Form of Government".[117] The introduction was authored by then-scholar Sir Kenneth Keith in 1990, and a revised version remains in the most recent edition of the Cabinet Manual.[118] The introduction purports to summarise New Zealand's constitution in a mere six pages. This guide is used not only by Cabinet ministers but as an educative tool for legislators generally and has been described by Matthew Palmer as '[t]he most elegant attempt to encapsulate the essence of New Zealand's constitution'.[119]

But constitutional education is not just (or even primarily) for government elites. The educative function is carried out with reference to at least two other audiences. First, the core audience of law teachers is law students. Academic institutions have a near-monopoly on professional legal education. Scholars provide formal education to law students through lectures, seminars, tutorials, as well as informed opportunities for advice and mentorship. This function has obvious constitutional implications. On an institutional level, the training of future lawyers makes possible a legal profession, a key component in maintaining a functioning constitutional system. More specifically, scholars are presented with an opportunity to shape lawyers' constitutional outlook from an early stage. As part of the core public law syllabus, an education in constitutional law is compulsory for all New Zealand-trained lawyers. Harris's influence over public law teaching, for example, is evident in the anecdotal observation that University of Auckland graduates are far more likely to be familiar with the 'third source' concept than their counterparts from other universities. Scholars thus discharge their function in shaping and perpetuating the unwritten constitution by inducting new generations of lawyers into its modes of discourse and reasoning.

Finally, scholars perform an educative function in relation to the general public, often mediated by media institutions. Academics are regularly called upon to explain elements of New Zealand's often-esoteric constitution to a wider audience. This has long been part of the scholarly role: books such as Geoffrey Palmer's *Unbridled Power* have been targeted at the general public, as have newspaper contributions, media interviews and addresses to community groups. The advent of the internet has opened up new opportunities for public engagement. Academics can provide

---

117 *Cabinet Manual 2017*, above n 25, at 1–6.

118 At 1.

119 Palmer, above n 4, at 137.

legal resources directly to the community;[120] legal blogs allow scholars to maintain regularly updated explanations of constitutional developments;[121] while social media sites such as Twitter offer unparalleled opportunities for real-time engagement between scholars and their public audiences.[122]

This engagement with a broad public audience best maps on to Jackson and Lazarus's discussions of academics' constitutional roles. Jackson and Lazarus both argue that the educative function is essential to the maintenance of a constitutional democracy. In this picture, the constitutional academic aspires to arm various audiences with objective knowledge, which in turn promotes better decision-making by both government actors and voters. Jackson, for example, argues that such knowledge equips voters with a necessary 'sound epistemic base' to 'resist manipulations, whether by those in high office, or running for high office, or foreign powers, or others, and – importantly – to be able to evaluate good faith arguments by opposing candidates for public office'.[123] The scholar – if not individually, as a member of an institution – in this picture is a purveyor of facts, the supply of which helps to defend against false information and promote a robust public sphere.

This is a picture of only one facet of a scholar's educational role: the best law teachers are also those who expose the indeterminacies and struggles in law, embracing the ways in which law is open to contest. Furthermore, it is a lofty ideal which is unlikely to be realised in practice. Scholars will often reach only a limited audience, as only one voice among many competing sources. But at the very least, scholars are able to provide fact-checking or accountability functions, for example by assessing the claims of politicians against constitutional principles or explaining the constitutional background to confusing political or legal developments. One such example was the challenge to New Zealand's 'lockdown' restrictions, imposed in response to the 2020 outbreak of the COVID-19 novel coronavirus. A legal challenge brought by a former civil servant contested the legality of these significant restrictions on personal

120 See for example the recent resources provided by the New Zealand Centre for Public Law on New Zealand's response to COVID-19. "COVID-19 and Beyond: Podcasts and webinars" New Zealand Centre for Public Law <wgtn.ac.nz/public-law/>.

121 See for example the contributions of Professor Andrew Geddis of Otago University on the "Pundit" blogging site. "Articles Written by Andrew Geddis" Pundit <www.pundit.co.nz>.

122 See for example the prolific Twitter presence of Dr Dean Knight of Victoria University Wellington. "@drdeanknight" Twitter <www.twitter.com>.

123 Jackson, "Knowledge Institutions", above n 6. See also Lazarus, above n 40, at 10.

liberties.[124] The challenge – *Borrowdale v Attorney-General* – was intended to stress-test New Zealand's legal framework for the exercise of emergency powers, and whether legislative reform was needed. The plaintiff did not intend to undermine New Zealand's public health measures. Nevertheless, the case was perceived by many as an attempt to sabotage New Zealand's (highly effective) public health response. Acting in their educative function and via the news media, scholars such as Professor Andrew Geddis sought to contextualise the challenge as a review of parliamentary processes and the rule of law, not an attack on the government's COVID-19 response.[125] In this way, scholars are at least able to explain what might otherwise be confusing events and can provide a counterpoint to more sensationalist media coverage.

3.3.2. Relationship to Other Functions

The communicative function performed by academics is intimately connected to the functions of interpretation and evaluation/prescription. In many instances, a particular scholarly intervention will perform all three functions simultaneously. The connections between these three functions may be explicit or implicit.

When intervening in public debates, scholarly contributions will often be explicitly tied to a prescriptive purpose. Interventions are often designed not only to convey information about basic constitutional facts and principles, but also to persuade readers of the propriety of a certain course of action. In Geddis's case, that course of action was to support judicial scrutiny of public powers. Geddis's intervention sought to provide information about constitutional principles (such as the 'rule of law'), but also to persuade readers that the *Borrowdale* litigation was appropriate, and that public scrutiny of extraordinary powers is desirable, no matter how popular or effective those powers might be.[126] In this way, as Fontana

---

124 *Borrowdale v Attorney-General* [2020] NZHC 2090.

125 Andrew Geddis "Today the legality of the lockdown will be sternly challenged. And so it should be" *The Spinoff* 27 July 2020 <www.thespinoff.co.nz>. See also Andrew Geddis and Claudia Geiringer "The legal basis of the lockdown may not be as solid as we've been led to believe" *The Spinoff* 28 April 2020 <www.thespinoff.co.nz>

126 Geddis "Today the legality of the lockdown will be sternly challenged", above n 124: 'in a rule of law society we try and put some limits on government power by requiring that it be both authorised by law (i.e. the law must recognise the power exists) and exercised according to law (i.e. the way the power is used must comply with legal constraints). This is by no means a total guarantee against power's misuse, but history shows that it's a pretty vital part of guarding against this'.

has observed, 'constitutional law scholars themselves ... not only generate the messages but may become the messengers'.[127]

Furthermore, education is necessarily tied to interpretation. The formal teaching process offers many examples. Rather than offering a didactic, one-way process for transmission of knowledge, many of the best public law teachers (including Harris) acknowledge the unavoidable uncertainty of the unwritten constitution. In the course of teaching about core but largely untested constitutional issues, such as Parliament's ability to bind itself or the possibility of fundamental common law rights, scholars have no choice but to acknowledge that they are offering a contestable interpretation of certain texts and practices, rather than authoritative information. A law teacher may attempt to stimulate class debate on these issues, inviting students to discuss the relative merits of competing interpretations and to consider possibilities for reform or transformation. The typical structure of a public law exam, which often includes a 'policy' question, recognises the open-ended nature of constitutional law and invites students to develop their own skills in interpretation and prescription. Harris freely acknowledges these challenge in *New Zealand Constitution*, noting that many of the principles he presents 'do not themselves have formal status'.[128] At best, they are 'community-agreed tenets around which the system of government operates', but their content depends on community needs, conflicts with other principles, and 'the myriad of factual contexts in which constitutional problems arise'.[129] As an educational text, *New Zealand Constitution* must necessarily be an interpretation of this complex picture.

This is not to say that New Zealand's constitution is unique: these problems of indeterminacy affect every area of law, to a greater or lesser extent. Nor is it to say that New Zealand's constitution has *no* objective, value-free content. But at the very least, there is a wide penumbra of uncertainty.[130] In all but the simplest of cases, the teaching or explanation of law will require the teacher to recognise that she is adopting an interpretive or even prescriptive position.

A final illustration is offered by the *Cabinet Manual*.[131] The *Cabinet Manual* self-consciously purports to be an educative tool and guide 'not just for those working in or with executive government, but for anyone

---

[127] Fontana, above n 67, at 328.

[128] Harris, *New Zealand Constitution*, above n 3, at 16.

[129] At 16.

[130] For discussion of the 'penumbra' in the context of judging, see HLA Hart "Positivism and the Separation of Law and Morals" (1958) 71 Harv L Rev 593 at 607–615.

[131] *Cabinet Manual 2017*, above n 25, at xvii.

who has an interest in New Zealand's constitutional arrangements'.[132] Yet the *Cabinet Manual*'s introduction, authored by Kenneth Keith, is necessarily an exercise in interpretation. The introduction adopts a functional approach. It recognises no formal source for its claims as to the elements of the constitution, but instead relies on normative reasoning and interpretation of past practice, conventions and several statutes. For example, Keith defines the constitution with reference to interpretation of principles such as democracy;[133] the neutrality, fairness and integrity of the public service;[134] transparency;[135] and 'autonomy'.[136] Keith moves from these principles toward a practical, working definition of the constitution, and simultaneously backwards from constitutional practice to arrive at these principles. This is a complex act of interpretation which is a necessary precondition for the *Cabinet Manual*'s functionality as an educational tool. The *Cabinet Manual* also illustrates how educational tools are guided by the scholar's own normative position: Keith is explicit in his argument that representative democracy is the principle which underpins and shapes the entirety of New Zealand's constitutional structure.[137]

4. WHAT DOES THIS MEAN FOR ACADEMIC PRACTICE?

Scholars are constitutional actors. They interpret the constitution, offer critique and prescriptions for change, and educate others on the operations of New Zealand's somewhat mysterious constitutional framework. They do so from a position of authority, as recognised experts. These three functions are closely interconnected. What does this all mean for New Zealand's constitutional scholars?

I make three observations. First, scholars should acknowledge their role as constitutional actors, and the academy ought to engage in constitutional functions across a range of different audiences. Conversely, other actors should recognise this role and ensure that the academy is appropriately resourced to discharge its functions. Secondly, scholarly interpretation is

---

132 At xvii.
133 At 3.
134 At 4.
135 At 5.
136 At 5.
137 At 3.

an exercise of power. Scholars should be cognisant of this power and be candid about the normative assumptions (and exclusions) which guide its exercise. Finally, scholars should recognise that they are part of a wide-ranging constitutional community, and that their roles in interpreting and shaping the community must be shared.

4.1. PARTICIPATION IN THE CONSTITUTIONAL ECOSYSTEM

Scholarly functions are vital in scrutinising political and judicial decisions, training lawyers and empowering voters. In the unwritten constitution, scholarly interpretation is also crucial in crystallising constitutional practice into a coherent set of norms, which can in turn guide government and judicial action. Not every scholarly act will have constitutional implications. But over time, the academy's output will have cumulative constitutional effects. It is thus incumbent on the academy to recognise its constitutional role. As an institution, the academy must discharge its responsibility across all functions and directed to several audiences (politicians, judges, students and the general public). This observation is uncontroversial. As the examples in this contribution demonstrate, New Zealand public law academics already produce a wide range of outputs in many different contexts. But the obligation should be stated clearly and recognised as an explicit part of the academy's constitutional role.

Furthermore, it should be recognised that this is a demanding set of obligations. Few scholars can simultaneously discharge all three, and it may be better to think of these as *institutional* rather than *individual* functions. These functions are not exhaustive of the academic role: indeed, despite the consequentialist functions performed by academics as part of a constitutional system, there is also value in knowledge produced for its own sake. Finally, recognition of the academy's role makes demands on other actors: it calls on them to safeguard the academy's viability, independence and freedom of expression, in much the same way as the constitutional importance of the judiciary justifies its continued independence.[138] This requirement is all the more pressing in the modern academic environment, where increasingly prescriptive demands are made on scholars' time.

---

[138] See further Lazarus, above n 40, for a similar argument in the context of populist threats to scholarly independence.

4.2. SCHOLARSHIP AS POWER

The nexus between education, interpretation and prescription demonstrates that scholars are powerful actors. The action-guiding nature of 'the constitution' means that even scholarly interpretations which purport merely to describe the constitution can have normative consequences. Furthermore, the knowledge-production role of scholars reveals that they are engaged in a constant process of debate and contestation as to the interpretation and reform of New Zealand's constitution. In other words, the work of academics has significant real-world consequences for the way that power is exercised: scholarship itself may be an exercise of power.

Scholars should consider the possible normative consequences of their constitutional interpretations. The choices that scholars make in their approach to interpretation can shift the future development of the constitution. In particular, scholars should think carefully about the reifying consequences of conservative interpretative approaches. The labelling of certain choices as 'unconstitutional' can severely weaken their normative appeal. In this way, constitutional interpretation may foreclose more imaginative possibilities for constitutional change. This is not to say that approaches to interpretation should be solely guided by their potential normative effects, but these prescriptive consequences should at least be considered. It is also important that the 'reform' standpoint not be the sole standpoint of scholarly analysis: standpoints of transformational change or foundational critique ought to be welcome in the constitutional academy.

Furthermore, the power to contest interpretation and effect change must be exercised responsibly. The power derives in part from the academic's position as an independent actor and trusted teacher. There is therefore a tension between the scholar's role as an advocate, and the need to maintain objectivity and credibility. Navigating this tension is a challenging, but ultimately essential task.

Finally, scholars ought to scrutinise the normative and value-based assumptions which influence their interpretations. Rather than presenting all interpretation as an inevitable or objective set of conclusions, normative assumptions should be acknowledged. This is standard practice among many scholars. Harris, for his part, has long recognised the instrumental nature of his functional approach, acknowledging that his interpretations are driven by the need for a particular form of nimble, responsive government, together with the desirability of incremental reform.[139] This transparency ensures that other constitutional actors (constitutional elites as well as the general public) can consider the extent to which they accept interpretations as action-guiding. It allows for a more democratic and honest approach to constitutional practice, in which different actors can fully evaluate possible constitutional futures.

4.3. COLLABORATION

Academics derive much of their power from their status as experts. Their interpretations are considered action-guiding because they are couched in an expert legal discourse; prescriptions are influential because of academics' institutional advantages; and academics, by virtue of their qualifications and university positions, have unique opportunities to take on the role of educators.

This legal expertise makes academic contributions valuable. But it can also narrow the range of constitutional possibilities offered by the academy. As Fontana argues (in the US context), it ties the academy closely to governmental and judicial elites ('it is hard to speak truth to power while one is also part of that power'),[140] and means that constitutional discourse is likely to become a technical legal one.[141]

Academics must ensure that the constitutional project is open, collaborative and inclusive. Public law academics are part of the constitutional ecosystem, but they are not exhaustive of it. This means that the academy must be diverse and welcoming to a range of backgrounds. It also means that academics should not seek to dominate the field of constitutional interpretation, prescription or education. This is particularly true when constitutional debate could most benefit from forms of knowledge – such as tikanga, history or experiences of exclusion from power – which falls outside the constitutional scholar's expertise. Academics must be willing to learn from the experiences of other disciplines and from non-academic voices, particularly from perspectives and identities which have historically be marginalised. Recognising the constitutional role of academics means ensuring that the power inherent in that role is fairly distributed with regard to broad representation.

139 See Harris, above n 2, at ch 1. See further Willis, above n 3.
140 Fontana, above n 67, at 319.
141 At 337.

INDEX

www.ingramcontent.com/pod-product-compliance
Ingram Content Group UK Ltd.
Pitfield, Milton Keynes, MK11 3LW, UK
UKHW051847100926
8556IPUK00005B/490

9 781839 701986